SOUTHEASTERN COMMUNITY COLLEGE

NORTH CAROLINA
STATE BOARD OF EDUCATION

SOUTHEASTERN COMMUNITY
COLLEGE, LRC
WHITEVILLE, N. C. 28472

ERA OF THE RUSSIAN BALLET

DA CAPO SERIES IN

GENERAL EDITOR: DALE HARRIS
SARAH LAWRENCE COLLEGE

SOUTHEASTERN COMMUNITY
COLLEGE, LRC
WHITEVILLE, N. C. 28472

GV
1787
R675
1979

ERA OF THE RUSSIAN BALLET

by

NATALIA ROSLAVLEVA

with a Foreword by
DAME NINETTE DE VALOIS

DA CAPO PRESS • NEW YORK • 1979

Library of Congress Cataloging in Publication Data

Roslavleva, Natal'ia Petrovna.
  Era of the Russian ballet.

  (Da Capo series in dance)
  Reprint of the ed. published by V. Gollancz, London.
  Bibliography: p.
  Includes index.
  1. Ballet—Russian—History. I. Title.
  [GV1663.R67 1979]   792.8'0947   79-11509
  ISBN 0-306-79536-1

This Da Capo Press edition of *Era of the Russian
Ballet* is an unabridged republication of the first
edition published in London in 1966. It is reprinted
by arrangement with Victor Gollancz Ltd.

©Victor Gollancz Ltd 1966

Published by Da Capo Press, Inc.
A Subsidiary of Plenum Publishing Corporation
227 West 17th Street, New York, N.Y. 10011

All Rights Reserved

Manufactured in the United States of America

ERA OF THE RUSSIAN BALLET

The Sleeping Beauty: Olga Moiseyeva and Yuri Solovyov in the "Blue Bird" *pas de deux* at the Kirov Theatre, Leningrad. (Photo S.C.R. London)

ERA OF THE RUSSIAN BALLET

by

NATALIA ROSLAVLEVA

with a Foreword by
DAME NINETTE DE VALOIS

LONDON
VICTOR GOLLANCZ LTD
1966

© Victor Gollancz Ltd. 1966

PUBLISHER'S NOTE

As is common practice in modern Russian books, all dates in this work that precede the Revolution (1917) are in Old Style, and all dates thereafter are in New Style. Old Style dates are thirteen days earlier than New Style dates: thus, January 14th (New Style) corresponds to January 1st (Old Style).

This book has been prepared and submitted for publishing by Novosti Press Agency (APN).

We wish to thank Mr. Cyril Beaumont for his generous assistance in seeing the work through the press.

CONTENTS

LIST OF ILLUSTRATIONS

FOREWORD

by Ninette de Valois, D.B.E.

ALTHOUGH this is not the first history of the Russian Ballet to be published in this country it is on a very much larger and more detailed scale than any that has appeared hitherto.

Madame Roslavleva impresses with her skill, her knowledge and her painstaking and rewarding research. We are absorbed by all that she has so faithfully unearthed and acutely aware of the craftsman-like simplicity with which she has constructed a book that is strictly historical. Never does she permit the more mundane side of her material to get the upper hand; she is always in complete control from the first page to the last. It is this never flagging example of technical skill that succeeds in making this monumental work such easy reading; it is further possible to admire it all afresh after one remembers that she has not written this book in her native language.

The great part in the history of the Russian Ballet played by the French ballet-masters and choreographers is dealt with very fairly. Yet we are made aware of the fact that there was an undercurrent at work—the slow but steady emerging of a group of creative Russian artists; thus Madame Roslavleva shows us, with the greatest conviction, the other side of the penny. She eventually stresses how the great Western ballet-masters were themselves, one by one, absorbed into the Russian scene. Yet on this point it must be conceded that a creative artist working outside his own country strengthens the value of the knowledge which he gives by making a study of what already exists in that country.

It is obvious in this book that nineteenth-century Russia offered foreign choreographers and visiting dancers a form of State Theatre organization that could be more than favourably compared with their own. Russian ballet today is prone to criticize its past tolerance of foreign artists. Why? Their nineteenth-century taste and judgement were certainly very catholic; yet it was this very objective attitude that in the end so strengthened the truly Russian scene that was so steadily and sturdily emerging.

Madame Roslavleva fails to convince me that the full development of the Romantic Ballet was ever really felt or accepted by the Russians. It would seem that it was the borderline between Classicism and true Romanticism (as shown to them in the ballet of Didelot) that they really understood:

"Russian romanticism, whether in literature or in the theatre had manifestations of its own. It was romanticism of high aspirations, of actual ideals searching for strong positive heroes, rather than the escapist romanticism of the much more decadent Western style."

Why decadent? Western romanticism completed a full cycle in time, through a form of tolerance that was foreign to the true Russian spirit. It was understandable that the Russian scene discarded the whole in favour of the part—for the whole was simply not suited to their outlook, not even for a brief period of time. The great Taglioni was worshipped as an individual by the public, but it is recorded that she was eventually frowned upon by the "direction".

Petipa's era is full of interesting sidelights on their great choreographer who perhaps ruled the Mariinsky Theatre rather longer than was wise or necessary. He is, though, most generously dealt with in the book. Yet you do not have to be a native of Russia to sense that Ivanov's career would have been a greater one if Petipa had been content with a little less glory.

The chapter on Ivanov is exactly what one has always hoped would emerge from the pen of someone with real insight into the history of Russian Ballet. His character comes completely and touchingly alive, and the following paragraph speaks for him:

"Was Lev Ivanov merely ill-starred? He could easily have fitted among Chekhov's characters. There was something of Uncle Vanya in him: a man of subtle, easily wounded nature, kind and benevolent, ready to sacrifice himself to the benefit of egotistic careerists exploiting his kindness without scruples."

Never do I see Ivanov's second and fourth acts of *Lac des Cygnes* without feeling that within these particular dance compositions there is to be found two perfect examples of real choreographic poetry.

The book takes us right up to the present day in Russia, giving us interesting facts about contemporary artists, choreographers and teachers. Yet outside Russia itself there is little known about the choreographic picture. We are given lists and very full descriptions of many ballets that have been produced in Russia during the last thirty to thirty-five years. How many of these really modern ones have been shown to the outside world? Very few—far too few. We are not therefore in the position to make comparison between Western and Eastern European choreography. It is surely time that these wonderful artists made a world tour that excluded, for once, the classics of the nineteenth century and works faithfully following in such a tradition. They could then present a repertoire of a more contemporary nature.

Diaghilev gave us the last picture of a "contemporary" Russian Ballet. That was in 1909—may we please now have another one?

CHAPTER I

FROM EARLY TIMES TO THE BEGINNING OF THE NINETEENTH CENTURY

THE WORD FOR "a dance", "*tanets*" in contemporary Russian, derives from the German "*tanz*", and was introduced into the language under the reforms of Peter the Great. "*Tanets*", however, implies a dance incorporating a series of steps, a dance embodying the rudiments of choreography. The Slavonic word "*pliaska*" is still used for folk dances composed spontaneously, the steps being arranged in any succession. In ancient Russia, moreover, there was also a distinction between two very different forms of dance—*pliasati* and *skakati*. The former indicated that the dance was slow and flowing, the latter, originally from the word "to jump", indicated that there would be plenty of hops and capers of all kinds. The first was usually (but not necessarily) danced by women, the second belonged to the domain of men.

Silver figurines of dancing men discovered in treasure-troves in the region of Kiev and belonging to the sixth century A.D. portray them in the familiar squatting poses of the "*prisiadka*", still considered (and by foreign audiences in particular), to be the most characteristic position in Russian folk dancing. These silver figurines have their arms akimbo, knees bent and well turned out, and feet on half point, as though the dance, stayed in a momentary pose, were about to continue.

Hence from earliest times the Russian folk dance existed, flourished and developed, never losing its national features, even during the Tartar and Mongol invasions and domination. Russian folk dance remained a special feature of Russian art, sometimes incorporating such attractive foreign elements as came its way, but never falling completely under their influence. The Russian people listened to the new melodies brought by the invaders, studied unfamiliar rhythms, and steps, but did not allow themselves to be charmed away by the seductive fragrant beauties of the Orient.

In the villages the people lived their normal lives. Each festive occasion was accompanied by songs and *khorovods*. The latter, the most ancient form of circular chain dance (which they also developed) to be found in the folklore of almost any nation, was particularly popular in Russia at every period. These ancient circle dances were performed to songs, usually slow and languid, and it is their close link with the musical structure, this stemming directly from the melody, that gave the Russian folk dance its flowing *cantilena* qualities, later reflected in the inimitable mastery of professional Russian dancers and indeed in the entire history of Ballet in Russia.

Early travellers to Russia noted in their memoirs these special features of the Russian national dance, particularly the ability of the performers to dance with their entire body (a quality noted by English ballet teachers and other professionals, following the Bolshoi Ballet season of November 1956). Thus Johann Bellerman, a German scientist and author, residing in Russia from 1778-1782, wrote in his *Bemerkungen über Russland in Rücksicht auf Wissenschaft, Kunst, Religion",* Vol. 1, published at Erfurt in 1788, as follows: "The Russian national dance is so eloquent, that I know of nothing to match it. . . . Its beauty is contained not merely in adroit steps, but in the fact that the head, shoulders, trunk, arms—in other words the whole of the body—participate in the dance to make an incomparable impression upon the spectator."[1] These remarks were made upon seeing ordinary village revels, danced by peasants. Professional dancers, on the other hand, existed in Russia from times immemorial. They usually joined troupes of entertainers or *skomorokhi,* famed for their virtuoso jumps and acrobatic capers. The art of the *skomorokhi* was largely in the grotesque and comic style, and most of their dancers were male. There also existed female professional dancers, for whom there were special terms in Old Russian: *pliassovitsa,* or *pliassitsa,* while the male dancer was called a *pliassun.* A chronicle of the beginning of the sixteenth century tells us that Ivan the Terrible's mother made what amounted to a court *entrée* at the wedding of her brother-in-law, when she was preceded by *pliassitsi* or professional dancing women, belonging to the court of the Grand Duke of Russia.

The *skomorokhi,* both men and women, frequently formed resident companies at the mansions of princes and boyars, while others, more restless, roved far westward, reaching even to Italy.

A relic of the *skomorokhi* art has been preserved for us in frescoes dating to the eleventh century A.D. on one of the walls of the St. Sophia Cathedral at Kiev, built in the reign of Yaroslav the Wise, known to have been an enlightened ruler interested in arts and letters. The frescoes depict different

[1] Quoted from the Russian translation in Abram Gozenpud's paper: "On the History of Ballet Theatre in the XVIIIth Century," published in *The Scientific Annals of the State Research Institute of Theatre, Music and Cinema,* Leningrad, 1958, p. 222.

types of dancing. One of the dancers, marking the rhythm with copper cymbals held in both hands, is preparing to execute a typical Russian squatting step. He is being accompanied by three other *skomorokhi* playing various kinds of wind instruments. But in the lower part of the picture two other men dance facing each other. One of them is waving a handkerchief in the traditional Russian way, while the other spreads his arms out in a broad gesture, also typically Russian. However crude, the painting proves that its author was aware that the two kinds of dancing existed in Russia already at that time: the languid *pliasati* and the fiery *skakati*.

The Russian people introduced *skomorokhi* into their epic songs (*byliny*), and left unforgettable memories of the great skill of these entertainers in such proverbs as: "Anyone can do a dance, but can they match a *skomorokh?*"

Skomorokhi did much to spread the art of dancing in ancient Russia, though dancing did exist in some rudimentary form in the folk theatre (both of the professional and amateur kind) and various puppet shows, particularly the "Petrushka".

And it was only after a long period of persecution by the church that the *skomorokhi*, particularly the roving ones, gradually lost their nationwide importance. A Church Council of 1551, convened in Moscow, forbade the *skomorokhi* to appear close to any church or to perform at weddings. Later the persecution of these actors, dancers and musicians became even more cruel. They migrated northward, settled on the estates of eminent people and became in a way even more professional, since they usually lost the many-sided nature of their art: those *skomorokhi* who knew how to play various instruments joined private orchestras in boyar's mansions, while *skomorokhi* dancers displayed their ability on the stages of the first private theatres alongside foreign artists, already finding their way into Russia.

In spite of the severe church rules that were outwardly strictly observed, tsars also invited *skomorokhi* and other entertainers to their courts. Ivan the Terrible organized revels and charades at his court.

The first tsar of the Romanov dynasty, Mikhail, set up in his palace a *Poteshnaia palata* or amusement room, the forerunner of the future Russian Court Theatre. The tsar was much pleased by the performance of a "German", Ivan Lodigin, who, in addition to tight-rope walking, demonstrated "dancing and all sorts of other antics". This Lodigin, obviously Russian by his name and surname, but called "German" because of his rather unfamiliar theatrical occupation ("German" stood for anything foreign in Old Russian), was entrusted in 1629 with the teaching of dancing to a group of children of humble origin, and thus became the first Russian dancing-master. The children in turn became the tsar's entertainers.

The next tsar, Alexei, went further than his father Mikhail. The first ballet performance on the Russian stage was presented in his reign on February 8, 1673, at the Preobrazhenskoye village near Moscow—the summer seat of the Russian tsars.

Neither the score nor any other record of the exact nature of this "Ballet of Orpheus and Euridice" has been preserved. It is not improbable, however, that it was produced after the pattern of the work of the same title by the German composer Heinrich Schütz, first performed at Dresden in 1638. Jacob Reitenfels, Roman ambassador to the Court of Moscow, left some information about this "choragium" as he termed it, in his memoirs: *De rebus Moschovitis ad Serenissimum magnum hetruriae ducem Cosmum Tertium*, 1680.

He says that upon hearing from ambassadors and other travellers that special entertainments were being arranged at European Courts, the Tsar ordered the presentation of "French dancing", and since the people entrusted with this production had only one week within which to prepare it, obviously they had to take for a model something already in existence. The first difficulty arose in finding a specialist in theatrical performances of this kind. Such a man was discovered in the person of Nicolai Lima, an engineer of foreign descent serving in the Tsar's army. Lima was responsible for the rather complicated settings and machinery, and, apparently, also for the production of the piece. Like all known first ballets, this one also included singing and speech. The ballet opened with an aria extolling the Tsar and sung by Orpheus who later danced "in the French manner" between "two pyramids"—that sounds like the numerous cars used in the first ballets in Italy and France (as well as in English masques) to carry various characters dressed as nymphs and other mythological figures.

The Tsar was delighted with the performance, never leaving it for ten hours at a time. He ordered urgently the training of children of humble origin in the art of dancing. This coincided with the founding, also in 1673, of a court dramatic theatre, for which its first "director", a German pastor by name of Gregori, trained a troupe of eighty Russians "from various walks of life". Thus one of the important features of the Russian ballet theatre was formed at a very early stage: while its themes and ballet-masters were often foreign, the main body of the troupe was always formed by Russian artists.

Tsar Alexei's death in 1676 put an end for a long time to any theatrical performances, and with them to the development of Court Ballet. Only a quarter of a century later a new attempt was made in Moscow on the initiative of Peter the Great. He founded a *Teatralnaia khoromina* (Theatre room) at the Kremlin, which remained in use until the capital was transferred to St. Petersburg. Here dancing took different forms of public activity and entertainment. Peter I was very fond of masquerades and revels. A grand masquerade which began on September 10, 1721, lasted, for instance, a whole week. We find the description of it in a diary of a courtier of Peter the Great, *kamer-junker* Bergholtz. The same courtier left valuable evidence that already, in the early part of the eighteenth century, dancing-masters were engaged by the Court and by some of the fashionable members of its retinue. During the same period Peter I introduced West European ballroom dancing at his famous "assemblies", attendance at which was obligatory for all the nobility. This led to the growth of a new attitude towards the very art of dancing in society. Dancing ceased to be a prohibited occupation, a thing of "low entertainment".

In Peter's reign dancing still took crude forms and there were hardly any attempts at making it into *theatre*. The first professional ballet in Russia was performed in the reign of Anna Ioanovna on January 29, 1736, when Francesco Araja's opera *La Forza dell'amore e dell'odio* was shown at Court, the finale containing "a most pleasant ballet" performed by over a hundred *Russian* (and not foreign) dancers. They were pupils from the *Corps des Cadets* (a Military School for young men of noble origin) who had been trained since 1734 by dancing-masters headed by Jean Baptiste Landé. It fell to him to become in addition the founder of the St. Petersburg Ballet School—the nucleus of professional ballet theatre in Russia.

Like anywhere else in Europe, at first dancing, singing, and declaiming existed side by side in the opera-ballet, and the artists were expected to be equally proficient in all these arts. Ballet was in fact an appendix to opera, dependent on it in many ways—either as an integral part of the action, or as a *divertissement* of dances, or as dance interludes with an independent subject and action, or as a brief résumé (usually in mime rather than dancing) of what had just been sung.

It was only in the eighteen-sixties that ballet in St. Petersburg began to be given more and more frequently as a spectacle existing on its own, quite apart from opera. The costumes were in the European tradition, closely resembling heavy court dress and fashioned after the French idea of seeing mythological characters through the eyes of eighteenth-century designers. But there is no documentary evidence of any sort to prove that Russian dancers used masks at any time—apparently their features were free to express their own feelings.

In 1794 a Russian teacher of dancing (the profession was no longer restricted to those of foreign extraction), Ivan Kuskov, published his *Dancing-master (Tantsevalny Uchitel)*. A record of dancing regulations and traditions as observed in St. Petersburg, it affords an idea of the state and technique of both ballroom and scenic dancing in Russia at the end of the eighteenth century. Much attention is paid in Kuskov's book to rules of deportment, to bows and reverences, and to how the minuet should be correctly performed.

Ballroom dancing was obligatory for the education of young noblemen of the time, and since it required a high standard of technique perfectly applicable to the contemporary stage, pupils from the *Corps des Cadets* participated in ballet performances, often competing quite successfully with professional dancers of foreign origin and at times exceeding their artistry. In September 1737 Landé petitioned the Empress Anna Ioanovna for permission to start a ballet school where the training of professional dancers for Court performances was to take, according to his plans, three years. The permission was granted, the number of pupils doubled (Landé asked for six boys and six girls), and in 1738 the first ballet school in Russia for twenty-four children of palace servants opened in two rooms of the house occupied by Landé and his wife, and later in one of the wings of the imperial palace.

Owing to the exceptional dancing abilities of the Russian pupils of Landé, they were able to take part in ballet performances at a very early stage, and some of them, for instance, Axinya Sergeyeva, Avdotia Timofeyeva, Afanasy Toporkov and Andrei Nesterov, won acclaim as first-class dancers quite capable of appearing side by side with Italian guests, brought in large numbers to St. Petersburg by roving choreographers such as Locatelli, Fusano, Canziani, Angiolini, and later Hilferding and Le Picq, who all found very good conditions on the Russian stage for fruitful work and good remuneration.

Landé taught his pupils the steps of the *danse d'école*, most of which has not changed to this day. It was the Russian dancers, however, who, so to speak, pronounced the new language in their own way; who, being directly versed in the Russian national dance, lent its inimitable features to classical ballet, thus creating from the very beginning the essence of the Russian school in the broad sense of the word.

With regard to the school as an educational institution, it was regularly filled with pupils and from then onwards supplied the Russian stage with home-trained dancers.

Ballets (for the most part in conjunction with opera) were shown much more frequently in St. Petersburg now that it had its own ballet company. The ballets belonged either to the comic and grotesque kind, in which Italian choreographers such as Fusano (his real name was Antonio Rinaldi) excelled because they were derived from their own *Commedia dell'Arte* with its popular characters, or to the "serious" style, that borrowed its subjects from Greek and Roman mythology in the tradition of classicism which reigned supreme over arts and letters of the period with its emphasis on conventional formality.

It was this serious *genre*, described in detail by Noverre in his famous *Letters on Dancing and Ballets* (*Lettres sur la danse et sur les ballets*, 1760) that gave birth to what we know as classical ballet.

In ballet at the Russian Court much importance was given to allegorical scenes, paying tribute to reigning figures.

Thus, in 1742, during the Coronation festivities of Elizaveta, Peter's daughter, which took place according to historical tradition in Moscow, two ballets by Fusano were performed to music by the Court violinist, Domenico dal'Oglio: *The Joy of the Peoples on the Occasion of Astreia's Appearance on the Russian Horizon and the Re-establishment of the Golden Age* and *The Golden Apple at the Feast of Gods and the Judgement of Paris*.

Landé's pupils danced in these two ballets with great success at the large theatre built on the River Yauza especially for the coronation.

It was not far from this site that the future Ballet of the Bolshoi Theatre was to take shape. The Moscow Orphanage was founded in 1764 in a set of white buildings stretching along the Moskva river. The first wards were children under four. When they grew up the trustees of the Orphanage decided to teach them dancing and acting, in addition to crafts and sciences. That was in 1773, when Filippo Beccari, one of the numerous Italian dancers and dancing masters who found their way to Russia, was engaged for the express purpose of training professional dancers in the course of three years. As in the case of Landé's pupils, the result exceeded all expectations, many more talents were discovered, and almost one-third of the orphans chosen to study ballet became soloists, soon to enter upon a professional career both in Moscow and St. Petersburg.

Moscow had already seen fairly good ballet at Giovanni Locatelli's theatre of 1759. It was Locatelli who had, three years earlier, founded an opera and ballet theatre at the Summer Garden in Petersburg, where any inhabitant of the capital could see a performance by paying for a ticket. The repertory consisted of ballets modelled on those presented at Court and the liberal amount of Italian text made them incomprehensible unless they were followed by a short pantomime. But the very novelty of a public theatre formed one of the main attractions; it was called the Italian *free* theatre to indicate the easy access in contrast to the former Court spectacles designed strictly for the select few. Also, aside from ballets about Persephone and Pluto, Cleopatra of Egypt, Cupid and Psyche, Locatelli would show comic ballets; for instance, *The Sailors' Return, London Fair*, and similar themes borrowed directly from life. Last, but not least, additional interest was provided by the rivalry of two parties of the first Petersburg balletomanes, followers of the beautiful Beluzzi, admired as Persephone or Cleopatra; and the impish Sacco, dancing Psyche and leading roles in comic ballets. These enterprising balletomanes from the highest possible society expressed their admiration by clapping not with their hands, but with the help of two wooden clappers tied with a ribbon bearing the name of the object of their adoration. Encouraged by the success of his first enterprise, Locatelli obtained a *privilège* for building his own theatre in Moscow, where regular performances of opera and ballet (freely merged) started in January 1759. The novelty, however, declined in Moscow even sooner than in Petersburg; the much broader and more democratic Moscow public soon lost interest in foreign themes and content. The time for a national lyric theatre in Moscow was still to come. Meanwhile Locatelli, having closed his theatre, returned to Petersburg, where attempts to regain his former success also failed.

A period of much deeper interests, greater dramatic content, and more perfect theatre was arising in Russian ballet. It was rapidly gaining importance as an independent phenomenon of the national theatre arts.

It is therefore not surprising that many precursors and disciples of the great reformer of the eighteenth century, Jean Georges Noverre, found support in Russia and a very fruitful field for their artistic inclinations. The ideas of the *ballet d'action* were welcomed by the Russian public, while Russian artists, brilliant talents both in mime and dancing, were there to endow with life the grand heroic tragedies of the classic ballet.

The Austrian choreographer, Frantz Hilferding van Weven, came to St. Petersburg in 1759. He had already made a name for himself: as early as 1752, in search of greater pantomime expression, he abolished the use of masks in all his ballets. Hilferding was an educated man, combining sound knowledge of his profession with the constant study of literature, music, and painting. Some twenty years before Noverre, he made the first attempts at creating pantomime ballet, wherein music, dance, mime, settings, and costumes were to be blended in one corporate whole. In reality Hilferding translated, often too literally, French classical tragedy into mime, and in actual practice achieved much less than he had envisaged in theory—but so did Noverre.

However, Hilferding was invited to Russia because he had the reputation of being a progressive choreographer working in a new style. Jacob von Staehlin, scientist, writer, musician, and teacher of Peter III, wrote in his valuable *Nachrichten von der Tanzkunst und Balleten in Russland* (1770) that Hilferding was invited "for the improvement of the ballet and introduction of a new taste" that consisted, among other things, of "village amusements".

Indeed, aside from numerous mythological and allegorical ballets— *The return of Spring or the Victory of Flora over Boreas* (1760), *Apollo and Daphne* (1762), *Cupid and Psyche* (1762), *Pygmalion* (1763)—Hilferding created in Russia many ballets in the comic *genre* such as *The Ridiculed Landowner* (1762), *The Isle of Fools* (1763), *The Lame Cavalier* (1766) and some *divertissements* using folk dances and scenes borrowed directly from life. Staehlin describes in his memoirs a ballet with fishing scenes and Tyrolean dances, performed by Russian dancers, and stresses in particular that ballets by Hilferding started having a special success at Court after Russian dancers, bearing the names of Petrushka, Vavila, Yevdokia and the like, began to take part in them side by side with the foreign artists, brought by Hilferding and the Austrian composer, Joseph Startzer, who provided the music for most of his productions.

Particularly prominent among Hilferding's pupils was Timofei Bublikov. A really outstanding soloist, he went to Vienna in 1764 and for two years danced there with great success. Apart from Staehlin who considered Bublikov "a young Russian of extraordinary talent", he is favourably mentioned in the memoirs of Semyon Poroshin (teacher of Paul I as heir-apparent).

Bublikov (who as a serf was known by the impolite diminutive of Timoshka) danced with grace and authority the leading role of Alcinde in the allegorical ballet *Prejudice Conquered* given on November 29, 1768. The ballet was created (together with the music) by Hilferding's successor and pupil, Gasparo Angiolini, who had arrived from Vienna in 1766 at the request of the Empress Catherine II, who desired to have for her Court Ballet a choreographer of no lesser talent.

Angiolini's first work was a ballet-pantomime in the opera *Didone*

Abbandonata. Staehlin testified that the ballet pantomime, which included the burning of Carthage, had a tremendous success, and, apart from its first performance as part of Catherine's Coronation festivities (autumn of 1766), it was often staged quite independently to follow operas and tragedies which had nothing in common with its subject.

Angiolini mounted many *ballets d'action* both in Petersburg and Moscow. Most of them were replicas of his earlier works created in Vienna during the fruitful period of his collaboration with Gluck, another important figure in the attempt to combine dance, mime, and music in the effort to portray the feelings and psychology of the characters, and the Italian poet Calzabigi, whose libretto contributed in no small measure to the attainment of a proper balance between music and drama.

It was in Russia, however, that Angiolini created new and original ballets: *Semira*[1] (1772) after the tragedy by Alexander Sumarokov, based on ancient Russian history, *The Chinese Orphan* (1776), and an original *divertissement*, based on Russian Yule-tide customs and revels, *Zabavy o sviatkakh*, produced in Moscow in 1767. The music and libretti of all these ballets were by Angiolini.

That he found favourable creative atmosphere in Russia is proved by the fact that he returned there three times, leaving the country finally in 1786.

In the course of his sojourns he taught at the Petersburg Ballet School.

Angiolini was a rabid opponent of Noverre (witness his published polemics with the reformer whom he accused, among other things, of plagiarising Hilferding). It was realized in Petersburg that the feud was more of a personal nature and that all three choreographers were striving in reality for the same cause, inspired by the progressive philosophy and aesthetics of the eighteenth century. The great Russian poet Alexander Radishchev, in one of his essays, compared the Angiolini–Noverre feud to two stubborn fisticuffers falling from exhaustion into poses that even these choreographers would fail to reconstruct "in their excellent ballets".

Angiolini's successor, Le Picq, was Noverre's direct pupil. He brought his master's ballets to Russia although he frequently failed to mention their source. In addition, these revivals often lacked the depth of Noverre's original intentions and were dressed up rather to dazzle the eye than to rouse the mind. . . .

[1] The story of the ballet *Semira*, as well as much interesting information on Opera and Ballet in Russia in the eighteenth century, may be found in the exhaustive work by Doctor A. Gozenpud: *Lyric Theatre in Russia* (*Muzikalny Teatr v Rossii*), Leningrad, Musical Publishing House, 1959.

However, three years after his arrival in Petersburg, in 1789, when Le Picq mounted one of Noverre's best ballets, *Médée et Jason*, several hundred people were turned away at the theatre doors and public opinion proclaimed it the best ballet ever to be shown on the capital's stage.

Thus, although Noverre never visited Russia in person, his works and his ideas on the *ballet d'action* were profoundly appreciated. The application of his theories throughout the entire history of Russian ballet finally achieved that complete realization only envisaged by the great master in his *Letters* in the best creations of Soviet choreographers.

The Russian appreciation of Noverre may also be seen from the fact that the most complete edition extant of his works (in four volumes) was published in St. Petersburg in 1803-1804, while another, important new edition has recently been prepared in Leningrad with a foreword by the eminent critic, Yuri Slonimsky.

Ballets with serious content existed in Petersburg of the eighteenth century together with spectacular allegories and *divertissements* dictated by the needs of the Court.

Theatre in Moscow was much less restricted in its development, particularly since up to the beginning of the nineteenth century it was in no way subject to the Court Ministry. Opera-ballet as well as dramatic theatre belonged in Moscow to free enterprise and in many ways was associated with advanced and enlightened circles, in particular with the Moscow University, whose role in the propagation of Russian lyric theatre can hardly be overestimated.

The University maintained two schools—one for boys of noble origin, and another for those from various strata. It is the second group that usually took an active part in the University theatre, as noblemen did not want their sons to appear on the stage. All pupils received an excellent musical education and were taught singing and dancing. A private theatre existed in the main University building. Tragedies, dramas, comedies and operas were presented both by students at the University and by the school pupils. Female roles were performed by boys. However, in 1757, one could see in the *Moscow Monitor* of July 27 an advertisement inviting "Women and young ladies desiring to take part in theatre presentations and possessing dramatic abilities, also able to sing and to teach the same to other persons", to call at the office of the Moscow Imperial University. Thus it came about that Tatiana Troepolskaya, one of the first to answer this advertisement, became one of the first women on the Russian dramatic stage. She might have taken part in the operas produced at the University, since *emplois* were not clearly distinguished in those times. The opera repertory of the University is not known, but most likely it was modelled after existing Italian examples. At any rate when Locatelli's enterprise failed in Moscow he became manager of the University company. It won such renown that in 1761 some of the Moscow artists trained by the University were transferred to Petersburg, which nearly put an end to the great amount of work that had been done.

New managers sprang up immediately in the theatre-conscious city. One was a Russian named Titov, the other two were the Italians Belmonti and Cinti. The latter rented one of the best opera buildings of Moscow— the Znamensky Opera House, owned by Prince Vorontsov. The next *privilège* for maintenance in Moscow of a public theatre was obtained by Prince Urusov, a great admirer of the histrionic arts. In 1776 he joined forces with Michael Maddox (1747-1822), an Englishman who came to Moscow shortly before for the purpose of demonstrating "mechanical and physical wonders", probably consisting of clever scenic illusions. (This Maddox is often confused with a British architect, George Maddox (1760-1843), designer of an opera house which was to have been erected in Leicester Square. His client died and so the theatre was never built. George Maddox never visited Russia, as may be seen from his biography, published in England in the nineteenth century. A study of Maddox's theatre in Moscow may be found in Olga Chayanova's *Teatr Maddoxa v Moskve*, Moscow, 1927.)

Michael Maddox did not build or design the Petrovsky Theatre, named after Petrovska Street (which still runs alongside the present Bolshoi Theatre building), but was its impressario and provided the funds for its erection. He himself probably designed the various mechanical transformations abounding in ballets shown at the Petrovsky Theatre, which opened on December 30, 1780. Before that date the partners owned the Znamensky Theatre, where ballets were shown regularly from 1776. Inasmuch as the present Bolshoi Ballet is the direct heir to that company, it dates its existence from the same year.

Apart from assembling at their theatre all the best artists residing in Moscow, the partners took over a group of dancers and actors trained at the Moscow Orphanage.

On February 26, 1780, the Znamensky Theatre was destroyed by fire together with all its costumes and properties. Suffering heavy losses, Urusov yielded his share of the *privilège* to Maddox, who, deciding to settle in Russia (he subsequently became a Russian subject, Russianizing his name to Mikhail Yegorovitch Maddox), invested considerable funds in a new theatre building. The Petrovsky Theatre seated 800, had three tiers of boxes (26 in each tier) and "a paradise"[1] for simple folk. The orchestra had twenty benches and several rows of armchairs in the front for privileged patrons. The name of the architect was Roseberg.

The Petrovsky Theatre was considered to be one of the best equipped in Europe. Its orchestra floor could be raised to form a ballroom to be used for fancy-dress balls. However, this building was also burned down on September 22, 1805.

It is interesting to note that for the opening performance of 1780 the Petrovsky Theatre presented a special prologue, *The Wanderers*, written for the occasion by Alexander Ablesimow, wherein Momus and Musa, two characters symbolizing histrionic arts, wander about, having been deprived by conflagration of their previous abode—the Znamensky Theatre. Apollo himself descends to earth in order to break the good news that Momus and Musa (Muse) now have a new home (the scenery changed for a backdrop with a view of Moscow and the Petrovsky Theatre) erected by a mortal (that is Michael Maddox) appointed by the deity in person.

After a grand apotheosis of Olympian gods there followed a pantomime ballet, *The Magic School*, with choreography by Leopold Paradis to music by Startzer and Paradis, and scenery by Friederic Hilferding. Other ballet-masters working during the twenty-five-year period of existence of the Petrovsky Theatre were the brothers Francesco and Cosimo Morelli, Pietro Pinucci—a *danseur* in the grotesque style, whose comic ballets were particularly popular with the Moscow audiences at large—and Guiseppe Solomoni.

An important change in the quality of ballet took place in 1784, when the ballet school of the Orphanage was completely turned over to Maddox for a lump sum and became a permanent school for training for the theatre.

The repertory of the Petrovsky Theatre was in accordance with the tastes of the democratic Moscow audiences and had its own distinctive features and peculiarities of performance.

As will be seen from the opening programme, many of the pieces were created by Russian authors—a tradition already predominant at the Znamensky Theatre, which may be considered the cradle of Russian national opera. As to ballet, while those in the "serious" style were also given, and the company could boast many good dancers, including the two first Moscow ballerinas (Mavra Poliskova and Matryona Andreyeva, trained at the Orphanage), the favourite and predominant *genre* was that

[1] A Russian expression for "the Gods", that is the gallery. Ed.

inspired by the national comic opera and influenced in form by the Italian grotesque ballets, but in spirit by the Russian folk dance.

A number of dance scenes were suggested by Russian folk festivals, national games, carnivals, revels, etc. Vassily Balashov, formerly of the Orphanage, choreographed many such *divertissements* for the Petrovsky Theatre. The roles of the courageous heroes, invariably escaping from all predicaments, were played by a popular danseur *buffo*, Gavrila Ivanov-Raikov, also a former ward of the Orphanage.

The titles of the ballets produced at the Petrovsky Theatre reveal the predominant style: *The Pretended Death of Harlequin, or the Deceived Pantaloon, The Deaf House-Owner* (both in 1782 by Francesco Morelli), and *The Deceived Village Doctor* (1796), *The Washerwomen* (1797), *The Miller* (1797)—all by Pinucci.

The last period of the Petrovsky Theatre Ballet was connected with the name of Guiseppe Solomoni who, in collaboration with the *décorateur* Bibiena, transferred one after another of Noverre's ballets to the Petrovsky stage—*Medée et Jason* (1800), *La Toilette de Vénus* (1802), *La Mort d'Agamemnon* (1805). These ballets, like Solomoni's independent experiments in "serious" dancing, did not win the heart of the Moscow audience, since they were contrary to firmly established traditions of the character style.

These traditions were also spread by serf dancers, trained at private theatres owned by rich landowners and sold not only to the Petrovsky, but to many other companies. This does not signify in any way that serf dancers were capable of nothing but folk dancing. They were highly trained professionals, often formed by foreign dancing-masters employed by their owners. Some serf theatres, such as that of Count Sheremetiev at Ostankino near Moscow (preserved as a museum to this day), had large companies and a repertory that could compete with Court theatres. Sheremetiev employed at different periods such celebrities as Le Picq, Morelli, Pinucci, and Solomoni. The ballet-masters gave daily classes (they were called "schools") according to contract and then passed on their knowledge to serf teachers. One such teacher was Sheremetiev's serf, Kuzma Serdolikov (from "cornelian" in Russian). His real name was Deulin, but the count's dancers were all given names after precious stones —hence the names of Sheremetiev's excellent ballerinas: Tatiana Granatova (from "garnet") and Mavra Biriuzova (from "turquoise" in Russian). A document preserved from Sheremetiev's archives shows that the Count gave strict orders that daily "schools" be given by Kuzma in the mornings —first for boys and then for girls, while the afternoons were occupied by rehearsals of the numerous ballets, for the most part created in the company, as was the case in other serf theatres.

While the training was strictly founded on the *danse d'école*, many of the ballets included Russian folk dances. And *danseuses* of the serf ballet, in hard work and in sorrow, often sold at the whim of their master, never lost the tradition of their national dance, passing it from one to another.

Folk songs and legends are connected with the name of Praskovia Zhemchugova (derived from "pearl"). Her real name was Kovaleva. She was an actress in Sheremetiev's serf theatre and her romantic marriage to the Count and early death through tuberculosis were all the talk at the time. For the most part the fate of serf dancers and actors was tragic. They were severely punished for any error and often had to do field work in addition to acting and rehearsing.

When the fashion for serf theatres dwindled and their owners had difficulty in selling even highly skilled troupes, many of their members were mercilessly sold as ordinary labourers.

In 1806 the management of the Imperial Theatres in Moscow purchased the last large group of thirty-six serf dancers and musicians from the estate of Stolypin. Other bankrupt landowners also destroyed their theatres.

By the first quarter of the nineteenth century the serf ballet—one of the most interesting indigenous phenomena of the national theatre—was no more.

CHAPTER II

THE IMPERIAL BALLET UNDER VALBERKH
AND DIDELOT

By THE BEGINNING of the nineteenth century Russian ballet was a strong, complete and rapidly developing institution, in line with the prevalent trends in arts and letters.

Its broader ties with life were explained, no doubt, by the important changes in the very system of organization. Ballet and opera became available to anybody who could afford a ticket. Prices were in no way prohibitive, while the presence of a *rayok* (paradise gallery) enabled people of the humblest means to see good theatre—and the rows of simple benches were always filled.

Public Theatres, whether dramatic or lyric, no longer depended entirely on private enterprise like that of Maddox in Moscow, or Kniepper in Petersburg.

True, Imperial theatres as a state system were established as early as 1756 by decree of Catherine II (a Russian dramatic theatre, consisting largely of serf actors and headed by the playwright Sumarokov). Ten years later, in 1766, Catherine II founded a *Directorate of the Imperial Theatres*. Its first Director, Ivan Yelagin, a writer of sorts and cabinet minister compiled a "List of the personnel of all theatres" that comprised: (*a*) Italian Opera and Chamber Music, (*b*) Ballet, (*c*) Ballroom Orchestras, (*d*) French Theatre, (*e*) Russian Dramatic Theatre, (*f*) Staff of artisans and other serfs needed by the respective theatres.

The same "Staff list" gave official status to the theatre school (of which the ballet division was an integral part) and instituted State pensions for the artists.

Of course the main purpose of such theatres in the eighteenth century was still to entertain the Court. But Russian dramatic actors, aside from performing on the palace stage in turn with other court companies, were obliged to "give public performances for money in the city theatres". This practice increased with the times and became prevalent in the nineteenth century.

The Imperial Theatres of Moscow were founded in 1806, soon after the failure of the Maddox enterprise. In the absence of a more suitable building, performances were given for the first two years in the grand

Skomorokhi in old Moscow. (Bakhrushin Theatre Museum, Moscow)
Ballet lesson of a serf ballerina. Lithograph from the Bakhrushin Theatre
Museum, Moscow

Tatiana Shlykova-Granatova, serf ballerina. Portrait by serf painter, A. Argunov.

mansion belonging to Pashkov (now housing the main section of the Lenin Library) and between 1808 and 1812 at the wooden Arbat Theatre, otherwise called the New Imperial. The first gala performance of opera and ballet took place at the New Bolshoi (big) Petrovsky Theatre on January 6 (19), 1825, with a grand prologue, *The Victory of the Muses* by Mikhail Dmitriyev to music by Alexei Verstovsky (composer and in 1848-1860 Director of the Moscow Imperial Theatres) and choreography by Felicité Hulin-Sor (a French *danseuse* who remained in Moscow to the end of her days, becoming a Russian subject). The prologue was followed by a grand ballet, *Cinderella*, with music by M. Sor, husband of Felicité Hulin, who in those days was still able to perform the title-role, as well as that of Terpsichore in the prologue.

The scale and grandeur of the theatre exceeded in every way its modest predecessor, the first Petrovsky Theatre, even though the architect Bovet used part of the old foundation and walls (found to be still there during the last big repairs of the present Bolshoi).

The new building was erected in the severe empire style with classical proportions. A quadriga driven by Apollo crowned its impressive colonnade for twenty-nine years until this theatre was also burnt to ashes on March 11, 1853. However, when Alexandre Benois' grandfather, the architect Alberto Cavos, rebuilt the Bolshoi—on an even grander scale—in 1856, the bronze horses were installed in their rightful place together with Apollo, and continue to adorn the building of the contemporary Bolshoi theatre.

There were two sides to the activity of the Imperial Theatres Directorate. Undoubtedly it consolidated national artistic talent and potentialities, assisting, whether deliberately or not, towards their development. On the other hand it conducted a policy of discrimination against native actors, however talented, in favour of foreign companies and guest-artists, giving the latter higher pay and better conditions in every respect. Artists in the service of the Imperial Theatres, whether in bondage of serfdom or not, could be arrested and detained at the offices of the Directorate, at police stations, prisons, or, as happened in the case of the famous tragic actor Karatygin, who dared to lean against a table in the presence of Director Maikov, even in the damp cells of the Peter and Paul fortress.

Another, earlier, Director of the Imperial Theatres, Prince Tyufiakin, hit an eight-year-old boy from the ballet school on the eye with a huge telescope (used in those days like binoculars), because the child ran across the back of the stage during the performance of a ballet. Vengeance, however, followed indirectly some years later, when Prince Tyufiakin lost his post: a sudden inspection of the School discovered it to be in a most deplorable state of dirt and mismanagement, with bad and insufficient food and poor bedding, outrageous in view of the funds allotted for maintenance. The situation was remedied. On the whole the Theatre School was well organized and provided sound professional training coupled with at least a reasonable amount of general education. Similarly, the Moscow school improved considerably upon passing under the control of the Imperial Theatres. (During Maddox's ownership of the school, he looked upon it in a purely commercial way. Any general education was discontinued and the pupils used for making props and as theatrical jacks-of-all-trades.)

The condition of the Moscow school improved in particular when Ivan Valberkh was sent there from St. Petersburg in 1807-1808 for the purpose of raising its standards.

Valberkh was the first Russian ballet-master and choreographer to make a name in history, though it is hard to say how many potential talents, like for instance Timofei Bublikov, were never given a proper chance in the time of the serf ballet or even in the Court theatre.

The origin of Ivan Valberkh (1766-1819) is still a matter of discussion. Yuri Slonimsky points out in his Introduction to *Ivan Valberkh. From the Archives of the Ballet-master* (Iskusstvo, Moscow–Leningrad, 1948) that the man's father was a theatrical tailor to the Imperial Theatres. Children of such employees were often placed in the Theatre School, from which Valberkh graduated in 1786. The ballet-master used the Russian ending of "kh" for his name, and was also known as "Liesogorov" a literal translation into Russian of "Wald-berg", or, as it may have been the case, vice versa—many artists invented for themselves foreign-sounding *noms de théâtre*.

Yuri Bakhrushin, the Moscow historian, on the other hand, supports the theory (mentioned as a fact in Pluchard's *Lexicon* of 1837) that Valberkh's great-grandfather served in the Swedish army, was taken prisoner on the battle-field of Poltava, and, after a period of service in Peter I's regiments, was granted Russian nobility. (Pluchard says the ancestor was a Swedish noble.) Whichever way it was, Valberkh or Valberg's genealogy is of no particular importance. Russian to the core, he took an important part in the independent development of national ballet, playing no mean role in the formation of the national style of Russian ballet.

A pupil of Angiolini and Canziani, and one who had danced in many ballets mounted by Le Picq, Valberkh was well acquainted with the ideas of Noverre's *ballet d'action* and carried them much further in his own ballets—always dramatically convincing, while his characters were based on actual persons, borrowed from history, or derived from literary works, or even from the life of the period.

A creative artist of Valberkh's type was needed by Russian ballet and he was brought forward by the current of the time. With the strengthening of indigenous ballet Russian composers created the first native works—not only in ballet, but in comic opera, where the action invariably changed from singing to dancing, and vice versa. One only has to mention the late eighteenth-century Russian operas of Mikhail Matinsky and Yevstignei Fomin, wherein Russian folk dancing was built into the *divertissements*, the first ballet compositions of Alexei and Sergei Titov, and, a little further into the nineteenth century, those of Alexander Aliabiev and Alexander Varlamov.

Now came a Russian choreographer. In many ways Valberkh was the last representative of the eighteenth century and the first one of the dawning nineteenth with its romantic ballet. He was still tied to the conventions of eighteenth-century classicism and his ballets tended to be a little heavy and pantomimic. He even resorted to lengthy written synopses explaining the action in accordance with old tradition.

On the other hand Valberkh, who was a self-educated man keeping abreast with the current literary trends and maintaining close friendship with many literary figures, reflected in his best works the new Sentimentalism, with its portrayal of the inner life of ordinary, small people, and its attempts at the presentation of realistic surroundings. It was but one step from there to Romanticism, which followed as a natural development of the preceding stage.

His ballets bore all the other typical features of Sentimentalism—the taste for melodramatic effect and the tendency towards the didactic and moralizing treatment of subjects, with Virtue invariably triumphing over Vice.

In order to augment his meagre salary (for carrying out the duties of dancer, choreographer, ballet-master and inspector of the ballet company, Valberkh was paid many times less than Canziani received just for heading the school) and to support an ever-growing family, the budding choreographer translated into Russian many French melodramas that remained in the repertory of Russian dramatic theatres many years after his death. Thus he became acquainted with the popular melodramas by Pixérécourt, such as *Le Pèlerin blanc, ou les Orphelins du Hameau* freely adapted by him in the ballet *Count Castelli or the Criminal Brother* (music by Martini,

Sarti and Davidov, 1804), and often borrowed from other dramatic and operatic works. Thus his *Romeo and Julia* (1809), "a tragic ballet with choruses", of which, unfortunately, no libretto had been preserved, was probably based not so much on Shakespeare's tragedy, as on Steibelt's opera of the same name which had a happy ending. (Valberkh himself danced or, probably, mimed the part of Romeo.)

While pantomime, of which he was past master, predominated in Valberkh's creations, and dance usually appeared in the form of *divertissements* at feasts, weddings and the like, at least one of them, *Blanca, or Marriage out of Revenge* (1803), with music by one of the very first Russian ballet composers, Alexei Titov, again freely adapted from Le Sage and other sources, was based on dance cleverly woven into the action and expressing its content in the true spirit of genuine *ballet d'action*.

Many titles of Valberkh's ballets—*Clara, or the Resort to Virtue, The American Heroine, or Perfidy Punished*—indicate their moralizing nature. On the other hand, as early as 1799, he created, together with composer Sergei Titov, the first ballet in Russia founded on a topical subject. Although the ballet was entitled *The New Werther*, its original theme was merely reminiscent of the succession of events in Goethe's famous novel that caused a veritable "Wertheriana" all over the world. In 1808, during his two years' stay in Moscow, Valberkh revived this production.

It was a truly bold undertaking. Valberkh ironically declared in 1815: "I dared to write the ballet *The New Werther* and Oh! how I was attacked by alleged wits and connoisseurs! What! A ballet that is going to be danced in frock-coats? I thought that I was finished: but *real connoisseurs* appeared and the ballet had a success. Nevertheless when I undertook another 'ballet of morals', I dared not use frock-coats any more but dressed myself and all the others in Spanish costume."[1] Valberkh termed anything portraying life, a "ballet of morals" in the spirit of the times. There is every evidence that in *The New Werther*, at any rate, he created a contemporary tragedy.

A special place in Valberkh's legacy must be given to his patriotic ballets of the 1812 war when the whole of Russia stood up against the Napoleonic invasion. Perhaps Valberkh's ballets were a trifle too literal and pedestrian, but they reflected his eagerness to join with his countrymen in their struggle and to publicize their victory.

During this period, spent partly in Moscow, Valberkh created such

[1] *Ivan Valberkh. From the Archives of the Ballet-master.* Edited by Yuri Slonimsky. Preparation of the text by A. A. Stepanov. Iskusstvo, Moscow–Leningrad, 1948, pp. 166-167.

ballets as *The New Heroine or the Woman Cossack*, the theme of which was connected with the story of Nadezhda Durova, heroine of the Patriotic War. The music of this ballet is unknown, or rather it consisted of assorted melodies. But another patriotic ballet, *Love for the Motherland*, staged by Valberkh in 1812 to music by Catarino Cavos, is known to have roused the feelings of the spectators to such an extent that, according to contemporary evidence, people went straight from the theatre to enlist in the army. Among other ballets of this kind, created by Valberkh, may be found *A Cossack in London, The Russians in Germany, or the Consequence of Love for the Motherland, A Festival in the Allied Armies Camp at Montmartre, Russia's Victory, or the Russians in Paris*, and *A Russian Village Fête*. The last named, containing Russian and Gypsy dancing, was choreographed, like *Russians in Germany* and several other pieces, in collaboration with Auguste Poireau, known as Auguste, who became one of the great character dancers on the Russian ballet stage and a real specialist in Russian folk dancing, of which he was such an expert performer that in 1839 he was recalled from retirement to teach a Russian dance to Marie Taglioni, and to perform it with her on the stage. Auguste did not count as a Frenchman, being one of those numerous foreigners who became thoroughly naturalized in Russia. Otherwise the period of the late eighteenth century, when the tsarist government feared the importation of anything even reminiscent of the dreaded French Revolution, and the early nineteenth, when patriotic feelings forbade the use of artists or works connected with an enemy country, proved beneficial for Russian ballet, which had the chance to develop its national school without the habitual restrictions on the part of officialdom, with its normal policy of preference for everything foreign.

So it came about that when Charles Louis Didelot, whose name became inseparably bound with an important era in Russian ballet, arrived in St. Petersburg, he found there a strong, well-trained professional company with its own repertory, and a well-organized school full of promising pupils. This was also due to the efforts of Ivan Valberkh, and perhaps represented the most important part of what he had done for Russian ballet.

Valberkh was appointed Director of the St. Petersburg School and Inspector (manager) of the ballet company performing at the St. Petersburg Bolshoi Theatre in 1794, when Canziani left and the school not only remained without a leader, but was in a most vulnerable state, as the Directorate of the Imperial Theatres had a new "bright idea": all ballet pupils were to be taught at the same time as singers, orchestra musicians, and painters of settings. These plans threatened the professionalism of

Russian ballet education, and Valberkh came to its rescue. In a short time he put the St. Petersburg School in perfect order, and it is not surprising that when the Directorate of the Moscow Theatres received the former Orphanage School in a deplorable state after the year of Maddox's ownership, it sent for Valberkh to reorganize it and place it on a proper footing.

Valberkh formed many outstanding dancers. However great was the talent of the outstanding actress and *danseuse* Eugenia Kolosova, it was Valberkh who not only taught her (he was a great mime himself) but gave her a place among his own family, for which she remained ever grateful. Valberkh kept as ward another orphan from the school—Anna Kontini. Among his pupils may be found such names as Anastasia Berilova and Arina Tumanova (these brilliant ballerinas died young of tuberculosis) and Isaak Ablets—a character dancer of repute, creator of national *divertissements* and patriotic spectacles in the Moscow ballet, thus continuing what his teacher had begun.

Last, but not least, Valberkh's activity as translator. The Moscow University printing shop published in 1790 a translation of Compan's *Dictionnaire de la Danse*. While anonymous, it is believed that the translation was done by Valberkh. He visited Paris—the first Russian choreographer to do so—later, in 1802, but he could have purchased the dictionary in Petersburg.

It is important to note that in his Paris diary Valberkh expresses great regret at his inability to visit, in his retirement at Saint Germain en Laye, Jean Georges Noverre, whom he revered. In another part of the diary Valberkh criticizes the Paris Opéra ballet for its superficiality and even goes so far as to express displeasure with the "grimacing and incessant whirling" of Auguste Vestris, whom he compares unfavourably with "the noble Deshayes".

Valberkh remained true to the tastes and aesthetics formed in the Russian ballet. He lived a fruitful if not always rewarding life, full of privations and ill health. He died of tuberculosis, abandoning teaching and the creation of new ballets just four months before his demise on July 14, 1819.

The circumstances and motives that brought Charles Louis Didelot (1767-1837) to Russia were not in any way extraordinary. Yuri Slonimsky quite justly points out in his definitive biography of the choreographer,[1]

[1] Yuri Slonimsky. *Didelot. Milestones of a Biography in Art.* Iskusstvo, Leningrad–Moscow, 1958.

the result of twenty years of research, that in the beginning St. Petersburg was visualized by Didelot as a purely temporary halt on the way to Paris with its *Académie de Musique* (the official name of the Opéra).

Already at that time Didelot was displeased with his lot. He dreamed of broad vistas, of personal success as a dancer, of great stages where he could implement his ideas for new ballets and new ways of composing them, with which he was literally seething. He hoped to find all this in Paris as Noverre did before him. But intrigue and professional envy repeatedly barred Didelot's attempts to enter the precincts of the *Académie*, jealously guarded by its current *maîtres de ballet* and *premiers danseurs*. He never recovered from the tremendous blow to his pride when, after a brilliant début in September 1788 on the boards of the Opéra, he was nevertheless refused a place in the company. He was now firmly determined to prove his merit there as a choreographer. That is why when he signed a contract, at first for a relatively minor position, to dance for three years in Petersburg as from September 1801; it was done largely because no other foreign country paid as well. Didelot expected to stay for a short time in Russia and find broader horizons elsewhere. Little did he envisage that eventually he was to settle in Russia for good, and that it was there that he would gain a name to remain for ever in the annals of the theatre, bringing him, albeit posthumously, the universal recognition of a stature he never dreamed of.

True, Didelot had considerable success in London, where he was first able to realize many of his ideas and create such ballets as *Flore et Zéphire* and *The Hungarian Hut*. But the conditions in London, with no state-owned ballet companies and repertory theatres, were not propitious for proper development of choreographic talent. Didelot was unable to carry out there half of what he had planned to do as choreographer, and was probably tormented by semi-dormant pedagogic and organizing talents.

It did not take him very long to realize that the Russia of the time was already an enlightened country with a flourishing theatrical culture of national and state importance, wherein ballet was given an equal and rightful position.

No less important for the full fruition of his talents and plans was the fact that the capital possessed an excellent opera house, with a stage so deep and so well equipped that he was able to organize aerial flights, at which he was such a past master, not only from one side of the stage to the other, as was done previously in the first London production of *Flore et Zéphire*, but from the back-cloth to the footlights, as occurred in the beautifully choreographed "Dance of the Winds", released from a cave, in the *divertissement* in Boieldieu's opera *Telemachus at the Isle of Calypso*. There was really no theatrical effect that the machinery of the Bolshoi Theatre of St. Petersburg could not supply, and whole mountains fell, ships sank, and dozens of cupids flew escorting aerial chariots driven by as many as sixty live doves in Didelot's anacreontic ballets, typical of his first period in Russia (1801-1811).

The Bolshoi Theatre of St. Petersburg was erected in 1783 under the name of the Kamenny or Stone Theatre, and already in those times seated about two thousand. In 1802 it was rebuilt by Thomas de Thomon on an even grander scale, but with the preservation of the classical traditional style, and acquired the name of Bolshoi or Big. This building suffered the fate of so many opera houses of the time, depending on candles and other primitive sources of lighting, and burned down on the night of January 1, 1811. However, in 1818, the Bolshoi Theatre was built anew and was thus again available during Didelot's second, much longer, sojourn in Russia (1816-1837).

One of the characteristic features of the large square in front of the Bolshoi Theatre was formed by the six stone pavillions or arbours, used for making bonfires in winter, when coachmen spent many long hours in bitter cold awaiting their masters' exit from the theatre.

At first operas, ballets and dramas were all given in succession at the St. Petersburg Bolshoi. After it was rebuilt once more in 1836 by Alberto Cavos, during which the ceiling was considerably raised in order to facilitate the use of new machines, the Bolshoi was used for nothing but opera and ballet. In 1889 the building was found to be unsafe for further use. It was rebuilt (by 1896 only) by the Russian Musical Society and still houses the Conservatoire. As to ballet performances, they continued from 1889 at the Mariinsky theatre alone (built in 1860 also by Cavos), while in the earlier part of the second half of the nineteenth century they may have been seen at both theatres.

Each of Didelot's periods in Russia has its own distinctive features, yet on the other hand, though separated by a lapse of five years, they cannot be considered quite in isolation from each other.

While Didelot did not create anything new in the first period, restricting himself to familiar mythological subjects—*Apollo and Daphne* (1802), *The Shepherd and the Hamadryads* (1803), *Zéphire et Flore* (1804), *Cupid and Psyche* (1809), the already mentioned "Dance of the Winds" from *Telemachus*, which in reality was a complete *ballet d'action*, and the like. However, even these old themes appeared in an entirely new guise.

Right: Ivan Valberkh.

Below: Charles Didelot in Petersburg. Water-colour by an unknown artist, 1841.

Scene from *Le Diable à Quatre* (*The Wilful Wife*). Kusilova and Alexandrov

Gone was the eighteenth-century convention of presenting even shepherds in thickly powdered wigs and buckled shoes. Characters from Didelot's anacreontic ballets wore light gauze tunics, that no longer restricted free movement: their arms and shoulders were bare, their feet shod in light slippers enabling them to dance on three-quarter point, while women even stood on full *pointe* for a fraction of a second.

These new costumes were in harmony with the new poetic quality of the choreography and treatment of subject. Pluchard's *Lexicon* made no bones about Valberkh's ballets in comparison with those of Didelot, who undoubtedly possessed greater choreographic talent. The *Lexicon* said: "Valberg's ballets had great dramatic interest and were arranged with great mastery, but they lacked those beautiful groupings and charming dances, through which Didelot's rich imagination lent the entire gamut of poetry to the art of ballet."

It was, indeed, this new quality in Didelot's creations that charmed the audience. Adam Gluszkowski, Didelot's closest Russian disciple, pointed out in his memoirs[1] that Didelot never tried to mask lack of talent by intricate stage effects and machinery, though he did use them in the right places when it was necessary to emphasize some development of the story. "He replaced all false opulence by the richness of his own fantasy," wrote Gluszkowski. "One could always do without velvet, brocade, and gilt in his subject-matter: life, interest, and grace stood in their stead. Picturesque arrangement of characters and groupings was always at his hand to conceal any external defects."

Didelot was a true follower of Noverre, whose precepts he acquired through his own teacher and the great reformer's pupil, Dauberval. There is no doubt that Didelot's creations found such great success with the Russian public because Noverre's ideas were very close to the ideals of the Russian ballet and Russian thought. Didelot strove to express the story through *action*, either in dance or in mime, that in his best works became danced mime.

Even the ballets of his first Russian period were, as a rule, new versions of his previous works because he, in turn, found in Russia an extremely beneficial field and material for carrying out his greatest hopes.

Of the new versions of the first period the most important was *Zéphire et Flore*. It is not accidental that the title placed Zéphire, the light and in-constant God of Wind, in the first place, instead of the *Flore et Zéphire* of the original London production. The St. Petersburg version of the

[1] A. P. Gluszkowski. *Memoirs of a Ballet-master*. Edited and prepared for publication by Yuri Slonimsky. Iskusstvo, Leningrad–Moscow, 1940.

ballet was newly recreated by Didelot for the illustrious guest-artist Duport, a virtuoso who in those times knew no equal and for a while took all theatre-going St. Petersburg by storm. Didelot was able to use to great advantage Duport's tremendous elevation. Although, as in the London production, Zéphire flew on to the stage of the Bolshoi Theatre on a wire, creating a tremendous sensation, and although Didelot was able to use dozens of children as flying cupids in his ballets, and even literally *hundreds* of supers whenever it was necessary to create impressive mass scenes, the real novelty was in the new technique of dancing, furthered and developed by the master in order to enhance the poetic qualities of ballet.

Didelot's choreography for Zéphire's solos made his dancer traverse the entire stage in several huge leaps and the dance itself became ethereal. Moreover, Didelot considerably deepened the very essence of the old mythological story. His characters were endowed with human feelings —they loved, they were inconstant and frivolous, but in the end, like Zéphire in the new version, having passed through the ennobling experience of suffering, they became true to their loves. Duport was not much of an actor, but Didelot's choreography was so arranged that it spoke for itself. Later, after coming into closer contact with Russian dancers and discovering their great talents for projection and identification with their assumed characters, he preferred to work with them and was ever opposed to the repeated attempts by the Directors of the Imperial Theatres to invite further guest-artists. Didelot created for Russian dancers and through their co-operation really exceptional choreographic images. One literally sees one of them from a brilliant contemporary description by an anonymous critic in the German-language magazine *Ryuthenia*, published in Petersburg. We may read in Number I for 1807: "In this spectacle [the talk is of *Telemachus at the Isle of Calypso*, Boieldieu's opera wherein Didelot had created the brilliant Ballet of the Winds and other dance interludes.—N.R.] the most droll part belongs to a little Bacchus, a girl from the Theatre School, who had been tasting too often from Hebe's cup. 'He' becomes inebriated and in this state dances a charming solo." The part of the small Bacchus was danced by Yekaterina Azarova, who later graduated from the school under Didelot in 1815. A more detailed description of the actual content of the dance created for her by Didelot is contained in the memoirs of a Russian dramatic actress, Alexandra Asenkova,[1] who, having been a pupil of the Theatre School,

[1] A. E. Asenkova. "Memoirs of a Russian Actress." In: *Theatrical and Musical Monitor* for 1857, SPB, No. 44, p. 607.

which did not draw a strict line between drama and ballet, was very closely acquainted with both arts: Asenkova wrote that Azarova was dressed as Bacchus in a blue tunic with a wreath of leaves and bunches of grapes on her curls. "Sipping wine from a gold cup, she, smilingly, watched the dances of the maenads, gradually falling under the influence of the inebriating drink. She traversed the stage in shaky but graceful steps, and, in the end, fell asleep in complete exhaustion, with her head leaning against the arm of one of the maenads."

Didelot created many parts for children in his ballets, some of them important ones, such as the son of Count Rackozski in *The Hungarian Hut*, or the seven-year-old son of Raoul de Créquis in the ballet of the same name.

The choreographer had plenty of youthful talent at his disposal. His activity at the Theatre School was perhaps the most important aspect of what he had done in Russia, though, quite naturally, all the sides of his many-faceted creative life were equally important and blended in one harmonious whole.

Rafail Zotov, a contemporary St. Petersburg theatre critic, pointed out[1] that "Didelot did not want to write big ballets until the dancing school was reformed", and in addition left the following reminiscences about the man's character: "People of genius possess an inborn ability of inspiring their surroundings. Didelot was far from sweet to his pupils, yet they obeyed him unconditionally, thinking of only one thing: how to please their master. Didelot had a fiery and often quite ungovernable temper— and yet he was loved and even adored by everybody."

This is a much more unbiassed opinion of Didelot as a man than the numerous anecdotes about his cruel stick (used even more liberally on the more gifted pupils) and endless hours of strict schooling. Apart from technique, justly considered by the master to be the cornerstone of future artistry, Didelot taught his pupils all the secrets of expressive acting through the body and face. Fedor Koni, one of the most enlightened theatre critics of the nineteenth century, understood full well that Didelot "wanted in every possible way to pass on his ideal and it was with this aim in mind that he spared neither pleas, nor tears, nor guile".[2]

Having been given a free hand at the School by the Directorate of the Imperial Theatres (his obligations as dancer and choreographer, according

[1] Rafail Zotov. "My Reminiscences of the Theatre". *Repertory of the Russian Theatre* for 1840, vol. II, book 7, p. 34.

[2] In: "Biography of N. O. Dure", see *Repertory of the Russian Theatre* for 1839, vol. II, book 7, p. 8.

to the contract that was renewed every three years, bound him to a much greater extent), Didelot started work with all the fanatical fervour of which he was capable. This was what he had hoped to have for so many years—a school full of young talents, trained according to precepts and ideals worked out by himself, but in accordance with those of his own predecessors in ballet such as Dauberval.

That these ideals coincided with the aesthetics of Russian ballet in its best manifestations was of paramount importance for Didelot's successful work in Russia.

In the first ten-year period he formed many brilliant pupils—Yakov Lustikh, Adam Gluszkowski who started under Valberkh, Maria Ikonina, Anastasia Novitskaya, and Maria Danilova (a *danseuse* of really outstanding talent, Duport's partner in *Zéphire et Flore*, immortalized by many contemporary poets after her untimely death from tuberculosis)—all dancers of distinct and varied individual personalities.

And yet Didelot left St. Petersburg rather in haste early in 1811, and it is not quite clear why. Perhaps because the Bolshoi Theatre was burned to ashes on New Year's Eve of 1811 and there was no other theatre with machinery and as large a stage enabling him to produce grand ballets. Or, as Borisoglebsky suggested in volume I of *Materials for the History of Russian Ballet* (1938, p. 63), perhaps he was deeply offended by a considerable reduction in pay. While his salary remained the same, after November 4, 1810, it was not paid in silver, but in paper money, and that made an appreciable difference.

Or perhaps the cherished desire to try his luck in Paris as choreographer still tormented Didelot—at any rate it was he who asked for release from his contract, which had been concluded for three more years not more than four months ago.

After a period of two years at the King's Theatre, London, where Didelot proved himself to be a mature choreographer, considerably enriched by his experience in Russia and creating, aside from the impressive pantomime ballet *The Hungarian Hut* (1813), a *divertissement* embodying Russian and other dances learnt by him during his Eastern travels, Didelot hastened to Paris as soon as the allied troops entered the French capital.

Didelot's Russian biographer, Nicolai Mundt, informs us that the choreographer's repeated attempts to mount his *Flore et Zéphire* at the Paris Opéra, again meeting with the die-hard resistance of Gardel, materialized only because of the intervention of Russian patrons heading the occupational troops of the period.

Didelot created, in an atmosphere of hostility and deliberate sabotage, an entirely new version of his *Zéphire* that had a brilliant première on December 15, 1815. At last Didelot in one crushing blow settled his ancient feud with Gardel and created a ballet that brought him European recognition. *Flore et Zéphire* became a classical model destined to attain one hundred and eighty-nine performances at the Opéra (up to March 1826) and to serve as a most important vehicle for Marie Taglioni's debut when it was revived in 1830-1831. Didelot was a true precursor of the Romantic Ballet, or rather the first choreographer of Romanticism and the last one of Classicism.

In spite of his triumph, Didelot could not possibly feel happy at the Opéra, though its directors now came forward with tempting offers. Success on the boards of the Opéra could have brought him nothing but new disillusionment and bitter opposition, as may be conjectured from the witty vaudeville by Scribe, *Flore et Zéphire* (1816), with a Flore who complains that they tried to separate her from her beloved Zéphire because he was not allowed at the Opéra, and a *maître de ballet* whose desire to meet the Parisian public encounters opposition.

Every circumstance indicated that it was better for Didelot to accept the invitation of the Directorate of the Imperial Theatres to return to Russia. However, this time it was he who dictated the conditions. He wanted a contract not for three years as was invariably customary for any foreign actor, but for six, so as to have enough time to mould his artists and carry out his plans for new ballets. He demanded a salary of 16,000 roubles annually for himself and his second wife Rose, née Colinette, a yearly benefit, recognition of his entire period of service in Russia with a view to a future pension, and many other just demands, that took the Directorate aback, but were subsequently agreed.

Didelot's great pantomimic ballets, created during his second period of work at the Imperial theatres, lasting for fifteen years, presented vehicles for the talents of Yevgenia (Eugenia) Kolosova (1780-1869) and other dancers for whom she served as a model, exerting considerable influence on the nature of Russian ballet of the period. The brilliant dancer-actress Kolosova was not only a great mime, she was also famed for her extremely graceful execution of the Russian dance, to which she added professional dexterity. In addition she sang well, appeared in opera and enacted *en travestie* the role of an officer in the comedy *Bridegrooms*. No wonder Didelot prized dancer-actors such as Kolosova and her like, because he was able to carry out with their help his vast new schemes.

Upon his return to Petersburg Didelot created several new works no longer connected with themes borrowed from mythology, though the first ballet, shown on August 30, 1816, to music by Cavos, was entitled *Acis and Galatea*, and belonged to the anacreontic *genre*.

Rafail Zotov pronounced it to be "worthy of Didelot's talent". The public was even more impressed in the following year by *The Hungarian Hut*, a grand "tragico-comic ballet" in four acts, created anew after the first London production of 1813 to music by Venua. London never possessed such dancer-actresses as Kolosova or Likhutina. Didelot was able considerably to enrich the production of his ballet at Petersburg, although, to his regret, the Bolshoi Theatre was not yet rebuilt after the fire and he had to be satisfied with a much smaller stage.[1] In his Preface to the Russian text of the libretto Didelot mentioned that he revived it expressly for Mme Kolosova (it was actually presented for her benefit performance on December 17, 1817, with her in the role of Count Rackozski's wife).

The Hungarian Hut was a pantomime ballet, intended to serve as a vehicle for Kolosova's great mimetic talents. But a study of the Venua score used in London, carried out by Doctor Gozenpud, proved that it was more than a pantomime with a few danced *divertissements*. Of the twenty-four "numbers" only four or five lack dance element and are intended for battle scenes and the like. Doctor Gozenpud found the music to be "lyrical and full of dramatism",[2] but, on the other hand, completely lacking any national Hungarian colour, though this would not be surprising at that time.

On the other hand the story of *The Hungarian Hut* was connected with actual historical events drawn from the life of the Hungarian hero, Ferenc Rakoczy (1676-1735), leader of an insurrection against the Austrians, though the libretto (Didelot gave him the name of Count Rackozski) did not in many ways faithfully reproduce historical events, inasmuch as all ends well in the ballet, while the real Rakoczy ended his days in exile.

The importance of *The Hungarian Hut* lay in its great dramatic conviction and Didelot's ability to mix with great intuition comic and tragic episodes so that the spectators laughed and cried in succession.

The ballet remained in the repertory for a long time and was last

[1] After the Bolshoi Theatre in Petersburg had burned down, opera and ballet (as well as drama) were presented from January 11, 1811, and up to the reopening of the reconstructed Bolshoi on February 3, 1818, at the "German theatre", belonging to the Directorate of the Imperial Theatres. It was located on Dvorzovaya (Palace) Square.

[2] A. Gozenpud. *Musical Theatre in Russia from its origins to Glinka*, Leningrad, 1958, p. 499. Contains a detailed account of the libretto (pp. 496-497).

revived in 1853, when Carlotta Grisi and Jules Perrot took part in the benefit of Yelena Andreyanova, with a brilliant cast of other Russian artists.

All that Didelot had at times merely traced in *The Hungarian Hut* was fully developed by him in his major and most important work: *Raoul de Créquis, or the Return from the Crusades.* This new grand pantomime ballet in five acts was shown at the Bolshoi Theatre, newly opened the previous year, on May 5, 1819, to music by Catarino Cavos and his pupil T. V. Zhuchkovsky.

The theme was not new—but there was a world of difference in its treatment by Didelot, who created a poetically romantic silent drama, and that of his predecessors, using the same subject. The opera by d'Alayrac (text by Monvel) produced in Paris in 1789, while very popular, was in the lyrical and sentimental vein. Viganò's ballet about the noble knight, thrown into prison by the tyrant, was of a much more dramatic nature. Viganò introduced changes into Monvel's libretto (while using d'Alayrac's music). Didelot's was an entirely new work. He said so in the Preface to the published programme: "My plan is quite different from the story of the opera written by Monvel. I borrowed from him one scene only: that when the keys are being stolen from the jailer. But even this scene appears in an entirely different form and with another ending than in the opera."

Didelot considerably developed the dramatic action in this scene, in many ways creating it anew. The stage in the fourth act of his *Raoul de Créquis* was divided into two parts: at the left was the jail where Raoul lay in chains on a bed of straw, and the guard-room occupied by the wicked prison jailer, Humbert (in the d'Alayrac opera there was a kind jailer, whose children released de Créquis). The introduction of the wicked Humbert increased the dramatic tension: the spectators' feelings were roused by this revolting character and they literally forgot the boundaries between real life and fiction in their anxiety for the successful completion of de Créquis' escape. This was done with the help of Alin, a soldier from de Créquis' camp, disguised as a sentinel, and his sweetheart Marguerite, who had to steal the keys to the knight's cell, which were attached to the scarf of the sleeping villain Humbert. In order to keep the spectators in a constant state of ever growing tension, Didelot made Marguerite drop the keys just after the release of Raoul, thus waking the jailer. However, after a skirmish, Humbert got himself locked up in the cell, where he was discovered at dawn by the arch-villain of the ballet, Baudouin, and the executioner.

The atmosphere of tension was both excellently conveyed and strengthened by the music. Gluszkowski tells that the score here was purposely arranged as a *quartetto*, while, in order to make it even more hushed, the violins had sordines to mute the sound. The noise made by prison locks and latches (performed by special machines located backstage) was very clearly heard with this hushed music as a background and was deliberately planned, inasmuch as the latches worked at a definite time in harmony with the score.

Didelot's collaboration with all his composers, but especially with Catarino Cavos, author of most of his St. Petersburg ballets, is a little-known subject that has been, however, studied by the Leningrad musicologist, A. S. Rabinovich,[1] and by Doctor Gozenpud. These studies have established that Cavos' operas were inferior musically and dramatically to his ballets, because the latter were composed after a detailed scenario supplied by Didelot, who worked out the sequence of scenes in the action and the nature and length of the musical "numbers". While Didelot treated music as the servant of choreography according to the custom of his time, he nevertheless paid far more attention to it than his other colleagues. All his choreography was extremely musical in the best sense of the word, and he demanded the same musicality from the dancers in his ballets. (It is impossible to go into greater detail here on the subject for lack of space, but the interested scholar may find analyses of the score of *Raoul de Créquis* in A. A. Gozenpud, *op. cit.*, pp. 509-512.)

In act III there was a scene in a tower, where Baudouin, in his effort to attain Adelaide's favours, kept her prisoner together with little Craon. There were many touching details here, such as when Craon, thinking that his mother was sleeping and tripping over her chains, touched his lips with his finger as if saying: "hush". The role of the Countess Adelaide, performed by Yevgenia Kolosova, afforded many occasions for her to exercise her exceptional dramatic gifts. The scene reached its climax when Baudouin, pretending that Raoul de Créquis (performed by Auguste Poireau) was killed, and showing his standard to the alleged widow, offered her the choice of wedding him or being put to death. It was at this point that an arrow flew into the window with a note from friends, promising rescue. The Countess rejoiced while trying to conceal her feelings. Desiring to have his revenge on the Countess, Baudouin ordered a soldier to throw Craon from the tower. Adelaide-Kolosova, begging for mercy, hugged her child. But the soldier tore it out of her arms. Then Adelaide, summoning all her strength, snatched up the de

[1] A. S. Rabinovich. *Russian Opera Before Glinka*. Musgiz, Leningrad, 1948.

Créquis standard and killed the soldier with a thrust of its pointed staff.

De Créquis's standard, incidentally, was adroitly introduced by Didelot in several crucial moments of the story and was first displayed at the very beginning of the ballet in the picturesque scene showing the sinking ship of returning crusaders. Thus Didelot continued using every theatrical effect and all types of mime and dancing in this ballet in order to bring closer to the public its noble ideals.

As usual comedy and tragedy were freely alternated in various scenes. Didelot was in no way averse to comedy and produced many original ballets in this style in Petersburg, such as *Strange Encounters* (1818) or *Nicette and Luke, or the Young Dairy Girl* (1817).

His most important contribution in this manner was the first production in Russia (and the first revival, so to speak, from the horse's mouth, since Didelot was Dauberval's pupil and worked under him at Bordeaux) of *La Fille Mal Gardée* (October 11, 1827).

Among other titles of Didelot's various Russian creations one comes across *The Fire-Bird*, a magic opera in three acts by Cavos, "with choruses, ballets, games, transformations and the parallel flight of the Fire-Bird and the Dragon by special machines". In this opera Didelot choreographed the Persian and Tartar ballets of the second act.

The master often resorted to various Oriental themes that were always popular, and was a connoisseur of all sorts of eastern dances.

It was in an entirely new quality, however, that he met with the theme of the East in *The Prisoner of the Caucasus* (1823). Taken from the poem by Russia's national poet Alexander Pushkin, the inspired imagery of *The Prisoner of the Caucasus* literally gave wings to the ageing master. Didelot could not read Russian, but he was very closely connected with Petersburg literary circles, with writers and artists of his day. Practically any representative of the Russian intelligentsia spoke French. And Didelot confirmed the source from which he got the suggestion to borrow poetical subjects from Pushkin, by saying in the Preface to the published programme that he used Pushkin's poem for his new ballet because "all men of letters praise this excellent creation of Russian poesy". It is important to note that the ballet (the music was again composed by Cavos) was created only four and a half months after the poem's first publication, so "the men of letters" were probably people very close to Pushkin and well acquainted with the poem before its actual publication.

Pushkin himself wrote that Didelot's ballets "are filled with lively imagination and extraordinary charm". In his *Eugene Onegin* he immortalized Didelot by saying that he was "winged by fame" in the Russian

Theatre. In the same poem, reflecting upon the Didelot ballets that he saw so many times at the Bolshoi Theatre, ballets that served as a vehicle for the inspired dancing of Russian ballerinas, Pushkin, with the insight of a genius, put into one sentence the entire essence of the Russian school by saying, "Shall I ever see the Russian Terpsichore's *soul-inspired flight?*" a definition whose value has remained constant to the present day.

Pushkin himself was exiled to Kishenyov at the time of the première of *The Prisoner of the Caucasus*, but he was eagerly interested and enquired about its reception in his letters.

In actual fact the scenario of Didelot's *The Prisoner of the Caucasus* departed in many ways from the original. To begin with, Didelot placed the action "in ancient times", roughly into Slav Russia of the ninth century.

There were some concessions to tradition in the bad sense: the ballet had a happy ending with the Shade of the Prisoner's dying bride blessing his marriage with the Circassian girl.

Despite this and other departures from the story of the poem, its romantic spirit nevertheless survived in the ballet. Avdotia Istomina (1799-1848), one of the greatest dancers ever produced by Russian ballet, was trained by Didelot's Russian collaborators at the Petersburg school during his absence, but as a dancer she was formed by Didelot, in whose first ballet of the second period, *Acis and Galatea*, she made her debut as Galatea in 1816.

From then on she performed numerous roles in Didelot's creations. Primarily a *demi-caractère* dancer, she had a very wide range and could perform "serious" dancing of the very highest order. Pushkin immortalized her in *Eugene Onegin*.

Istomina created an unforgettable image of the Circassian Girl, which remained identified with her ever afterwards. The Prisoner was Nicolai Goltz, a pupil of Didelot, just out of school; he was to become one of the greatest mimes of Russian ballet.

Didelot was helped in the Russian *divertissements* by Auguste, a specialist in this kind of dancing. But the master created many highly romantic scenes that suggested the Caucasus of his time, rather than that of ancient Russia.

The settings closely resembled the wild and picturesque nature of the Caucasus. The artist, Nicolai Orlovsky, a great personal friend of Didelot, who took drawing lessons from him, designed at the choreographer's request some figurines of Caucasian warriors in costume, also far removed from the ancient Slavs.

And with this background at his disposal, Didelot created scenes which revealed the stature of his talent. An eagle flew down to a cradle in the mountain camp of the Circassians and carried off a young woman's baby. The cradle itself was poetically conceived by Didelot: it was attached to a sabre, stuck in the trunk of a tree, and represented a "burka" or Caucasian male cloak, attached to the sabre with the help of trappings taken from a war horse.

The child was lying in this improvised cradle, which was eloquent of the people's habits, of their nature and way of life. When the eagle flew away with the child, the Circassian mother followed the bird like a tigress, climbing the high mountain and rescuing her baby. It was this and similar scenes, and not the artificial "apotheosis" wherein the Circassian "Khan" (there was no such thing) became a Russian subject, that brought *The Prisoner of the Caucasus* lasting fame.

This was Didelot's last great victory. He had many other plans including one for a historical ballet about the taking of Kazan by Ivan the Terrible, and another based on *Macbeth*, but his further fate was becoming more and more tragic.

Since it was really impossible to find fault with his ballets, the Directorate of the Imperial Theatres started persecuting the "tiresome" master, ever seeking for perfection and too independent, in every other possible way. The pupils trained by him with such care in ballet classes were sent to dramatic theatres. The curriculum of the Theatre School was once more changed in order to give ballet an inferior position.

Yuri Slonimsky points out that as soon as Didelot became accepted as one of their own by the progressive artistic intelligentsia, as soon as he identified himself in spirit and in essence with Russian culture—and he really did—he became undesirable for the Court circles that engaged him. The more Didelot tried to be useful to Russian art, the less chance he was given to carry out his intentions.

Prince Gagarin, the newly appointed Director of the Imperial Theatres, was a man half the age of Didelot, and of ruthless manner and character. True, Didelot's final feud with Gagarin was merely the last of a long line of grievances. Didelot sent repeated memoranda to the Directorate, which increased in the final two years, wherein, apart from complaints, he expresses the assurance that the judgement of future generations will be in his favour. He was ready to give up any personal claims had he been given a chance to foster the school, to sacrifice all for the art he loved, for Russia that he considered to be his new home. That chance never came.

On October 31, 1829, Didelot was ordered by Gagarin to reduce the intermission during the performance of *Thésée et Arianne*. Didelot gave no such orders—the *danseuses* were not ready. Then the Prince ordered servants of the Bolshoi Theatre to arrest the *maître de ballet*. Didelot refused to follow them and, apparently, rendered some resistance to the men, who lifted him, carried him into the Director's office and locked him up. Having spent about 48 hours under arrest, Didelot immediately filed a petition asking to be released from his services. Every morning the official carriage of the Imperial Theatres arrived to take him to work and left empty.

This was followed by a year and a half of obstinate resistance. Didelot demanded full satisfaction of all points of his contract, which was at last granted in May 1831. He got his benefit, however, only in 1833. Yet the public had not forgotten him and a veritable ovation was arranged after a performance of *The Hungarian Hut* on October 4, 1833. The spectators clapped and shouted for fifteen minutes. The Directorate of the Imperial Theatres did not want to allow Didelot's appearance on the stage, but it was obliged to give way to public demand. The artists had obviously prepared everything in spite of the ban. As soon as Didelot came on to the stage, two large wreaths and one small one were handed to him from the orchestra. One of the *danseuses* crowned the old man with the wreath. A young actor read a scroll, signed by all the company. Didelot was embraced by all present: children from the school kissed his hands.[1]

Didelot started a life of forced inertia that was unbearable. He read and wrote much. When passing through Moscow in December 1836 *en route* to Kiev, where he hoped to improve his health, Didelot was taken to the Kremlin by Adam Gluszkowski, his devoted pupil, almost an adopted son. The latter thought that he would have to play the role of a guide, but Didelot showed excellent knowledge of Russian history and various stages in the development of Moscow. And at Kiev Didelot started research on its historical treasures. But on November 7, 1837, he died, being literally suffocated by a boil in his throat.

He was survived by his son, Karl Karlovitch Didelot (1801-1855)[2] (Didelot-Père was also known in Russia as Karl), also an excellent dancer formed by him, but forced to retire early because of ill-health.

[1] The ceremony is described in the memoirs of Avdotia Golovacheva-Panayeva (1819-1893), Didelot's former pupil and one of the first Russian women-writers. See: A. Y. Panayeva (Golovacheva). *Memoirs*. Goslitizdat, Moscow, 1956.

[2] Son of his first wife, Rose Paul, who died soon after he came to Russia.

He bequeathed to the Directorate of the Imperial Theatres the five-floor house belonging to his father, in the hope that it would be sold and the funds used for a Didelot scholarship at the school.

Didelot's real disciple and follower was Adam Gluszkowski (1793-*circa* 1870). Had Gluszkowski left nothing but his invaluable memoirs, first published in the *Pantheon and Repertory of the Russian Stage*, 1851, and reprinted in 1940 on the initiative of the Bolshoi Theatre School with an introductory article by Slonimsky, he would have made an important contribution to the history of ballet.

But Gluszkowski, upon graduating from the Petersburg school in 1809 and dancing in the Petersburg company, was delegated to Moscow in 1812 and remained there up to 1839 as *premier danseur*, head of the school, and principal ballet-master of the Bolshoi Theatre. It was Gluszkowski who restored the ballet company of Moscow after the events of 1812. And it was he who created the numerous *divertissements* based on Russian folk dances and customs, so popular at the time of the patriotic upsurge of feelings after 1812. Isak Ablets, a talented character dancer formed by Valberkh (who was Gluszkowski's first teacher), also created in Moscow many folk-dance *divertissements* and worked mainly in this style during the period between 1813 and 1815.

But Gluszkowski was also the first to use Pushkin's poems in ballet and to resort to national rather than foreign literature for subject matter. His *Ruslan and Lyudmila* (1821) after Pushkin's romantic work with music by Scholtz, Gluszkowski's permanent collaborator, was, for the most part, choreographed in accordance with eighteenth-century recipes, and could not match Didelot's poetical imagination. But it was the first Pushkin ballet, to be revived in a somewhat changed version by Didelot in St. Petersburg in 1824 (in collaboration with Auguste). This was a token of respect for Gluszkowski's priority in the matter.

Gluszkowski created another ballet, *The Black Scarf* (1831), music by Zhukovsky, that was inspired by Pushkin's poem of the same name. Altogether Gluszkowski created over thirty original ballets and revived in Moscow all of Didelot's best ballets, including *The Prisoner of the Caucasus*.

A modest and hard-working man, devoted to the art he served in no less degree than his great teacher, he revered Didelot and gave a very detailed professional analysis of the master's methods and best works in his reminiscences and contemporary articles.

Like Didelot he was creatively somewhere on the borderline between the ballet of Classicism and that of Romanticism. However, while his talents could not be compared to those of Didelot, Gluszkowski's understanding of national problems was undoubtedly greater, though he failed, as his master did, to see certain limitations of the grand pantomimic spectacles that were very soon to give place to the Romantic Ballet with its predominance of danced action.

CHAPTER III

THE ROMANTIC BALLET IN RUSSIA: I

In Russia the seeds of Romantic Ballet fell on fertile ground. The way was paved by Didelot's ballets which already contained the elements of Romanticism: the interest in human characters, the use of *couleur locale* and folk dancing, according the body greater freedom, and introducing the rudiments of *pointe* technique that finally placed the ballerina on full point, thus creating the impression of inspired elevation.

Moreover, the greatest achievement of Romantic Ballet so far as the new dance idiom was concerned—dancing on point or high three-quarter point—existed in ballets by Didelot as performed by Russian ballerinas since the early twenties of the nineteenth century. It is known that some Italian dancers, such as Fanny Bias, also demonstrated dancing on point as early as 1820. But they did this as a new trick, whereas the Russian dancers taught by Didelot resorted to *pointes* as a means of artistic expression, standing on the point of one foot at moments of emotional climax.

Russian Romanticism, whether in literature or in the theatre, had manifestations of its own. It was a romanticism of high aspirations, of active ideals searching for strong positive heroes, rather than the escapist romanticism of the much more decadent Western kind.

Contemporaries did not realize that Didelot's ballets were romantic in essence even when they presented characters from life, such as Count Rackozski or Raoul de Créquis. But they did miss something when the new fashion set in. They missed the full-blooded realism of Didelot's dramas and the noble ideals pursued by their characters. The reign of reaction that set in after the defeat of the Decembrist uprising of 1825 prevented the Russian ballet from continuing the line of development indicated in ballets on Pushkin themes and Didelot's dramatic creations such as *The Hungarian Hut*. True, they lacked danced action and the story was too often told in mime. However, had he been given the chance, Didelot would probably have developed the *ballet d'action* element that also existed in his dramatic ballets, while *Zéphire and Flore* was a veritable dance poem.

Marie Taglioni's personal success in Petersburg was beyond any doubt. But serious critics realized full well that all the Taglioni ballets were nothing but "frames for her portraits",[1] providing a pretext for Marie's dances. Rafail Zotov compared unfavourably the two trends: "In Didelot's time we demanded that ballet should contain dramatic interest, intrigue, poetry. . . . Now . . . we need pictures, dances, settings, music, luxury, and brilliance, but we do not bother at all about the content of the ballets."[2]

The anonymous author of the first article from the *Artistic Gazette* added in nostalgia that ballet had had its own Shakespeares and Racines, naming in this connection Didelot and summing-up in the following manner: "No! Say what you will, the previous ballet belonged to the dramatic art and comprised one of its most beautiful parts."

This does not in any sense belittle the significance of the Romantic Ballet and its new discoveries. But it does show that there were many minds in Russia who understood the value of content in ballet and were unwilling to accept anything superfluous.

Again, although at first the Russian Lyric Theatre had to be satisfied with existing Western works by learning the Romantic repertory with a critical eye and selecting its own favourite ballets, the St. Petersburg company (and that of Moscow in the person of its great Romantic ballerina, Sankovskaya) refused to be satisfied with any empty spectacles and unfailingly strived for expressive and "soul-inspiring" dancing. Thus Russian Romantic Ballet had distinct features of its own.

The trends in Russian Romantic Ballet were closely connected with the new developments in music. The Russian Lyric Theatre acquired examples of great dance music in the operas of Glinka (1804-1857).

Glinka introduced principles of symphonic development of the score, and, while he did not leave a single complete ballet, the dance scenes in his operas no longer were in the nature of accidental *divertissements*, they were woven into the action and grew out of it as an integral part of the whole. Mikhail Glinka was a great admirer of ballet and had first-hand knowledge of its powers of expression. In his youth, he even took dancing lessons from Nicolai Goltz. The future composer made considerable progress in the course of the studies that lasted for two years, by the end of which he was able to perform *entrechats doubles, ailes de pigeon* and other difficult steps. Glinka was also very much interested in folk dances, particularly Russian ones. He frequently used dance forms and rhythms in many of his compositions.

There is no doubt that this intimate knowledge of dance in varied form

[1] *Artistic Gazette*, SPB, 1838, No. 5, article "The Ballet", p. 48.
[2] Rafail Zotov, *op. cit.*, p. 48.

Jules Perrot. Water-colour by A. Charlemagne (Bakhrushin Theatre Museum, Moscow). The picture is inscribed: "A ma chère petite Prikhunova (Anna Ivanovna), ce souvenir du passé, en temoignage de ma sincère et constante affection, St Petersbourg, 1er Janvier 1861." Anna Prikhunova was Perrot's favourite ballerina at the time of his work in the Petersburg ballet.

Anna Prikhunova. Water-colour by Zakharov. (Bakhrushin Theatre Museum, Moscow)

was of great help to the composer when he created his poetical dance scenes in the operas *Ivan Susanin* (1836) and *Ruslan and Lyudmila* (1842). This was a new kind of ballet music, calling for new methods on the part of the choreographer. Glinka was, as a matter of fact, considerably in advance of the ballet of his time, and the symphonic music of his opera *ballets d'action* was not to be adequately choreographed for years to come. Antoine Titus, the mediocre *maître de ballet* from Paris, a "yes-man" very much more to the taste of the Directorate of the Imperial Theatres than the insubordinate Didelot, was utterly incapable of coping even in some small degree with the symphonic beauties and expressive powers of the "Polish" act from *Ivan Susanin*, or with "Naina's Magic" in *Ruslan and Lyudmila*. Probably Glinka created the visions of lovely flying maidens in the latter opera while influenced by what he saw during Marie Taglioni's first visit to St. Petersburg. But he saw Romantic Ballet with his own poetic eye and introduced a new quality into the music, which otherwise played a very secondary role in all the works of the Romantic Ballet.

Titus was able to reproduce in dance form nothing but the obvious rhythms of Glinka's Polish suite, depriving it both of national character and of that dramatic content that was only to reach full realization a hundred years later in a production by the Bolshoi Ballet. And the dances of the third act in *Ruslan and Lyudmila* were also inadequately choreographed at the time of the opera's birth. However profound the poetical idea underlying this beautiful scene, the weak choreography prevented not only such great and serious critics as Serov and Stasov, but the young Tchaikovsky himself, from comprehending the music's true worth.

Neither was the famous suite of national and character dances in the Palace of Chernomor properly done at that time. Glinka, realizing that Titus was a man of limited talent, even asked his friend Kamensky to dance the "Lezghinka" for the *maître de ballet*, who arranged something to that effect for Yelena Andreyanova. But even the appearance of this ballerina in the dance created by Glinka, in the spirit of genuine rhythms from the Caucasus, failed to rouse the public's interest. It remained indifferent and raved about the artificial *cachuchas* and *cracoviennes* of imported Romantic Ballet.

Yet it was Glinka who created a very important bridge leading to the future flowering of the symphonic dance. Had his really remarkable dance suites been understood and properly choreographed, they might have become the crowning achievement of Romantic Ballet. Musically they did attain a height of perfection undreamed of by composers of the Romantic Ballet.

Glinka's discoveries opened a new period in the Russian lyric theatre and were later developed in full measure in Tchaikovsky's work.

It is a pity that Taglioni never had a chance to dance to music by Glinka. These two geniuses would have understood one another beyond any doubt as Taglioni was far above the general level even of the Romantic Ballet of her time.

Marie Taglioni (1804-1884) arrived in Russia in 1837 while still at the height of her fame.

She made her début in *La Sylphide* on September 6, 1837, and achieved an instant success. Petersburg was aware of the existence of this great dancer. Some had seen her in Paris, others had heard of her. For months in advance the Petersburg Press printed eulogies of the ballerina, announcing her forthcoming arrival.

After the début Taglioni was pronounced by the *Northern Bee* "an ideal of grace, ideal of dance, ideal of mime" with each pose or movement worthy of a painter's brush. From then on Taglioni's successes increased and the Bolshoi Theatre was always filled for her performances—for her, as the *Northern Bee* put it, "there were no ballets, no ballet-masters, no dances—nothing, but Taglioni, and that was more than enough!"

Taglioni danced in Petersburg (she never got to Moscow) for five seasons, arriving each September at the beginning of the season and departing at Lent (when the Imperial Theatres were closed for performances of local companies) to dance in Vienna, London, or Paris. Over this period she succeeded in appearing about 200 times, dancing usually every other day. This is an extraordinary feat, particularly since it is known how hard this ballerina worked. The daily classes taken by her unrelenting father often drove the ballerina to a state of exhaustion —and this practice continued in Petersburg.

Taglioni had such great success with Russian audiences because her art was very close to the nature of the Russian school. It was found that she danced as the nightingale sings, as the butterfly flies, that dancing was her language, her life, her happiness—was not this the very substance of the dance of Russian ballerinas? It was not accidental that Mundt, the biographer of Maria Danilova, the first Russian Flore, wrote:

"Who of the inhabitants of Petersburg, visiting the theatre, did not admire the charm of the incomparable Marie Taglioni, this personification of grace in dance, combining both the ethereal lightness of the Sylphide and a certain purity of movements that belongs to her alone. All those who had seen her had long ago named her the queen of ballet who had had no precursors, who knows no rivals. All this might be so, but there was a time, when our theatre possessed its own Russian Taglioni, who was given equal praise and applause, who captivated everyone by her charm, when the appearance alone of this sorceress roused the admiration of a huge public. This Taglioni was called, like the present one, Maria; but she was Russian, she was one of us by heart and origin, she was born under our severe sky, on our cold shores—but with a burning soul. Youthful, beautiful, charming, she flitted about the stage of our theatre like a poet's dream, and, unfortunately, was stolen from art too prematurely by cruel death. This Taglioni was our Danilova."[1]

Danilova was no more, but the linking of the name of this dancer of thirty years ago with Taglioni of the Romantic period was very significant. And did not Taglioni dance in the numerous romantic ballets mounted by her father in Petersburg, in the midst of a company of Russian dancers?

The great Russian writer, Nicolai Gogol, wrote of the nature of Taglioni's dancing: "Taglioni is the synonym of Air! Nothing more ethereal had existed heretofore on the stage." On the other hand, inasmuch as Taglioni's style of dancing was part of the choreography of Filippo Taglioni's ballets, blending into an inseparable unity with the dances for the *corps de ballet*, it was far from an indifferent matter who performed this choreographic accompaniment. Marie Taglioni knew this full well and that is probably one of the main reasons (aside from the exceptional response of the Russian audiences) why she was so anxious to dance in Russia for as long as possible. But by 1842 her success began to decline. Contemporary critics complained that her repertory—an endless succession of more than a dozen of her father's ballets, all following a similar pattern, but none as inspired as *La Sylphide*—was becoming dull and monotonous. Fedor Koni, the venerable critic, wrote somewhat later that "Marie Taglioni's talent breathed life into the moonlit fantastic characters of her father's ballets. As soon as she was gone, the spectators realized the depressing stupidity of the ballet".[2]

Neither were the Directors of the Imperial Theatres very willing to renew contracts with a ballerina lacking youth or any personal attraction. Taglioni had passed her prime and this was becoming evident.

All Russian contemporaries of Taglioni, on the other hand, agreed unanimously that on the stage her features became completely transformed by the inspiration that lent them charm and beauty.

Moreover, Taglioni had no intention of dancing forever. It is little

[1] Nicolai Mundt, "Biography of Famous Russian Artist Maria Danilova". *Pantheon of the Russian and all European Theatres*, 1840, vol. I, p. 121.

[2] *Repertoire and Pantheon*, 1847, vol. II, p. 31.

known that both she and her father wanted to stay in Russia in order
to teach at the school and create ballets. In a letter to the Director of the
Imperial Theatres in Moscow about a proposed tour in that city that did
not materialize for financial reasons, Taglioni wrote: "le désir de voir
Moscou, désir bien vif pour moi qui ai trouvé en Russie une nouvelle
patrie"[1] (the desire to see Moscow, a desire so strong in me, who have
found a new motherland in Russia) left proof that she, like many other
foreign artists, valued Russia for the artistic satisfaction it gave her. But
the Directorate of the Imperial Theatres paid no heed to Taglioni's
offer. Her services were no longer wanted, and that was all.

The audiences in St. Petersburg saw differently. Taglioni remained
their favourite to the very end. Her last benefit on January 26 (*Gerta, the
Queen of the Elfrides*—one of Filippo Taglioni's tedious repetitions of the
"Sylphide" theme), was followed by single farewell presentations of
each of her ballets. For the final performance on March 1, 1842, she had
eighteen curtain calls. Moved to tears, Taglioni, approaching close to the
footlights, said in French: "You will remain engraved upon my heart
for ever."

The public would not part with Taglioni so easily, and the Directorate
was obliged to grant, as a great exception, two more farewell performances, officially "for spectators of other denominations", in the first week
of Lent. This time the enthusiasm was unsurpassed. There were numerous
encores and thirty curtain calls, after which Taglioni said, this time in
German: "I hope to come back."

But she never did.

The Taglioni era had spent itself. Now came *Giselle*, the greatest
achievement of the Romantic Ballet.

The first performance of *Giselle* in Petersburg took place in December
1842. The ballet was laboriously reproduced from the original production,
Titus having been delegated to Paris for the purpose.

In the person of the first Russian Giselle, Yelena Andreyanova (1819-
1857), Russian ballet acquired its own Romantic ballerina. Beyond doubt,
the example of Taglioni's inspired art had a great deal to do with the
development of home talent. But Taglioni herself singled out Andreyanova and another promising dancer, Tatiana Smirnova (the first
Myrtha in the Petersburg ballet), as talents in her own, ethereal romantic
style. Andreyanova not only succeeded in acquiring the Romantic style
to perfection. She was a gifted actress with a strong power of projection.
It was she who started the tradition, continued by an endless line of Russian

[1] Published in: *Marie Taglioni* by Nicolai Soloviev, Petersburg, 1912, p. 50.

Giselles, of attaching equal importance to both parts of the role. Her mad scene was moving and convincing. Her wili was ethereal and spiritual.

Comparing the performances of various ballerinas in this ballet, Rafail Zotov would write as late as 1856: "The famous Fanny Elssler was incomparable in the first act, but already much weaker in the second; Mlles Grahn and Richard were more outstanding in the second act; Mlle Andreyanova alone was equally superb in both acts."[1]

Andreyanova created many roles of the romantic repertoire in Russia, notably the name-part in *La Péri* (this ballet of Jean Coralli was reproduced on the St. Petersburg stage in 1844 by Frederic), and those of the Black Fairy in *La Filleule des Fées*, and Bertha the Countess in *Le Diable à Quatre* (known in Russia as *The Wilful Wife*), mounted by Jules Perrot especially for her.

She was honoured by Petipa as his partner in *Paquita* for his St. Petersburg debut of 1847, and danced with him for her own benefit, the ballet *Satanilla* in the next year. In all these roles she was able to display not only a fine technique, but outstanding dramatic talent. Andreyanova danced in Moscow on several occasions for a long period and received enthusiastic notices, particularly in *La Péri* and *L'Ombre*.

In 1845 she danced with great success in Paris and in London, returning to the latter in the summer of 1852 to attain particular success at Covent Garden in the opera by Julien, *Peter the Great*, dancing a "Mazurka" and "Minuet" the rendering of which was found to be highly poetic. By earning this kind of praise Andreyanova proved that she was a real dancer of the Russian school.

Ill health forced her to retire in 1855 after successful performances in the Russian provinces, to which she brought classical ballet of the highest order. She spent her last years in Paris and died there on October 26 (new style), 1857.

Yekaterina Sankovskaya (1816-1878), the romantic ballerina formed in the Moscow ballet, was even more endowed than Andreyanova, though there was no cause for actual rivalry between them, as both dancers were of an entirely different type—Andreyanova was more lyrical and ethereal, Sankovskaya a little more earthbound, but capable of creating stronger characters, though both dancers, aside from good technique, possessed a dramatic talent. Sankovskaya as a pupil (she entered the Moscow school in 1825) performed the role of Count Rackoszky's younger son in *The Hungarian Hut* in her second year. At that time there was no

[1] R. Z. (Rafail Zotov) in the *Northern Bee* for 1856, No. 55 of March 9, p. 287.

strict distinction between ballet and drama tuition, and the child acted in plays at the Maly theatre, appearing as the Infanta in Schiller's *Don Carlos* with the great tragic actor Mochalov.

When she graduated in 1836, her teacher, Hulin-Sor, who a year previously had retired from her own position as ballerina of the Moscow ballet, now passed it on to her talented successor, who in reality was many times more expressive. The atmosphere of the Moscow ballet, where dramatic gifts were always valued, the tastes of the democratic Moscow audiences, her own associations with the great traditions of the Russian drama—all this moulded Sankovskaya into one of the most outstanding ballerinas of Russian ballet history.

Sankovskaya introduced new aspects into the dance technique of her time, always making it her servant, completely subjugating it to the general requirements of the role. All these new qualities stood out when Sankovskaya performed the title role in *La Sylphide*, produced at the Bolshoi by Hulin on the very day when Marie Taglioni danced the same ballet for the first time in St. Petersburg. Sankovskaya considerably deepened the role of the Sylphide. She showed that the supernatural heroine suffered deeply as a result of her tragic love for a human being. She was particularly impressive in the scene where the Sylphide loses her wings, her love, and life itself.

While not being blessed with natural elevation, Sankovskaya created an ethereal impression through her mastery of technique and acting. She danced almost the whole of the Taglioni repertory, and by her performance imbued the poetic and fantastic images of the romantic ballets with the truth of human passions. It was for these qualities that this plain woman with huge tragic eyes became the idol of Moscow audiences and particularly of the students at the University. The secret of her popularity lay in the great emotional impact she made on the spectators. The great literary critic, Vissarion Belinsky, wrote that her dances were full of soul and grace. The writer, Saltykov-Shchedrin, said she was a herald of truth, beauty and goodness. Her contemporary N. Dmitriev, to whom she meant so much when he was a student in Moscow because of these qualities, left important evidence in his memoirs *The Recent Past* (SPB, 1865), that Fanny Elssler had been heard to say that she had seen only two Sylphides in her life: Taglioni and Sankovskaya. At the same time Sankovskaya, who first saw Elssler in Paris when just out of school, was very much the same type of dancer, more emotional than lyrical, interested in the human side of her characters.

These qualities of Sankovskaya came to full fruition in *Giselle*, performed by her soon after Andreyanova's departure. She never feared comparisons with other dancers since she rendered every new part in her own inimitable manner. Thus she successfully danced Esmeralda after Fanny Elssler, and *La Fille du Danube* after Taglioni.

Sankovskaya made new but mature attempts at choreography. She produced *Le Diable à Quatre* on the Moscow stage four years before Perrot mounted this ballet in St. Petersburg. In 1849 she herself choreographed dances for her benefit performance.

Sankovskaya's career was not an easy one. The Directorate of the Imperial Theatres dismissed in 1845 Theodore Guerino, a talented Romantic dancer who had been her partner for seven years and had much in common artistically with the ballerina. The void left by the loss of this partner was never properly filled. In December 1854 Sankovskaya retired, having danced for the last time in *Giselle*. In retirement she lived in obscurity and poverty. The founder of the Moscow Arts Theatre, Stanislavsky, was her pupil when she taught dancing in the families of rich Moscow merchants.

Fanny Elssler (1810-1884), whom Sankovskaya resembled, though in a very indirect way, had her greatest successes in Moscow, where she was particularly valued for "harmony of simplicity and charm". Moscow remained Elssler's particular love, and it is here that she said farewell to dancing. She felt more at home on the Moscow stage, where her emotional impact was particularly well recognized and appreciated. This does not imply that she had lesser successes in Petersburg.

After having made the *faux pas* of appearing in *Giselle*, which was not really suited to her style, she rehabilitated herself in *Le Délire d'un Peintre*, which she mounted in 1848 (the year of her arrival in Russia) some months before Perrot, the author of its choreography, came to assist her in the production of *La Esmeralda*, which became her crowning glory.

Before that she proved her real worth in *La Fille Mal Gardée*, creating a life-loving and charming portrayal of Lise that became a model for many generations afterwards. Russian critics wrote that the way Elssler fed chickens in the first act was unforgettable, while another scene, in which Lise was dreaming of her future children, became a classic. With great warmth she acted a simple and loving daughter of the people.

Elssler represented another facet of the Romantic Ballet that was very close both to Russian artists and audiences. This was an art of many romantic exaggerations, but it was closer to reality and often inspired by life itself, like the characters of Esmeralda or Lise, or that of Giselle in the first act. Russian critics noted that Elssler's Giselle was a real peasant girl, naïvely happy when seeing Albrecht, losing her reason because of disillusionment upon his betrayal.

Elssler's execution of character dances, a vital component of the Romantic Ballet, and which also played an important part in her repertory, was duly appraised in Russia. Critics wrote that her execution of the "Cachucha" was a veritable poem of a young woman's passionate love.

Elssler's greatest achievements were connected with the ballets by Jules Perrot. It was he who introduced the new realistic trends in Romantic Ballet, to which Elssler gave life. It is important to note that in Russia Perrot created many of his ballets anew, thus taking the opportunity to carry out many of his unrealized ideals.

This particularly applies to *Giselle* and *Esmeralda*, so that they may be regarded as new versions of those ballets.

Perrot worked in the St. Petersburg company in the capacity of its *maître de ballet* and dancer-mime from 1848 to 1859, except for a short interval in 1851, when the post of *maître de ballet* was occupied by Mazilier. When Perrot arrived in St. Petersburg only two weeks after Fanny Elssler, to complete the staging of *La Esmeralda* begun without him, he found a group of talented responsive dancers, eager to understand his artistic principles.

The atmosphere of Russian ballet was very different from that of Paris and even of London, where, in spite of the success of the Romantic Ballet and his own creations, Perrot was allowed to leave, his great talents not fully exploited.

In Petersburg Perrot discovered ideal surroundings. No longer the brilliant dancer that he was in earlier days, he had the chance to play character roles with excellent partners in many of his own ballets. But more important than that was the fact that he met experienced first-class artists, who were fully capable of creating roles in his works, choreographed according to the true principles of the *danse d'action*, in which the dance not only grew out of the action, but furthered it as an integral part of the plot.

Having understood all this, Perrot enthusiastically started to produce *Giselle*. It meant so much to him. While it was common knowledge that he had created all the dances for the first Giselle—Carlotta Grisi—Jean Coralli remained officially author of the entire choreography and Perrot, far from being mentioned on the programmes and posters, had to remain very much in the shade. Therefore the St. Petersburg *Giselle* was in many ways a new production.

What was at times merely sketched in Paris, and not fully carried out

Ballerina A. Danilova. (Bakhrushin Theatre Museum, Moscow)

Klavdia Kanzyreva as the Gold-
fish in *The Goldfish*, ballet by
Saint-Léon, music by Minkus.
Saint Petersburg, 1867.

Marfa Muravieva. (Bakhrushin
Theatre Museum, Moscow)

in London, was at last realized in Petersburg. Perrot not only edited the dances created by him in the Opéra production of 1841, but choreographed many of them in a new way. He considerably strengthened the dramatic action of the ballet, deepened Giselle's mad scene, and made all the secondary characters more convincing.

Fanny Elssler was unable to satisfy fully either Perrot or the Petersburg public in this 1848 production, particularly in the second act. But in 1850 Perrot mounted the ballet all over again for Carlotta Grisi's tour in Petersburg. This time he achieved much more, working with the original creator of Giselle.

Yet the exacting Russian critics were not entirely satisfied with Grisi. Rafail Zotov found that when Myrtha, the Queen of Wilis, gave wings to Grisi-Giselle, the dancer might have invested the famous *pirouette en arabesque* "with greater speed and fire, as it used to be done by Mlle Andreyanova". He also expressed a desire to see a demonstration of greater sorrow and compassion for Albrecht, when Myrtha commands Giselle to dance him to death. The venerable Fedor Koni fully supported him in this opinion, accusing Grisi of neglecting Giselle's inner state, and of a certain amount of affectation. Koni summed up the attitude of Russian audiences to the artist's responsibility for his role in the following words: "we think that in all kinds of dramatic creation, including even ballet, nature [which Koni apparently interpreted as true feelings] should reign supreme, if the artist wishes to make enduring . . . conquests".

Some of the guest-artists who later danced in Perrot's ballets also disappointed Russian connoisseurs. But Perrot himself was the personification of dramatic truth, at times to the detriment of dance in the numerous character ballets mounted by him in Russia, where he was so happy.

The attitude of the Directorate of the Imperial Theatres in the person of the then Director, Saburov, alone forced him to retire, hurt and disillusioned. His democratic tendencies, his delight in devising dramatic (and melodramatic) ballets about simple people, his affection for the *ballet d'action* were considered both harmful and out-moded.

Perrot actually ceased his activities in 1859, having produced *Eoline, ou la Dryade* for his last ballet, his official dismissal taking effect in 1860. But Perrot remained in Russia until the summer of 1861, spending some of that time as a private person in Moscow, where according to information supplied by the well-known ballet historian, Yuri Bakhrushin, he conducted negotiations about his possible employment.

The Bakhrushin Theatre Museum, founded by the historian's father, has in its possession a rare portrait (in water-colours) of Perrot in a red Russian blouse. The inscription: "To my dear little Prikhunova,[1] this memory of the past" reveals Perrot's nostalgia for the days spent in the Russian ballet. The inscription is dated "St. Petersburg, January 1, 1861". The portrait found its way into Moscow because Anna Prikhunova, Perrot's favourite Russian exponent of his creative aims, married Prince Gagarin, leader of the Moscow nobility. The date is also interesting because it confirms that Perrot spent a long time in Russia after his official retirement. Moreover we know that Perrot arrived in Paris only in the *summer of 1861*, when he was guest at the wedding of his former Russian pupil, Zina Richard, with Louis Merante. From then on the creator of *Giselle*, forgotten by all, spent the time with his fishing-rod at Paramé. And only visiting Russian ballerinas came to study roles from his ballets under the master's guidance. . . .

And, today, Perrot is still remembered in the country he loved so dearly. In Soviet ballet his name, with great respect to the memory of this outstanding choreographer, is invariably mentioned on the programmes of *Giselle* as the legitimate joint author of this gem among ballet classics.

Perrot contributed much to Russian ballet, but received no less. By the end of the eighteen-fifties, when Théophile Gautier, one of the leading figures in the Romantic Movement, visited Russia, he was greatly impressed by the performances of the St. Petersburg company. In his book, *Voyage en Russie*, Paris, 1858, the author and critic of Romantic Ballet admitted that the art was very much more developed in Russia than in France, and that ballets in several acts, with involved dramatic plots and plenty of dancing, made Russian ballet a self-sufficient art, in no way dependent on opera or any other kind of spectacle.

Gautier offered the highest possible praise to the nature of Russian ballet theatre. "In Petersburg it is not easy to win applause for a *pas*," he wrote. "The Russians are great connoisseurs of ballets and the dancer who has withstood the marksmanship of their opera-glasses must be very confident of herself. Their Conservatory of Dance [Theatre School—N.R.] supplies excellent soloists and a *corps de ballet* knowing no equal for perfection and speed of their evolutions. . . . There is no talk, giggling, amorous glances at spectators or the orchestra. It is in truth the world of pantomime, where words are absent and action never transcends its

---

[1] In brackets Perrot wrote: "Anna Ivanovna" to distinguish Anna Prikhunova (1830-1887), singled out, by Marie Taglioni, at the age of nine for outstanding talent, from her sister Alexandra (1843-1900), a mediocre dancer.

boundaries. This *corps de ballet* is carefully chosen from pupils of the Conservatory: there are plenty of beauties, while all are young, perfectly built and know their profession, or their art, if you will, to perfection."

Thus the die-hard conservative of Romantic Ballet succeeded in distinguishing the progressive precepts of Russian Ballet, often overlooked by many of its nineteenth-century contemporaries.

CHAPTER IV

THE ROMANTIC BALLET IN RUSSIA: II

When Arthur Saint-Léon (1821-1870), born in Paris in the family of an Opéra dancer, Arthur Victor Michel, offered his services as ballet-master to the Directorate of the Imperial Theatres in 1859, he was just the man they wanted. Gone were the days when choreographers who claimed artistic independence, such as Didelot or Perrot, were tolerated and even allowed to go their own way. Nothing of the kind was going to be permitted for the future. Ballet was "to be shown its place": it had to entertain, to present a fascinating and dazzling spectacle for the pleasure of the first few rows of stalls, and, in particular, the Imperial boxes.

The prolific Saint-Léon was willing to mount any number of new ballets (in reality they were often his own old ones, given new names), to dance, play the violin (the contract specified this), and, when necessary, revive ballets belonging to other choreographers. This jack of all trades was in addition a composer with a number of pieces to his credit. As a dancer he was of a good school, as a choreographer he knew how to produce suitable impressive spectacles, not requiring extra expenditure,[1] and to exploit to mutual advantage the steel points and vertiginous pirouettes of the Italian ballerinas from the Milan school that were rapidly coming into fashion.

His ballets were really protracted *divertissements*. Khudekov, reminiscing in 1896, appraised him in the following manner: "He was a past master at inventing separate dances and in particular *variations*, devised to suit the talents of particular dancers. Soloists always said that it was easy for them to dance this ballet master's *enchaînements*. On the other hand he did not know how to manage crowds. His *ensembles* were lifeless and devoid of colour."[2]

His predecessor, Perrot, could work only at moments of inspiration and was known to cancel rehearsals when it did not come. Saint-Léon

---

[1] From Saint-Léon's letter to his agent in Paris, preserved in the Archives of the Directorate of the Imperial Theatres (Leningrad).

[2] Sergei Khudekov. "Reminiscences about the première of 'The Hump-Backed Horse' ", *Petersburg Gazette*, No. 20, 1896.

Anna Sobeshchanskaya as Odette in *Swan Lake*. Bolshoi Theatre,
Moscow, 1877.

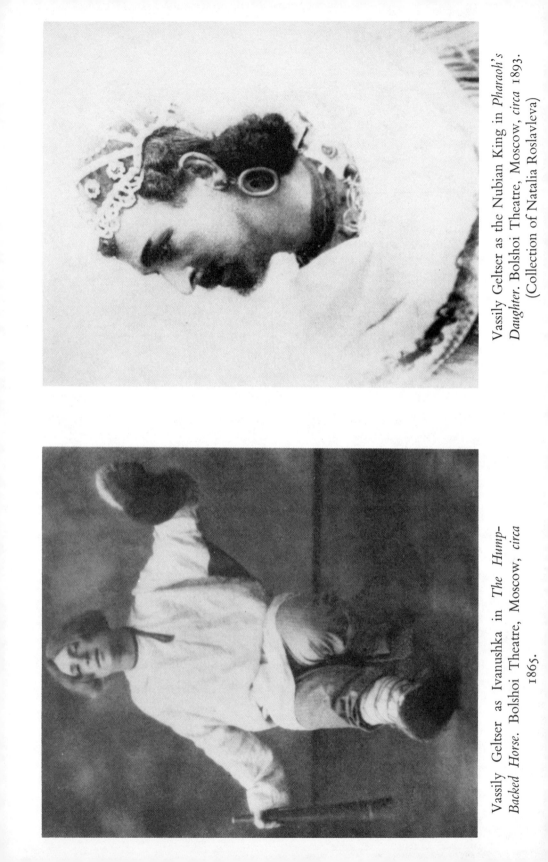

Vassily Geltser as the Nubian King in *Pharaoh's Daughter*. Bolshoi Theatre, Moscow, *circa* 1893. (Collection of Natalia Roslavleva)

Vassily Geltser as Ivanushka in *The Hump-Backed Horse*. Bolshoi Theatre, Moscow, *circa* 1865.

was ready to work at any hour, and, not dependent on the creation of poetic images, knew no lapses of inspiration.

There is no doubt that he did have choreographic talent and professionally his standards were very high. But, always in a hurry and ever ready to please, he borrowed dance idiom for his ballets from anywhere, including the cancan, which was rapidly gaining popularity. Having travelled widely, he was well acquainted with various folk dances and used them liberally in his ballets. This was one of the positive sides of his activity, yet so many of these dances lost their national character or were introduced without rhyme or reason. However, Saint-Léon did build up a new variety of steps, often retaining their true national spirit in a stylized form.

Character dancing was, however, the least important element in Saint-Léon's works. New and original tricks—this is what mattered most, and he racked his brains inventing processions of weird characters with lanterns on their heads, dances of wines, represented by *danseuses* dressed as bottles with corks for headgear, dances in sacks hindering freedom of movement, and so forth.

Jovita, ou Les Boucaniers, freely borrowed from the Mazilier ballet of the same title, *Saltarello, or a Passion for Dancing*, and a scene from *Graciella* that was shown in full a year later, were all produced at the very beginning of his first season in St. Petersburg, between September and November 1859.

The impression made by these ballets was rather superficial. Thus the author of the "Theatre Chronicle" in the *Northern Bee* admitted that, in *Saltarello*, Saint-Léon had demonstrated all his varied abilities: composed the dances, the music, and even played upon the violin two pieces: a concerto and "Hymn to Terpsichore", a brilliant fantasy with Paganini-like difficult passages! But when it came to appraisal of the actual choreography, plenty of criticism arose.

Saint Petersburg Monitor found that while there were plenty of dances in *Saltarello*, it lacked "those dancing masses, to which M. Perrot had accustomed us. It is only the soloists who dance."

After reviving *Paquerette* early in 1860 (written for him by Gautier as early as 1851), Saint-Léon moved on to Moscow, where he was obliged to work according to his contract, depending on the needs of the Directorate.

None of Saint-Léon's work was admired in Moscow. The choreographer was accused of creating a set of dances that did not suit one another, of looking for cheap success and composing in haste.

Moscow audiences and critics always expected a ballet to contain a dramatic plot and sustained action. But many of the more progressive St. Petersburg critics also severely criticized the emptiness of Saint-Léon's compositions, far from agreeing with the official attitude.

Some of the St. Petersburg critics were fully in agreement with the new current, and even insisted on ballets without subject or any common sense, but with plenty of dances. Another, and considerable, part of the Press and of the world of arts and letters was bitterly opposed to the existing state of things. The revolutionary wave of the late fifties and early sixties; the emancipation movement that ended in 1861 with freedom for the serfs, bringing in reality no actual relief to the peasant; the opposition to the political reaction that set in immediately after a certain amount of liberty was granted—all this gave birth to a new type of Russian intelligentsia known as the revolutionary democrats. These people came from different walks of life, burning with noble ideals and ready to spare no efforts in their struggle for a better lot for the people, whom they identified with the peasants.

They had ideals in literature, expressed in full measure by their recognized leader, Nikolai Chernyshevsky, in his famous thesis, *Aesthetic Relations of Art to Reality* (1855), where he said that art should depict life, explain it, and pronounce a verdict. Russian literature and arts of the nineteenth century conformed to these ideals, and inspired many great writers and dramatists who not only pronounced verdicts, but tried to show possible solutions. Ballet alone remained segregated and quite indifferent to any new movement.

It is not surprising, therefore, that leading Russian writers and the whole progressive intelligentsia had no use for ballet and lost any interest whatsoever in it. Saltykov-Shchedrin, once writing so favourably of Sankovskaya, signifying ideals of goodness and truth, now spared no irony in one bitter attack after another on ballet.

The poet Nekrasov left evidence in many of his stanzas of the attitude to ballet prevalent in his circle. In the magazine *Sovremennik* for February 1866 he published a satirical poem directly entitled "Ballet", attacking the "diamond row", the "starched dandies, youthful old men", and officers of high rank that formed its spectators.

A little later, upon seeing Maria Surovshchikova-Petipa in her popular dance, "The Little Mujik", performed *en travestie* first at concerts and later as an interpolated number in *The Beauty of Lebanon*, Nekrasov begged her "to dance *La Fille du Danube*, but to leave the mujik alone!"

The repertory of ballet was such that it invited opposition on the part of anyone possessing common sense. Neither did the situation improve after Saint-Léon's attempt to resort to Russian subjects.

The popular fairy-tale by Yershov, *The Little Hump-Backed Horse* (*Koniok-Gorbunok*), was suggested to Saint-Léon by some Petersburg friends as a suitable story for a Russian ballet. The choreographer did not know the language, therefore the fairy-tale was translated and explained to him. Khudekov stated that the general outline of the ballet and the idea of the *grand divertissement* of different nations living in Russia (it included a Ukrainian, Urals, Lettish dance and a Lezghinka, while the number later multiplied with further interpolations) was supplied by the balletomane Lopukhin.

It is doubtful, however, whether even the most conservative among Saint-Léon's Russian friends could have devised the ensuing concoction, wherein the stupid Russian Tsar of Yershov's tale became an Oriental Khan and the Tsar-Maiden was placed among nereids having nothing in common with Russian folklore. It is most likely that any spectacular tableaux, contrary to Russian imagery, but typical of Saint-Léon's style, were introduced by the choreographer, while other changes were ordered by officialdom.

With all its absurdities and very scant music by Pugni, who, not knowing sufficient Russian tunes, succeeded in working a part of the overture from Rossini's *Tancredi* into *The Hump-Backed Horse*, its première on December 3, 1864, had immediate success. The ballet on a Russian theme attracted such attention that for months it was impossible to get a ticket. Anyone expecting a truly Russian creation might have been disappointed.

The pseudo-patriotic and pseudo-Russian flavour of *The Hump-Backed Horse* was bitterly criticized and satirized by the progressive Press in feuilletons, verses and caricatures.

Yet *The Hump-Backed Horse* remained in the repertory for many generations, a great favourite with the dancers and the general public. The reason was simple—within the obvious limitations of its libretto, it became more and more Russian in fact. This Russian spirit was brought in by the numerous performers of all the roles. The first Tsar-Maiden—the outstanding ballerina, Marfa Muravieva—did much to make her heroine into a genuine Russian fairy-tale character.

Marfa Muravieva (1838-1879) attracted the attention of the public and critics when she first appeared at the age of ten as the Cupid in *Le Délire d'un Peintre*. Fanny Elssler, who staged the ballet and danced the leading role, embraced the child in the wings. By 1856 Muravieva was very much praised for dancing "La Diablotine" in *La Vivandière* with Lev Ivanov, quite on a par with fully-fledged dancers. She graduated in 1857 but remained at school for one more year in the *classe de perfectionnement*. Muravieva's first year of service as soloist on the Imperial stage was exceptionally difficult as she had to compete with such ballerinas as Ferraris and Rosati.

Muravieva was very small and not endowed with physical beauty (and that was a drawback from the point of view of the Court circles), neither did she possess a gift for expressive mime, but talent and hard work enabled her to develop into a brilliant ballerina—ethereal, soft, musical, and technically very strong. Her *pointes* were hard as steel and she performed virtuoso feats without any visible difficulty. In spite of all these qualities Muravieva was not given the leading ballerina position she deserved. Moreover, in 1860, she was sent to Moscow to work there for one year (she was born in that city).

In many ways Muravieva was formed as a dancer by Saint-Léon who exploited her brilliant technique to full measure in his ballets; and in her he had a ballerina to be proud of. In 1863 she was invited (on his recommendation) to dance at the Paris Opéra, where she had her debut in a revival of *Giselle*. Jules Janin compared her to a "Dream come forth from gates of ivory, whose whiteness she retains". Muravieva was one of the first Russian dancers to tour extensively abroad. In the summer of 1864 she again danced in Paris in *Néméa*, a shortened version of Saint-Léon's *Fiametta* (in Moscow it was called *The Salamander*!) that he had mounted specially for Muravieva in St. Petersburg the previous winter. The ballerina did not return to Paris in the next season of 1865, merely because she married a rich nobleman, N. K. Ziefert, and, at the request of her mother-in-law, retired from the stage, at 27, at the zenith of her creative power. In retirement Muravieva, whenever she visited the theatre as a member of the audience, seldom stayed until the end of the performance, often returning home in tears. Upon her death from consumption her husband donated a large sum to the Theatre School to institute a scholarship, from which many dancers, afterwards well-known, benefited.

Russian ballet lost in Muravieva one of its great ballerinas, but other talents were there to step into her place. Graceful Matilda Madayeva was the next Tsar-Maiden, continuing the line of her predecessor. It was at Madayeva's request that Saint-Léon introduced into the last act the "Slav Fantasy" dance, that added more national colour to the leading role. So many interpolations followed in ensuing years that in the end the

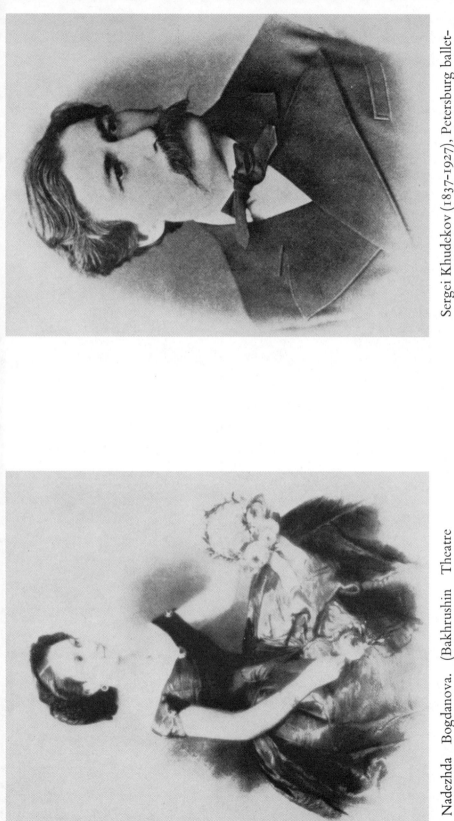

Nadezhda Bogdanova. (Bakhrushin Theatre Museum, Moscow)

Sergei Khudekov (1837–1927), Petersburg ballet-omane, publisher of the *Petersburg Gazette*, author of ballet scenarii and of a *History of Dancing* in four volumes. (Collection of Natalia Roslavleva)

The Awakening of Flora. Ballet by Marius Petipa, Mariinsky Theatre, 1896. Kshesinskaya I and Soliannikov I.

Pupils of the Theatre School in the mazurka from *Paquita*, Mariinsky Theatre, Petersburg.

music of eighteen composers was to be found in what was still called the Pugni score! Among these interpolations were Liszt's *Second Hungarian Rhapsody* with choreography by Lev Ivanov, and Tchaikovsky's "Russian Dance" from *Swan Lake*, known as the "Melancholia" of the captive Tsar-Maiden.[1]

All these new pieces were necessitated by changes in choreography and *mises en scène* introduced in the course of the ballet's long history. These also improved the Saint-Léon work as first conceived, leaving practically nothing of the original production. Petipa revised the ballet in 1895, choreographing many of the dances anew, while Gorsky's entirely new Moscow production of 1901, with settings by Konstantin Korovin, breathed new life into the old ballet, creating many picturesque and genuine scenes of peasant life even if many of the old weaknesses inevitably remained.

It was the Moscow ballet and the Moscow dancers headed by their first Ivanushka, Vassily Geltser, who really made *The Hump-Backed Horse* into a Russian ballet. Saint-Léon paid no heed to the advice of friends and warning of Russian critics that it was Ivanushka, and not the Tsar-Maiden, who is the central figure of the ballet. For him choreography existed as a vehicle for the ballerina. Perhaps things would have taken a different turn, had Timofei Stukolkin (1829-1894), the leading character dancer of St. Petersburg ballet, been able to undertake the role of Ivanushka at the time of its creation. But Stukolkin was taken ill shortly before the first performance, and the role was danced by Nicolai Troitsky (1838-1903), a much poorer actor.

When Saint-Léon was sent to produce his ballet in Moscow,[2] events took an even sadder course. He intended to entrust the role of Ivanushka to Wilhelm Vanner (1820-1889), a member of the Bolshoi ballet, German by nationality, but as *danseur buffo* brought up entirely in the traditions of the Italian Commedia dell'Arte. However worthy an actor in his own style that was always popular in Moscow, through a long line of Italian dancers and choreographers, Vanner could not possibily create anything credible from material entirely unfamiliar to him. Both the Bolshoi dancers and their friends, in particular those from the Maly Dramatic Theatre, opposed Saint-Léon in this case. And it was on their insistence

[1] The old *Hump-Backed Horse* in Gorsky's version is still in the repertory of the Kirov Theatre in Leningrad, while its Maly Opera and the Bolshoi in Moscow use Shchedrin's new score, with new choreography by Bielsky and Radunsky respectively.

[2] First performance in Moscow was on November 26, 1866.

that Vassily Geltser (1840-1908) became the first Moscow Invanushka, only pretending to be a Fool, and fooling in reality all those around him. The spectators loved Geltser's Ivanushka and the Moscow *Hump-Backed Horse* won the reputation of being better than the St. Petersburg one. Geltser performed this role more than three hundred and fifty times, and only in the nineties passed it on to the remarkable dancer and mime, Nicolai Domashov (1861-1916), while brilliantly enacting the role of the old Khan up to his last year of service. From Domashov, Geltser's traditions passed to the next Ivanushka—Vladimir Riabtsev, who invariably performed it for many years. When Gorsky's version of *The Hump-Backed Horse* was revived in the season of 1947-1948, Nicolai Popko, a talented mime of the new Soviet generation, continued playing Ivanushka in the Geltser tradition, introducing at the same time his own, contemporary attitude to the character, which was endowed with an even greater share of peasant humour and wit.

Geltser was one of the most extraordinary mimes, not only of his own times, but in the entire history of ballet. He possessed the exceptional quality of acting while dancing. He danced with each mimed gesture; a great dancer-actor who belonged to ballet.

He completely identified himself with each assumed character, and his range was limitless. He created a whole gallery of portraits—from the tragic figure of Claude Frollo in *Esmeralda* to the ludicrous policeman in *The Two Thieves*. In *Pygmalion*, a very third-rate ballet, he formed a picture of untold beauty. When he appeared on the stage in a chariot, crowned with a laurel wreath, the audience gasped and accorded him an ovation. He knew how to make them believe that his Pygmalion was a great sculptor, capable of creating the statue of Galatea. And later, in the same ballet, according to the whims of the story, he transformed himself into a pitiful beggar.

Geltser's rendering of the Malayan Mute in *The Song of Victorious Love* was quite unparalleled. Spectators came not so much to hear this mediocre opera by Simon, as to see Geltser perform, particularly in the scene when the Malayan, by power of magic hypnosis, resurrected his dead master.

At the beginning of 1889 Vassily Geltser started teaching plastique and mime at the Moscow Theatre School and conducted this course until his retirement in 1906. Not only ballet dancers, but many dramatic actors of Moscow learned much from his inspired tuition and example.

Such were the artists helping Saint-Léon to create *The Hump-Backed*

Horse. They and their like saved it from failure and made it into a Russian ballet of their own.

In the same year Saint-Léon attempted another ballet on a Russian theme. Immediately upon his return from the Moscow *première* of *The Hump-Backed Horse* he completed *The Goldfish*, supposedly inspired by Pushkin's poetic fairy-tale, but so altered that no one was able to recognize it. The old Russian woman from Pushkin's poem became a Ukrainian girl; the old fisherman—her young cossack husband, Taras. Obviously in preparing *The Goldfish* Saint-Léon did not enjoy even the amateur advice he had had at the time of the creation of *The Hump-Backed Horse*. Nor could he expect any co-operation from Guglielmina Salvioni, a much advertised Italian ballerina who performed many technical feats in the leading role of the cossack wife, Galia, but could not possibily create a Ukrainian character. The ballet was packed with inconsequences of every kind. None of the tricks performed by machines, such as a flight on a magic carpet, the sudden rising up of a diamond castle and the like, could save *The Goldfish* from dismal failure. It served for repeated attacks by the democratic authors and it was *The Goldfish* that was used by Saltykov-Shchedrin as the point of issue in his bitter pamphlet, *Project of a Contemporary Ballet*, where all the absurdities of Saint-Léon were set down with most sarcastic remarks.

After *The Goldfish* Saint-Léon produced three more ballets in St. Petersburg: two curtain-raisers and one monumental four-act concoction, *The Lily*, to music by Minkus.

In vain did he rack his brains for novelties. His ballets, repeating one and the same pattern, were now played to half-empty houses. In 1869 the Directorate did not renew Saint-Léon's contract, and he left for Paris to create, shortly before his death in 1870, *Coppélia*, which in the eighties found its way to Russia, there to attain a long and successful existence.

Of course Saint-Léon was not alone instrumental in the decline of the Russian ballet and its temporary loss of a positive ideal. *Coppélia* proved that he was capable of much more. But he was typical of the popular taste and was willing to be a useful tool in the hands of the Directorate.

It was the Russian dancers and the two Russian schools, ever preserving the national tradition, who saved the ballet of that period from complete decline.

Much in this respect was done by the Moscow ballet—further removed from officialdom and less under the obligation to amuse at all expense.

Of course the Moscow ballet of the sixties also suffered from the inevitable influence of the St. Petersburg repertory and official tastes. It was not so advanced as in the period between the thirties and the fifties, which had the outstanding romantic ballerina, Sankovskaya, and dancers like Irakly Nikitin, St. Petersburg trained (and later Augusta Maywood's partner in Vienna), who was sent to work in Moscow where he performed *premier danseur* roles in the romantic repertory, Fedor Manokhin, *demi-caractère* dancer of a wide range, and Nikita Peshkov, a really outstanding mime who started his career early in ballets by Valberkh, Gluszkowski, and Didelot, and the Russian *divertissements* of Balashov and Lobanov.

The Bogdanov family, whose name occupies a very definite place in the annals of Russian ballet, started its activity in Moscow at this same period. Konstantin Bogdanov (*circa* 1809-1877) enjoyed in his youth the tuition of Didelot, under whose guidance he perfected his talents in St. Petersburg after graduating from the Moscow school. In May 1839, upon the retirement of Gluszkowski, Bogdanov became manager (*régisseur*) of the Moscow ballet.

During his career as a dancer he partnered all the Moscow ballerinas of the time: Hulin, Voronina-Ivanova, Sankovskaya, and Tatiana Karpak-ova—his future wife. He danced every kind of role according to the custom of the period, but was strongest in those requiring characterization. Bogdanov was the first Gurn in the Moscow production of *La Sylphide*, and the character of the simple peasant youth created by him was recalled for years afterwards by critics as being a model for future performers.

Bogdanov taught at the Theatre School in Moscow, but after the premature death of Tatiana Karpakova in 1842, when he had a large family to support and bring up, Bogdanov opened a private ballet school of a sort, where he taught his own daughter Nadezhda. She soon proved to be its best pupil and by 1849 Bogdanov retired altogether, devoting the rest of his life to his daughter's career.

Nadezhda Bogdanova (1836-1867) was formed by her father into a prominent ballerina of the Moscow ballet. While in her 'teens she danced ballerina roles in a small company organized by her father for the purpose of touring the provinces. On the recommendation of Fanny Elssler, who saw Nadezhda dance in Moscow, Bogdanov sent his daughter to Paris, where she studied and danced at the Opéra (1850-1855).

Upon returing to Russia, Bogdanova danced in Petersburg and Moscow in all the ballets of the period. She was predominantly a lyrical ballerina. Her Giselle was exceptionally pure and warm, her acting sincere and natural. There were other facets to her talent: she could be vivacious and gay in *La Vivandière*, which had such a success when she danced in Paris.[1]

Yet Bogdanova was unable to show all her worth in Russia. When the interest in native dancers dwindled after the temporary upsurge of patriotic feelings connected with the Crimean War, and the Directorate of the Imperial Theatres again started giving preference to foreign guest-artists, Nadezhda Bogdanova resumed her tours in Germany, Hungary, and Italy. Her last appearances took place in Warsaw in 1867. The career of this remarkable dancer was cut short while she was still at the height of her powers. . . .[2]

Another prominent Moscow ballerina of the sixties was Praskovia Lebedeva (1838-1917). She danced leading roles in romantic ballets while still at school, where she was taught by Frederic Montessu, a French dancer and teacher working in Moscow between 1846 and 1860. After Lebedeva's début in the title role of *Gitana*, Alexander Verstovsky, the composer and manager of the Moscow Theatres, wrote to the all-powerful Gedeonov, Director of the Imperial Theatres: "A wonderful future in Russian ballet is seen in this girl."

This was in 1854, and although Lebedeva remained a pupil until 1857, she added the principal roles in *Giselle*, *Katarina*, *Esmeralda*, *Gazelda* and *Paquita* to her repertory—all without any remuneration, while lauded by the Press as the only attraction in the Bolshoi Theatre of those times. Lebedeva was a dramatically expressive dancer often compared with Elssler, while her friend, Muravieva, recalled memories of Taglioni. In many ways Lebedeva was continuing the traditions started by Sankovskaya, and like her predecessor sought depth of feeling and strong passions, which she portrayed through her powers of mime. Lebedeva was never a technical virtuoso, yet, after certain weaknesses of the first years, when she was allowed to dance leading roles instead of concentrating on studies, she perfected her standards. Lebedeva often danced with success in St. Petersburg, particularly after the retirement of Muravieva, a dancer of a different style, for whom everything was conveyed through dance movement. They were dancers of two schools—both valuable, each enriching the other. After Lebedeva studied in the St. Petersburg school under Huguet and Johansson she was written of as "a charming dancer

[1] See *Ballet of the Second Empire* (1847-1848) by Ivor Guest, p. 57.

[2] More about Bogdanova in: "The Artistic Family of Bogdanovs"—see *Musical and Theatre Monitor* for 1856, Nos. 30 and 31. Also "The Dancer Nadezhda Bogdanova", by V. M. Krasovskaya in: *Scientific Papers of the Leningrad Institute of Theatre and Music*, vol. 1, 1958, pp. 295-322.

united in one person with an excellent actress". However, Lebedeva's tastes and inclinations in ballet were connected with roles requiring characterization and sincerity of portrayal. Faced by the necessity to take part in Saint-Léon's *Goldfish* intended for her benefit performance in St. Petersburg, Lebedeva preferred to retire rather than betray her own artistic principles. She was remembered for a long time as the "unforgettable and irreplaceable Lebedeva", as one who had introduced drama, life, and energy into ballet.

Lebedeva's talents were fully appreciated by Carlo Blasis who cast her as Marguerite in *Faust* during his work for the Moscow ballet (1861-1864).

By the time Blasis came to Russia his powers had declined. The ballets he produced made no particular impression, while the claim that his version of *Faust* was different from that of Perrot met with nothing but cold indifference. The book published by Blasis in Moscow in 1864 under the title *Dances in general, ballet celebrities, and national dances* was a partial re-hash of some of his other works, without any merit, of such books as *The Code of Terpsichore* and other earlier technical manuals. Yet this book is an interesting historical document, inasmuch as it contains Blasis' evaluation of members of the Moscow ballet; Lebedeva: "Through gesture and facial mime she expresses everything just as if it were said in words. Her dances are picturesque, brilliant, passionate and ravishing, if the role calls for these qualities"; Sobeshchanskaya: "Although still very young, Mlle Sobeshchanskaya does not yield in the art of dancing to many favourites of Terpsichore and may be counted among the most sparkling stars"; Nikolayeva: "A clever and inspired dancer, she has become the favourite of the Moscow public because her dancing is so lively and captivating", and others.

Blasis taught at the Moscow school and actively participated in the internal designing of the new building on Neglinnaya street, opened in 1866, two years after his departure. At first the reorganized school had three departments: ballet, opera and drama. At the end of the sixties the school curriculum was restricted to ballet, and remained thus until the new reform of 1888, when educational subjects were made obligatory (within the programme of the elementary school) and the dramatic department reinstated. The course of ballet education lasted seven years.

Memoirs of a former pupil of the Moscow school, published in 1910 in the *Annual of the Imperial Theatres*, give some amusing details of the period when the school moved to the new building. All the windows facing the street were of opaque glass. In order to look out into the street, girls broke the windowpanes "by accident". For these and other pranks they were ordered to wear a dirty apron and a dunce's cap and spend several hours thus attired at the recreation hall. All the pupils' relations were personally known to the management of the school and no visitors from outside were permitted. Once the schoolmistress noticed that her charges were particularly agitated, and, recognizing in a pieman standing on the landing a member of the gilded youth of Moscow, the hussar K., she requested him to leave the school immediately. He retired, forgetting his wares. Officers dressed as chimneysweeps and furnace-men tried to penetrate into the building, but were invariably recognized. These "balletomanes" considered it their duty to parade under the school's windows or on the other side of the street, and even run beside the large carriage that took the pupils to the theatre.

Konstantin Stanislavsky left us in his book, *My Life in Art*, many charming remembrances of the life of a young balletomane of the Bolshoi in the seventies and eighties.[1]

The Bolshoi ballet of the sixties and the seventies had every reason to be proud of its male contingent.

Sergei Sokolov (1830-1893), who graduated in 1850, was soon promoted to be partner of all the leading ballerinas, dancing with Lebedeva and Muravieva, and later with the guest-artist Adele Grantzow, and Sobeshchanskaya. Sokolov's brilliant gifts as a dancer, his grace, lightness, and elegance, coupled with a more than ordinary mimetic talent reached full development by the sixties. Blasis wrote of him in his book: "M. Sokolov (as Faustus) fully revealed the drama of the role and the movements of the soul that should accompany it." A contemporary writer, A. M. Dmitriev, admired Sokolov's speed, freedom of dancing, excellent partnering, and, especially, the musicality of his dance.

At times, Sokolov was obliged to give way to bad taste in dances of the Saint-Léon style, such as the "Polka Folichon" choreographed by Frederic Montessu, and containing too much cancan according to the criticism of V. I. Rodislavsky in the journal *Entr'acte*.

Doubtless Sokolov was obliged to dance such numbers on the orders of the management, yielding to the current fashion.

He was very much interested in choreography, and, apart from revivals, such as that of *La Sylphide* in 1866 for his own benefit, he choreographed a ballet to a Russian theme and with music by a Russian composer, Yuri Gerber. *The Fern* was first shown on December 27, 1867, at the Bolshoi

[1] See *Stanislavsky and the Ballet* by Natalia Roslavleva. *Dance Perspectives*, No. 23, N.Y., 1965.

Theatre. Sokolov was not an outstanding choreographer, moreover, as such, he was considerably influenced by Saint-Léon's *Hump-Backed Horse*. On the other hand he had a better understanding of Russian folklore and this constituted the merit of his work. It is interesting to learn from the memoirs of Karl Valtz, formerly in charge of the theatrical machines at the Bolshoi Theatre for sixty-five years,[1] that the idea of *The Fern* was born in the "salon" of V. P. Begichev, inspector of the repertory of Moscow Imperial Theatres and, later, one of the authors of the scenario of *Swan Lake*. Moreover, Valtz states that the first draft of *The Fern* was initiated by Begichev's wife, the talented amateur singer M. L. Shilovskaya, the soul and inspiration of the Begichev circle. Every member of it took part in the making of the ballet—Begichev, his wife, her son Konstantin Shilovsky, and Sokolov who, as author of the choreography to be, had his own ideas about the ballet. In the end the story was credited on the posters to Konstantin Shilovsky, then a nineteen-year-old student of the Moscow University, thus re-creating its old ties with the Bolshoi ballet.

The story was founded on the poetical Russian legend that the fern flowers but once a year on Midsummer night, and those who have the good fortune to find it discover treasures. However, the authors of the scenario modelled it on all the existing clichés. Thus the actual heroine of the ballet—The Genie of the Fern—fell in love with Stepan the peasant, gave him the treasure and died—in the manner of the Sylphide. There were other scenes quite contrary to the nature of Russian fairy-tales and rather in the style of traditional "*féerie*". In the subterranean kingdom of the third act, precious stones and metals danced their *variations*, gold and silver warriors marched, while the Genie of the Fern tried to persuade Stepan to stay in her kingdom. The dances in this and other scenes were in the nature of *divertissements* not linked directly with the action. Nevertheless, some of the dances had success—the Russian "Kamarinskaya" was invariably encored, while the virtuoso *variations* of the Genie of the Fern were choreographed with Sobeshchanskaya's special talents in mind.

While Sokolov's attempt to create a Russian ballet with the help of Gerber (first violin and conductor of the Bolshoi orchestra) was inspired by the best of intentions, these did not materialize. Russian in subject-matter, *The Fern* failed to be Russian in spirit.

Another ballet created in Moscow was destined to become one of the greatest achievements of Russian ballet.

[1] K. Valtz. *Sixty-Five Years in the Theatre*. Academia, Leningrad, 1928.

True, the contemporaries of Tchaikovsky failed to distinguish in *Swan Lake* its great musical and poetic merits at the first showing, neither did they see that in the guise of a German fairy-tale they were given a story about love conquering death which could compare with the best of Russian literature and lore.

Again the Begichev *salon* had its finger in the creation of the ballet. Tchaikovsky was very closely connected with the family. He taught music to the younger son, and was great friends with the elder. The composition of *Swan Lake* was started by Tchaikovsky in 1875. Kashkin, the composer's biographer, said that before actually starting his work in the spring of that year Tchaikovsky had long sessions with the choreographer, assisting in details of the programme. By August two acts were completed, and on March 23, 1876, rehearsals of *Swan Lake* soon began in the Bolshoi Theatre. The ballet did not take very long to compose—apparently Tchaikovsky was very much attracted by its general poetic idea which, beyond any doubt, belonged to him and him alone. Perhaps the theme had pursued him ever since he had written a small children's ballet, *The Lake of Swans*, when staying for a summer at Kamenka, the Ukrainian estate of his sister Anna. One of Tchaikovsky's nephews declared that the central "swan song" from the ballet of his childhood was immediately recognized by him as the main theme of the completed *Swan Lake* of 1877.[1]

No less important is the evidence of Anna Mekk-Davydova, Tchaikovsky's niece: "He (Tchaikovsky) liked to arrange home performances. The first production that I remember was *The Lake of Swans*. My sister, who was about six at the time, took part, and so did Uncle Modest who performed the role of the Prince. I was the Cupid. . . . This was probably in 1867".[2]

So the main theme of *Swan Lake* haunted Tchaikovsky for many years, growing in his poetic imagination. What he may have wanted from his friends in the Begichev circle was the mere skeleton of a plot. This was probably worked out by all the friends in co-operation. Moreover, none of them had any claims to authorship.

Yuri Slonimsky suggests in his study *Tchaikovsky and the Ballet Theatre of his Time* that the authors might have had at their disposal the fairy tales

[1] *Days and Years of P. I. Tchaikovsky*. Chronicle of his life and work. Musgis, Moscow, 1940, p. 75.

[2] Preserved in the State Central Museum for Culture of Music, the extract from these memoirs was first published in Yuri Slonimsky's *Tchaikovsky and the Ballet Theatre of his Time*, Musgis, Moscow, 1956, p. 89.

collected by Johann Musäus in the eighteenth century and known in the German original to any schoolboy from an educated Russian family.[1]

There is no proof, however, that the authors did resort to this source, neither is it of any great importance. The image of a White Swan, of maidens shedding their wings at night, recurs in many Russian fairy tales in a much more poetic imagery, that was closer to Tchaikovsky's musical thought. Neither could he have missed Pushkin's *Tale of the Tsar Saltan* with its wonderful stanzas about the White Swan of Russian folklore saved by the Prince from the wicked Hawk and then appearing as a beautiful maiden.

Tchaikovsky used the scenario offered to him as a point of issue in his work. He created one of the greatest poems without words about the search of true happiness and love as an issue of desperate psychological struggle. This portrayal of the inner spiritual state of the heroes through music was an important discovery destined to turn over a new leaf in the history of ballet music and upset customary ballet clichés.[2]

Tchaikovsky's immediate contemporaries were unable to distinguish this upon first hearing, with the exception of a few initiated ones, such as the music critic Laroche, who wrote: ". . . At the presentation of Tchaikovsky's ballet I listened much more than looked. . . . The musical side decisively surpassed the choreography. For its music *Swan Lake* is the best ballet ever heard by this author. . . ."

On the other hand Tchaikovsky's popularity in Moscow was great, and the interest of the public was attracted in no small measure by the fact that the music was written by a favourite Russian composer. Although the tickets were sold at prohibitive prices, the Bolshoi Theatre was packed on the night of the première of February 20, 1877.

Even if the new symphonic qualities of Tchaikovsky's ballet music could not be fully appraised, the real disappointment was the choreography. Wenzel Reisinger (1827-1892) the current ballet-master of the Bolshoi theatre, was really quite incapable of coping with the beauty of

[1] The first edition of Musäus' *Volksmärchen des Deutschen* (1782-1786) in Russian translation was published only in 1880, five years after the book of *Swan Lake* had been completed.

[2] A definitive analysis of the score of *Swan Lake* may be found in Daniel Zhytomirsky's *Tchaikovsky's Ballets*, Musgis, Moscow, 1951 and 1957.

Greater detail may be also found in the monumental *Tchaikovsky's Musical Legacy* prepared by the Tchaikovsky Museum at Klin in 1951. It was during the preparation of this work that the *répétiteur* (for two violins) from the Sobeshchanskaya *pas de deux* was discovered (see p. 83).

the work. The journal, *World Illustration*, that obliged us by printing the only two available drawings of that production, wrote of it in No. 434 for 1877: "M. Reisinger (called in irony by wits 'a choreographic virtuoso') has long ago proved to the Muscovites his complete inability to produce ballets, in which he strives to replace dances either by ugly processions or some sort of calisthenics. The only things alive were two 'national' dances, but M. Reisinger is not to be 'blamed' for their composition."

The anonymous writer does not say who was responsible for the national dances, including the Russian one. Most likely they were choreographed by members of the company, among whom there were several excellent character dancers, while the first Siegfried, Sergei Sokolov, is known to have been an aspiring choreographer.

The distinction of being the first Russian Odette fell to Pelageia Karpakova (1845-1920), lauded by Blasis while still at school, but not quite suited for the role, since she was a poor mime and not really a dancer of ballerina standards. Anna Sobeshchanskaya (1842-1918), the second Odette, created a much deeper character. But Sobeshchanskaya had already passed her prime as a dancer.

However, realizing that nothing could be expected from Reisinger, she went to St. Petersburg to seek Petipa's co-operation shortly before her first appearance in *Swan Lake* at its fourth performance, on April 28, 1877. Sobeshchanskaya wanted to have a *pas de deux* of greater virtuosity than Reisinger could provide. Petipa did compose such a *pas de deux* on the usual pattern, with *variations* and a coda, to music by Minkus. When Sobeshchanskaya returned to Moscow with the intention of inserting this *pas de deux* in her role, Tchaikovsky, not wishing to have alien matter in his score, composed new music on the same rhythmic pattern for Sobeshchanskaya and her partner Gillert. Having been performed only a few times by Sobeshchanskaya and her successor, Yevdokia Kalmykova, the *pas de deux* was dropped from the repertory,[1] to be discovered only in our own time in the score of *Le Corsaire* at the Bolshoi music library. (Orchestrated by Vissation Shebalin, part of this *pas de deux* was used by Vladimir Bourmeister in his 1953 version of *Swan Lake*, based on the original Tchaikovsky score.)

New interpolations, this time by other composers, crept into *Swan*

[1] In his later work, *Swan Lake* (State Musical Publishing House, Leningrad, 1962), Yuri Slonimsky included some new facts about this *pas de deux* and other aspects, unknown to him at the time of the publication of the chapter on *Swan Lake* in *Tchaikovsky and the Ballet Theatre of his Time*.

Lake in the eighties, when it was presented with choreography by J. Hansen. Again the great musical and spiritual beauties of *Swan Lake* failed to be implemented in visual images.

The choreographer capable of this historic mission was yet to be brought forth by the tide of development of the Russian school.

CHAPTER V

THE AGE OF PETIPA

THE SECOND HALF of the nineteenth century is associated in the history of Russian Ballet with the name of Marius Petipa (1819-1910).[1] Many authors have called it "the Petipa era", and such a term was justified. But what would seem, at first glance, a monolithic edifice created through the sole efforts and will power of a ballet-master of genius was, in fact, the product of an historical evolution and of circumstances and the taste of the times.

Petipa devoted fifty-six years of his life to the Russian stage working for the benefit of the Russian art with which he identified himself. He had lived in Russia for sixty-three years—the greater portion of his span of life. And though never bothering to master the intricacies of the language, he became deeply attached to this country, earning in full justice the name of Master of the Russian Ballet. It is this period of his biography that made his name immortal.

The atmosphere of the Russian ballet, particularly favourable for artistic work, enabled Petipa, like a long line of his predecessors (and some of them, such as Perrot, had in a way greater genius) to create, with the help of a pleiad of brilliant artists, a repertory of ballets that will go down to posterity.

Petipa's genius brought the art of choreography to the apex of achievement in some of his best works. Many of Petipa's early dance compositions, built on the polyphonic principle, consciously or not, anticipated the symphonic construction of great ballets yet to be created by Russian composers and prepared the Russian Ballet for this historical encounter.

Petipa was always in search of dramatic content expressed through

[1] Petipa gave the year of his birth as 1822 in his memoirs. It was customary, however, for actors to reduce their age. Biographical facts confirm that when Jean Petipa, the choreographer's father, moved with his family to Brussels in May 1819, his son, Alphonse Victor Marius, took part in the journey from Marseilles as a baby.

According to other statements, for which it is impossible to find documentary proof, Petipa was perhaps born even earlier than 1819. Sergei Khudekov, the publisher and balletomane, in polemics over the book of *La Bayadère* in the *Petersburg Gazette* of December 7, 1900, said that the "venerable ballet-master was eighty-nine years old".

choreographic idiom. A true disciple of Perrot he preferred to deal with three-dimensional characters, being interested in portraying the emotional side of their psychology. The fact that as choreographer he by far surpassed his great teacher in the art of creating endless dance patterns, original *enchaînements*, and *ballabili*[1] was only to his credit. Petipa definitely represented a new step in the development of the very art of making dances. Also at times he succeeded in achieving a remarkable fusion of emotional content expressed both in dance and in music.

But how often Petipa the entertainer, Petipa the obedient servant of the Court, would fall into an abyss of banality bordering on vulgarity and downright bad taste, continuing in the wake of his immediate predecessor Saint-Léon.

These two trends were ever in conflict, and it is because of Petipa's readiness to please and amuse the eye rather than rouse the mind, that few of his ballets have actually withstood the test of time. Yet those of his masterpieces that have survived: *The Sleeping Beauty*, *La Bayadère*, *Raymonda*, the *grand pas* created for the wilis in the second act of *Giselle*, "Le Jardin Animé" from *Le Corsaire* and other compositions in this style, brought by him to heights of perfection, are quite sufficient to place him among the greatest choreographers of all time.

Petipa's activity as teacher, his firm leadership and clarity of direction welded the Petersburg company into a unity of unprecedented strength.

His collaboration with great Russian composers such as Tchaikovsky and Glasunov yielded epoch-making results equalling that of a reform in ballet.

These unquestionable merits are seen in historical perspective. Petipa's immediate contemporaries, the progressive Russian intellectuals, refused to see anything positive in what he did. For Russian men of letters Petipa's ballets were just as absurd as those of Saint-Léon.

Petipa began his career in St. Petersburg. A young and practically unknown dancer, he obtained a very good position in view of the departure of Emile Gredlu (the *premier danseur*), on the initiative of Titus, as early as May 1847. His debut as Lucien d'Hervilly in *Paquita* on September 24, 1847, brought him immediate recognition, though largely for his mimetic powers and ability to perform character dances, for the role of Count d'Hervilly belonged to the sphere of pantomime with just two dances—"Pas de folie" and "El haleo". His next brilliant

---

[1] A dance executed by a large number of persons such as the *corps de ballet*. The term *ballabile* (plural *ballabili,* derived from Ital. *ballare*, to dance, was introduced into France and other countries by Carlo Blasis—Ed.

success was in *Satanilla*[1] (partnering Andreyanova, as in *Paquita*)—
again in a *demi-caractère* role requiring much verve and projection. As a
dancer Pepita was never a great classical virtuoso though, being engaged
as a *premier danseur*, he had to perform *danseur noble* roles in addition, and
could acquit himself quite well. Nevertheless, it was only a year after his
arrival in the country, when Perrot came to head the Petersburg company
for almost eleven years, that Petipa found his true calling. He performed dramatically charged roles in many of Perrot's ballets, for
instance, *Armida*, *Catarina*, *Le Délire d'un Peintre*, *Esmeralda*, *Faust*, and
La Péri.

During Fanny Elssler's tour in Russia, Petipa partnered her in some of
these ballets. Ballerinas liked to dance with him because they were sure
that with his help any difficulties that might arise would be overcome—
he was as reliable as a rock, being thoroughly trained in his profession.
But he was more than just a good dancer. Petipa was a first-class mime,
and this talent matured with the years, enabling him to take mime roles
when no longer young, and to lead a class in mime at the Theatre School.
He particularly fascinated the audience by his incomparable miming in
the part of Conrad in *Le Corsaire*. Here he reached heights of Byronic
romanticism. His acting was so natural that the ballerina, Vazem, admitted
having had a feeling of real awe when playing opposite him in *Le Corsaire*.
He seemed to identify himself with the character and, according to the
evidence of another ballerina, Yevgenia Sokolova, many times his
partner, he indeed became a noble and temperamental corsair, capable of
taming a crowd of brigands by the mere force of his glance! His treatment of roles was deeply thought out and psychologically motivated.
The scene of Faust's repenting and suffering upon meeting Margarita in
prison was particularly moving and served as a contrast to the earlier
scenes of love and infatuation. Petipa's close association with Perrot while
the latter was in Petersburg had a great influence on the future choreographer. He never abandoned the idea of preparing himself for this
vocation,—ever since staging the two Mazilier ballets *Paquita* and *Satanilla*
—apart from appearing in the leading roles. Of course he had attempted
earlier ventures in choreography, in Madrid and Bordeaux;[2] but here, in

---

[1] *Le Diable Amoureux.*

[2] We do not go into details of Petipa's biography since they are now available
in English in: *Russian Ballet Master: The Memoirs of Marius Petipa*. Edited by
Lillian Moore. Translated by Helen Whittaker. A. & C. Black, London,
1958. Also: Yuri Slonimsky. *Marius Petipa*. Translated by Anatole Chujoy.
Dance Index, N.Y., May-June, 1947.

Russia, he met, for the first time, ideal conditions and first-class dancers to work with.

It took him, however, a full twenty years to achieve his ambition. In the meantime he was ready to be satisfied with modest assignments that provided a wealth of experience.

In 1850 Petipa produced *Giselle* for Carlotta Grisi after Perrot's indications, but introducing many of his own independent touches in the dances of the wilis (act 2). (Later, in a production of 1884, he expanded these into the famous "Grand Pas des Wilis".) Perrot used Petipa as his assistant when putting on *The Naiad and the Fisherman* (*Undine*), *Faust* (1854), and other ballets on the St. Petersburg stage. It was from his association with Perrot that Petipa acquired a preference for dramatically convincing plots, development of the story through *pas d'action*, a love for various national dances and moving mime scenes.

But Perrot's was not the only influence. Upon the arrival of Saint-Léon, under whom he had to serve also for a number of years, Petipa immediately felt a change of trend and taste that he was willing to follow.

He was attracted by the Saint-Léon style of ballet containing a variety of *divertissements* and large-scale *ballabili* and himself became a past master in the composition of these, transcending the art of both Perrot and Saint-Léon.

Petipa the choreographer was beginning to develop his own style of classical ballet: *à grand spectacle*—in its best manifestations a magnificent spectacle, a superb creation.

But repercussions of "Saint-Léonism" (which in itself had little to do with Saint-Léon—he merely faithfully expressed the current trends) were constantly repeating themselves in Petipa's work, often peacefully existing side by side with real strokes of genius.

Presentation of ballet as means of diversion and amusement, with one striking *divertissement* being strung upon another—this new and latest fashion had already crept into Petipa's first Petersburg works. True, the plots of *Paquita* and *Satanilla* were sufficiently dramatic in the traditions of Romantic Ballet. However, in *Paquita*, particularly, the interest was concentrated on all sorts of *variations* and *pas*.

In time Petipa introduced more and more brilliant dances into *Paquita*, providing a chance for many a ballerina to show her virtuosity. The famous "Grand Pas" from Paquita, created by the great master in the last version of 1881 for the ballerina, six *premières danseuses* and eight second soloists to new music by Minkus (the original score was by Deldevez) is preserved to this day as one of the gems of the classical legacy. It was in

Marius Petipa in 1869.

Marius Petipa with his son and daughter.

the same year that Petipa introduced into *Paquita* a *mazurka* for eighty pupils of the school, still danced although the ballet has long vanished from the repertory.

It is not easy to classify Petipa's ballets according to definite types, since these are often combined in one and the same work. His works included fairy-tales and *féeries*, fantasies of all kinds, including revivals of the best creations of the Romantic Ballet; historical subjects, wherein history was treated rather loosely; classical subjects, that is stories borrowed from tales of ancient Greece or Rome; and a long line of character ballets at times based entirely on the national dances of a given country.

While Petipa was always ready to borrow from the works of his predecessors and contemporaries, he never copied anyone, but used definite elements from the creations of other choreographers, changing them according to his own artistic credo and needs. Petipa was truly a direct heir of the great choreographers of the past and a preserver of their traditions.

A prolific worker, Petipa created forty-six original ballets in Russia, most of them comprising several acts, while outside Russia, his compositions number only twelve short pieces. He revived seventeen ballets by other choreographers, frequently creating new scenes and dances as in the cases of *Giselle* and *Le Corsaire*. He also choreographed in Russia thirty-five dances in operas and five ballet *divertissements* in the nature of *pièces d'occasion*.

His first important creation was *Pharaoh's Daughter*. Much was at stake in 1862 when Petipa conceived his ballet. Suffice it to recall that Saint-Léon was as yet the official ballet-master, fearing his budding competitor and conscious of his rival's greater talent.

Petipa was not at all sure of his position. As late as 1867 he was on the verge of being transferred for permanent work in Moscow, and that the transfer did not take place was merely due to a deficit in the budget of the Moscow Bolshoi Theatre, which could not afford the expense of a highly skilled ballet-master. Ballet cognoscenti, however, hinted that the idea of Petipa's transfer to Moscow, with a subsequent termination of his contract altogether, was adroitly suggested to the Directorate of the Imperial Theatres by Saint-Léon, acting through a henchman, who himself had claims (but not enough talent) for the post of second ballet-master in Petersburg.

Such was the atmosphere in which Petipa began his career. The future all-powerful leader of the Petersburg ballet was supported at the time by a very modest (but more unbiased) group of balletomanes, while

Saint-Léon's ballets, and particularly the ballerinas appearing in them, received ovations from the so-called "infernal box" (the one almost overlooking the stage of the Bolshoi Theatre on the prompt side) hired for a whole season by rich and influential *habitués*.

Petipa completed *Pharaoh's Daughter* in the unprecedented short period of six weeks. Circumstances forced him to work at the pace of two rehearsals a day: the contract of Carolina Rosati, the Italian ballerina and excellent mime, for whom the principal role of Aspicia was being created, was running out. Moreover, less than two months remained till Butter Week (Shrovetide) preceding Lent, when all performances at the Imperial Theatres were interrupted. It was either then or never. Should the ballet not be ready shortly before the departure of Rosati (who was retiring), its first performance would have to be postponed until some time in the autumn, and the principal role given to some other artist. That spelled failure and probable cancellation. The Director of the Imperial Theatres, Saburov, was very much against the creation of a new ballet for Rosati, either because he was egged on by Petipa's opponents, or for the reason that Rosati came to Petersburg at the decline of her career, and, according to contemporary critics, could hardly "get off" the floor, performing brief *variations* that could not satisfy the exacting Petersburg balletomanes.

Yet Rosati regained her dramatic powers, and Petipa tailored his ballet with them in mind. When Saburov, in an effort to ward off Rosati's request, asked whether the ballet could be prepared in six weeks, Petipa said "yes". He knew the company he was going to work with and *Pharaoh's Daughter* was ready in time for the première on January 18 (30), 1862—exactly six weeks later.

The music by Cesare Pugni, the staff ballet composer of the Imperial Theatres, was being written simultaneously with the choreographer's work, in other words made to fit in rhythm and tempo the dances that had already been performed in the rehearsal room. Newspaper notices described the music as "lively and vivacious". It did not even attempt to convey national character or psychological motivation. The composer was not expected to supply anything but "danceable" accompaniment, and this was Pugni's speciality. For years many tunes from *Pharaoh's Daughter* were used in the ballrooms in the form of various dances and quadrilles and gained wide popularity, though admittedly in the field of light music.

On the other hand the plot of *Pharaoh's Daughter* by Petipa and Vernoy de Saint-Georges, who based their prologue on Gautier's *Le Roman de la Momie,* contained many scenes affording strong dramatic situations, even if the entire action frequently lacked logic. This was a concoction wherein Perrot's dramatic principles (still accepted by Petipa) were blended at random with fantastic *divertissements,* exotic scenes, and no less than three impressive apotheoses.

This was the first ballet *à grand spectacle* whose pattern was afterwards repeated by Petipa, with few changes, on innumerable occasions.

Each of the five acts had some effective *pas d'action* or *ballabile.* In the first act there was an impressive "Pas d'action of Huntresses" performed by Aspicia, the Pharaoh's daughter, and her retinue; and a *grand pas* for the ballerina, several soloists, and the *corps de ballet.*

Dances for the *corps de ballet* were specially beautifully designed, providing interweaving symmetrical groups carefully worked out by the choreographer. The "Grand ballabile des cariatides animées" was performed by eighteen pairs of *danseuses* and *danseurs.* They carried on their heads baskets of flowers, which concealed thirty-six children, who revealed their presence on the last beat of the music in the final grouping.

This was one of the first fruits of Petipa's inexhaustible inventiveness. Later, in *Trilby,* he created a large golden cage, from which were released numerous "birds"—dancers of the *corps de ballet.* But every now and then he fell victim to very bad taste, as in the earlier *Blue Dahlia,* where the ballerina watered a "bed of dahlias", again represented by the *corps de ballet,* from a real watering-can.

Pharaoh's Daughter became a lasting favourite with its numerous dances, processions, *ballabili,* camels, monkeys, and prancing lion. The setting, a huge pillared hall with mysterious hieroglyphics done in great detail, was provided by the official *décorateur,* Roller, who was elected to the Academy of Arts for this work. This was about the only authentically Egyptian touch. The tutus for the ballerina had vaguely Egyptian ornaments on the border. The coiffure followed contemporary fashion. However, the costumes of the purely mime characters—the Pharaoh (Nicolai Goltz, relic of the Didelot era), the High Priests and Courtiers— to a certain extent created the exotic atmosphere. This impression was enhanced by various theatrical effects—there was a simoom in the prologue, a sparkling fountain of water in the Nile scene that brought Aspicia back to earth, and a three-level apotheosis in the finale, showing the entire areopagus of ancient Egyptian gods.

However impressive were all these attractions, the actual success was won by the performers of the ballet. Rosati, who performed the title role exactly eight times for every night in the course of Shrovetide and then left for Paris and complete retirement, surpassed herself in the mime scenes, while her dances were artfully composed so as to conceal her defects and display her virtues. Petipa himself performed the role of an Englishman (Lord Wilson) and Ta-Hor (a noble Egyptian youth) with great success. Better still, moreover, after *Pharaoh's Daughter* he was officially appointed to the post of second ballet-master.

All the remaining roles in the ballet were assigned to first-class soloists of which the Petersburg ballet could justly boast. The River Neva was danced by Matilda Madayeva, one of the most popular *danseuses* of the day. The River Congo was Kosheva, the Tiber—Sokolova I, the Thames —Yefremova, the Rhine—Nikitina Ramseya, Aspicia's favourite slave and confidante, was Radina I. Lev Ivanov took the mime role of the Fisherman, while Alexandra Kemerer was his wife. Thus the smallest role in this long ballet (it lasted for five hours) was performed by excellent artists, welded into a homogeneous ensemble.

In the autumn of the same year, when the question of the revival of *Pharaoh's Daughter* presented no problem in view of its overwhelming success, the role of Aspicia passed to Petipa's wife and pupil, Maria Surovshchikova-Petipa. Though the role was created for Rosati, it fitted Maria Petipa to perfection, and the young dancer became a *prima ballerina* almost overnight. She owed this to the guidance of her husband, who knew how to exploit to advantage her natural gifts.

Petipa married Maria Surovshchikova in 1854, when she was just out of school. She was endowed with a beautiful figure, a pleasing face, charming smile, and a more than average ability for mime. Petipa created for her dances that were technically easy but contained pretty plastic poses, and made every effort to show her off in dramatic or comic scenes. He choreographed for her such ballets as *The Blue Dahlia*, *Un Mariage sous la Régence*, *The Beauty of Lebanon*, *Le Marché des Innocents*, *Camargo*, and *The Travelling Danseuse*. In each of these ballets he introduced some special dance such as the "Charmeuse" in *The Beauty of Lebanon* that was later chosen by Anna Pavlova for its languid grace; the "Pas de Sabre" in *Pharaoh's Daughter* and, particularly, the numbers *en travestie*—"Le petit Corsaire" and "Mujichok" ("The Little Mujik")—that pleased the chauvinistic part of the audience in the early sixties, but roused indignant protests on the part of the democratic defenders of the peasants.

Maria Petipa's repertory included the role of Margarita in *Faust*; this she performed brilliantly under the guidance of her husband. She was an outstanding ballerina in her own sphere, but many balletomanes criticized her "cotton-wool *pointes*" (Petipa avoided them by choreographing most

Maria Petipa as the Lilac Fairy in the first performance of *The Sleeping Beauty*, 1890. (Collection of Natalia Roslavleva)

Virginia Zucchi as Esmeralda. Petersburg, 1886. (Collection of Natalia Roslavleva)

of her popular dances on half-point), and other technical weaknesses, drawing comparisons with Muravieva, a real *prima ballerina* with a wide range of virtuosity. The ballet audience was divided into "Petipists" and "Muravievists". Verses were composed in a popular vaudeville about the rivalry, in which Surovshchikova-Petipa spared no intrigues. Upon her parting with Marius Petipa in 1869 she soon declined as a dancer, and, after making a pitifully unsuccessful attempt to appear on the St. Petersburg dramatic stage, moved to Novocherkassk. There she died of smallpox in 1882, when Marius Petipa was enabled to legalize his union with the Moscow dancer, Savitskaya, who became his second wife, and with whom, according to his own words, he experienced true marital bliss, raising a large family.

All this happened much later. In the sixties Marius Petipa was still engaged in the rivalry with Saint-Léon. Saint-Léon, following the lesson of *Pharaoh's Daughter*, endeavoured to improve his *ballabili* and general choreographic design, that was evident in *The Hump-Backed Horse*. Petipa, in his turn, racked his brain for new and striking subjects. In 1868, on the suggestion of Gedeonov, Director of the Imperial Theatres, he chose a historical episode from the life of the ancient King of Lydia for his new grand ballet *King Candaules*. The novelty of this ballet was its tragic end, wherein Nisia, the guest-artist Henriette d'Or, for whom the ballet was created, lost her reason at the sight of the ghost of her murdered husband. The première of the ballet took place in Moscow, where it had an outstanding success, that was considerably heightened by a train-load of Petersburg balletomanes arriving for the occasion. Yet, while d'Or was praised for her great mimetic talent, so much needed in the role of Nisia, serious critics pointed out the complete absence of the softness and feminine grace equally essential in the scene where she had to replace Aphrodite on her pedestal. It was this steel hardness that gave the "infernal box" the pretext for giving d'Or the nickname of "the man in skirts", while their favourite Adele Grantzow was called by the "Dorists", "the German stocking". This was a hint that Grantzow, like a true German, took to knitting stockings and embroidering souvenirs as soon as she was home, and subsequently gave them away to admirers of her talents.

In *King Candaules* Petipa continued to develop his main formula. He created a "Ballabile Lydien" wherein one could see simultaneously two nymphs, three graces, a bayadère, a negro, eight mulattoes, sixteen *danseuses* with parasols, sixteen girl-pupils, sixteen boy-pupils dressed as black slaves, and eighteen male dancers in Lydian costume.

This was a beautiful ensemble composition in the vocabulary of the *danse d'école*, given a slightly Oriental flavour.

The "Ballabile" was immediately followed by a "Grand Pas d'action" in the ancient Greek style, representing one of Petipa's greatest classical *grand pas*. The centre piece of this *pas d'action*, with numerous cupids, nymphs, and various mythological characters taking part, was the "Pas de Vénus" that brought d'Or particular renown. A decade or so later, when the invasion of Italian virtuosity dancers started in Petersburg, the feat performed by d'Or—a series of five *pirouettes sur la pointe* on the right foot, affording a chance to demonstrate her steel toes, was no longer so astounding. At the time it made, and justly, a great impression.

There was more than virtuosity to the "Pas de Vénus". In the true tradition of the *ballet d'action* it furthered the action and stemmed directly from it. After Nisia's dance her husband, Candaules, proclaimed her to be the true Venus, upon which the statue of the goddess was removed from its pedestal and the queen placed upon it in her stead. The sky grew dark at this act of defiance and later in the ballet punishment ensued from Venus-Aphrodite herself.

Other dances in the classical ensemble composed by Petipa enabled budding Russian soloists to show their worth. While the Directors of the Imperial Theatres concentrated attention on foreign guest-artists, Petipa created *pas* for his pupils. Yevgenia Sokolova, the future pride of the St. Petersburg stage, was entrusted with the *pas*, "Les Amours de Diane", and another, very soft and poetic number, "La Graziosa", while still in the last year at school.

These purely classical *divertissements* were skilfully alternated by Petipa with mimed scenes and processions such as the triumphant return of Candaules' troops. Petipa also could not refrain from introducing at least one banality (bordering on the vulgar), being influenced by the current demand.

This sensation was provided in *King Candaules*, act III, the set representing a bathing-pool of pink-and-white marble with a group of beautiful slave girls bathing in it and attending on Nisia (standing beneath a curtain).

King Candaules was again a mixture of good and bad taste, dramatic and purely entertaining scenes, and a wealth of choreographic invention that drove Saint-Léon to create for Adele Grantzow the already mentioned *The Lily*. The music and dances of this ballet were mostly borrowed from *La Source*, produced earlier at the Paris Opéra, but the new book, according to the desire of the choreographer, placed the action in China, and this gave him the chance to make Adele Grantzow "dance out" a whole melody on a specially invented "Chinese" musical instrument. However, this was an inventiveness that could not compete with the choreographic genius of Petipa, and it was soon after the dismal failure of *The Lily* (in October 1869) that Saint-Léon left the field free—at long last.

However, before he became the unconditional master of the Petersburg company, Petipa had to do another major work in Moscow on the orders of the Directorate of the Imperial Theatres.

This was *Don Quixote*, with music by Minkus that provided a mere suggestion of Spanish themes. Yet it became one of Petipa's greatest realistic creations. The reason for the success of this work, that stood even at the time quite apart from his Petersburg assignments, was embodied in the simple fact that Petipa knew full well the difference between the respective requirements of the Moscow and Petersburg public. He realized that for Moscow he had to provide a ballet with a logically developing plot, a ballet in the nature of a good play, with three-dimensional characters, and, at the same time, plenty of colourful dances. This he set out to produce, and the Moscow *Don Quixote* was in no way the same as the Petersburg version that was revived in 1871—two years after the ballet had been staged in Moscow.

The Moscow version of *Don Quixote*, in four acts and eight scenes, was a robust comedy. It followed (but not minutely) the inserted story about the love of Quiteria and Basilio (in the ballet they became Kitri and Basil) from the second volume of Cervantes' monumental novel. The accent was on the merry *quid pro quo* into which either the lovers or Don Quixote with his Sancho Panza kept falling, and Kitri (Anna Sobeshchanskaya) together with Basil (Sergei Sokolov) enjoyed support and benefaction from Don Quixote. Thus it was a true story about simple people striving for their happiness, something quite unusual for the late sixties in Russian ballet.

There were some scenes of fantasy, but these were treated with a touch of humour. In the colourful and picturesque encounter with a wandering troupe of actors, the deranged Don Quixote took the rising moon for his beloved Dulcinea, for some reason in a sad mood. The Moon indeed started weeping (this was adroitly arranged by Karl Waltz, the chief machinist of the Bolshoi Theatre). Big tears rolled down the Moon's cheeks, but then its grief changed to laughter, to the general merriment of the entire audience.

In this scene Don Quixote again met Kitri. Disguised as a man (here Petipa's addiction to dancers *en travestie* was at any rate justified by the action) she ran away from home in order to escape marriage with the hateful rich nobleman, Gamache. The players guessed she was a girl and asked her to stay with them.

In this scene Kitri-Sobeshchanskaya took part in a charming comic dance in which the famous *danseur grotesque*, Espinosa, dressed as Harlequin, and armed with a cage, tried to catch "larks"—Sobeshchanskaya and six *coryphées* in appropriate bird-like costumes.

After Don Quixote's delirious fight with the windmills (he tried to save the Moon from imaginary giants) and his subsequent injuries, there ensued a dream in the woods, also presented in a humorous vein. In his nightmare Don Quixote fought with droll cacti, with various monsters of unbelievable shape, and only at the end of that dream saw his Dulcinea, represented by Pelageia Karpakova. (In this production Don Quixote did not confuse Dulcinea with his protégée, Kitri.)

All the characters met once more at the forced marriage of Kitri to Gamache. Basil faked suicide, Don Quixote insisted that the dying barber and Kitri be united by the alcalde, Basil immediately jumped up quite safe and sound, and the newly-weds, together with their friends, merrily said goodbye to Don Quixote and Sancho Panza, departing for new and even more wondrous adventures.

The Moscow version of *Don Quixote* was packed with Spanish and other character dances of all kinds,—even for the leading *sujets*. There were a "Morena" for Kitri and Basil; a "Zingara", "Jota", and "Lola" for the company, including an impressive dance of *torreros* with swords for the male *corps de ballet*. Petipa borrowed amply from his earlier experiences in Spain where in his youth as a dancer he boasted of having danced and played the castanets no worse than the first dancers of Andalusia.

The whole Moscow Press was most favourable. The chronicler of the *Universal Gazette* for 1869 (No. 109 of December 16), expressed the opinion that "all the dances in *Don Quixote* possess the character of the country where the action is taking place. Languid grace, passion, and pulsating life are all reflected in them. We hear castanets, accompaniments of Spanish dancing."

Beyond doubt these qualities were introduced not only by choreography, but by the music as well. In this ballet made for Petipa (after Pugni's death in 1870 Minkus became the choreographer's principal musical collaborator and wrote sixteen compositions for him) Minkus revealed in full his understanding of dance requirements, a variety of melody, and, above all, that general emotional upsurge that was and is so typical of the *Don Quixote* score, making its music infectious both for

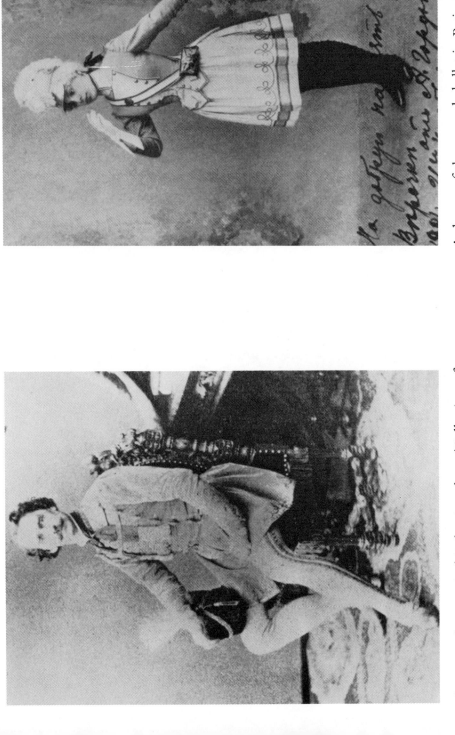

A dancer of the corps de ballet in Petipa's time. (Apollinaria Gordova.) Probably *La Halte de Cavalerie*. (Collection of Natalia Roslavleva)

Christian Johansson in his dancing days. (Collection of Natalia Roslavleva)

The Naïad and the Fisherman as presented in 1851 on a lake near Petersburg. (Bakhrushin Theatre Museum, Moscow)

audience and dancers. Moreover, Petipa's scenario, to which the score was composed, ensured that the dances really did follow from the action and sprang from it, while the action itself was charged with merry feeling. That is how *Don Quixote* in its Moscow version became a *ballet d'action* in the true sense.

When the production was being transferred to the Petersburg stage in 1871 the situation was quite different. Petipa, who had been sole head of the Petersburg ballet since 1869, had to produce something to the taste of the "diamond row". Minkus was asked to compose a fifth act of three scenes. Quite a few changes were made in the story. Don Quixote's interest in Kitri was no longer that of a patron: he mistook her for Dulcinea, and thus the double role was taken by one ballerina, Alexandra Vergina, providing her with more varied material. The accent was now made on the big classical scene of Don Quixote's dream, where Kitri-Dulcinea was surrounded by a large *corps de ballet* and seventy-two children costumed as cupids.

The cupids also appeared in the new fifth act, at the Court of the newly introduced Duke and Duchess, unknown in the Moscow version. It is interesting to note that the "Grand Pas de Deux" (accompanied by soloists and the *corps de ballet*) was danced by Vergina, not with Lev Ivanov performing the part of Basil, but with the then young classical dancer Pavel Gerdt, brought in for the sake of partnering as sometimes happened in those days.

All the comic scenes and many of the character dances from the Moscow version had disappeared in the Petersburg production, while those that remained became firmly welded with classical steps and style, losing much of their national character, but, on the other hand, gradually evolving into that special academic character dancing that is a special feature of the Petipa choreography and a valuable part of Russian classical heritage.

The ballet was not too popular and local wits made wry jokes about the only success of Sancho Panza's donkey in a "classical *pas* made by Petipa".

Its continued life on the Russian stage proved that *Don Quixote* withstood the test of time—through the exuberant, life-asserting and life-loving nature of its dances, carefully preserved in its essence, though much changed by generations of Russian dancers and ballet-masters.

Having been officially placed at the head of the Petersburg ballet, Petipa undertook the colossal task of moulding it into the company he needed for his numerous projects.

He never left anything to chance and appeared at rehearsals with the entire choreography which he had worked out at home, usually with the help of small figurines arranged on his table in the place of dancers. Well versed in every possible resource of the theatre, he liked to use all sorts of props and accessories in the form of garlands of flowers, baskets, and tabourets used for placing the *corps de ballet* at different levels.

His main concern, however, was with the classical dance proper. His ability to create endless new *enchaînements* that never repeated themselves was really extraordinary. He used the entire gamut of the classical school, alternating quick and slow *tempi*, and contrasting steps *à terre* and elevation in a dance pattern of great beauty. In his best *pas d'action* and dance miniatures, such as *A Midsummer Night's Dream* to music by Mendelssohn, or "Le Jardin Animé" to that by Delibes, he attained perfect fusion of the music of sounds with the music of movement.

The Leningrad historian, Vera Krasovskaya, D.A., gives in her valuable book, *Russian Ballet Theatre of the Second Half of the XIXth Century* (Iskusstvo, Leningrad, 1963), an analysis of what she terms Petipa's principle of orchestrating the dancing ensemble. Krasovskaya says: "Petipa disposed the dancing groups of soloists and the *corps de ballet* in the same way that a composer arranges separate solos and various groups of instruments in the orchestra. He knew how to obtain remarkable plastic results by placing side by side similar, or, on the contrary, acutely different dance elements. Dividing the stage into several levels, he filled each of them with groups of dancers. These groups, either staying on place, or moving, or merging with others, or separating once more, reached at times the greatest possible force of expression. A dance movement or a 'dance phrase' was repeated by one group, either contrasting with the dance pattern of neighbouring ones, or interrupting and breaking it, or merging with it in perfect harmony. There were some groups, whose task consisted in forming a harmonious background, serving as a reliable monotone rhythmic point of issue for the flowering of intricate dance melodies. In their turn, the 'voices' of soloists, at once independent and interwoven with it, could emerge against the background of this dance melody."

Vera Krasovskaya considers that the method of creation of dance imagery in Petipa's works with time equalled that of the most complicated and developed musical imagery. And if at first the music proper was very simple, even almost primitive, later, when Petipa had consolidated his searches for the complex orchestration of *dance*, he arrived at true *choreo-*

graphic symphonism in his best works, created in association with great Russian composers.

Perhaps Petipa's method of "orchestration" arose from the fact that he was a musically educated man, having studied at the conservatoire in Brussels. However, so far as ballet was concerned, he left but a subsidiary and secondary role to music, and, outwardly at least, seemed to conduct his choreographic experiments quite separated from the score. On the other hand, he was concerned about finding good music much earlier than is usually realized. In 1870 Petipa had plans for creating a new ballet to a Slav theme with music by the famous composer Serov, whose sudden death prevented its composition. However, Petipa had time to send, through the Directorate of the Imperial Theatres, a memorandum to Serov, wherein, aside from a request that the composer should be present at rehearsals for explanation of the nature of his music and necessary cuts, he was also entreated to "compose melodious music, as this is the most important requisite for the production of dances".

The opportunity of obtaining a score by a first-class composer was put off for another twenty years, until his collaboration with Tchaikovsky.

But in the same year of 1877 which marked the unsuccessful first Moscow production of *Swan Lake*, Petipa created a ballet, where one scene, at least, despite the mediocre Minkus music, was much closer to symphonism than Reisinger's pedestrian treatment of Tchaikovsky. This was "The Shades" from *La Bayadère*.

This work, arranged to a programme by the balletomane and publisher, Sergei Khudekov, and Petipa, had much in common with the Parisian *Sacountala* of Lucien Petipa. It was also based on the famous play by the Indian classical poet and dramatist, Kalidasa. There were some similarities, and many differences. *La Bayadère* was a tragedy about a dancer. The bayadère Nikia, forced to dance at the wedding festivity for her lover Solor and the King's daughter Gamsatti, was handed a basket with a snake hidden among the flowers. In the course of a beautiful dance expressing anguish, jealousy, and suffering, Nikia was bitten by the snake. Before she expired the great Brahmin offered her an antidote—on condition that she surrendered herself to him. Nikia refused and died of the bite.

In the next scene Solor, tormented by pangs of conscience, dreams of Nikia in the Kingdom of the Shades, surrounded by wraiths.

The ballet ended with an impressive scene (omitted in present revivals) during the wedding of Gamsatti and Solor, when the walls of the temple collapsed as a sign of punishment from the gods.

La Bayadère offered Petipa the chance to exploit exotic dances to full measure, and he did not miss the opportunity. The ballet was packed with pseudo-Indian dances. There was a temperamental "Hindu Dance", in Kathak style, with bells attached to the ankles, performed by Lubov Radina (later the role passed to the choreographer's daughter, Maria Petipa) with Felix Kshesinski and Alexander Pichaud. Matilda Madayeva danced "Jampé", a dance of unidentified origin, in which one end of a transparent scarf was attached to the performer's leg, the other to her head. A popular number was the "Danse Manu", in which the *danseuse* (Vera Zhukova), bearing a pitcher on her head, teased two little girls who asked her for a drop of water. (This dance provided early theatrical experience for generations of pupils from the school. Many a ballerina of today of the Kirov Theatre appeared as a child in "Danse Manu", and so did Galina Ulanova.)

The "Manu" was merely a part of a *grand divertissement* in the second act, which opened with a ceremonial procession, with Solor mounting a huge artificial elephant while King Dugmanta and Princess Gamsatti were carried in palanquins.

Demi-caractère dances were followed by a magnificent classical "Grand Pas", one of Petipa's greatest works, for twenty-four *danseuses*, twelve *danseurs*, twelve small and twelve average pupils, two senior girl-pupils as *bayadères* and two *coryphées*. This grand ensemble, now filling the entire stage, and now leaving it free for the two bayadères, was but a preliminary for the *grand pas de deux* performed by Maria Gorshenkova and Pavel Gerdt (while Lev Ivanov *acted* the part of Solor).

After the "Danse Manu" and a general coda followed Nikia's tragic dance, beautifully choreographed by Petipa in the spirit of genuine *danse d'action*, with the feelings expressed directly through movement.

Her dying scene was beautifully done. She stood alone in the centre of the stage. The crowd stepped far back. Nikia raised her arm to the sky, drew herself up as if defying those who had betrayed her, and collapsed.

Everything in the choreography was calculated to lead to this moment of ultimate tragedy.

The next act started with the "Shades"—a superb achievement of Petipa, preserved to this day as one of the greatest gems of the classical legacy of all times.

The scene was originally a vision seen by Solor, drugging himself with opium, but this detail is now omitted, and rightly.

Down a high ramp, seemingly from nowhere (Petipa's contemporaries said that visually he was influenced in this scene by Gustave Doré's designs for Dante's *Divine Comedy*—Paradise), stepped one by one the dancers of the *corps de ballet* in white tutus, with white scarfs attached to their heads and wrists. As in a musical scale, they all performed one and the same movement: *arabesque-renversée*. When the complete first line had descended the ramp, with the next one in its wake, it continued the same pattern *par terre*, until the entire stage was filled with figures moving in symphonic harmony to the same haunting melody. The *soli* that followed stemmed from this background.

In the already quoted book Doctor Krasovskaya offers an original concept that Petipa created in "The Shades" the first successful experiments in the symphonization of the dance. While it has been customary to think that this process was brought about by music alone at the time of the creation of the great Tchaikovsky symphonic ballets, in reality Russian choreography was gradually evolving symphonic idiom with its own means, even to the simplest of musical forms.

"Choreography could have arrived at symphonic imagery only with its own armament" says Doctor Krasovskaya, confirming her postulate by an analysis of the "Shades" and its choreography, from which there was but one step to a future encounter with great symphonic music.

In many ways *La Bayadère* remained Petipa's ultimate achievement. Its unity of drama and lyrical dance revealed a strong, if indirect, influence of Russian dramatic theatre and the Russian school of symphonic music that was being evolved in those years.

At the time of the creation of *La Bayadère* Petipa had lived in Russia and had worked in Russian ballet for thirty years. The general trends of Russian art could not fail to exert an impact upon so sensitive an artist. He came to love and understand the country that had adopted him. Petipa's friend and collaborator Khudekov writes in the fourth volume of his *History of Dancing*, a great bibliographic rarity: "A Frenchman by birth, Petipa was Russian at heart from head to foot."

La Bayadère served as a vehicle for many Russian ballerinas, and it is significant that in 1903 it became the first ballet to bring Anna Pavlova fame as a great dramatic dancer.

This could not be said of Yekaterina Vazem, the first Nikia. She was a considerable virtuoso, particularly for the time, a typical Petipa ballerina, whose well-trained supple body was an obedient instrument in the hands of the choreographer—and for the "Shades" this was of paramount importance, where the entire idea of the ballet and the fine texture of sustained feelings was conveyed through dance. But Vazem was not an actress. Her range of expressiveness came through the body and that counted most in the kind of choreography created by Petipa.

Yekaterina (Matilda) Vazem (1848-1937) entered the Theatre School in 1857. She attracted attention while still at school by performing the title-role in the ballet *Teolinda* (Pugni–Saint-Léon), and was lucky to have taken part in Perrot's ballets. Shortly before graduation in 1867, she attended the *classe de perfectionnement* of Huguet, who accepted only the best pupils that could be made into ballerinas, so Vazem's career was assured. She had her debut on September 10, 1867, in *The Naiad and the Fisherman* (*Ondine*) and was given many responsible roles in the first two seasons. Although not Petipa-trained she became a true Petipa ballerina because her career for the most part coincided with the period when the choreographer was at the height of his creative ability. Vazem performed leading roles in twenty-eight ballets. Many of Petipa's works had been created especially for her: *Les Bandits*, *Le Papillon*, *La Bayadère*, *The Daughter of the Snows* (a fantasy inspired by the Nordenskjöld Arctic expedition in the eighties), *Zoraya*, the one-act ballet *Night and Day*, and the famous "grand pas" from the 1881 version of *Paquita*, to name but the most important ones.

Vazem was a *terre à terre* ballerina, a *danseuse de force* for whom no difficulty existed in repeating a technically trying *variation* on her steel *pointes*, or performing double pirouettes, considered a great rarity at this time. In *La Bayadère* she decided to prove that she was not only a *terre à terre* dancer, and surprised even Petipa by traversing in three leaps the huge stage of the Bolshoi Theatre, with its seven wings. Appearances on such a huge stage quite naturally required from the ballerina especial skill and unusual presence. On a stage of these dimensions it was possible to present spectacular productions such as *Pharaoh's Daughter* or *La Bayadère*.

It was for Vazem that Petipa composed many *pas* of extreme difficulty, such as the "Pas des Eventails" in *Le Corsaire*, in after years not danced by any other ballerina. While Vazem was not a great mime, through hard work she achieved success in parts requiring acting ability: *Pharaoh's Daughter* and *La Bayadère*, and was even entrusted in 1876 with the purely mimed name part in the opera *Fenella* (*The Dumb Girl of Portici*), performing it with success in the company of brilliant singers of the Italian opera such as Patti, Lucca, and Mazini.

News of Vazem's brilliance as a dancer reached Europe through many visitors to Petersburg, and in the spring of 1873 she received an advantageous offer to dance in the course of three years for three summer months of every year in the United States of America. This engagement was to include appearances at the Universal Exhibtion of 1876 in Philadelphia.

The management of the Imperial Theatres would not let Vazem accept this offer, as the transatlantic crossing was considered dangerous, and it did not want to risk the loss of its *prima ballerina*.

On another occasion, while staying in Paris at the end of the seventies, Vazem obtained permission through Zina Mérante (née Richard and a former Petersburg dancer) to attend the dancers' classes at the Opéra, in order to keep in training. No sooner did the Opéra Director, Galantier, see Vazem's merits as a dancer, than he offered her a contract. This was strongly opposed by the *premières danseuses* headed by Rita Sangalli, fearing the emergence of a dangerous rival. Thus the Opéra public was denied the chance of seeing a great Russian ballerina.

Vazem retired from the stage in 1884, but continued to teach until 1896 in the responsible intermediary classes. Here she taught Pavlova and Vaganova. The latter wrote of her as of a teacher with a remarkable eye for noticing any defect and error, and one who paid particular attention to the development of good technique.

After the Revolution of 1917 Vazem returned to private teaching and gave wonderful lessons sitting in an armchair. She spent the last years of her life in the Leningrad Home for Veterans of the Stage where, with the help of her son N. I. Nosilov, she wrote *Memoirs of a Ballerina of the St. Petersburg Bolshoi Theatre* (Iskusstvo, Leningrad, 1937), containing a wealth of valuable material.

Another "Petipa ballerina" was Yevgenia Sokolova (1850-1925). Like Vazem, she began her career in Saint-Léon's day, performing in 1862 with great success the role of Cupid in his ballet *The Pearl of Seville*, receiving the "pink dress" of distinction given to pupils. (She studied in Lev Ivanov's class.) Again in 1864 she received an even higher reward—the "white dress" (these were worn only in class) for dancing the *Malo-rossian* dance from *The Hump-Backed Horse*. On October 22, 1868, one year before her official graduation, she had what amounted to a début on the stage of the Bolshoi Theatre, St. Petersburg, when, at short notice, she replaced Kemerer I in "Les Amours de Diane"—an important *divertissement* from *King Candaules*. The young dancer was acclaimed as an artiste of exceptional promise that was soon fulfilled. In 1870 she performed with great dramatic impact the title-role of *Esmeralda*. Here she revealed the grace and softness of dancing that made her such a typical representative of the Russian school. In many ways she was the same kind of dancer as Maria Surovshchikova-Petipa, and inherited most of her roles.

Petipa created a number of ballets with Sokolova's talent in view. The first one—*L'Amour Bienfaiteur*, in which Sokolova danced the title-role—was composed by him for her graduation performance in 1868.

In later years Sokolova performed leading roles in the following Petipa ballets: *A Midsummer Night's Dream* (Titania), *The Adventures of Peleus* (Thetis)—both in 1876; *Roxana, the Beauty of Montenegro*, in 1878; *Mlada* in 1879; *The Cyprus Statue* (Galatea) in 1883; *Trilby* in 1884. She was also a brilliant Queen of the Night against Vazem's Queen of the Day in *Night and Day*, and a charming Chloe in the one act *Les Offrandes à l'Amour ou le Bonheur est d'aimer*, choreographed by Petipa in the style of the anacreontic ballets. It was in this ballet that Sokolova bowed to the public for the last time on November 25, 1886, after exactly twenty years of service, in the course of which she danced in a great many ballets apart from those specially created for her.

As Aspicia in *Pharaoh's Daughter*, she was praised by Sergei Khudekov for her "rounded poses", her grace of body and enchanting personality. Sokolova never possessed the steel technique of Vazem, but her school was very good, and with perseverance she improved her natural abilities, in particular the expressiveness of mime that in time became quite outstanding. She was not a tragic actress and preferred light roles, such as Lise in *La Fille Mal Gardée*, first performed in 1879 with Petipa's choreography, or the title-role in *Paquerette*, the old Saint-Léon ballet revived in 1882 for her benefit. Yet she could perform highly dramatic roles as well: in 1871 the Alexandrinsky Theatre revived especially for Sokolova the famous melodrama by Scribe, Villeneuve, and Desverges, *Olga, the Russian Orphan*, and she performed with great success the role of the Dumb Girl that used to win ovations for Fanny Elssler.

In her lifetime Sokolova received three offers to dance abroad: in 1869 at the Paris Opéra, in 1879 at Milan and Florence. However, since on each occasion the invitations were for the winter season, the Directorate of the Imperial Theatres did not wish to part with so valuable a ballerina.

She retired while still at the height of her talents, desiring to leave a lasting good impression. In 1902 Sokolova was appointed ballet-mistress of the Mariinsky Theatre in place of Johansson, but retired in 1904 passing the post to Nicolai Legat. She taught Anna Pavlova, Tamara Karsavina, Lubov Yegorova and many other dancers of the coming new generation. Between 1920 and 1923 Sokolova returned to the same post at the State Academic Theatre of Opera and Ballet (the former Mariinsky) and to private teaching. She was an excellent pedagogue and an invaluable adviser for the revival of classical ballets. In her old age she could hardly walk, and taught sitting in an armchair. In spite of this many pupils

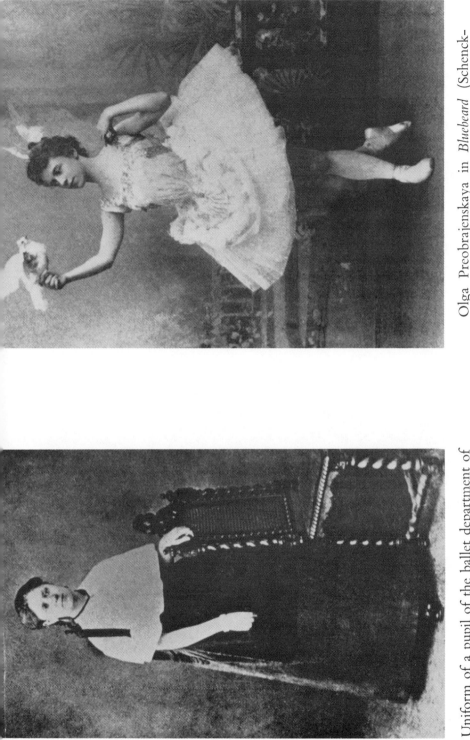

Olga Preobrajenskaya in *Bluebeard* (Schenck-Petipa, 1896). (Collection of Natalia Roslavleva)

Uniform of a pupil of the ballet department of the Bolshoi Theatre School, Moscow, in the late sixties. (Collection of Natalia Roslavleva)

Pavel Gerdt. (Collection of Natalia Roslavleva)

Ballerina Yevgenia Sokolova (1850–1925).

benefited from her method, and she died surrounded by respect and admiration for fifty-four years of devoted service to the art of ballet.

Vazem and Sokolova were perfect mediums with whose help Petipa could easily bring to life the fruit of his choreographic imagination. Vazem in particular, with her amazing command of the entire range of classical technique, was of the greatest possible help in the realization of his far-reaching aims.

One more ballerina, Varvara Nikitina, meant a great deal to the versatile master when he wanted to create roles in the lyrical vein or revive ballets of the romantic repertory. Nikitina (1857-1920) came to the Theatre School from the Orphanage. A pupil of Lev Ivanov, she graduated in the spring of 1873, and in the autumn of the same year was taken into the *corps de ballet*. While showing exceptional promise as an ethereal, lyrical dancer with a lovely line and strong technique, she was kept well in the background and given very small parts until Vazem retired in 1884. Petipa was preparing a production of *Coppélia*. He entrusted Nikitina with the part of Swanilda and she had an immediate success at the first performance of November 25, 1884, with her lightness, grace and coquettish charm, just right for the style of the ballet. With time, on the other hand, Nikitina also proved herself to be invaluable in romantic ballets. As Ondine and Sylphide she had no peer in the entire company. The balletomane Bezobrazov, writing for the *Petersburg Gazette*, expressed the opinion that none of the foreign stages of the period could boast of a better Sylphide. He particularly praised the adagio of the first act, danced with Maria Anderson and Pavel Gerdt, for its elegance and perfection of execution and the beauty of the poses and "groups" (i.e. dance patterns formed by the three partners and due, no doubt, to the genius of Petipa).

The master did not fail to exploit Nikitina's special talents. She was not only a graceful lyrical dancer. At a time when Italian virtuosity was rapidly coming into fashion, she developed a very strong technique without sacrificing any of the soft *cantilena* qualities of the Russian school. Yet she was officially given ballerina status only in 1889—four years before the expiration of her term of service.

In that year Petipa created for her the role of the Butterfly in *The Caprices of the Butterfly* (also known as *The Grasshopper Musician*) to music by N. Krotkov, and in the next year Nikitina became the first Princess Florine in the famous "Blue Bird" *pas de deux* danced with Enrico Cecchetti. The delicate, elegant pattern of the Princess Florine's dancing, and the soaring leaps and *batterie* of the Blue Bird, were conceived by Petipa (as in the case of all other characters from Perrault's fairy-tales) with the special talents of these two performers in view.

Why did Nikitina retire, refusing to stay a day longer than the official twenty years, and why did she not attain all the honours due to a *prima ballerina*? Alexander Pleshcheyev bitterly answered this question in one of his contemporary articles: it was the Italian guest-artists who received fabulous pay for a technical virtuosity that had been mastered by Nikitina to an extent where she could have said: "The boldest of Italians could be envious of her". The Directorate of the Imperial Theatres underpaid and undervalued native talent. All that Nikitina could expect was to alternate with Italian ballerinas in new ballets. Thus, while Elena Cornalba, technically brilliant but very cold, performed the role of Niriti in *The Talisman*, Nikitina appeared in the same role after the première, matching Cornalba technically and outshining her in grace and expressiveness.

When she was denied the privilege of creating the title role in *Cinderella*, Nikitina retired without waiting for a farewell benefit performance and flatly refused prolongation of her contract.

Petipa for ever continued to count her among his most talented pupils.

There were many others—the expressive Alexandra Vergina (1848-1898)—Vazem's rival in mime but not in virtuosity; the really excellent ballerina, Maria Gorshenkova (1857-1938), compared by contemporary critics with Adele Grantzow and Marfa Muravieva, and one who received her due to a smaller measure even than Nikitina. Gorshenkova was given either secondary new roles (though requiring considerable artistry and technique, like that of Gamsatti in *La Bayadère*) or inserted solos. She danced leading roles in all the ballets of the repertory, but only after Italian ballerinas had appeared in them. Thus, while being given ballerina status, like Nikitina, after Vazem's retirement in 1884, Gorshenkova did not properly enjoy this position. She was twice sent to Moscow where she had great popularity. Gorshenkova's span on the stage was too short.

Very much a "Petipa ballerina", although actually a private pupil of her father (of whom more later) was Anna Johansson (1860-1917), a dancer of perfect sculptured grace, though a trifle too cold. Anna Christianovna Johansson went only through the final examinations at the Theatre School, and upon winning the highest marks was accepted into the company in 1878. While she had her début in *Esmeralda* her true merits shone in parts requiring perfection of the academic classical school and grace. She was therefore incomparable in *The Cyprus Statue* (Pygmalion), *The Tulip of Harlem*, and "The Shades" in *La Bayadère*, which was also in her repertory.

A complete contrast to a dancer of Anna Johansson's style was provided by Maria Petipa (1857-1930), the choreographer's daughter. She was a private pupil of Johannson and her father, who moulded her into a leading soloist by adroitly exploiting her individual gifts.

He even gave her a début in 1875 as the Blue Dahlia in the ballet of the same title, created fifteen years earlier for her mother in the same role. Maria Petipa (Maria Mariusovna Petipa) was not endowed with abilities or figure for classical dancing. The most she could do with her stature was to appear as various Good Fairies and other roles requiring a certain majestic command. In this type of role she went down in history as the original Lilac Fairy in *The Sleeping Beauty* (the part was mostly mimed and posed and contained very little dancing). Her true calling was in the sphere of character dancing, which she rendered with much *brio* and temperament. Having created an endless amount of national dances in ballets and operas, specially choreographed by her father, she was equally good in the Lezghinka from *Ruslan and Lyudmilla*, the Mazurka from *A Life for the Tsar* (*Ivan Susanin*), or the "Spanish Dance" from *Carmen*. Unkind critics said that she danced mostly with her hands and arms (as her technique was far from strong), but that required a talent of its own kind,

Maria Petipa was one of the first Russian artists to perform Russian national dances on foreign stages with the idea of introducing them to the public. She organized two tours to Budapest of a fairly large group of Mariinsky dancers (1899 and 1901), when caricatures compared the "invasion of Russian ballet" to that of the Cossacks. In 1902 and 1903 she danced Russian dances at the *Opéra Comique* with Sergei Legat, scoring great success and surprising all Paris by appearing in the Bois de Boulogne in a Russian *troika*.

Both Legats, Sergei (1875-1905) and Nicolai (1869-1937), were excellent dancers whose technical prowess already spoke of the new, budding generation of twentieth-century ballet.

The leading male dancer of the late nineteenth century was Pavel Gerdt, one of the greatest names in Russian ballet. Petipa was not particularly interested in male dancing; the interest in the second half of the nineteenth century in general was definitely concentrated on the ballerina and therefore Russian ballet of the time, though full of properly trained dancers and dancer-actors, had but one *premier danseur* of distinction. Pavel Gerdt (1844-1917) was of German origin, although his father, a pinmaker, had become thoroughly Russian. The father's name was Johannes. The son was named Pavel Andreyevich after the name and patronymic of his godfather, Count Pavel Andreyevich Shuvalov. Perhaps it was Gerdt's godfather who got the idea of placing him as a state-supported pupil in the Theatre School. Gerdt graduated from it in 1864, having studied under Jean Petipa, Marius Petipa, and Christian Johansson. Through these teachers he received an excellent schooling in the pure, classical tradition. Russian to the core, Gerdt lent his own qualities to the acquired knowledge. He was expressive, noble in bearing, an excellent mime at any time, but particularly in the latter part of his career, a partner with whom any ballerina—and in the course of forty years he danced with all the leading danseuses of at least two generations—considered it a privilege to appear. Gerdt's handsome face, blue eyes, blond hair and perfect figure had a lot to do with his success. With such wonderful assets he seemed to have been born for ballet. He knew how to exploit and enhance his natural gifts and through constant perfectioning became the great artist he was.

No one in the company could wear a costume with the nobility and manner of Gerdt. However handsome, Gerdt made up with great care, applying it himself; he was also a good artist and known to paint pictures in his spare time. Through no fault of his own he was deprived of the chance fully to reveal his acting capacity and power of projection in the earlier part of his career. A *premier danseur* was expected to dance and provide an attractive and reliable background for the ballerina. The tradition of classical ballets of the second half of the nineteenth century—to name but *King Candaules* and *La Bayadère*—was to entrust the principal role to a mime, while the difficult *pas* were danced by the actual *premier danseur*. So it came about that Lev Ivanov was Solor the Indian warrior, while it was Gerdt who danced the important *pas de deux* with Gorshenkova-Gamsatti in the "Grand Pas". Towards the end of Gerdt's career as *premier danseur* Petipa might have trimmed the choreography of his roles in order to make them a little easier. But the practice of dividing the role into two parts—the mimed and the danced—was not connected with the dwindling powers of Gerdt or anybody else. The difference was that, at the height of his powers, Gerdt, the *premier danseur*, stepped in to partner the ballerina at the proper moment, while later it was he who performed the mimed part of the role, to be relieved by a young and technically stronger dancer for the *pas de deux*. And only once was Gerdt, in his prime, given a role that really pleased him, both as actor and dancer: when Petipa revived Filippo Taglioni's *La Fille du Danube* in 1880, affording Gerdt the possibility of carrying the public away in the mad scene of Rudolph the hero, choreographed so as to blend mime with dancing. So it came about that Gerdt was able to reach a full flowering of dramatic ability only after he had given up dancing. Then he created the part of

Abderahman in *Raymonda*, and started teaching (from 1909) a class in mime at the school. Gerdt was a mime in the old tradition, concerned mainly with a definite set of stylized gestures. Yet he was able to give them clear meaning and considerable expressiveness.

Gerdt spent all his life in the theatre as a model of discipline and conscientious attitude to work. In 1910, shortly after he had celebrated his jubilee, he was thrown out of a chariot during a rehearsal and seriously injured. He continued to serve the chosen art in spite of the fact that a handsome pension could have enabled him to live in comfort. He appeared for the last time on November 27, 1916, in *Don Quixote* in the mimed role of Gamache, with Karsavina as Kitri. In the course of his glorious career Gerdt performed in 108 ballets on the stage of the Mariinsky Theatre alone.

Pavel Gerdt established a tradition and an elegance of manner that continues to influence *premiers danseurs* of the Leningrad ballet, particularly when they prepare roles created by their illustrious predecessor.

It is worth noting that Diaghilev intended to invite Gerdt to participate in his first season of ballet in Paris (1909) when he wanted to show five performances of *Raymonda*, the zenith of the classical school, with Gerdt as Abderahman. These plans did not materialize, but Diaghilev's letter of September 16, 1909, wherein he invited Gerdt to appear in "one of your most brilliant roles", is preserved in the Leningrad archives.

Gerdt's importance and influence as a teacher can hardly be overestimated. He taught until 1904, forming such celebrities as Anna Pavlova; Tamara Karsavina; his daughter, Yelizaveta Gerdt; Lydia Kyaksht; Michail Fokine; the brothers Nicolai and Sergei Legat; Vassily Tikhomirov; and many, many others.

Gerdt taught beauty of line, expressiveness of movement, softness of *port de bras* (his pupils were famous for their arms), and, above all, a *cantilena* flow of dancing interwoven with acting. His memory held a real treasury of famous dances from the old repertory, which he used for the benefit of his pupils. He taught both men and women, strictly distinguishing between male and female grace. His men-pupils were masculine, while the ballerinas trained by Gerdt for ever retained a feminine softness and poise, coupled with beauty and perfection of *épaulement*.

Another great teacher and collaborator of Petipa was Christian Johansson (1817-1903). A Swede by birth, a former dancer of the Royal Opera House in Stockholm where his début took place in 1836, he became associated at an early stage of his career with the Danish ballet, having been sent to Copenhagen to perfect his talents under the guidance of Auguste Bournonville.

Johansson parted early with the Danish ballet and remained closer to the French school of Vestris so far as the first part of his career was concerned. He arrived in St. Petersburg as a private traveller in 1841 with the aim of seeing Marie Taglioni dance, and to take some classes from Titus. Through the latter he met Gedeonov (Director of the Imperial Theatres), and asked for a chance to appear in a ballet without any claims for an engagement. After a very successful début as partner of Olga Shlefogt and Natalia Apollonskaya—two good young soloists—an official proposal followed that he should appear with the *prima ballerina*, Yelena Andreyanova, in Filippo Taglioni's *La Gitana*. This proper début on October 31, 1841, led to the signing of a contract. Johansson soon occupied the position of one of the leading male dancers; he was on the stage of the Imperial Theatres for forty-three years, becoming a Russian subject and remaining in Russia to the end of his days.

Johansson danced in all the ballets of the period and was Taglioni's partner when she came to Petersburg. He partnered all the famous ballerinas in the course of his long and glorious career. Johansson was a dancer of an impeccably correct style, possessing a virtuosity that never transgressed the borders of grace and elegance. He had an outstanding elevation, enabling him to rise into the air lightly, without any visible *préparation*.

His dancing was virile and strong, his pirouettes and beats flawless. With all these qualities Khudekov wrote of Johansson that his dancing "reminded one of a clockwork machine: he would start his *variation* at a definite place and when asked for an encore would repeat it in exactly the same way".

It was not as a dancer that Johansson made himself a name in history, however. He was a teacher of genius. At an early stage of his career he became interested in teaching. Many of the younger dancers asked for his advice and started taking lessons from him. For fully twenty years Johansson, on the other hand, studied the special features of the Russian school with its "soul-inspired flight". Not only did he change as a dancer, moving closer to the spirit of the Russian school as a result of his having worked for a long time in Russia, but he introduced some changes into the Vestris stystem as he knew it, bringing it nearer to the style of the company he worked in. In 1860 he started teaching at the Petersburg school, at first unofficially. It was only in 1869, twenty-eight years after his arrival in Petersburg, that Johansson was officially made a member of the school's faculty.

The great practical value of Johansson's method consisted in the very fact that he had not invented it. It arose as a result of selection and systematic arranging of all that was necessary for the education of Russian dancers. The same was done by many generations of teachers of the Russian school before Johansson. It fell to him to complete the work of his predecessors.

His pedagogical genius naturally enabled Johansson to achieve great results. His aim was to develop strength, equilibrium, stamina, and correct breathing in the pupils. The critic, Akim Volynsky, recalled how Johansson would purposely make pools on the floor of the classroom with the ubiquitous watering-can, saying: "Slippery? You should know how to maintain equilibrium under any conditions!"[1]

The same author quoted Johansson as saying to his pupils: "Do not look at the spot to which you have to jump. You must 'look' with your legs, not with your eyes."[2] This great teacher understood muscular sensations.

The highest praise one could win from Johansson, even in the *classe de perfectionnement* for advanced artists, was: "All right, you can now do this on the stage." He demanded that at any given moment the pupil could be stopped to form a sculptured pose in the air or *par terre*.

In the entire course of his pedagogical career Johansson *never* repeated a single *enchaînement*—every lesson was created anew, for the pupils he was working with.

As a very old man, being hardly able to move his legs, Johansson would daily climb up the steep stairs to the classroom, with the small fiddle that provided the only accompaniment, tucked under his arm. As soon as he entered the classroom a veritable transformation took place: his eyes burned with the fire of inspiration and he demonstrated steps when necessary.

Johansson's method was individual, based on a close study of each pupil, whose faults, such as absence of elevation, he knew how to correct. On the other hand, while in favour of ideal classical line, he did not interfere with such natural defects as Pavlova's lack of good turn-out, because he considered it to be part of her personality.

Like Gerdt, Johansson, in keeping with the precepts of the Russian school, strictly distinguished between male and female style of dancing.

[1] A. Volynsky. *Book of Exultation*. Leningrad, 1925, p. 164.
[2] *Op. cit.*, p. 99.

While teaching only the *"classe de perfectionnement"* for *danseuses*, he had considerable influence on male dancers and teachers such as Pavel Gerdt, Nicolai Legat, and Vassily Tikhomirov. He encouraged the first teaching efforts of the latter two, and they considered themselves among his pupils, furthering Johansson's system according to the needs of Russian ballet.

Petipa had a deep respect for Johansson and frequently visited his lessons, borrowing interesting *enchaînements* for a new ballet.

Such was the school that never ceased to develop its national tradition, even in periods of decline, among Russian dancers. Together they formed an artistic whole with which one could truly perform miracles. The tradition of the Petersburg company was such that everybody was expected to be fully versed in the entire vocabulary of the *danse d'école*. Any *coryphée* was capable of replacing a soloist at short notice, and any soloist could replace a ballerina and sustain a full-length ballet.

Without such a company and without the fundamentals of its school Petipa could not have arrived at the creation of masterpieces like *The Sleeping Beauty*, and the artists would have been unable to give life to the remarkable images of the Tchaikovsky ballets.

While *The Sleeping Beauty* was destined to become Petipa's crowning achievement, at the time of its conception it was to him simply a new assignment from his betters, that he was ready to fulfil to the best of his ability.

The idea belonged to Ivan Vsevolojsky (1835-1909), Director of the Imperial Theatres since 1881. This post was frequently given to former high officials and military men. Vsevolojsky belonged to the first category. When appointed to the new post he had a long diplomatic career behind him, in the course of which he was on the staff of the Russian embassy in Paris and served in St. Petersburg in the capacity of special functionary.

On the other hand, Vsevolojsky was a University man, a writer (two of his plays were produced under the initials of I.V.), and a prolific designer of costumes, having no less than 1,087 sketches to his credit.

Vsevolojsky proved himself to be a gifted administrator. In his second year of service his salary was doubled "for excellent management". Many of the measures carried out in the course of his term were extremely beneficent. The two-tier rehearsal hall on Rossi (Theatre) Street, used to this day for rehearsals and classes, was instituted on his initiative, also the publication of the *Annual of the Imperial Theatres* (1890-1915), an invaluable source of information. The first ballet syllabus at the Theatre School was compiled on his orders, and he also created an advisory panel consisting of the author of the scenario, the composer, the designer of the settings, the choreographer, and the stage manager. These members were expected to collaborate in the course of the production of a ballet, in order to reach a homogeneity of style.

Being an artist (though far from a brilliant one), Vsevolojsky understood full well the importance of painting as one of the composite parts of ballet, and strictly forbade the commissioning of settings from three or four different designers for one production, as practised by his predecessors.

As to his personal tastes, they were very much in line with those in circulation. He was interested largely in purely external elegance and beauty. The content of ballet did not concern him to any extent and any semblance of a plot existed merely for the purpose of stringing one amusing set of dances upon another. Pronounced francophil inclinations brought about Vsevolojsky's special partiality to the latest Parisian diversion: the *féerie*. In the eighties this style, with its predominance of spectacular *divertissements*, expected to be as varied as possible, gained wide popularity, particularly after the success of Manzotti's *Excelsior* (Milan, 1881), produced on many other stages, including those of Paris and London. In Petersburg this ballet (in the nature of a revue extolling the progress of civilization and showing such novelties as the invention of electricity and the construction of the Suez Canal), was produced by visiting Italian companies at two private stages simultaneously in the summer of 1887. The one at the "Arcadia" was done by Enrico Cecchetti, who only two years before had performed the leading part in the London production of *Excelsior*.

Spectacles of the type of *Excelsior, Round the World in Eighty Days* (borrowing its semblance of a plot from Jules Verne), or *Voyage à la Lune* wherein Petersburg saw Virginia Zucchi for the first time at the "Abandon Sorrow" summer cabaret, attempted to impress their audiences by huge masses of supers representing various groups of costumed characters. They were not expected to know much about dancing. That was left to the one or two stars of the revue, invited as a special attraction, and not, by any means, for any artistic reason. The general public liked the new entertainment, while some theatre critics even predicted that it would soon absorb ballet, thus making it quite unnecessary.

Petipa's attitude to these latest importations was, on the contrary, quite negative. He denied any artistic value in *Excelsior* and its like, expressing sincere regret at the sight of its invasion of the ballet stage in addition to pleasure gardens.

He considered that *féeries* corrupted the audience by diverting them from serious ballets. In an interesting interview published by the *Petersburg Gazette* on December 2, 1896, Petipa emphatically expressed an opinion that he considered the Petersburg ballet "to be the first in the world, just because it has preserved the serious art that has been lost abroad, where art is being replaced by dancing of a vulgar nature or by acrobatic exercises".

Yet Petipa had to produce quite a number of *ballet-féeries* on the orders of the Directorate of the Imperial Theatres in the person of Vsevolojsky. Not for nothing did Petipa confide to Bournonville that he abhorred the "new vulgarities", but was obliged to satisfy the corrupted tastes of the public and obey the orders of the officials.[1]

However, being a true artist, Petipa used all novelties (his eye was always open for them) with discretion, transforming anything borrowed from other sources into something artistically his own and suitable for ballet. After the advent of the *féerie* he re-arranged crowd scenes and *ensembles* in some of his old productions, such as *King Candaules*, on a grander scale.

In *The Magic Pills*, a French *féerie* produced on the orders of Vsevolojsky on February 9, 1886, at the Mariinsky Theatre with the participation of dramatic actors and singers, but with the entire ballet company also taking part, Petipa utilized the chance to create varied dances. In "the games" scene he used thirty-two "playing cards" in appropriate velvet costumes and wigs the colour of which corresponded to the suit—thus the spades were brunettes while the hearts had golden hair. Moreover, dancers of the *corps de ballet* were arranged in patterns reminiscent of the game of preference, while several dozen pieces of "domino", wearing the proper number of dots on special panels attached to their chests, had to recline on the floor forming sets of the game.

Using to advantage the experience gained from Italian virtuoso guest-artists, Petipa created for the brilliant young soloist, Zinaida Frolova, a "Spinning-Top Dance" consisting of vertiginous *tours*, in the course of which the multi-coloured ribbons sewn on to the bodice of the dancer became blurred into one pattern, as happens with real toys, while the dance ended with the Spinning-Top falling on its side.

The "Kingdom of Lace" afforded the choreographer a chance of producing a varied suite that formed a unified whole with its inventive *variations* of Lace from different countries, all choreographed to convey,

[1] See Auguste Bournonville's *Mit Teaterliv*, Copenhagen, 1858.

through the vocabulary of the classical ballet, one or other national character.

In this *féerie*, which was far removed not only from ballet but from art altogether, Petipa, as ever, used the opportunity of exercising his creative powers and furthering them.

The idea of using Perrault's *La Belle au Bois Dormant* for a ballet belonged to Vsevolojsky, who obviously intended to produce one more *féerie*, a gala spectacle in the style of his favourite period of Louis XIV. Petipa could easily have fallen here into the abyss prepared for him, and, by repeating all his former tried methods, produce something quite ordinary and uninspired.

Vsevolojsky had nothing out of the ordinary in mind. But he had commissioned the new ballet from Tchaikovsky—by that time a widely-known composer. Desiring to have the best of talents, Vsevolojsky invited Tchaikovsky (in a letter of May 13, 1888) to write the ballet if the idea appealed to him. As described by Vsevolojsky, it consisted of a ballet in the style of Louis XIV, with melodies in the spirit of Lulli, Bach, and Rameau, and a quadrille of characters from all the fairy-tales of Perrault in the last act. Such was the order. While Tchaikovsky did carry it out, following very closely Vsevolojsky's "book" and, particularly, Petipa's detailed draft of the future ballet, indicating the nature and duration of every dance,[1] in reality he created a work that amounted to a reform in ballet.

The great Russian music critic, Stasov, wrote of Glinka: "He thought that he was only creating a Russian opera [*Ivan Susanin*—N.R.] but he was wrong: he was creating Russian music, a whole Russian school of music." Paraphrasing this, one might say that Tchaikovsky thought he was creating a ballet to stories from Perrault's tales. In reality he was creating a new school of Russian ballet, promising it new vistas for years to come. He was also creating a great symphonic work for Russian music as a whole.

The subject appealed to Tchaikovsky's genius by its poetic charm. He said in a letter to Nadezhda von Mekk of July 25, 1889, that he wrote the music with warmth and eagerness that always ensure beneficent results.

[1] In Russian the full text of Petipa's original programme for *The Sleeping Beauty* was published for the first time in: *Tchaikovsky and the Theatre*, Iskusstvo, Moscow, 1940, pp. 245-257. The original (a handsewn exercise book) is preserved in the manuscript department of the Bakhrushin Theatre Museum, Moscow.

In English a full translation by Joan Lawson may be found in *The Dancing Times* for December 1942, January, February, and March 1943.

The musical richness of *The Sleeping Beauty* is inseparable from the extraordinary wealth and variety of its dancing roles. These are composed with the sweeping breadth of a symphony and are literally charged with depth of musical content.

Petipa found himself, as it were, in the position of the sorcerer's disciple who had released magic forces without being able to make them obey his orders. It would appear that the experienced ballet-master had foreseen everything in his detailed draft. And Tchaikovsky did follow it out religiously. When asked to write a *variation* for the Breadcrumb Fairy he created music imitating the staccato of falling crumbs. Each of the fairy *variations* bore the imprint of some trait of character that the fairy-god-mothers were giving to the Princess. Yet Petipa, author of the programme, did not recognize in many cases the children of his own imagination. Yuri Slonimsky, the well-known Soviet ballet critic and historian, was quite right when he wrote: "Petipa saw that he was participating in the creation of music of such force, that not infrequently he was unable to cope with it."[1]

Academician Boris Asafiev considered that with *The Sleeping Beauty* "a new form of musical-choreographic action", a new form of Russian music, was born.[2]

As in a symphony, each of the four parts of *The Sleeping Beauty* (prologue and three acts), while being quite complete and capable of existing apart from the remaining three, may be properly understood and valued only in the light of the entire work.

The importance of the music was embodied in its spirit, in the victory of life over death, goodness over evil.

The Aurora of the ballet was a young girl, awakening to maturity under the influence of deep feelings that were unknown to her until that moment. Academician Asafiev pointed out in his remarkable and since unmatched analysis of the score that if one relied on nothing but the four great *adagios* (B flat *adagio* and the *variations* of the six fairies bringing gifts to Aurora in the prologue; E flat *adagio*, known as the "Rose *Adagio*" with the four princes in the first act, F major of the second— vision of Aurora to Prince Charming; and the grand C major *adagio* in the wedding of the last, fourth act), it would be possible to perceive, through

[1] Yuri Slonimsky. *Tchaikovsky and the Ballet Theatre of His Times*, Music Publishing House, Moscow, 1956, p. 196.

[2] Igor Glebov (Boris Asafiev). "The Sleeping Beauty". In: *Letters on Russian Opera and Ballet*, Letter No. 3, Weekly of the Petrograd State Academic Theatres, 1922, No. 5, p. 28.

means of symphonic music, the story of a whole life—the growth and development of a playful and carefree child into a young woman, learning to know great love through tribulations. Asafiev moreover remarked that, "by starting from them [the four adagios—N.R.] and studying the rhythms of adjoining scenes and dances one learns to know, step by step, the great riches of the composition of this superb ballet".[1]

Indeed, Petipa had to employ all his creative abilities to cope with this great music. He admitted to his contemporaries that work on *The Sleeping Beauty* was very difficult for him.[2] The choreography created does not quite reach the heights of the overwhelmingly great spiritual world embodied in the music. It is possible to doubt whether the choreographer capable of rising to the same height as Tchaikovsky will ever be born.

Yet Petipa's choreography for *The Sleeping Beauty* is finely constructed, developing as logically and as gradually as Aurora's character in the ballet. The choreography of *The Sleeping Beauty* is built, to continue using musical terms, on the *accelerando* principle, changing from the more simple forms and patterns to complicated ones. Thus, he did not over-burden the "Rose Adagio" with high lifts and other technical feats, because he wanted to show the state of a young and life-embracing girl, whose confidence has never been shaken. More complicated lifts were reserved by the choreographer for the grand adagio of the third act, which expresses the ecstasy of the mature love of Aurora and Prince Désiré.

What ballerina of generations past was not happy to dance the part of Aurora? A smile, a glance, a gesture—all this enriched the portrait of the slightly spoilt child, while the role offered untold possibilities for demonstrating technical merits and called for virtuosity of the highest order. The first Aurora was Carlotta Brianza (1867-1930) the youthful Italian guest-artist (when she arrived in Petersburg a year earlier, in 1889, she was only twenty-two).

Petipa exploited Brianza's merits and created the role for her. As always, he thought of the constellation of excellent soloists available in the company led by him, and, although obliged to give the title role to an

[1] Igor Glebov. *Op. cit.*, pp. 35-36.

[2] Alexander Shiryaev. *From the Memoirs of an Artist of the Mariinsky Theatre*, VTO, Leningrad, 1941. Photostat copy of the galley-proofs of this book, the publication of which was prevented by the outbreak of war, is preserved at the Saltykov-Shchedrin Public Library, Leningrad, Is 70, G-3/31. Full quote is to be found in *Russian Ballet Theatre of the Second Half of the Nineteenth Century* by Vera Krasovskaya, D.A., Iskusstvo, M.–L., 1963, p. 297.

Italian ballerina invited by the Directorate of the Imperial Theatres for another season, he created a plethora of roles for all of them, also with individual talents in view.

The parts of the six good fairies were impersonated by the following *danseuses*: Fairy of the Song-birds—Anna Johansson, Fairy Violante—Vera Zhukova, the Breadcrumb Fairy—Klavdia Kulichevskaya, Fairy Candide—Alexandra Nedremskaya, Fairy Fleur de Farine—Marie Anderson, while the part of the Lilac Fairy was created by Petipa's daughter, Maria Petipa, whose role was mostly mime, with very little dancing. (In the "Vision Scene", as a contemporary photograph shows, Maria Petipa wore high-heeled shoes.)

There were classical dances and period dances, introduced with great feeling for the period (it is through them that the choreographer showed the passage of one hundred years).

The elaborate costumes by Vsevolojsky were appropriate, though uninspired, and definitely showed that the designer had thoroughly acquainted himself with Ciceri's sketches for the earlier Paris production in 1829 of *La Belle au Bois Dormant*, with music by Hérold and choreography by Aumer.

The remarkable suite of Precious Stones was danced as brilliantly as the sparkle of their facets by Anna Johansson—Diamond Fairy, Klavdia Kulichevskaya—Gold Fairy, Yelizaveta Kruger—Silver Fairy, Maria Tistrova—Sapphire Fairy.

The gallery of characters from Perrault's fairy-tales was created by the following artists: Maria Anderson as the Cat and Alfred Bekefi as Puss-in-Boots, Vera Zhukova as Little Red Riding Hood and Sergei Lukianov as the Wolf, Maria Petipa as Cinderella and Joseph Kshesinski as Prince Fortune, while this "quadrille of fairy-tale characters" was topped by the incomparable Enrico Cecchetti as the first Blue Bird and the exquisite Varvara Nikitina, who could have easily created the title role, as the first Princess Florine.

As if to prove his great range, Cecchetti also mimed the role of Carabosse, the evil fairy. Catalabute, the Master of Ceremonies, was Timofei Stukolkin.

The good King Florestan XIVth was played by Felix Kshesinski, the venerable head of the family of dancers among whom Mathilde was rapidly reaching ballerina status. Prince Désiré, the hero, was Pavel Gerdt, who knew how to exploit even the meagre choreographic text to his great advantage. The four princes of the "Rose Adagio" were Alfred Bekefi, Platon Karsavin, Alexander Oblakov, and Stanislaus Gillert.

The ballet was conducted by Riccardo Drigo, who had occupied the post of chief conductor to the ballet company since 1886 (alternating during a performance of an opera with the operatic conductor, if there was a dance *divertissement* in it).

The musical and choreographic beauties of the ballet were not immediately appreciated. The contemporary critique was far from favourable. "Brother-composers" accused Tchaikovsky of disgracing himself merely by agreeing to write a ballet. Progressive *literati* and other intellectuals had no use whatsoever for the ballet, which they associated with the Court and its amusements. Stasov, the great, uncompromising, and vehemently temperamental supporter of the Russian school, failed to see that in *The Sleeping Beauty* Tchaikovsky had created in the guise of a French fairy-tale a beautiful work bearing all the best features of Russian art. Naming Vsevolojsky "that insipid Frenchman" Stasov wrote to Nicolai Findeisen in 1893 that the Director of the Imperial Theatres thought of nothing but "French operettas", "porcelain dolls", and "Tchaikovsky's music for them".[1]

That Stasov, in all his highly commendable earnestness, in this case made a fatal mistake, was proved by the fact that critics of the opposite camp, ready to support the idea of ballet as a source of amusement and spectacular entertainment, found *The Sleeping Beauty* to be "much too serious".

Meanwhile the dancers soon came to love the ballet that gave them an opportunity to display the Russian school at its best. It was no accident that Carlotta Brianza changed her style and manner of performance considerably upon appearing in the title role of *The Sleeping Beauty*. Sergei Khudekov wrote of her in volume four of his *"History of Dancing"* (Petrograd, 1918): "Brianza was the first Italian dancer on whom the Russian school exerted a beneficent influence. When criticized for the extreme angularity and brittle quality of her dancing, she endeavoured to get rid of these typical defects of the Milanese school through strenuous exercise. Her work was rewarded by success. She introduced into her performance greater softness, roundness and elasticity, i.e. those very features that are in general inherent in representatives of the Russian school. Her technically perfect dancing gained much, because she took the trouble to study carefully the graceful Russian ballerinas, who never permitted themselves any deviations from the classical precepts of choreography."

[1] See: Yuri Slonimsky, *Tchaikovsky and the Ballet Theatre of his Time.* Musical Publishing House, 1956, p. 168.

The Sleeping Beauty performed by Russian ballerinas (the role of Aurora passed to Mathilde Kshesinska on the day of Brianza's departure) won itself a permanent niche in the repertory. A year later the newspapers noted that the "The *danseuses* have become inseparable from the music of Tchaikovsky, and *The Sleeping Beauty* is now being excellently performed." (Newspaper *Novoye Vremya*, 5/10/1891.)

Three years later *The Sleeping Beauty* continued to draw full houses. The masterpiece became part of the great legacy of Russian ballet and Russian national art in general, serving as a source of development and training for endless successions of dancers. It received full recognition at first in Russia and years later it won its permanent place in the repertory of the British ballet—at the Sadler's Wells Theatre and at the Royal Opera House, Covent Garden.

In *The Sleeping Beauty* Petipa amalgamated all his personal achievements and those of nineteenth-century ballet as a whole. His eclipse was pending because very soon he would be behind the times with his old-fashioned aesthetic ideas and precepts.

After *The Sleeping Beauty* Petipa, the choreographer, existed by borrowing tried-out methods and situations. They kept recurring in several (at times quite charming) one act ballets, such as the *Nénuphar* to music by Krotkov (1891), *La Halte de Cavalerie* to music by Armsheimer (1896), *The Pearl* by Drigo, created as a *pièce d'occasion* for the Coronation festivities in Moscow of 1896, and in multi-act works, such as *Kalkabrino* by Minkus (1891) and *Bluebeard* by Schenck (1896), that were protracted and short-lived.

But before the final dismal failure of *The Magic Mirror*, to music by Koreshchenko, in 1903, after which followed retirement and life in Gurzuf (the Crimea), Petipa was destined to create one more masterpiece. This was *Raymonda*, whose success was brought about by collaboration with another great Russian composer, Alexander Glasunov.

An outstanding Professor of the Petersburg Conservatoire, a pupil of Rimsky-Korsakov and a follower of that great man's tradition, Glasunov excelled himself in following the symphonic laws discovered by Tchaikovsky in his ballet scores. Glasunov in fact furthered the musical reform in ballet initiated by the author of *Swan Lake*, *The Sleeping Beauty* and *The Nutcracker*.

Raymonda, Glasunov's first attempt at a ballet score, proved to be also one of his greatest symphonic works. The beauty of its melody and musical imagery, richness of orchestral palette and sweeping symphonic breadth brought the composer universal recognition.

Varvara Nikitina and Pavel Gerdt in *The Nutcracker*,
Mariinsky Theatre, Petersburg, 1892.

The Sleeping Beauty. First production at the Mariinsky Theatre, Petersburg,
1890. Carlotta Brianza as Aurora in the centre.

Vladimir Yakovlev and two pupils in *The Nutcracker*, Mariinsky Theatre (Mother Gigogne and her children).

Alfred Bekefi (1873–1925) in the "Pas Indien" from *Bluebeard*, music by Schenck, choreography by Petipa, 1896. (Collection of Natalia Roslavleva)

The score was commissioned to an already written "book" by L. Pashkova (Glinskaya). A woman writer was a rarity in those days. The libretto is a heavy concoction about a châtelaine of the Middle Ages, patronized by a mysterious "White Lady" invariably appearing at critical moments, such as when Raymonda was almost abducted by the Moor Abderahman and was conveniently saved by her fiancé Jean de Brienne, returning from the Crusades just at the right time. No attempts at breathing real life and action into it have ever done this ballet any good. Yet it continues to exist, and first of all because of the music, wherein old French dances are interwoven with fine lyrical episodes and scenes of typical ballet fantasy. The music was created in close collaboration with Petipa, perhaps even closer than in the case of Tchaikovsky's music, inasmuch as Glasunov was working at his first ballet composition. This was confirmed by Glasunov himself as quoted by Asafiev in an article "From My Conversations With Glasunov" (*Selected Works of Academician Asafiev*, Vol. II, p. 209).

Petipa worked out a programme built on the traditional lines of nineteenth-century ballet, with classical and historical dances, a vision scene, numerous dances and *variations* for the ballerina and soloists, and, a harbinger of changing times, a *pas de quatre* for four male dancers, while the highlight of the ballet was a *grand pas classique hongroise* wherein the great man of ballet surpassed himself in a beautiful composition, cunningly welding into a true gem of academic ballet steps of classical and character dancing. Yet Glasunov succeeded, like Tchaikovsky before him, in creating an artistic work of his own within the strict boundaries of the given frame.

Glasunov worked on *Raymonda* in 1896-1897. Its première took place on January 7, 1898.

The title role was again taken by an Italian, Pierrina Legnani, who had spent so many seasons in the midst of the Russian ballet (and had created the dual role of Odette-Odile in the Petersburg production of *Swan Lake*) that she almost ceased being treated as a guest-artist. Like Brianza, Legnani experienced the beneficent influence of the Russian school. Her brittle Milanese style of dancing mellowed under the influence of the Petersburg company. She knew this, and, having come to love Russia dearly, liked to perform in the Russian style that she had assimilated.

The choreography of Raymonda's part contained all the traditional adagios and *variations* of classical ballet. The ballerina was given plenty of rewarding material. After Legnani the role was entrusted to Yekaterina Geltser, the budding Moscow ballerina sent to Petersburg to perfect her technique under Johansson's guidance, and to Olga Preobrajenskaya, whose name became particularly identified with this ballet.

Raymonda was conceived by Glasunov and Petipa as a succession of dance suites: one based on character dancing, another in the style of *demi-caractère* and a purely classical one, wherein Glasunov often resorted to waltz forms frequently used by him in earlier symphonic compositions for the concert stage.

A classical dance suite occurred in the vision scene of the first act (Raymonda dreamt of her fiancé), and another, grandiose classical *pas d'action* started the second act (when Abderahman tried to woo Raymonda). Then the languid tempo of the *pas d'action* suddenly gave way to a temperamental *ballabile* of Abderahman's retinue and a brilliant suite of pseudo-Spanish and Oriental dances.

The already mentioned *grand pas* of the third act seemed to absorb all of the best in Petipa's achievements over half a century. The *grand pas hongroise* was choreographed for the ballerina and her partner, four pairs of first soloists (both male and female) and, likewise, four pairs of second soloists, who actually opened the dance with beautifully conceived steps taken from the Hungarian dance and transformed into something even more perfect through fusion with classical ballet.

Preobrajenskaya, who inherited the title role in the autumn of 1903, performed the part of Henriette, Raymonda's confidante, while the other friend was danced by Klavdia Kulichevskaya, one of the most gifted soloists in the company. Maria Petipa danced, with her usual *brio*, the Spanish "Panaderos" in the second act and a "Mazurka" with Joseph Kshesinski in the second. Another Spanish dance, the "Palotas", was danced, with Alfred Bekefi, the superb character soloist, by Olga Preobrajenskaya, equally brilliant in classical and character style. As was mentioned earlier, Abderahman became one of the best mime roles of Pavel Gerdt. The importance of the ballet so far as its male contingent was concerned was connected with the fact that a group of young and promising dancers—Sergei Legat (Jean de Brienne) Nicolai Legat, Alexander Gorsky and Georgi Kyaksht—performed for the first time with brilliant success the famous *variation*, repeating it at public request, for whom this virtuoso male dance abounding in *batterie* and *tempi* of elevation was quite a novelty after the unquestioned supremacy of the ballerina. It is a known fact that Petipa was not a connoisseur of male dancing and the composition of such a *variation* required some study on his part and visits to Gerdt's class.

Petipa received a gold wreath from the company inscribed: "To the great master and artist." Glasunov was given a scroll and a wreath.

This was the final triumph of the old master. In July 1899 Vsevolojsky became Director of the Hermitage Museum. This was a sign of the changing times; his dictatorship was no longer appropriate. The new Director of the Imperial Theatres, Prince Sergei Volkonsky, was in advance of his time, a follower of Dalcroze, author of a book on his eurythmics, and several others on Delsarte and the art of expressive gesture.

Petipa and Volkonsky seemed to have established cordial relations. So they had, but the old ballet-master was now entrusted with small ballets for the Hermitage stage—such as the charming *Ruses d'Amour* and *Les Saisons* (both produced in 1900 to music by Glasunov), which were transferred to the Mariinsky stage, and *Harlequinade* to music by Drigo, also transferred to the Mariinsky after its initial success in the same year at the beautifully designed Hermitage Theatre.

It is true that these pretty ballets were successful, and that Glasunov's music added considerably to the lasting interest in the first two pieces, but Petipa was repeating old "recipes". This was particularly applicable to his methods of ballet production, which were becoming exhausted by the turn of the century. Whatever he put into the classical school and the purity of its idiom continued living, growing, and developing in the Theatre School and the company. But the time of "Petipa theatre" was over. The old man, as set down in his published memoirs (SPB, 1906), was convinced that the catastrophe was due to the advent of a new Director in the person of Teliakovsky, who in 1902 came to replace Volkonsky after the latter's quarrel with the then all-powerful Kshesinskaya.

The attempt to rehabilitate himself with the help of *The Magic Mirror* became for Petipa what Moscow was to Napoleon. This medley of every known nineteenth-century cliché with modern scenery by Golovine simply could not have weathered criticism. The expensive production was shown only once more after the première of February 9, 1903. On February 17, Petipa was informed that his contract would not be renewed after September 1 of the same year, though he would receive the same salary for life. He lived until July 1, 1910. His passing at Gursuf was practically unnoticed, particularly since it happened during the summer holidays. At that time, his former pupils from the Mariinsky company were appearing in the fabulously successful "Saisons Russes" at Paris. A new era was about to begin.

CHAPTER VI

THE BALLETS OF IVANOV

As many a genius before him, Lev Ivanov (1834-1901) was completely unconscious of the great historical role he was destined to fulfil, or the permanent place he would occupy in the Pantheon of universal art.

He began a modest and hardworking career in 1852 by entering the ballet company of the Bolshoi Theatre, St. Petersburg, as a rank-and-file member of the *corps de ballet*. His actual début took place two years earlier, when on June 7, 1850, on the recommendation of his teacher, Jean Petipa, the pupil Ivanov danced a *pas de deux* in *The Millers*[1] with his classmate Nadezhda Amosova. The ballet was not presented at the Bolshoi, but at the Alexandrinsky drama theatre. In the Imperial Theatres the term of service for ballet dancers, the year of graduation notwithstanding, began at the age of sixteen. Ivanov reached that age in 1850. His service was counted from that year, and he was frequently given small parts in the current repertory.

While a member of the Bolshoi Theatre ballet, Ivanov danced for the first two years only at the Alexandrinsky and Mikhailovsky theatres in ballets obviously of a secondary nature. He was also directed to partner pupils not excluding those of promise. Thus, in August 1852, he danced a *pas de deux* at the Alexandrinsky theatre (in a mixed programme) with Maria Surovshchikova, Petipa's future wife, destined to shine, for some years at least, as the *prima ballerina* of the Petersburg ballet.

On another occasion he danced a *pas de deux* in *La Péri* (Perrot headed the company at that time) with Marfa Muravieva.

Russian ballerinas remarked Ivanov's talents and gave him his first roles, choosing the young dancer to partner them at benefit performances. Yelena Andreyanova, reviving Didelot's *Hungarian Hut* with new music by Lyadov, for her benefit in 1853, suggested that the young dancer Ivanov be entrusted with the role of Ulrich, the peasant. Tatiana Smirnova (1821-1871), later one of the first Russian ballerinas to tour abroad, invited him to partner her in a *grand pas de deux* interpolated for her benefit performance into *La Fille Mal Gardée* later in the same year. A wonderful

[1] *The Millers*, an old comic ballet by Poireau, music by Tivolsky, was given a new score by Pugni and choreography by Gredlu in 1845. The story of this ballet came from the play by Alexander Ablesimow.

cast took part in this memorable presentation on November 3, 1853: Jules Perrot as Marceline, Christian Johansson as Colin, and Rosa Giraud (a guest-artist of inferior quality) as Lise, while Nicaise was mimed by the incomparable Timofei Stukolkin.

Small promotions followed after these initial successes, promotions that might have taken place earlier, but for the extreme shyness and modesty of the young dancer. By nature rather lackadaisical, and something of a *bon viveur*, he did not want to bother about anything that required serious effort so far as career-making was concerned. In his own memoirs (preserved in the Leningrad Theatre Museum and published in part in the *Petersburg Gazette*, January 13, 1901, p. 5), he admitted ignoring the chance to remain in Petersburg in 1856 in the capacity of stage manager and ballet-master, because he was very eager to go to Moscow with the rest of the company for the Coronation festivities of Alexander II. The opportunity was snatched by Alexei Bogdanov.

All this does not imply that Ivanov was not devoted to his art. He considered ballet his only true calling and literally lived in the theatre. From February 1858 he started teaching in the lower forms of the Theatre School and with time matured into a good teacher, responsible for the first forming of such outstanding dancers as Yevgenia Sokolova, Alexandra Vergina, Varvara Nikitina, Olga Preobrajenskaya, and many others. However, he failed to acquire a reputation in this field, and was frequently criticized for not being strict enough and for showing too much leniency in the course of a lesson, again a trait of his character.

Music, perhaps his true calling, was the source of constant trouble ever since he was at school, where P. S. Fedorov (1803-1879), the Director, threatened to "make Ivanov suffer for his irrepressible infatuation with music". Indeed, Ivanov's musical abilities were quite extraordinary. His memory was such that after hearing a piece only once, he was capable of repeating it in detail. Joseph Kshesinski, in his memoirs, said: "We seldom had piano accompaniment during rehearsals, usually the music was provided by two violins. Once the first violin did not come. Then Lev Ivanov calmly sat at the grand piano and played the whole of the ballet from beginning to end, as if he were looking into sheet music."[1]

Another colleague, Shiryaev, told of another legend in connection with Ivanov's phenomenal musicality: "Once Anton Rubinstein was playing his ballet *The Vine* in the rehearsal hall. He hardly had time to leave the room, when Ivanov sat at the piano and, by ear, reproduced

[1] M. Borisoglebsky. *Materials for the History of Russian Ballet*. The Past of the Ballet Department of the Petersburg Theatre School. Vol. I, Leningrad, 1938.

almost the whole of the Rubinstein composition."[1] Rubinstein heard this, and was astounded and delighted, confirming that he had never met anything comparable in the course of his life in music.

The Director of the Musical Society was told of Ivanov's musical talent and made an attempt to place him in the Conservatoire, but the Theatre School would not release its ward, neither did the pupil in question show any particular anxiety to study music seriously. Ivanov for ever remained a dilettante in music, he could neither write down his compositions nor could he orchestrate them. But composer he was. As early as 1858 Lyadova (his future wife) and Bogdanov danced a mazurka "Petulance", the music being composed by Lev Ivanov. In 1878 Yevgenia Sokolova danced a new *variation* interpolated into *The Hump-Backed Horse* by Petipa; the music was also composed by Lev Ivanov.

Possessing such an excellent musical memory, being thoroughly professional as far as the *danse d'école* was concerned, and never missing a single rehearsal or performance, the young Ivanov knew the whole repertory by heart. It would seem that his chance came when Petipa suddenly fell ill on the day when *La Vivandière* was to be performed and Ivanov was asked to take over the principal role. Upon rehearsing in the morning with Anna Prikhunova as Kathi, the *vivandière*, he appeared successfully in the evening as Hans, the postman. In a short time he had another chance to replace Petipa as Phoebus in *La Esmeralda*. The Director-ate of the Imperial Theatres, realizing that in Ivanov it had a willing and hardworking man, started to exploit him in every possible manner. He was given all sorts of roles, often of a secondary nature and mostly contrary to his personal tastes. He was a romantic dancer by inclination; instead he had to impersonate a whole gallery of character roles and gained quite a reputation as a character dancer. At last in 1869 he was given the position of *premier danseur*, made vacant when Petipa replaced Saint-Léon as chief ballet-master. Yet Ivanov received a salary that was in no way commensurate with this position and his repeated petitions to the Directorate for modest increases and benefits remained unsatisfied. His wife, Vera Lyadova, a gifted dancer and attractive woman, refused to continue this kind of life, and left him to become a brilliant Operetta star —one of the first in Russia. In 1870 his former wife died. Seven years elapsed before Ivanov petitioned for permission to marry a *coryphée*, Varvara Ivanova-Malchugina, transferred to Petersburg from the Moscow

[1] Alexander Shiryaev. *From the Memoirs of an Artist of the Mariinsky Theatre.* VTO, Leningrad, 1941. For quote see V. M. Krasovskaya. *Russian Ballet Theatre of the Second Half of the Nineteenth Century,* p. 347.

ballet. This marriage was happier—but hardships and disillusionment had done their work. Gone was the happy-go-lucky youth of the fifties.

A higher salary did come, but rather late and still out of proportion with the actual position occupied. Ivanov performed leading roles as dancer and mime in: *Faust, Esmeralda, Catarina* and *Le Corsaire, Fiametta, Satanilla, Le Diable à Quatre, Pharaoh's Daughter, La Bayadère*. His execution of the Russian and the Urals dances in *The Hump-Backed Horse* (he performed these roles in the first instance with Madayeva and in the second with Kosheva at the première of the ballet in 1864) was considered exemplary.

As a classical dancer and partner Ivanov was soon outshone by Gerdt. Ivanov did not possess the grace, the figure, the perfect manner of the great *premier danseur* of the Russian school. Moreover, he was near-sighted and always afraid of dropping his ballerina, though this never occurred. But as a mime he was second to none, having created a whole gallery of various characters, from the Duke in *Catarina* to the Chief of the Moors in *Zoraia*.

On January 3, 1893, at a benefit performance—how he craved for them when he was younger—Ivanov bowed to the public for the last time after a forty-year career as a dancer, in a "Pas Espagnol" with Maria Petipa, the choreographer's daughter.

Ivanov passed on to other duties without any visible repercussions. He had occupied the post of *régisseur* (stage manager) of the Petersburg ballet since 1882, when Alexei Bogdanov was transferred to Moscow. Ivanov was not happy at this appointment; he revealed in his memoirs that he feared any responsibilities, knowing his own "too kind and weak disposition". Three years passed quickly. The company loved and respected its *régisseur*, arranging a celebration of his thirty-fifth jubilee on February 18, 1885. Exactly one month later Ivanov was removed from that post and made second ballet-master. It did not mean much to the disillusioned man. He merely recorded that the job of assistant ballet-master, while also troublesome, was, however, a little more peaceful than the previous one. . . . And that was all he thought of it.

Psychologically the chances to create, in view of the absolute dictatorship of Petipa, were not great. Ivanov was entrusted for the most part with revivals of old ballets (he held an untold number of these in his memory) and the choreography of dances in operas. Among the numerous character *divertissements* produced by him, the "Polovetsian Dances" in *Prince Igor* (1890) passed practically unnoticed. Hardly anybody, including the choreographer, realized that they were witnessing a major event. The

"Polovetsian Dances", created by Ivanov twenty years before Fokine, held the core of what was heralded as the greatest possible revelation of twentieth-century ballet in the Paris season of 1909. Alexander Shiryaev, a participant in the Ivanov production, wrote: "It is customary to think that the honour of the creation of the Polovetsian dances belongs to Fokine alone. In fact he merely strengthened, enlivened, adorned with numerous details, the dance patterns composed by Lev Ivanov for the old production of *Prince Igor* in 1890. I remember these very well, as I danced the solo of the Chief."[1]

When Nicolai Sergeyev, who had in his possession records of the Ivanov production notated in Petersburg by Rakhmanov and Chekrygin in the Stepanov dance notation, reproduced it for the International Ballet, its similarities with the well-known definitive Fokine "Polovetsian Dances" struck the eye of anyone who had seen them.

With his inborn feeling for music Ivanov reached the very heart of Borodin's composition. His earlier experience and inclination towards character dancing supplied him with the necessary idiom, expanded and developed together with the soaring, boundless, sensuous rhythms and melodies of Borodin. To this typically symphonic score with the richest possible orchestral colours Ivanov created a dance suite of equal beauty and harmony, artfully blending classical steps with purely character ones. The dances from *Prince Igor* had a tremendous success with the audience. Contemporary critics, however, for the most part forgot to mention the name of their producer.

Was Lev Ivanov merely ill-starred? He could easily have fitted among Chekhov's characters. There was something of Uncle Vanya in him: a man of subtle, easily wounded nature, kind and benevolent, ready to sacrifice himself for the benefit of egoistic careerists exploiting his kindness without scruple.

This fine and sensitive artist could and would have achieved much more under more favourable circumstances. The supposed bad luck arose from his character: he was not a fighter and, besides, fighting could hardly have helped in his position.

One thing gave him wings and strength; and that was music. Not every kind of music: he sometimes encountered mediocre ballet scores. His first major effort—*The Tulip of Harlem* (1887) to monotonous tinkling by Baron Fitingoff-Shell—was choreographed with taste and contained many elaborately conceived dances, but Ivanov was quite naturally handicapped

[1] Alexander Shiryaev. *Op. cit.* Quoted from: V. M. Krasovskaya. *The Russian Ballet Theatre of the Second Half of the Nineteenth Century*, p. 59.

Scene from *The Nutcracker*, Mariinsky Theatre, 1892.

Scene from *The Nutcracker*, choreography by Lev Ivanov. Mariinsky Theatre, Petersburg.

La Halte de Cavalerie, music by Armsheimer, choreography by Marius Petipa, St. Petersburg, 1896. Alexandrov, Rubtsova, Colubeva, Legat (Sergei), Kshesinski (Joseph) and Kunitskaya.

Stars, music by A. Simon, choreography by Ivan Clustine, Bolshoi Theatre, Moscow, 1898. Vassily Tikhomirov as Mars surrounded by his satellites.

by this lack of inspiring material. Ivanov's inspiration had to grow directly out of music. He knew how to interpret it. His greatest achievements were connected with Tchaikovsky's music. With his Russian soul and enormous talent Ivanov responded to the call of Tchaikovsky's genius, a genius equally Russian by its very nature. Tchaikovsky once wrote about himself: "I passionately love Russians, the Russian language, the Russian way of thinking, Russian facial beauty, Russian customs. . . ."

Even if appearing in the guise of foreign fairy-tales, Tchaikovsky's heroes and heroines remained Russian in spirit, just as his music never lost its national character. Tchaikovsky made an immense contribution to world culture through being true to his own national character.

Could there be anything more Russian in its essence than the poetic Odette? Yuri Slonimsky was quite right in saying:[1] "Odette's world of emotions is typical for Tchaikovsky. It is filled with the restless, pure sadness of a maiden's lyricism. Odette's musical theme is akin to that of Francesca de Rimini (in its first A minor part). Odette's musical portrait reminds us of that of Tatiana [heroine of *Eugene Onegin*—N.R.], in particular the D minor theme from the letter scene. This affinity pertains not only to some of the episodes, but to the work as a whole. *Swan Lake* is closely linked with the operatic, symphonic and chamber works of Tchaikovsky at that period: it has the same youthful enthusiasm, a serenely lyrical perception of life, breadth, and purity of feelings, so typical of *The Snowmaiden, Eugene Onegin,* and the early symphonies and quartets." "*Swan Lake,*" continues Yuri Slonimsky, "belongs to the circle of themes that were central in Tchaikovsky's creation. They were connected with the urge for true happiness and love in the eternal struggle of the soul, with the maxim that love is stronger than death."

Could Lev Ivanov fail to respond to such imagery, could he fail to understand what Tchaikovsky's music was saying?

He came into contact with Tchaikovsky's scores earlier than is supposed. Vassily Tikhomirov, a contemporary of the first production of *The Sleeping Beauty*, told this writer that Lev Ivanov was to a considerable extent responsible for the poetic "Vision Scene" of that ballet, when the vision of the sleeping Princess, shown to the Prince through the magical powers of the Lilac Fairy, now floats into his arms and then escapes his embrace in an intangibly elusive dream. In his position of assistant to Petipa, Ivanov was never credited for what he had done, and who knows how many more small masterpieces of his were buried for ever?

[1] Yuri Slonimsky. *Swan Lake.* State Music Publishing House, Leningrad, 1962, pp. 13–14.

In 1892, however, came the chance to work independently at a full-length Tchaikovsky ballet. The music of *The Nutcracker* was first heard in Petersburg on March 7, 1892, in one of the concerts of the Russian Musical Society, when the author conducted the overture-fantasia, *Romeo and Juliet* and a suite from his new ballet, commissioned in 1891 by the Directorate of the Imperial Theatres together with the opera, *Iolanta*. Tchaikovsky received from Petipa a programme as detailed as that of *The Sleeping Beauty* and followed it.

The "book" was compiled by Petipa not from the original tale by Hoffmann, but after a version by Alexandre Dumas. The seventy-year-old ballet-master was to have started production of the new ballet early in the season of 1892-1893. Only his sudden illness provided Ivanov with the opportunity to produce his own choreography to a major musical creation by Tchaikovsky. Naturally he was very much limited by the detailed programme of Petipa who continued supervision of the production. The music, on the other hand, suggested much broader vistas and a greater range of human feelings. Ivanov's musical genius could not fail to fathom this. Like Tchaikovsky, who had great difficulty in transgressing the narrow boundaries of the scenario in the process of composition, so Ivanov had to limit himself to the purely outward visualizations of Petipa, when the mature symphonic score suggested the inner world "Of the ripening soul of a little girl, at first playing with dolls, and then arriving at the dawn of love through dreams of a brave and manly hero —in other words the process of the 'education of sentiments' ".[1]

Everything that Lev Ivanov created in *The Nutcracker* was born out of the music. He could not work otherwise. However, the numerous *divertissements*, conceived by Petipa, limited his creative imagination, even if the dances conveyed to perfection the rhythmic pattern. In some cases Ivanov had great difficulty, such as with the traditionally conceived "Chocolate" with its Spanish theme, or the "Trepak", which also seemed out of proportion in the lyrical texture of the score. Shiryaev confirms this in his memoirs, and one may believe him, as it was he who took part in the first performance of December 7, 1892, having composed for himself a "Jester's Dance" with a hoop, to the music of the "Trepak".

It was in the "Waltz of the Snowflakes" that Ivanov created his first symphonic masterpiece. Here he was able to compose freely, without being hampered by the idiosyncrasies of the scenario. He listened to the music and obeyed it, creating in visual form a scene of a snowstorm.

[1] Academician B. V. Asafiev. *Selected Works*, Vol. IV, pp. 107-109, Moscow, 1955, Publishing House of the Academy of Sciences of the U.S.S.R.

Perhaps the simple idiom and patterns used by him were not completely on a par with the complex symphonic structure of Tchaikovsky's score. The choreographer who is completely capable of tackling all of Tchaikovsky's symphonic richness has yet to come.

But Ivanov did succeed in creating, through the type of classical steps used, and in the ever changing dance pattern, an illusion of falling snow, with soft, large flakes drifting in the frosty air. The Snowflakes (dancers of the *corps de ballet*) carried in their hands wands with spherical flakes attached to quivering wires, while similar wires and small white balls were attached to their headgear. As they formed intricate groups and moved across the stage in various patterns, the "snowflakes" quivered and seemed to be floating through the air. The dancers formed now a star and then assembled into one huge snowball, and in the end stood still in a compact group, as if chased by the wind into one large heap of snow, formed by no less than sixty dancers headed by eight soloists. This composition was named by the critic Akim Volynsky "a *chef d'oeuvre* of *plastique*".

The rest of the ballet, including the famous Sugar-Plum Fairy *adagio*, created for the popular guest-artist Antonietta Dell-Era, was done in a more traditional manner according to Petipa's programme. It was impossible to follow the music more closely when a traditional *pas de deux* was strictly indicated and had to be choreographed with the needs of the ballerina in view.

But the dance of the snowflakes remained a classical masterpiece, and, according to the late Agrippina Vaganova, connoisseurs of ballet purposely took seats in the upper tier to admire its beautiful patterns, wherein the movements were at one with the music.

This dance was, beyond any doubt, a step towards Ivanov's great achievements in *Swan Lake*.

Lev Ivanov was probably nursing the idea of this ballet, at least of its second act, for several years. As early as March 1886, Tchaikovsky received a letter from his publisher, Jurgenson, informing him that Vsevolojsky intended to show one act from *Swan Lake* in a special performance for the Tsar at the Krasnoye-Selo Summer Theatre and was asking for the orchestra parts of act four. Tchaikovsky replied on April 4 of the same year that the second act, being the best in his view, had to be taken from the score, kept at the time in the Maidanovo estate.

Lev Ivanov, in his capacity of second ballet-master, choreographed all the Krasnoye-Selo Theatre ballets (usually one-act ones) for a number of years. There is no documentary evidence that *Swan Lake*, act II, was ever produced at that theatre. But Yuri Slonimsky says in his *Swan Lake* book[1] that in his youth he heard from veterans of the Russian ballet that, at the end of the eighties or the beginning of the nineties, the second act of *Swan Lake* was shown on an island in a lake either at Peterhof or Tsarskoye Selo—and it is known that such performances were given on those lakes on more than one occasion. Xenia Davydova, the composer's grand-niece, who was on the staff of the Tchaikovsky museum in Klin, had also heard such reports.

There is evidence, however, that the production of *Swan Lake* was in preparation while the composer was still alive. The Leningrad Theatre Museum has in its possession a sketch for a costume of the swan *corps de ballet* signed by Ponomaryov, staff designer of the Imperial Theatres in 1892. Tchaikovsky's disciple, composer A. Koreshchenko, wrote in a notice two years after the Petersburg première of *Swan Lake*: "Since its first production this work has been subjected to many changes, both as regards the *mise en scène* and the music, if we are not mistaken, *still with the consent of P. I. Tchaikovsky*. . . . The order of some dances had been changed, a few numbers, taken from the author's pianoforte compositions, had been added. . . . These numbers have been selected very successfully and are excellently orchestrated by M. Drigo."[2]

Yuri Slonimsky, while considering that Koreshchenko's evidence is quite valid, draws attention to the fact that Tchaikovsky's publisher, Jurgenson, printed the numbers, inserted in *Swan Lake* from opus 72 (composed in April 1893), as separate sheet music with the following title: "*Swan Lake*. Grand ballet in four acts. Music by P. I. Tchaikovsky. Numbers, inserted into the ballet by the author himself (orchestration by R. Drigo), 1895."

The list of Tchaikovsky's works, appended by his brother Modest to *The Life of Pyotr Ilyich Tchaikovsky* published by Jurgenson in Moscow in 1900-1902, Vol. III, pp. 26-27, includes three numbers from opus 72 under the general title of *Swan Lake*. Slonimsky considers this to be ample evidence of the fact that both Jurgenson and the composer's brother knew full well that the insertions were made with the consent of the composer and perhaps even selected by himself.

These changes were carried out, most likely, as the result of negotiations with Petipa, who insisted on providing the ballerina with a suitable number of *variations*.

  [1] Yuri Slonimsky. *Op. cit.*, p. 40.
  [2] Arseny Koreshchenko. "The Bolshoi Theatre". *Moscow Monitor* No. 125 of 8/5/1896 and No. 124 of the same year. Quoted from: Yuri Slonimsky. *Tchaikovsky and the Ballet Theatre of his Time*, p. 134.

Edition „Richard" St. Pétersbourg. 176

фотогр. Императорскихъ ТЕАТРОВЪ.

С. Легатъ и Леньяни

Pierrina Legnani and Sergei Legat in *Camargo*. Legnani's farewell benefit performance. (Collection of Natalia Roslavleva)

Goldfish, ballet by A. Gorsky. Bolshoi Theatre, 1903. Yekaterina Geltser and Vassily Tikhomirov.

Lyubov Roslavleva as Swanilda in *Coppélia*. Bolshoi Theatre, Moscow, *circa* 1895. (Collection of Natalia Roslavleva)

In act III Odile was given a *variation* to the music of No. 12, opus 72 "L'Espiègle", and the last act was expanded by the addition of Numbers 11 and 15 from the same work ("Valse Bluette" and "A Little of Chopin"). Aside from additions, there were many deletions interfering with the author's original score to a considerable extent and interrupting the natural flow of dramatic rise and fall. Such were the demands of the time, and apparently Tchaikovsky and, after him, his brother and executor Modest had to give in, so as to realize a new scenic version of the work. On the other hand some of the cuts were for the better, while Slonimsky reminds us in his book that Tchaikovsky's friend and great admirer, Laroche, insisted on the necessity of some excisions and insertions as early as the seventies.

Available correspondence between Vsevolojsky and Modest Tchaikovsky seems to indicate that the decision to achieve the complete production of *Swan Lake* in Petersburg was made only after the great success of the second act, shown at the Mariinsky theatre on February 17, 1894, in a gala concert dedicated to Tchaikovsky's memory. Petipa was ill at the time. Lev Ivanov had only two months in which to prepare the second act, the most important in the entire ballet according to the opinion of the composer. Works of genius have been created in an even shorter time; and it is likely that Ivanov was already well acquainted with the score, and had already arranged a version of the second act. At any rate the *Petersburg Gazette* reported rumours that *Swan Lake* was to be given at the Mariinsky theatre exactly two weeks after the composer's death in October 1893. In two more weeks the same paper informed its readers that *Swan Lake*, the production of which was scheduled for the next season (1893-1894), was to be shown in February of 1894.[1]

Either the second act alone was ready by February, or it was considered more appropriate to give only one act from *Swan Lake* (together with the first act of *The Maid of Orleans* and excerpts from *Eugene Onegin*) at the memorial concert.

The overwhelming success of Lev Ivanov's inspired "*Swan*" compositions and the general veneration of the Russian public at large for the name and legacy of Tchaikovsky convinced Vsevolojsky that the time had come to stage *Swan Lake* in full. Negotiations between him and Modest Tchaikovsky on changes in the scenario were followed by negotiations between the librettist (and author's executor), on the one side, with Petipa and Drigo, on the other, about the order of the musical numbers in the entire score.

[1] *Petersburg Gazette* of November 30, 1893, and December 16, 1893.

Modest Tchaikovsky was requested to delete the tragic final scene and replace it with a sentimental apotheosis, in which Odette and Siegfried sailed in a golden boat driven by swans to an unknown land "of eternal bliss".

Upon receiving the new scenario (in August 1894), wherein Modest Tchaikovsky deleted some irrelevances and made the story clearer while at the same time introducing some banalities, to please the Directorate, Petipa, who by that time had regained his health, started preparing a new programme. The notes preserved in his archives at the Bakhrushin Museum in Moscow are not as full as those for *The Sleeping Beauty*, but are capable of providing sufficient evidence that Petipa had given much thought to the future production.

In the first act he wanted to create something in the nature of peasant revels around a May-pole. He visualized pretty costumes of six cantons with twenty-four women carrying small baskets of flowers and twenty-four men with ribbons tied to sticks. He visualized the peasant waltz as a grand character ensemble, using very few classical steps, which were to be reserved for the main protagonists. In reality Petipa produced something less interesting, probably in the constant effort to please his Imperial patrons. There was a May-pole, indeed, but the *corps de ballet* around it formed very ordinary groups, wherein, in order to place the dancers at different levels, Petipa introduced the ubiquitous small stools (*tabourets*) that had to be carried by the men from one place to another. The baskets of flowers and beflowered hats soon introduced a monotonous similarity, rather than the desired variety.

While working out in detail all the scenes, Petipa did not touch the swan scene of act II, he merely recorded: "the second scene has already been done". This shows that the chief choreographer accepted Ivanov's work without any changes. In this case Ivanov's choreography, being born out of the music and literally corresponding in its inspiration to that of the composer, was head and shoulders above what Petipa could have achieved, and the old choreographer made way for this new development of Russian ballet. Petipa was over seventy-two: he had great experience, but was weighed down by clichés and stereotyped methods of production. However, his notes show that the master did his utmost to penetrate and match the depth of Tchaikovsky's music.

He left sketches for a dance of white swans and black swans, in order to introduce a tragic note. He showed Siegfried in the ball of act III wearing a swan feather in his cap, a sign of his pledge to Odette. He wanted to order fancy-dress ball costumes for the guests in this act, in accordance with Tchaikovsky's concept. And he created a remarkable *bravura* characterization of Odile in the same scene.

According to the unwritten law of the Imperial Theatres, the leading role of the new production had to be given to the current Italian guest-artist—in this case Pierrina Legnani. Of all the Italian ballerinas she was the one who had experienced the beneficent influence of the Russian school to the greatest extent. The virtuosity part of Odile with its *fouettés* and other technical feats was closer to the Italian manner. It was the role of Odette that required particular effort and much work with the ballerina on the part of the choreographer. Legnani, who had spent several seasons in the midst of the Russian ballet, was ready to absorb its precepts. Her dancing became much more expressive, her movements much softer. Vassily Tikhomirov, talking to this author about the 1895 première of *Swan Lake*[1] (he frequently danced in Petersburg in those years), remembered that Legnani's back quivered like that of a bird, and that her pruning of feathers was a remarkable sight. That Legnani's dancing experienced the influence of the Russian school is confirmed in print by her contemporary, Sergei Khudekov, who wrote in vol. IV of his *History of Dancing* (Petrograd, 1918, p. 132): "Odette beyond any doubt became her best role. Here Legnani became literally transformed. One could not recognize the former impassionate Legnani."

And, seemingly in recognition of the debt she owed to the masters of the Russian school, Legnani sent to Lev Ivanov, for his benefit of 1899, a small gold souvenir with an inscription: *"De la part d'Odette"*.

Apparently Legnani satisfied the ideals of the choreographer. One could hardly say that of Gerdt, who by that time was in his fifty-first year and appeared in the role of Siegfried with a beard and moustache. We know from the account of earlier Petipa ballets that the *premier danseur* was frequently replaced in *pas de deux*, requiring virtuosity and knowledge of partnering, by another dancer. It used to take place on many occasions and there came a day when the young Gerdt danced an interpolated *pas de deux* to replace Lev Ivanov in *La Bayadère*. Now this was done not only as a tribute to an old custom. The young Alexander Oblakov was called in out of necessity to relieve the *premier danseur* (in the role of Benno, the Prince's esquire). Naturally this interfered with the romantic *adagio* of the second act (*Andante non troppo*, G flat major), which was originally written by Tchaikovsky as a final duo of Undine and Gulbrandt for

[1] The première took place on January 15, 1895. Scheduled for the season of 1894, the production might have been postponed because of court mourning on the occasion of the death of Alexander III in 1894.

the opera *Undine*. (Its score was burnt by the author and this theme reappeared as one of the most poetic themes of love in *Swan Lake*.)

To a certain extent the artists with whom Ivanov had to work did not implement his ideas as fully as he would have liked. But so far as choreography was concerned he was able, for the first time, to achieve dance images according to the laws of the symphonic music that engendered them.

This was symphonization of the dance of the highest possible order. Lev Ivanov arrived at it with the inborn sense of a real artist. What amounted to one of the greatest reforms of ballet was not understood by his contemporaries. He was ahead of his times. The remarkable polyphonic dance patterns of his choreography for the second act of *Swan Lake* developed plastic *leitmotivs*, in which the *arabesque*, in a slightly changed form, became a symbol of the Swan-maiden and her sad, tormented soul. Familiar classical steps were used in repeated succession so as to convey a new content, the psychological state of the protagonists, the theme of love that could not be fully happy, the current of unrest that ran through the entire composition. The scene started with a traditional mime sequence (Odette's story of the circumstances of her enchantment) carried out by Lev Ivanov with the help of conventional mime of nineteenth-century ballet—he was still bound by its conventions. But everything that took place further on was carrying him directly into the twentieth century.

The famous pose of Odette, when, half maiden and half swan, she softly reclined on her bent leg, and lowered her body and arms, gracefully arched to frame the head, one leg over the other, stretched out and pointed, became identified with the image of the Swan in future choreography. It served as a point of issue for Fokine in his dance, "The Dying Swan"— he merely changed its serene tranquillity for more tragic notes. It has been immortalized for ever by Anna Pavlova. She would have made an ideal Odette of Lev Ivanov's dreams but never had the chance to dance the full *Swan Lake*.

Generations of Russian dancers have performed the dual role of Odette-Odile. In Soviet ballet it acquired a new, deeper reading. The Odettes of Marina Semenova, Galina Ulanova, and Maya Plisetskaya are unforgettable—each in its own way. A majestically graceful Odette was that of Marina Semenova; Galina Ulanova's Swan-maiden was lyrically sorrowful; Maya Plisetskaya's is romantically clouded in mystery.

The role allows many interpretations if the ballerina grasps and understands the emotional meaning of Tchaikovsky's music. Such is the nature of Ivanov's symphonism. It does not stop at reproducing the rhythmic pattern and structure of the score—though it does that to perfection. The form, the dance pattern, became in Lev Ivanov's greatest creation an exact expression of the psychological and emotional content of the music. The musical dramaturgy found reproduction in choreography that had similar dramatic rises and falls, climaxes and dénouements.

Lev Ivanov's choreography for *Swan Lake*, act II (he staged many beautiful dances in the fourth act, but was unable to implement his ideas as fully because of the considerable changes introduced at the request of the Directorate of the Imperial Theatres), may serve as an object lesson of *Russian* dance symphonism. It is inseparably bound with Russian symphonism in general—with the breadth of its canvases, the poetic warmth of its imagery, the wide expanse of themes posing important ideas, portraying a noble human spirit. Those Russian choreographers who approached symphonic music in ballet, for the purpose of reaching the heart and mind of the audience by deeply probing into its content, followed the national tradition of which Lev Ivanov is by right the greatest disciple.

It is this life of the human spirit that contains the answer to the secret of the eternal impact of Tchaikovsky's ballets.

After *Swan Lake* Ivanov did not come into contact with music of appreciable quality and never reached the same summit of inspiration. There were several one-act trifles and a full-length ballet, *The Daughter of the Mikado* (1897), to music by Wrangel and book by Langammer, trounced by the critics as unprecedented trash. Ivanov could not possibly be blamed for failing to create anything worthy to the colourless score produced by Wrangel, but he was criticized and for four years after the failure of *The Daughter of the Mikado* (it received only a few performances) he revived old ballets.

His health was failing; the burden of supporting a large family (three children by the first marriage, one of them deaf-and-dumb, and three by the second one) was too heavy.

In the conclusion to his memoirs (completed in February 1899) Ivanov wrote: "How much has been experienced, how much blood has been soured because of hurt pride and humiliated human dignity. . . ." Yet he expressed great admiration and devotion to the art he served and, addressing future generations of ballet, wished them success. Little did he know that for many generations to come he would ever be regarded as a lodestar in the art of making dances.

Though when writing the bitter epitaph to his life Ivanov did not expect to achieve anything worthy, he did create one more masterpiece shortly before the end: the "Csardas" to Liszt's *Second Rhapsody*, inter-polated in *The Hump-backed Horse* for the performance of October 11, 1900, with Olga Preobrajenskaya as soloist. The beautiful suite of stylized character dances created by Ivanov was symphonically constructed in harmony with the music. It had great success with the public and was encored at each presentation, yet Ivanov's name was not even mentioned on the posters, and justice was done to him only in Soviet time.

Ivanov's "Rhapsody" is preserved to this day in Soviet ballet as one of the classical gems and has been frequently revived in Leningrad.

In 1900 Lev Ivanov was also preparing Arensky's *Les Nuits d'Egypte*, but this production was repeatedly postponed, never to be achieved. There is no doubt, however, that Ivanov did most of the work and that rehearsals of the new ballet were started. Delibes' *Sylvia*, produced on December 2, 1901, jointly with Pavel Gerdt, whose choreographic talents were slight, did not succeed—ancient Greece seen through the eyes of nineteenth-century classicism appeared naïve and outdated.

Lev Ivanov's life was nearing its ebb. The year of 1901 was filled with illness and petitions for help after fifty years of service for the Imperial Theatres. The master died on December 11, 1901 (Old Style), leaving his family penniless.

It is hard to believe that not a single obituary mentioned *Swan Lake* among the choreographer's works, which were spoken of only briefly and without much respect.

Posterity has accorded proper due to Lev Ivanov, great master of the nineteenth century. His work has withstood the most difficult test—that of Time.

CHAPTER VII

GORSKY AND THE DRAMATIC MOVEMENT IN BALLET[1]

TOWARDS THE END of the nineteenth century the Moscow ballet was going through a very difficult period. At the beginning of the eighties, ballet at the Bolshoi theatre was on the decline and failed to produce anything of even average interest. The Belgian choreographer, Joseph Hansen (1842-1907), chief ballet-master of the company from 1879, was unable to lead the Moscow ballet artistically. As choreographer he relied to a considerable extent on effects, in the producing of which he depended in no small measure on Karl Waltz, the chief machinist.

Hansen's first ballet, *La Fille d'Inferno*, first performed on November 16, 1879, did not pursue any serious artistic purpose and was shockingly eclectic. While its story was laid in India and the chief protagonist, Radomani, impersonated by Maria Stanislavskaya, a gifted dancer of the period, was supposed to be an Indian goddess, her retinue of "infernal maidens" wore powdered wigs, black masks, and black elbow-high gloves. Hansen relied on his previous music hall experience and paraded dozens of dancers in multi-coloured costumes, in lieu of proper choreography.

La Fille d'Inferno was nothing but a thinly disguised *féerie*. However, Hansen, while not belonging to the ranks of great masters of the ballet, was sufficiently professional to please the Moscow office of the Directorate of the Imperial Theatres. He was not the person badly needed to lead the Bolshoi ballet out of its blind alley. He did his job fairly well, at least better than his predecessor, Reisinger. Hansen's production of *Swan Lake* (on January 13, 1880), with settings and costumes used in 1877, but with new choreography, again centred the main interest on dances of the *corps de ballet*. The role of Odette was now taken by Yevdokia Kalmykova, a dancer who was really not fit to occupy ballerina status. There is no indication that Tchaikovsky's score had inspired the choreographer to

---

[1] Gorsky's choreography is sometimes regarded as naturalist, sometimes as realist. In the Russian Theatre "naturalism" implies exact reproduction of episodes, whereas "realism" presents life as seen by a creative artist. Gorsky sometimes deviated to naturalism, e.g. the torture scenes in *Gudule's Daughter*, but such lapses were rare. His prime interest was dramatic content and the realist motivations governing a character's actions.—N.R.

create anything worthy of the composer's genius. It probably meant nothing to Hansen since, having reproduced a ballet called *Swans* at the Alhambra, immediately upon his arrival in London from Moscow, he readily used music by that music hall's prolific and permanent musical director, Jacobi.

The Moscow audiences were not so easy to please. They were accustomed to, and expected, some meaning in ballet, associated with some poetic idea.

One of Hansen's last productions for the Bolshoi theatre (1881), *Arifax, the Pearl of Aden*, to music by Gerber, was gravely censured by the writer Boborykin. The author did pay tribute to Hansen's professional merits, but he considered that "there would be more sense and better sales of tickets if the public were interested in the content of ballets. This may be achieved only in connection with all that is being given on other Russian stages and with the public interest in literature and other artistic spheres."[1]

Close ties with all other branches of arts and letters were a tradition of the Russian ballet ensuring its place in the national art treasury. Those foreign choreographers who either worked in Russia for a length of time, or made the country their second home, accepted and followed this custom. For Hansen the contract with the Imperial Theatres was a matter of business. He had no clear artistic purpose. The Moscow ballet did not improve in any way during his term of service. The situation remained critical. While Hansen alone was not responsible for this state of affairs, he was obviously incapable of improving it. His contract was not renewed. Hansen left for London and ultimately for Paris, where he headed the Opéra ballet from 1889 to his death in 1907.

Upon his departure the Moscow ballet was subjected to a "reform" that nearly put an end to its existence altogether. The reform of 1882, carried out in the season of 1882–1883, was conceived by officials, who wanted to balance the considerable deficit incurred by the Moscow office of the Imperial Theatres. It was no longer headed by Begichev, an educated man genuinely interested in the arts. P. M. Pchelnikov, the new chief, a former military man, was altogether different. The artists of all the Moscow theatres hated him, and Prov Sadovsky, a leading dramatic actor of the Maly Theatre and a great wit, wrote caustic verses about "infantry delegated to introduce order into art". Pchelnikov had his own ideas as to the kind of order needed. He reduced the personnel of the Moscow ballet by ninety-two persons and transferred a number of other

[1] The newspaper *Russkie Vedomosti*, No. 39 of February 8, 1881.

Scene from *Salammbô*, music by A. Arends, chorography by A. Gorsky. Yekaterina Geltser as Salammbô (centre). Bolshoi Theatre, Moscow, 1910.

Above: Don Quixote, version
by Alexander Gorsky. Bolshoi
Theatre, Moscow, 1900.
Sophia Fedorova and Mikhail
Mordkin.

Right: Sophia Fedorova II as
Esmeralda. (Collection of
Natalia Roslavleva)

dancers and mimes to Petersburg. Such leading artists as Sokolov, Wanner, Yermolov, Reinsgausen, and the ballerina Karpakova were among those to go first. Genuine ballets could no longer be given, nor did the officials consider them necessary. They intended to limit the role of ballet in Moscow to appearances in opera *divertissements* and ballet's very right of existence as an independent art was questioned. The Bolshoi Theatre school, that continued to graduate thoroughly educated professionals, was also in danger. When told that small trained children were needed in every ballet, an official from the Court Ministry replied that plenty of even prettier child supers could be found at any time in the streets.

The financial state of the rank-and-file members of the Moscow ballet was at times desperate. Moscow intellectuals sympathized with their plight and the young Chekhov wrote a sarcastic feuilleton in the humorist magazine *Oskolki* about "ill-mannered" dancers daring to express displeasure at being dismissed, while the playwright, Ostrovsky, expressed serious anxiety at the position of the Moscow theatres as a whole.

As to the Bolshoi ballet company, it remained without any ballet-master whatsoever for almost a year, until October 1883, when the Petersburg dancer and manager of the ballet, Alexei Bogdanov (1830-1907), was transferred to work in Moscow. Bogdanov possessed no choreographic or artistic talents whatsoever, but knew how to take care of his career. Had he had at least some talent, he could have occupied Petipa's post as second ballet-master to Saint-Léon in the Petersburg ballet as early as 1867. These plans having failed, Bogdanov worked his way up to the position of chief *régisseur* (manager) of the Petersburg company. The promotion to Moscow placed him, for the first time, at the head of an entire company. Having been trained at the Petersburg school and served a full term as a dancer, Bogdanov at least knew what was lacking in the Moscow ballet. He started his duties by ordering that the whole company must attend daily classes and rehearsals.

The general level of the company improved and so did the attendance at performances. Being incapable of creating his own ballets, Bogdanov revived a succession of those in the Petersburg repertory: Petipa's *Don Quixote* (though it was staged in Moscow in a better version), *Roxana, the Beauty of Montenegro, King Candaules*, and Perrot's *The Naiad and the Fisherman (Undine)*, all within a very short time.

These copies lacked artistic unity and the performance was still very poor. As might have been expected, Bogdanov failed to breathe new life into the Moscow ballet. Neither did his own productions, *The Charms of Hashisch, or the Island of Roses* and *Svetlana* (both to music by N. Klenovsky), staged in 1885 and 1886 respectively, improve the situation. Bogdanov had to retire on August 1, 1889.

The situation of chief ballet-master of the Moscow ballet was again vacant. This time it was occupied by a foreigner.

José Mendez (1843-1905), while of Spanish origin,[1] was an international roving ballet-master who had worked on many stages. Having started in his youth as a pupil and apprentice of Carlo Blasis, he also worked and studied under Paul Taglioni. He was thoroughly *au courant* with the latest novelties in ballet. After meeting Virginia Zucchi during the ballerina's tour in Warsaw, he was invited by her to be ballet-master of the company formed in Italy for the purpose of touring Russia. Having shown his worth during that company's appearances in Moscow at the private theatre owned by Rodon, Mendes was invited by the Moscow office of the Imperial theatres to sign a contract, according to which his duties consisted not only of choreographing ballets, but also of staging dances in operas and conducting classes for pupils and members of the comany.

While never becoming truly identified with the Russian ballet, Mendes spent almost ten years in Moscow, retiring in 1898 at the time of the retirement of Pchelnikov, his benefactor. He was responsible for the training of many good dancers, including his two daughters—Julietta and Angelica,[2] and his sister-in-law Adelina Giuri, who became a brilliant *prima ballerina* of the Bolshoi theatre.

Lyubov Roslavleva, an outstanding Russian ballerina, also owed her development to Mendes. A good teacher, Mendes provided his pupils with strong technique of the Italian school, but failed to give them the softness and grace of Russian *ports de bras*. Those of Mendes pupils who were considered as promising either had to be sent to Petersburg for the perfection of their art under such masters as Gerdt and Johansson, as happened in the case of Geltser and Mosolova, or, on the strength of their talent, succeeded in overcoming the brittle quality of the Mendes school as Roslavleva did.

The activity of Mendes at the school on the whole was rather fruitful, but his work at the Bolshoi theatre was very much out of harmony with its traditions and the national character of the Russian ballet. Mendes, even more than Hansen, introduced the latest fashions of European ballet, which by the eighties was in decline.

[1] He used a French version of his name "Joseph Mendes".

[2] Both were members of the Bolshoi ballet, remaining there after their father's departure from Russia.

Mendes's first big production was the ballet *India* staged in February 1890 as a popular "exotic" piece. *India* was a *ballet-féerie* consisting of a set of *divertissements* that were expected to be as varied as possible. True, probably as a concession to the tastes of the Moscow public, accustomed to ballets with serious content and sufficiently high artistic level, Mendes revived *Esmeralda*, freely borrowing the choreography of separate dances from the version by Petipa. In 1891 he showed in Moscow Paul Taglioni's popular ballet *The Adventures of Flik and Flok*. This was also a fantastic ballet in the nature of a *féerie* to music by Hertel. Mendes, who knew very well the greatest *féerie* of the time, Manzotti's *Excelsior*, attempted to make *Flik and Flok* into something similar. With this in view he added many other pieces to the music and choreographed new dances, including those to music from the Klenovsky–Bogdanov ballet, *The Charms of Hashisch*.

The spectacle was rather impressive. In the submarine scene the stage was filled with the *corps de ballet* in the form of sea-shells, corals, goldfish, and the like. Additional effect was produced by human seaweeds, iridescent in ever-changing light (electricity was a great novelty in those days). In the apotheosis a "live ship" was formed by all the dancers, while "animated caryatids" bore a huge silver sail, also lavishly lit by electric bulbs. There were other scenes designed to dazzle the eye to the greatest possible extent. But there was very little dancing.

Those who liked spectacular effects approved of the ballet. The more serious critics, however, expressed alarm at the direction in which the Moscow ballet was being led, saying openly that productions like *Flik and Flok* followed tendencies which "had already brought about a rapid disintegration of ballet in the West". This alarm was sounded by a critic who preferred to remain anonymous, in the *Moskovsky Listok* (a daily newspaper) of September 18, 1892. The discerning critic said that external glitter served in European ballets of that period (particularly those by Manzotti) to conceal absence of any content whatsoever, and although Russian ballet had succeeded in avoiding this "fatal path" in the past years, the new Mendes ballet placed it in a similarly vulnerable position. Wisely the author of the article pointed out that *féeries*, with their endless marching in file that replaced dancing, threatened the professional integrity of the Moscow ballet—its gifted dancers, accustomed to expressing through the dance a certain idea, now had none to create. The author of the article regretted that "separate talents, that strike the eye among the mass of the *corps de ballet*, are doomed . . . to senseless waving about of arms, legs, and heads".

Indeed, the Moscow ballet even in that unfortunate period contained many outstanding personalities, while potential ones simply did not get the chance to show their worth. It is these dancers of the Russian ballet, fervently devoted to their art, who maintained it at a proper professional level and helped the Bolshoi company of the late eighties and the early nineties to survive these trials and tribulations. Until late in the nineties the fate of ballet in Moscow was still hanging on a thread. The Directorate of the Imperial Theatres continued questioning the desirability of its existence. This was done at a time when the company still had a Lydia Geiten, a Vassily Geltser, a Nicolai Domashov (1861-1916), and brilliant young talents (Vassily Tikhomirov, Lyubov Roslavleva, Yekaterina Geltser and many others) were about to leave school or had already shown their worth.

Lydia Geiten (1857-1920), with her great temperament and expressive face, was a typically Moscow ballerina, though she graduated from the Bolshoi school in 1874 from the class of Gustave Legat—a teacher whose method was closer to that current in Petersburg. Dark, well-built, with huge grey eyes that seemed to illumine her face, Geiten was at her best in strong roles—when she got them.

Her histrionic abilities were first noticed by Petipa when he produced his ballets in Moscow. At the age of twelve Lydia Geiten was given the role of the mischievous spirit in *Trilby* and succeeded in creating a charming character. Not surprisingly she was asked to dance the "Diablotine" (Little Devil) in 1871—also while still at school—for the benefit performance of Ivan Yermolov, the mime and teacher. Thus started a career that took place under difficult circumstances, in lean times for the Moscow ballet. Yet Geiten carried on, with the same amount of devotion and talent, in the course of the twenty years of her service. She was essentially a *terre à terre* dancer, best in such roles as the tragic Esmeralda and Nisia (*King Candaules*), the vivacious Kitri (*Don Quixote*), Medora in *Le Corsaire*, the famous mimed role of Fenella (*The Dumb Girl of Portici*), and numerous other leading parts in ballets that had to be charged with dramatic content in order to allow this excellent dancer-actress to shine. Geiten's first role, Esmeralda, was danced at the age of fifteen, and permanently remained in her repertory. She was also the first Swanilda of the Moscow ballet, a role that afforded her the opportunity to act with conviction. This does not imply that Geiten was not a good dancer; she constantly perfected her technique, when already firmly occupying the position of *prima ballerina*. Geiten was often compared to Zucchi, but a Moscow critic, writing about this ballerina in 1885, at a time when Zucchi's success in Petersburg was enormous, noted that Geiten, while being a good mime, was also a meticulous classical dancer with perfect sense of style and proportion.

It is interesting to note that Geiten's dramatic abilities, probably because they did not get full opportunities in the Bolshoi theatre of the time, led her to a liaison with the dramatic theatre. Like Fanny Elssler before her, she performed the title role in Scribe's play *Olga, the Russian Orphan*, and also undertook two dramatic roles in summer theatres during her vacation. Konstantin Stanislavsky recorded in his diary of the late eighties that he was advised to take part in the presentation of the drama *Vasantasena* (this tragedy of an Indian temple dancer was partly used by Khudekov for the "book" of *La Bayadère*), together with Geiten in the title role. The play was translated from the French adaptation by Emil Paul (in verse) of the Indian classical drama by Shudraka, *The Clay Cart*, especially for Geiten, but the interesting project did not materialize.

Geiten was equally good in classical and character dances; she performed many of these with great *brio* and power of projection in the operas at the Bolshoi Theatre.

In 1887 Geiten was invited to dance in operas at Covent Garden and was lauded for the expressiveness of her dancing and a technique that was quite astounding in the London of those days; she surprised the critic of *The Times* by performing an entire solo *sur les pointes*.

In 1890 Geiten ventured to dance in St. Petersburg with Alfred Bekefi, the brilliant Hungarian character dancer (whom she knew in the Moscow company before he was transferred to Petersburg as an outcome of the notorious reform), and Platon Karsavin, her partners in characters and classical numbers respectively, and was very well received. Alexander Pleshcheyev, the prominent Petersburg balletomane and author, found Geiten to be "one of the most gifted Russian ballerinas, brilliant in dance and mime".[1]

Geiten retired in 1893 while still at the height of her powers. She formed a company of sixty dancers, largely of her colleagues from the Bolshoi Theatre, and toured the provinces in the summer of 1894, fulfilling the important mission of bringing ballet to towns where it had never been seen before. She had a colossal success in shortened versions of *Pharaoh's Daughter*, *Coppélia* and even *Giselle*, though the latter ballet, particularly its second, ethereal act, was not suited to her kind of talent.

No ballets had been created for Geiten during her career, the Moscow stage could boast of no outstanding choreographer in the course of these twenty years. Yet Geiten's role can hardly be exaggerated in the history

[1] Alexander Pleshcheyev. *Nash Balet (Our Ballet)*, SPB, 1899, p. 373.

of Moscow ballet. At a time when it had no leader to take care of its precious traditions, she preserved and furthered the performing style associated with the Moscow ballet stage since its inception.

Geiten's qualities were hard to compete with and for a number of years she remained unchallenged. Lydia Nelidova (1863-1929), her contemporary, had some claims to the position of *prima ballerina* upon Geiten's retirement, but failed to erase impressions of that ballerina's impersonations from the memory of the Bolshoi Theatre spectators.

Nelidova was half-English by birth. Her father, Richard Barto, was a British manufacturer who had settled in Russia for good. She was placed at the age of ten in the Moscow school and graduated from it in 1884. Having spent thirteen years in the Bolshoi Theatre Ballet, she was given in the first six years secondary parts in all the current ballets—*Satanilla, The Naiad and the Fisherman, Le Corsaire*, and the like. However, after having danced in London in 1890 at the Empire Theatre, she had a new debut in the principal role of *La Fille Mal Gardée* and acquitted herself quite well. After this success as Lise, Nelidova insistently claimed the title of bona fide ballerina, but her petitions were rejected. Then, she decided to apply her energy elsewhere. She published a small book wherein she posed some theoretical problems of ballet (L. Nelidova. *Letters on Ballet*, Moscow, 1894), and opened a school that existed for many years and provided training for numerous aspiring dancers. Among its teachers was the former ballerina, Sobeshchanskaya. It was from Nelidova's school that Diaghilev acquired many new members of his Russian Ballet when it became difficult to employ dancers from the Imperial Ballet all the year round. The original Nymph in *L'Après-Midi d'un Faune*, Lydia Redega, was Nelidova's daughter.

Upon the short interregnum that followed Geiten's retirement, three dancers rose, almost simultaneously, to ballerina rank.

Adelina Giuri (1872-1963), fragile and ethereal, possessed steel *pointes* and excellent *tours* acquired from her teacher and brother-in-law Mendes. Upon graduating from the Moscow school in 1891 she spent three years at La Scala, Milan, and on other European stages. Giuri signed a contract with the Bolshoi Theatre as from January 1, 1894, upon Geiten's retirement.

Her dancing was rather cold, but it was the coldness of beautifully cut diamonds. While the young Giuri was slightly critized by the Moscow Press for the accent on virtuosity, typical of the Italian school to which she belonged, so to speak, by inheritance, she never allowed herself to sacrifice grace and elegance to technical prowess, and, with time, having spent a number of years in Russian ballet, she developed expressiveness and was praised in 1897 for outstanding mimetic talent in the role of Padmana from Monplaisir's *Bramah*, a daring undertaking since it was created by none other than Virginia Zucchi.

Giuri was destined to perform the roles of Raymonda and Odette-Odile (*Swan Lake*) in the Gorsky productions of these ballets. She was also a lovely Aurora (*The Sleeping Beauty*), dancing this part after the *prima ballerina* Roslavleva.

Though Giuri did not become a "Gorsky ballerina" (she was too much of a classical *danseuse* for that), the chance to take part in the great Tchaikovsky and Glasunov ballets, and the creative atmosphere that at last reigned in the Moscow ballet with the advent of Gorsky, meant a great deal in her artistic life. It was, unfortunately, short, as she retired in 1903 after having seriously injured her foot.

After the Revolution, Giuri taught in various studios and at the Bolshoi school. She lived for ninety-one years, retaining full mental capacity, and shortly before her death completed a book of memoirs.

Lyubov Roslavleva (1874-1904), one of the greatest ballerinas ever reared by the Moscow ballet, was a superb artist in a class by herself. Premature death from an unsuccessful operation deprived the Russian ballet as a whole of a precious talent. Lyubov Roslavleva possessed the rare gift of capturing the attention of the entire audience by her mere entrance upon the stage. Her dancing was imbued with a sun-lit warmth and spiritual truth that could not fail to endear her to the public.

Every movement of this ballerina was linked with the next, flowing smoothly with the *cantilena plastique* typical of the Russian school and born out of the Russian dance.

To say that Roslavleva was essentially a Russian ballerina would not be enough. She was a great dancer by any standards, possessing a first-class technique equal to that of the Italian virtuosity ballerinas of her time, but without their hardness and lack of refinement.

The life story of Lyubov Roslavleva was not ordinary. Usually children of humble folk, and very often those in service at the Imperial theatres, were placed in ballet schools. Lyubov Roslavleva came from the nobility. Her father served with the Lancers, and for a number of years was leader of the nobility in their province, a post occupied by wealthy nobles enjoying the respect and popularity of their peers. But when the little Lyubov was only eleven, her father lost his fortune. Her mother, forced to give music lessons, placed the girl in the Moscow Theatre School on the advice of some friends. Within seven months the talented child danced a solo in the Petipa version of *Don Quixote*. In another year she was made a ward of the State. Upon graduation in 1892 Lyubov Roslavleva received several small solo roles, and in October 1893 danced her first Swanilda. The real victory came when the Directorate of the Imperial Theatres repeatedly started delegating her to dance in Petersburg. She took the advantage of studying and rehearsing under masters of the Petersburg ballet. Her talent matured and she danced better than ever.

The Petersburg critic and balletomane, Bezobrazov, wrote in the *Petersburg Gazette* of 1899 that "this talented artiste is at present the best and the most talented of Russian ballerinas".

Roslavleva had greater dramatic abilities and inclinations than was customary among Petersburg dancers. She was a true artist of the Moscow tradition in ballet. She was married to the leading actor of the Maly Theatre, Prov Sadovsky, and was closely connected with the dramatic art, learning much from the pleiades of brilliant actors forming at that time the company of the Maly.

Roslavleva died when she was only thirty, and could not have achieved all that she had the power to express. Had she lived, the history of the Moscow company might have taken a different turn, at least as far as its leading dancers were concerned.

But Lyubov Roslavleva did have time to dance in the two Tchaikovsky ballets produced by Gorsky at the Bolshoi Theatre, in *The Sleeping Beauty* and *Swan Lake*. With her absolute musicality this became the greatest event of her life in art.

In 1902 Lyubov Roslavleva danced with overwhelming success at Monte Carlo during the summer vacations. Probably other foreign tours were awaiting her, but early in 1903 her health deteriorated and in 1904 she died in Switzerland.

Yekaterina Geltser (1876-1962) came of the same generation as Roslavleva, but, having lived a very long and fruitful life, she belonged more to twentieth-century ballet, though as a dancer she was formed completely at the end of the nineteenth. A whole epoch of Russian ballet is connected with this grand ballerina. She danced at the Bolshoi theatre for forty-one years. But her influence and the personification of her remarkable dramatic style was felt for a much longer period. Yekaterina Geltser was in no small measure responsible for that blending of dramatic impact, projection, and great *brio* that became over the years the hallmark of the Bolshoi ballet in the twentieth century.

Yekaterina Geltser, born on November 14, 1876, was the daughter of Vassily Geltser (1840-1908), one of the greatest mimes of the Russian

Mikhail Mordkin as Albrecht in the Gorsky version of *Giselle*, 1911. The action was transferred into the Directoire period and the costumes changed accordingly. (Collection of Natalia Roslavleva)

Setting by Konstantin Korovine for *Salammbô*, Act III; 1910.

La Fille Mal Gardée, Act I. Revived by Gorsky. Bolshoi Theatre, Moscow, *circa* 1920. Lise: Anastasia Abramova, Colin: Victor Smoltsov, Marcelline: Vladimir Riabtsev, Lise's four girl-friends: Yelena Ilyushchenko, Maria Gorshkova, Lyudmila Alexandrova, Tamara Nikitina.

ballet. His talent was so exceptional that when he appeared in the opera by Simon, *The Song of Triumphant Love* (after the story by Ivan Turgenev of the same title), as the deaf-mute Malay, spectators would arrive only for the second act to see him in this otherwise rather tedious opera. He also created a profound, deep impersonation of Claud Frollo in *Esmeralda*, and, as we know already, was the first Ivanushka—the Fool—of *The Hump-Backed Horse*.

Vassily Geltser was an enlightened man, in whose house one could meet the best of the Moscow intelligentsia. He formed a lasting friendship with Tchaikovsky after he had collaborated with Begichev on the book of *Swan Lake*, and was asked by the composer to choreograph the dances in the first production (at the Moscow Conservatoire) of *Eugene Onegin*.

Vassily Geltser occupied in the second part of his artistic career the important position of *régisseur* of the Moscow ballet. He could easily have placed his daughter at the ballet school. Yet when she begged him to do so, he was reticent. He explained to her the great amount of work and responsibility that a dancer had to undertake. Moreover, the girl's physique was not ideally suited for ballet. At last the eight-year-old girl succeeded in persuading her father and became a pupil of the Theatre School's ballet department. She graduated from it in 1894 and had her debut in the "animated frescoes" of *The Hump-Backed Horse* with her father as Ivanushka, who animated the figures of four dancers on the wall through the force of magic given to him by the Hump-Backed Horse.

Everything went well. She received more solo roles. But after having seen Pierrina Legnani with Mathilde Kshesinskaya in Petipa's *The Two Pearls* on the occasion of the Coronation performances in 1896, when the Petersburg ballet came almost *in toto*, and having witnessed the general higher level of the capital's company she begged her father to send her to Petersburg to study under Johansson and her father's old friend, Petipa. Mendes, from whose class she graduated in Moscow, had provided her with a sufficiently sound technical foundation. However, a general improvement in style, and, particularly, of the arms, was very much indicated. Vassily Geltser himself intended to send his daughter for further study in Petersburg, so this time it was not difficult to persuade him.

In 1896 Yekaterina Geltser departed for the capital with her friend Vera Mosolova—an excellent classical *danseuse*—to attend Johansson's *classe de perfectionnement*. This is what she said about it: "Johansson's class was so different from what I was accustomed that at first I was unable to do anything, I just looked at what others were doing. His *enchaînements* were exceedingly complicated and he changed them every day. I consider this one of the main conditions for successful work in a ballet school. Thanks to this you will later easily overcome any difficulties invented by the choreographer, and therefore be able always to preserve on the stage the joy and freshness of your feelings.

"Johansson would torment us with various *tempi*. He would accelerate them on his little violin, and then again slow them. This was extremely difficult to follow in such quick succession, but how easy it was to dance afterwards in an even *tempo*!"

While in Petersburg, Geltser took part (dancing one of the *variations*) in the first performance of *Raymonda* (August 7, 1898) with Legnani in the title role. When Legnani left in 1901, Geltser was asked by Petipa to return from Moscow for a triumphant performance of the title role in *Raymonda* that brought her the rank of ballerina.

A brilliant career was launched. It is difficult to define exactly what Yekaterina Geltser was as a dancer. While possessing the strong technique of the old school, steel *pointes* acquired from Mendes and elegant grace learnt from Johansson's lessons, while being a recognized "queen of *adage*", she really never excelled in *ballet blanc*, though she had danced all the big classical roles, Aurora and Odette-Odile and Raymonda. Her real forte was in roles charged with drama, such as her Esmeralda that always drew tears, Kitri of *Don Quixote*, Salammbô, one of Gorsky's greatest creations, and a whole gallery of roles that might better be classed as *demi-caractère*: the Hebrew "Bacchanale" from Saint-Saëns' opera, *Samson and Delilah*—another Gorsky masterpiece, in which she was inimitable (critics said her body "laughed" in this dance), the "Spirit of Belgium" to the music of Schubert's "Marche Militaire", and many others. And in each of these portrayals the ballerina, according to the expression of her celebrated partner Tikhomirov, had "another face, and, so to speak, another body". She possessed the rare gift (developed by hard work and utmost devotion to her art) of making her body convey what she wanted. She was capable of dancing in acute contrast: in the Gorsky version of *Le Corsaire*, Geltser, after all the plastic languid elegance of the preceding dances of Medora depicted as a "truly Byronic portrayal", suddenly performed *en travestie* "Le Petit Corsaire", a charming and graceful joke of a dance, at the end of which the dancer shouted: "*A bord!*"

Yekaterina Geltser, the company's favourite ballerina, readily participated in Gorsky's pursuit of the new, and took part in all his creations and innovations much more willingly and with a greater sense of collaboration than some of her other colleagues, though she was also steeped in the nineteenth-century tradition by force of her ballet education.

She showed a broadness of outlook and an ability to walk in step with the times that later made her a great ballerina of the Soviet ballet. She was able to give her spectators many moments of the greatest possible emotional uplift until her very last appearance.

At the very beginning of her career Yekaterina Geltser met a perfect teacher and partner in the person of Vassily Tikhomirov, one of the greatest dancers of the Russian ballet.

Vassily Tikhomirov (1876-1956) graduated from the Moscow school in 1891 from the class of Ivan Yermolov. He was only fifteen at the time. Since the required age for joining the ballet company was sixteen, he was sent to Petersburg for a year's "perfectioning" under Gerdt and Johansson, actually staying there for a further year.

In Gerdt's class Tikhomirov learned those secrets of special plastic expressiveness of the male body which he later perfected in his own practice. From the boys' class of the school in Teatralnaya Street it was possible to pass on to the gallery of the double-tiered rehearsal hall, where the *classe de perfectionnement* for ballerinas of the Mariinsky ballet was taken by Christian Johansson.

Tikhomirov spent all his spare hours in that gallery, observing everything that was valuable in Johansson's method, particularly the extraordinary variety of his *enchaînements*, never repeated.

In Petersburg Tikhomirov had his debut at the Mariinsky Theatre and was cast for gala performances. A brilliant career awaited him. He was to remain in the Mariinsky company, which needed a *premier danseur* of his merits. Tikhomirov, however, used every means to return to Moscow. Pleading that the damp climate of Petersburg had an ill effect on his health (in reality he was as strong as an athlete) he obtained a transfer back to Moscow. There he became a member of the Bolshoi ballet company beginning with September 1, 1893, and on the same date had his début in a difficult *pas de deux* (with his classmate of the Moscow days, Lyubov Roslavleva) interpolated into the one-act ballet, *Robert and Bertram* (music by Schmidt, new choreography by Mendes).

Soon afterwards he started teaching at the school, at first quite unofficially. The Moscow Inspector Tcheremukhin, on whose initiative Tikhomirov was sent to Petersburg for perfectioning, asked him to pass on the knowledge acquired to the school. Tikhomirov was only too happy to show his gratitude in this way. He started teaching enthusiastically, preparing himself in every possible way for the difficult profession of a teacher, which was to become one of the main activities of his life. He studied the history of ballet and anatomy. He did something quite unprecedented when he asked the Moscow University for permission to attend lectures of the famous physiologist, Ivan Sechenov, the founder of the Russian school of Physiology.

When Tikhomirov returned to Moscow in 1893, the Moscow school was still living a very patriarchal life. The teachers did not spare much effort and the pupils worked very hard. Old Nikitin and Yermolov taught dressed in tail coats, slowly tinkling primitive rhythmic accompaniment on their tiny violins—relics of an old tradition.

Old ballet dancers of the Bolshoi remembered for many years afterwards Tikhomirov's first appearance in class. He was clad in a neat ballet costume with short breeches and white shirt. His feet were shod in ballet shoes. Moreover, he brought with him an accompanist and the tinkling of violins was never heard again—at any rate not in his class. In the course of his lessons Tikhomirov widely applied what he had learnt in Petersburg, introducing much that was his own, and working out a system that yielded excellent results. Teaching both boys and girls, Tikhomirov strictly distinguished between the method in both classes and never imposed on male dancers an effeminate and affected manner. He demanded great plastic expressiveness from all his pupils, but maintained that the plastic expressiveness of men and women should be different. Possessing an enormous erudition and the gift of composition, he never repeated a class, and many of his *enchaînements*, which he liked to compose around a definite set of steps for the day, were worth seeing as a spectacle.

In 1896, after having taught unofficially (and without pay) for a couple of years, Tikhomirov became a member of the school staff (and eventually its director). His work yielded results in a short time: in 1898 he danced in the new ballet *Stars*, by Ivan Clustine, the role of Mars, with technical prowess unprecedented on the Bolshoi stage of those years, being surrounded by four of his pupils, all to become, in turn, outstanding male dancers of the twentieth century. Mikhail Mordkin was one of them.

Tikhomirov's own career as a dancer, long and brilliant, served for ever as an example to his numerous pupils. There was something of a lion in his great soaring leaps, though in reality he was not endowed with great elevation. His figure was that of an athlete of ancient Greece. When he first appeared in Gorsky's *The Dance Dream* at the Alhambra Theatre, London (1911), British newspapers wrote that suffragettes would have readily given up their "man-hating", had they seen Tikhomirov dance. Of the numerous roles performed by Tikhomirov in classical ballets, the noble knight Jean de Brienne (*Raymonda*) and the pirate Conrad from *Le Corsaire*, whom Tikhomirov made into a truly Byronic character, were particularly memorable. He was a classically perfect Phoebus in *La Esmeralda*, a manly Ta Hor in *Pharaoh's Daughter*.

It was Tikhomirov who created the special "Moscow style" of male dancing, manly and heroic, a style that was to be cleverly utilized by Gorsky in his productions. Tikhomirov trained the constellation of male dancers adorning the Moscow ballet at the beginning of the twentieth century—Mordkin, Novikov, Volinin, Fyedor and Alexei Kozlov, Zhukov, Ivan and Victor Smoltsov.

Anna Pavlova preferred to chose partners from among the Moscow ballet—their great plastic expressiveness and style, their sense of characterization were much closer to her own ideas than the academically routine Petersburg ballet at the turn of the century. For one season (1914) Tikhomirov himself was her partner, and he might have stayed on in Pavlova's company, but hastened to return to Russia.

As a teacher Tikhomirov did not limit himself to dancing. He formed a long line of ballerinas, among them being Caralli, Balashova, Makletsova, Krieger, Reisen, and the famous *pas de quatre* of the early twenties— Abramova, Bank, Kudriavtseva, and Podgoretskaya. Each of these dancers possessed an individual quality of her own.

Tikhomirov's main works as choreographer belong to the period after the Revolution, and will be considered in another chapter.

His role in the preservation of the Russian school of classical ballet and the continuation of its great traditions through a period when even the company's right to existence was being questioned, can hardly be exaggerated.

With the great reserve of talent being regularly supplied to the Bolshoi company by the school, ballet in Moscow could not cease existing in spite of the repeated efforts of the Directorate of the Imperial Theatres. On the other hand the talents needed an outlet that could not be found in the stale and mediocre repertory and the musty atmosphere of the Bolshoi Theatre during Mendes' term of service.

On April 30, 1898, Mendes was officially released from his duties by a written order signed by Vsevolojsky.

Mendes was the last foreign choreographer to head the company in Moscow. The new Director of the Moscow Office of the Imperial Theatres, Vladimir Teliakovsky (1861-1924), held that post from 1898 to 1901. He was much more interested in the arts than his predecessor Pchelnikov. His appointment looked, on the surface, quite unsuitable— he was a retired cavalry colonel, and this gave rise to new quips about infantry having surrendered to cavalry so far as the governing of fine arts in Moscow was concerned. But in reality Teliakovsky was not as unsuited to the position as it seemed. While still in the army, he seriously studied pianoforte and even the composition and theory of music. He came from an enlightened family that maintained contact with many artists and composers, including Tchaikovsky. In his youth Teliakovsky played on two grand pianos with Nicolai Rubinstein, the illustrious director of the Moscow Conservatoire.

During his long career—first as Director of the Moscow Office, and, from 1901, as the last Director of the Imperial Theatres as a whole, Teliakovsky kept a diary that now serves as a valuable source of study for materials on the history of Russian ballet in the twentieth century.[1]

While Teliakovsky could not have been responsible personally for the changes in the Moscow ballet, he was, however, capable of understanding the lively creative atmosphere that existed at the time of his appointment in Moscow—at the newly-born Art Theatre, in the Mamontov private Opera that was the first to exploit the genius of Chaliapin, an atmosphere felt everywhere, with the exception of the Bolshoi ballet. Something had to be done about it. To begin with, the company needed a new ballet-master.

Ivan Clustine (1862-1941), apart from being a very good dancer in the *danseur noble* style that did not find sufficient application in the predominately *demi-caractère* repertory of the Moscow ballet, had already shown some pronounced choreographic abilities. He created many *variations* for dancers taking part in the pedestrian Mendes ballets, and staged in January 1898, his own version of the Polovetsian dances in *Prince Igor*, which received very favourable notices.

On January 21, 1898, Clustine presented his first four-act ballet *Stars* to music by the Bolshoi composer, A. Simon. The scenario by Karl Waltz, which set the theme in the eighteenth century, did not offer anything new. The story was connected with the delusions of Count de Castro (portrayed by Clustine himself) who fell in love with the Star Venus (Lyubov Roslavleva), forgetting his bride, Clairemonde (Adelina Giuri). In the course of his dreams the Count saw visions of stars that afforded the opportunity for staging a varied *divertissement*—we already mentioned the sensational appearance of Tikhomirov as Mars with his four pupils,

---

[1] The complete diary of 16,000 pages is preserved in the manuscript department of the Bakhrushin Theatre Museum, Moscow. Parts of it have appeared in: V. Teliakovsky. *Memoirs.* Vremia Publishing House, Petrograd, 1924, and: V. Teliakovsky. *Imperial Theatres and the year of 1905.* Academia Publishing House, Leningrad, 1926.

while the sisters Mendes as the Double Star turned around each other in a rapid succession of *pirouettes*. In the spectacular scene of the Stars, the Queen of Night descended from the skies in a chariot pulled by gigantic butterflies. Live stars were placed in each wing, shaped in the form of the crescent of the moon.

In the final act there was a *divertissement* of Wines, arranged by Clustine as a suite of character dances that might have been out of place in the eighteenth-century castle (the Don Wine was represented by a Cossack dance, and the Caucasian one by a Circassian), but introduced a medium that had not been exploited in the Moscow ballet for some time.

There was also, in the first act, an impressive *pas de trois* in the romantic style, in which the Count danced with his fiancée, but was constantly disturbed by the vision of Venus, seen by him alone.

A year later Clustine showed another big ballet, *Magic Dreams*, using a Russian fairy-tale story about two peasant children lost in the woods and involved in the struggle of Frost with Spring. The story was by M. Popello-Davydov, a Russian writer with a poetic imagination, and the music was by a young composer, Yuri Pomerantsev. Pomerantsev was far from being a new Tchaikovsky, nor was Clustine experienced or talented enough to inspire the composer and teach him, in collaboration, the rudiments of ballet composition.

Magic Dreams did not prove successful, either musically or choreographically. Clustine, unable to find adequate form and idiom for the Russian theme of the ballet, resorted to the well tried methods of the *féerie*.

It was not Clustine who was destined to turn a new page in the life of the Moscow ballet, although the authorities were willing to retain him and he was even commissioned to create a new production of *Swan Lake*.

Illness prevented Clustine from completing even the production of *Don Quixote* upon which he was engaged, neither was he particularly interested from any point of view in the post of choreographer.[1] The times called for an innovator, and such a one did arrive in the person of Gorsky.

Alexander Gorsky (1871-1924) was born in Petersburg. His father was a book-keeper and the boy's early years might have been passed in a most uninspiring atmosphere. As it was, Gorsky's father was occupied in

[1] Clustine retired after having celebrated his twentieth jubilee of service in the Imperial Theatres in January 1899. He spent the second half of his career abroad, as *maître de ballet* at the Paris Opéra in 1903-1904, and in the same position for the Pavlova company, 1914-1922.

book-keeping for his livelihood. In his spare time he liked to visit picture galleries, to paint a little, and to embroider whole pictures in silk with such dexterity and art that they were accepted at exhibitions. The boy became interested in painting and tried to follow his father.

At the age of eight Gorsky's parents decided to place him at the Commercial School in Petersburg. His health was weak, and they thought that book-keeping, a profession not requiring great physical effort, would be a suitable, quiet occupation for the frail child. They also had a daughter. The mother decided to make use of an old acquaintance, O. B. Adams, then *inspectrice* of the Petersburg Ballet School, and ask for her help in placing her daughter at the school. They went along with the son. After the girl had been accepted, the *inspectrice* inquired about the graceful boy, with his curly hair and blue eyes. The mother answered that they had already filed a petition about him at the Commercial School on the way to Theatre Street. The *inspectrice* said that this could be arranged and that the children would be happier learning together. She obtained the permission of Frolov, director of the school, and the boy's fate was settled.

So it happened that in the autumn of 1880 Gorsky entered the Theatre School as a paying pupil in the class of Platon Karsavin. In a year's time Gorsky was entered on the list of state-supported pupils for excellent progress in all studies. He graduated in 1889 from the class of Marius Petipa into the *corps de ballet* of the Mariinsky Theatre. There he was a witness of and a participant in the creation of *The Sleeping Beauty*. Having started with insignificant parts, Gorsky was soon entrusted with good roles. In those first years he danced, both in the purely classical style (Prince Fortune in *The Sleeping Beauty*, Aquilon in *The Awakening of Flora*) and in character and grotesque numbers such as the Satyr in *Tannhäuser*, Genie of the Wood in *Le Diable à Quatre*, and the "Chinese Dance" in *The Nutcracker*. In 1895 he was made second soloist and received leading roles in *La Fille Mal Gardée* and *The Magic Flute*.

The young dancer purposely attempted all styles and was also praised for being a good mime. He was dissatisfied with the career of a dancer and was ever trying to extend his activities. He formed a lasting friendship with Vladimir Stepanov (1866-1896), author of an original dance notation system based on musical symbols. Stepanov obtained permission to attend lectures in anatomy at the Petersburg University and was helped by the famous professor Lesgaft in working out his *Alphabet of movements of the human body*. In 1891 Stepanov went to Paris, where several scientists, including the celebrated Charcot, showed interest in his invention. In

"Fruits of a ballet strike". Cartoon by Miguel, Petersburg, 1905.

The cartoon is concerned with the events that took place in the Petersburg ballet during the Revolution of 1905. Nicolai Sergeyev, *régisseur* of the Petersburg company, is shown holding the artists' "petition", in which they dared to enumerate their claims. Teliakovsky, Director of the Imperial Theatres, is shown sitting in a baby-chair. Krupensky, official of the Imperial Theatres, is dressed in woman's Boyard costume. Pavel Gerdt (who withdrew his signature from the petition) is shown in a court dress. In the centre of the cartoon Olga Preobrajenskaya is being flogged. (Reproduced from *Materials for the History of Russian Ballet*, Volume II, page 120.)

Corner of the drawing-room in the Diaghilev ancestral home, Perm, *circa* 1880. (Collection of Natalia Roslavleva)

spite of untold material hardships (he fainted in his hotel from malnutrition) Stepanov succeeded in publishing a French description of his system,[1] dedicating it to the Theatre School. Upon returning to Petersburg he attained only partial recognition after many years of hardship. However, his system was entered on the syllabus of the Petersburg school and some successful recordings of ballets made. In 1895 Stepanov was sent to teach notation at the Moscow school. There he contracted pneumonia; his exhausted organism was unable to combat it, and on January 16, 1896, he died in hospital. He had many friends in the Petersburg company. *Premier danseur* Oblakov paid his debts. Alexander Gorsky apparently considered it his moral duty to continue in Stepanov's steps. He made a thorough study of his system and prepared, together with the pupils of the Petersburg school, a one-act ballet *Clorinda, Queen of the Mountain Fairies* (music by E. Keller), the parts of which were learnt from notation in the course of the scholastic year. This ballet was shown in a graduation performance at the Mikhailovsky Theatre on April 11, 1899. Gorsky succeeded in publishing, at the expense of the Petersburg school, a brief résumé in Russian of the Stepanov system.[2]

Gorsky asked the Directorate of the Imperial Theatres for 800 roubles and two assistants in order to notate the whole of *The Sleeping Beauty*. His request was not granted. Then he recorded *The Sleeping Beauty* on his own initiative. In 1898, when the new management of the Bolshoi Theatre in Moscow wanted to include Tchaikovsky ballets in its repertory, Gorsky was delegated to mount *The Sleeping Beauty* from his records, with the help of the Stepanov notation.

This mission turned a new leaf in Gorsky's life.

When he arrived in Moscow he found there an artistic atmosphere that was a great contrast to St. Petersburg. Life in general, and that of the theatre in particular, was less conventional and more democratic than that of Imperial Petersburg. The first All-Russian Congress of Artists, convened unofficially in 1897, was a great event in theatre life.

Gorsky came into contact with the Art Theatre that had just been opened by Stanislavsky and Nemirovich-Danchenko. He saw the remarkable productions of the Mamontov private Opera that had invited such

[1] "J. Stepanov", Artiste des Théâtres Impériaux de Saint Petersbourg, *Alphabet des Mouvements du Corps Humain*, Essai d'enregistrement des mouvements du corps humain au moyen des signes musicaux. Paris, 1892.

[2] *Tablitsa znakov dlia zapisyvania dvijeniy chelovecheskogo tela po systeme artista imperatorskikh S. Peterburghskikh teatrov V. I. Stepanov.* Isdanie Imperatorskogo S. Peterburgskogo Teatralnogo Uchilishcha, SPB, 1899.

outstanding painters as Korovine and Golovine as its decorative artists.

The criterion of the Art Theatre consisted in showing the "truth of life" in scenic images. Its founders wanted to create a *public* theatre accessible to everyone and recognized as its own by the democratic intelligentsia. This new "art of truth" greatly impressed Gorsky. After having achieved the staging of *The Sleeping Beauty* in three weeks, Gorsky came back to Petersburg with unforgettable impressions of Moscow. He returned in a year (in the course of which he danced in Budapest and visited Vienna, Paris, London, and Berlin) to produce Petipa's *Raymonda*, in collaboration with Clustine. Such productions, however, introduced only a temporary improvement in the repertory of the Bolshoi Theatre. Something much more radical was needed.

Though he was promoted as from September 1, 1900, to the rank of first soloist, and could have stayed on in Petersburg as a dancer, Gorsky readily accepted the offer that followed in the same month, to become *régisseur* of the Moscow company. While this did not authorize him to create his own ballets (and in the first part of his work in Moscow Gorsky had to content himself with giving new readings to old ones) he was able, however, to apply his artistic ideas, thoroughly developed by that time, on a much broader scale than he might have expected in Petersburg. In the course of his previous trips to Moscow Gorsky became acquainted with all spheres of its cultural life. Apart from the Art Theatre and the Mamontov Opera, the great tradition of the Maly Theatre was being maintained by such brilliant actors as Yermolova, Fedotova, Lensky, Sumbatov-Yuzhin, and the Sadovsky family. The Moscow University, which was closely bound with the theatre at all periods of its existence, continued this contact through the outstanding personalities of Professors Kliuchevsky and Kovalevsky, their lectures being attended not only by students of the University. Moscow was seething with literary groups of a progressive nature. Chekhov lived in Moscow, Gorky frequently came there. Everything they wrote was immediately seized upon, studied and discussed. In Abramtsevo, the Mamontov estate some sixty miles away from Moscow, there was a group of talented painters with Serov and Vrubel almost permanent members, while Repin frequently came from Petersburg for the entire summer. The canvases of Korovine, Levitan, Vrubel, and Serov presented a daring riot of colours or novelty of deeply searching themes at exhibitions of easel painting. The young Leonid Sobinov and Antonina Nezhdanova, the great Fyodor Chaliapin, now readily engaged anew by the Imperial Theatres following his successes at the Mamontov Opera, rang a new note even in the stale routine of the

Bolshoi Theatre opera productions. . . . The ballet alone seemed to be immune to all these novelties and took no part whatsoever in this general enlivening of Russian art.

Gorsky was thoroughly aware of this and considered the task doubly interesting because of the difficulties it entailed. There were times when only one-third of the Bolshoi Theatre auditorium was filled on ballet Sundays and Wednesdays.

For his first assignment in the new position (virtually it amounted to that of ballet-master of the Moscow company) Gorsky was invited to revive Petipa's *Don Quixote* with the right of introducing any changes he desired. Ivan Clustine was supposed to have collaborated with Gorsky on this production but pleaded sickness at the very beginning, apparently failing to understand Gorsky's far-reaching plans. Indeed, the choreographer decided to break with all accepted clichés of ballet and create a new production based on the new principles of the Art Theatre. Gorsky was the first to treat the *corps de ballet* and the whole ensemble on the stage as members of a choreographic drama, according to the principles of Stanislavsky, expecting them to act and be natural. Instead of frozen symmetrical lines of the *corps de ballet* he presented a living crowd. Every actor was given a task, however small. The impersonators of the fruit seller, the barber on the *piazza* of the first act, the inn-keeper—all knew not only what to do but the why and the wherefore of it. This made a great impression on the company and immediately brought Gorsky many staunch followers and no smaller number of enemies and opponents.

It sounds surprising today, but even the colourful and realistic settings of the young designers, Korovine and Golovine, were criticized for being supposedly quite unsuitable. For the first time the square in Barcelona represented real-life sunlit stone of Spain in a white and bright-blue colour scheme by Golovine. The tavern by night in the next scene was conceived by Korovine with brightly coloured costumes contrasted with subdued lighting. The third, fantastic act, with its scene in the woods followed immediately by Don Quixote's dream of Dulcinea surrounded by Dryads, was again designed by Golovine.

Every costume was designed in accordance with the style of the period and the country concerned. There was no question of the casual attire that was customary for ballet performances of previous years.

What Gorsky had done in ballet amounted to a reform carried out four years before Fokine had conceived his own innovations, and eight years before he had the opportunity to implement them.

Gorsky met great difficulties at the beginning of his work in the

Moscow ballet. Those who were in favour of the old tradition and failed to see the value and importance of Gorsky's novelties met changes in the old *Don Quixote* either with caution or direct hostility. There were plenty of conservatives outside the company in theatrical circles. Gorsky's first act in *Don Quixote*, that lives to this day in the Bolshoi ballet's repertory, was pronounced to be "a mess having nothing to do with ballet".

And only the younger part of the company, eager for the new, happy to work with a choreographer who knew his mission and was ready to explain it to them and make them share in it, enthusiastically stood up for Gorsky. At this time Gorsky made a speech to the company in which he summed up his artistic credo. This speech was not recorded, but some notes by Gorsky preserved in the Bolshoi Theatre Museum apparently refer to that occasion. This is what Gorsky wrote: "There are many people in the ballet profession who love art not for art's sake, but because *they* take part in it. Do these people bring any good, do they develop art and forward it? Alas, of course they don't. Eveything they do is done for their own benefit. They have no concern for the meaning of art, for its roots. . . ."[1]

In his reminiscences about Gorsky's early activity in Moscow, Vladimir Ryabtsev (1880-1945), the well-known mime, said: "We, at that time very young artists, sooner felt, rather than understood, that Gorsky was right and readily followed him."[2]

Margarita Vassilieva, the incomparable performer of the leading role in Gorsky's *Les Petits Riens* (1922), thus spoke of Gorsky's method of work: "He always arrived at rehearsals with the score under his arm, with every scene quite ready and worked out, with sketches for separate dances and a complete plan of the whole production. And when work actually started, one only had to see his burning eyes, his state of creative fervour that seemed to possess him completely, to the oblivion of everything else."[3]

Gorsky endeavoured to improve the repertory of the Bolshoi Theatre with ballets to great music. When he undertook a new production of *Swan Lake* in January 1901, he was unanimously pronounced crazy— for since the failure of all the previous versions of that ballet, it was considered unsuited for the stage. Gorsky himself recalled: "I was predicted complete failure with *Swan Lake*."[4] In reality it proved to be a favourite of the public for many years to come. Gorsky carried out five

[1] Quoted from: Yuri Bakhrushin. *A. A. Gorsky*. Iskusstvo, Moscow, 1946, p. 19.
[2] *Op. cit.*, p. 20.   [3] *Op. cit.*, p. 20.   [4] *Op. cit.*, p. 22.

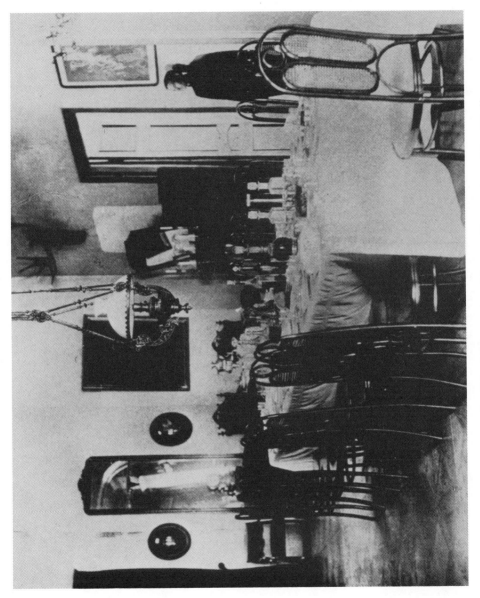

Dining-room in the Diaghilev ancestral home, Perm, *circa* 1880. (Collection of Natalia Roslavleva)

Corner of the two-tiered ballroom in the Diaghilev ancestral home, Perm, 1880. Grand-piano used by Sergei Diaghilev. (Collection of Natalia Roslavleva)

productions of *Swan Lake* in the course of his life. In the production of 1901 he preserved the general outline of the Petersburg production, being fully aware of its merits. The greatest changes were introduced into the first act, to which he added a lively scene of revels on the occasion of the Prince's birthday. As in *Don Quixote*, each character was given a task to fulfil, and many colourful *mises en scène* appeared in *Swan Lake* for the first time, to remain in the Moscow productions of the ballet as a tradition. There was more logic of action, more attention to the content, in Gorsky's reading of *Swan Lake*, and this was observed by the more unbiased critics. As to Lev Ivanov's second act, Gorsky only slightly changed the pattern of the choreography and arranged a dance for six, rather than four, small swans, probably because of the dimensions of the Bolshoi stage. The role of the Jester, now introduced in practically all of the versions of *Swan Lake*, was created by Gorsky in 1920 for the brilliant dancer, Vassily Yefimov.

In 1901 Gorsky produced five more ballets, all with great success. The old *Hump-Backed Horse* was particularly popular; again it got a realistic reading, was charged with humour and action, had many new original character dances by Gorsky and a brilliantly choreographed new classical suite of "Nereids". It was not so easy for Gorsky to attain the desired effects: the supers used in those days were completely untrained. More often than not the "crowd" was formed by some 150 soldiers brought from the barracks for the occasion and standing in strict formation. Gorsky despaired of getting any life into the picturesque market scene of the first act. He would don a bright gown over his suit, come out on to the stage and start pushing the soldiers about. They would turn, complain at being knocked about, and push back—and the crowd looked much more animated!

Gorksy's work in Moscow could no longer miss the attention of the Directorate of the Imperial Theatres. At the beginning of 1902, he was officially nominated ballet-master of the Moscow Bolshoi Theatre. His version of *Don Quixote* was simultaneously transferred to the Mariinsky Theatre, where it caused even greater resistance on the part of the company and the critics than it had in Moscow.

But Gorsky paid no heed to these attacks. He was carried away by the idea of a new creation. No longer was he obliged to mount old ballets in a new way, but had the right to create something of his own. Ever since *Don Quixote* Gorsky wanted to compose a ballet on the theme of Hugo's *Notre Dame de Paris*. He did not want to repeat the old *Esmeralda* in any way and, in the effort to bring his ballet closer to Hugo, entitled it

Gudule's Daughter. He conceived it as a "mimodrama with dances", following the principles of the Art Theatre production to a greater extent than in any of his previous works.

The book was written by Gorsky after a careful study of historical material and a trip to Paris made in the summer of 1902, together with Konstantin Korovine, designer of the ballet. The music was specially commissioned from A. Simon, a Bolshoi theatre musician and composer. The première took place on November 24, 1902, and caused a new wave of indignation. When one reads the accusations directed at Gorsky's new work by contemporary criticism, they serve as a vivid proof of the work's merits: "Ballet with a realistic menacing crowd. . . . Ballet, that required conferences with archaeologists. . . . This is the Art Theatre. This is like Stanislavsky! This is an undermining of the very fundamentals of ballet. Its carefree art has been turned into a chronicle of human suffering. The scene of Esmeralda's death has upset all the tried rules of the art of choreography. Go away with your 'Stanislavsky Esmeralda'." There were many other expressions of indignation at the realistic scenes in *Gudule's Daughter*, that were justified only to some extent. Gorsky at times overdid realism to the point of naturalism, contrary, indeed, to the very nature of ballet, and used the medium of pantomime more often than dancing. But the critics somehow neglected to mention the classical suite "Time", consisting of eighteen numbers danced by leading soloists of the company in the castle of Fleur de Lys.

If Gorsky had not possessed a suitable dancer for the title-role he would probably never have attempted this work. But he did have an Esmeralda such as he had conceived her, in the person of Sophia Fedorova.

Sophia Fedorova II[1] (1879-1963) graduated from the Moscow school in 1899. Her mother, daughter of a serf theatre actress by the owner of the estate, had to struggle with poverty, having five children on her hands. The widowed woman opened a small laundry establishment but it did not provide enough means to support a large family. Some friends advised her to place the children at the Theatre School. Thus it happened that no less than three of them—Olga, Sophia, and Fedor found their way into the ballet.

Sophia's talent was observed by Gorsky immediately upon graduation, he noticed her expressive face and enormous wistful eyes while she was

[1] Her sister, Olga, graduated earlier—hence the "II" added to the name. It was done by order of succession of graduates and concerned namesakes, not relatives. Coryphée V. Pavlova I was not related to the famous ballerina Anna Pavlova II.

still in the *corps de ballet*. In her he found the ideal actress of his dreams: musical, temperamental, inspired, and possessing an expressive *plastique* that was very much valued by this master.

In the sphere of character dancing Fedorova II had no peer. Her Wife of the Khan and, particularly, the "Tartar Dance" (both in *The Hump-Backed Horse*), the Slave Hita in Gorsky's version of *Pharaoh's Daughter*, the Snake-charmer in *Salammbô* were unforgettable. She also danced classical roles: Lise in *La Fille Mal Gardée*, Giselle in Gorsky's original version of that ballet (1911) wherein the action was placed in the Directoire period with appropriate costumes; while only illness (she suffered from nervous breakdowns) prevented her from making the expected appearance as Odette-Odile.

However, Fedorova's most memorable part (not counting the Polovetsian Girl created for the original Fokine production in the Paris season of 1909), was that of Esmeralda in *Gudule's Daughter*. In the execution scene, she was dressed in rags, a tiny tortured woman with a huge candle roughly put in her hands by the executioner. Around her neck was a thick rope, dragging after her with each of her steps. Her numb fingers were no longer able to hold the candle and it fell to the ground. But with every faltering step her face gained greater and greater spiritual calm. She seemed to be seeing something, that the rest of the crowd was not given to see. The climax of this scene came when soldiers tore Esmeralda out of the arms of her mother Gudule, who had just found her lost child. Esmeralda's slim body was thrown about from one soldier to another while some of the crowd tried to win her back. It is important to note that Gorsky used here for the first time high lifts, bordering on acrobatics, that were ahead of his time—he was very much criticized for "risking the health of the ballerina". In spite of the intense difficulties of this scene Fedorova remained the Esmeralda she was playing. She continued portraying the tortured half-child, half-woman, with terror and suffering in her eyes and a mouth that seemed to emit silent cries.

Gorsky considered *Gudule's Daughter* to be one of his most important creations. It was a complete work with the title-role created on and for an ideal protagonist. Circumstances prevented Gorsky from working with Fedorova on many more roles. After her great success as the Polovetsian Girl, and as Ta-Hor in *Cleopatra*, she took part in every Diaghilev season up to 1913 inclusively. Grave illness, connected with a nervous disorder, inherited from her tragic grandmother, cut her career short. She developed acute stage fright and retired from the Bolshoi Theatre. Although she spent two years (1925 and 1926) in the Anna Pavlova Company and danced the Polovetsian Girl in a Diaghilev Paris season of 1928 (at the age of 49), in the course of her life abroad (where she went in 1922 for reasons of health) Sophia Fedorova had no active dancing career. She spent her last years in Paris, at first in a nursing home, and then living quietly in complete retirement, and only periodically recovering full mental capacity.

Gorsky's other major created work was *Salammbô*, after Flaubert's novel of the same title. He again sought a subject of high dramatic tension. In *Salammbô* Gorsky applied the principles of a "mimed drama" first revealed in *Gudule's Daughter*, but this time he created a different kind of spectacle. He worked on *Salammbô* for six months (to his own book) in unity with Konstantin Korovine, the designer, and Andrei Arends (1855-1924), the composer of the music. While Arends was not endowed with an outstanding talent for composition he was a highly professional musician, a pupil of Tchaikovsky's class in composition at the Moscow Conservatoire. He started his career in 1889 as conductor of the Maly dramatic theatre, but frequently performed at the Bolshoi. He was appointed chief ballet conductor in 1900 and held this post for almost a quarter of a century (he died in 1924). He understood Gorsky's ideas and inclinations, and this understanding, coupled with a fine professional knowledge of ballet, brought about a truly fruitful collaboration between Arends and Gorsky.

The première of *Salammbô* on January 10, 1910, was again accompanied by mixtures of attack and admiration. Gorsky had carried his reforming activity much further in this work. He completely gave up *tutus* and, on his suggestion, the dancers were dressed in appropriate stylized long robes. Some of the *corps de ballet* danced in sandals—a thing unprecedented in Russian ballet. There were no traditional *divertissements*, no sterotyped *pas de deux*, no *variations*. Instead, Gorsky created a unique spectacle, dramatically charged and telling the story of Salammbô, Princess of Carthage, in impressive and colourful scenes abounding in what the choreographer himself termed "mimodrama". The importance of *Salammbô* lay in the unity of the production.

Salammbô—the heroine of the ballet—was created by Yekaterina Geltser, and the production succeeded to a great extent because of the famous dancer-actress. Gorsky admitted: "Ballet owes much to Yekaterina Geltser." She readily went ahead along new paths. Her appearance in *Salammbô* served as an impetus for this turn towards a new trend.

Participation in *Salammbô* certainly presented new and complicated artistic problems to each of the protagonists. The ballet started with a feast of mercenaries in the gardens of Hamilkar, Salammbô's father. When it grew to the dimensions of a riotous orgy, Geltser-Salammbô appeared at the top of a huge staircase in the centre of the stage and slowly descended from it, holding a small black lyre. A long black robe with a large red mantle on her shoulders gave her a majestic appearance. The golden chain binding her feet made her step even more measured and serene. Her face was lit with inspiration. In this scene, purely mimetic, it was extremely difficult to convey its content and only an actress of Geltser's merits was capable of making the necessary impact in an almost static pose. This episode was considered by the critics to be one of the best in the whole ballet.

While everything in Gorsky's production was interrelated and each scene was important in its way, the climax came in the love duet between Salammbô and Matho (Mikhail Mordkin) when the Princess of Carthage stole into Matho's tent in the enemy's camp in order to retrieve the magic veil of the goddess Tanit. In the *adagio* the choreographer wanted to show that, for Matho, Salammbô was more than a woman of his desires—she was a supreme being, whom he was ready to worship.

This *mise en scène* was beautifully enacted by Geltser and Mordkin who formed a remarkable partnership. But it had to be first conceived by Gorsky the choreographer.

Salammbô, as conceived by Gorsky and interpreted by Geltser, was a heroic, full-blooded character, leaving far behind the impassive priestess, Tanit, Goddess of the Moon, coming from the pen of Flaubert. An equally human character was Matho as created by Mordkin.

Mikhail Mordkin (1881-1944), graduating from the class of Vassily Tikhomirov in 1899, received from that great teacher, like the group of other male dancers adorning the Bolshoi theatre at the beginning of the twentieth century, a solid classical training coupled with that manly *plastique* that was the hallmark of Tikhomirov-trained aritsts. But, as an artist, Mordkin was formed by Gorsky. His temperament and dramatic talent found a full application in the Gorsky ballets. He was equally good in classical roles, and, as a matter of fact, had his début at the Bolshoi Theatre as Siegfried in *Swan Lake*. He created Albrecht in Gorsky's version of *Giselle*, where greater stress was laid on the disguise of the fickle Count in the first act, and Mordkin presented him as a simple peasant. In every new role Mordkin looked for psychological motivation, giving his own version even in classical ballets. With great feeling of plastic beauty he performed the role of Petronius in Gorsky's *Eunice and*

Petronius (1915), a ballet wherein the idiom was very much influenced by Isadora Duncan, whose art had made a lasting impact on Gorsky.

Mordkin took part in the first Paris season of the Russian Ballet and was Pavlova's partner in 1910. He attempted his own choreography with *Axiade* in 1912 (to music by Hertel). In later years, in the "Mordkin Ballet", founded in 1926 in the United States, he introduced many motifs of Gorsky's choreography into his own productions, for instance, *The Goldfish*, directly inspired by Gorsky's ballet of the same title. Mordkin remained true to Gorsky's principles of dramatic truth in ballet to the end of his days, and, while being unable to march in step with modern trends in ballet, passed on these valuable precepts to his American pupils who, in turn, founded the "American Ballet Theatre".

Some of Gorsky's works created shortly before World War I showed the influence of *art nouveau*. His last version of *Raymonda* (1908) had "dances in colour" entitled *"en blanc"*, *"en orange"*, *"en bleu"*. He was the first to use music of a whole symphony for dance visualization, by producing a ballet to Glasunov's *Fifth Symphony* in 1916.

Gorsky's work was less well known abroad than that of Fokine. *The Dance Dream* commissioned for the Alhambra music hall in 1911 was composed, for the most part, in the old tradition and to a medley of music. The choreographer had to work with the Alhambra *corps de ballet*, who could not possibly implement anything more serious or artistic. But Diaghilev had invited Gorsky in 1913 to stage a ballet for his company to Tcherepnin's *The Red Masks*, and only the composer's failure to complete the score in time coupled with the advent of the war in 1914 prevented the presentation of a Gorsky ballet in Western Europe.

Gorsky's significance in the history of Russian ballet is immense. He was the first Russian choreographer with a definite artistic programme that made a significant imprint on the whole history of ballet. He led the Moscow ballet out of a blind alley to the position of a mature artistic ensemble capable of seriously competing with the ballet in Petersburg.

Although an innovator and fighter against routine, Gorsky was ever ready to preserve and revere all that was truly precious in the classical legacy.

CHAPTER VIII

THE IMPERIAL BALLET IN ITS HEYDAY AND THE EMERGENCE OF FOKINE

THE EARLY YEARS of the twentieth century found the Petersburg ballet in a state of uncertainty. There was a strong and beautifully trained company. A varied repertory contained over fifty ballets including such gems of the classical ballet as *La Fille Mal Gardée, Le Corsaire, Giselle, Esmeralda, The Naiad and the Fisherman, et alia*, that otherwise would have been lost for ever because their choreography was forgotten in the country of their creation.[1] These ballets were given in Petipa versions that in turn became classical models, to a greater extent, perhaps, than the originals.

Petipa's own monumental creations, *Pharaoh's Daughter, King Candaules, La Bayadère, The Sleeping Beauty,* and *Swan Lake,* which was only partly his, were also carefully preserved in the Mariinsky Theatre even after its doors were closed to the venerable choreographer.

Had Petipa returned, he could not have improved the situation. His time was over. The Petersburg ballet was in desperate need of a leader with definite artistic ideas, and the ideas themselves had to be new. A new generation was growing up both inside and outside the ballet that realized full well the necessity for drastic reforms. Towards the turn of the nineteenth century the artistic and cultural activities were more developed in Moscow. But it could not fail to be felt in Petersburg.

The air of the pending 1905 Revolution penetrated even beyond the musty windows in Theatre Street, however strictly guarded from reality were its wards. There was a pronounced feeling of unrest in the Mariinsky company. From early childhood ballet dancers had been kept away from progressive thought, from advancing developments in their country. Their outlook was usually limited to what took place within the enclosure of the school and, later, the theatre they worked in.

Now interests were rapidly expanding. Some dancers, desiring to

---

[1] *Giselle*, for instance, was shown for the last time at the Paris Opéra in 1868. Its revival in 1924 for Olga Spesivtseva became possible only because of a dance score (notated after the Stepanov system) of the Coralli–Perrot–Petipa version from the Mariinsky theatre repertory that was in the possession of Nicolai Sergeyev, former *régisseur* of the Petersburg company.

improve their range of knowledge, attended the Petersburg University as external students, others did the same at the Conservatoire. A group of six joined the Dramatic Courses of the Theatre School, and two women entered the Bestuzhev Higher Courses that were founded in those years as a result of a long campaign for the right of the weaker sex to higher education.

In the period just preceding the 1905 Revolution the Directorate of the Imperial Theatres was obliged to permit at least some public activity among the artists. They were allowed to open a kind of mutual aid bank that in reality collected funds in order to purchase books and help workers. An officially sponsored Philanthropic Society opened a Gogol School in Greblovo (a village near Petersburg). They gave concerts in order to support the school. Officials from the Directorate were placed at the head of this Society in order to prevent the penetration of anything radical. Yet in a short time the police reported that a group of artists taking part in the formation of the Gogol School in Greblovo (hence they were called "Greblovtsy") had its own library containing political literature that was being spread among members of the company.

It is significant that the most active organizers of the Greblovo school, Pyotr Mikhailov (1883-?) and Valentin Presniakov (1877-1956), were among the first to lead the strike of dancers in 1905, and it is also significant that political unrest during the revolutionary events took place mostly in the ballet company of the Mariinsky Theatre, the opera remaining practically immune to any political influence.

Mikhailov headed the elected council of the Mariinsky ballet and directed the strike. Presniakov was also among its initiators. Both were discharged from the Imperial Theatres.[1] Teliakovsky, the Director, tried to prove that only the talentless and the mediocre were among the dissenters. In reality they included Olga Preobrajenskaya, the brilliant *prima ballerina* at that time having reached the summit of her career, and great young talents in the persons of Anna Pavlova, Mikhail Fokine, Tamara Karsavina and Sergei Legat.

Sergei Legat (1875-1905) was one of the most gifted dancers of the new generation. Equally good in classical and character roles, he was also a first-class partner, a talented mime, a caricaturist (the caricatures of the

---

[1] Mikhailov entered the Petersburg University in 1906, and, having graduated from it brilliantly, was offered a chair. He left for Paris where, reportedly, he became a Doctor of Law. Presniakov conducted a class in *plastique* at the Conservatoire in Petersburg, became its Professor and Director of the Opera studio. Later he organized ballet studios in many provincial towns.

Above left: Mikhail Fokine in 1898.
(Collection of Natalia Roslavleva)

Above right: Uniform of a pupil of
the Ballet Department of the
Theatre School, Petersburg (Pierre
Vladimirov in the graduating class,
1911). (Collection of Natalia
Roslavleva)

Right: Caricature of Sergei
Volkonsky, Director of the
Imperial Theatres, by Nicolai
Legat. Published for the first time.
(Collection of Natalia Roslavleva)

Anna Pavlova and Nicolai Legat. (Collection of Natalia Roslavleva)

Petersburg ballet by him and his brother Nicolai were published as an album in 1903) and promising choreographer.

Taking the company as a whole, Sergei Legat's revolutionary inclinations were probably the most earnest. He took part in workers' meetings and manifestations, was ready to fight for the artists' rights, and was one of the first to sign the collective protest of the company against various injustices. Pressure exerted by his wife, Maria Petipa (probably instigated by the Directorate), drove Sergei Legat to suicide by cutting his throat. Teliakovsky recorded in his Diary that Legat's funeral took the form of a revolutionary protest, and that Anna Pavlova kept demonstratively arranging more prominently the red ribbons on a wreath from the company with the following inscription: "To the first victim at the dawn of freedom of art from the newly united ballet company."[1]

These words about "freedom of art", written at a time of extreme rise in revolutionary feelings, at a time when meetings of dramatic actors demanded the liberation of political prisoners and the abolition of capital punishment, indicate how very mild in reality were the requests of ballet dancers. They were connected with various professional problems and the dire necessity for improvement in their material position.

They demanded a rise in the salaries of certain categories, one more free day a week, the right to choose their own *régisseurs* (company managers), and so forth. The petition was drafted after a six-hour meeting in the big rehearsal hall, on October 15, 1905. Among the first items on the paper was a request for the return of Marius Petipa, Alexander Shiryaev (of whom more later), and the character dancer, Alfred Bekefi. However, when ballet dancers wanted to have another meeting the next day, they were not let in. They then organized a meeting in the yard. Their speeches attracted pupils of the Theatre School. Lessons were stopped and many of the pupils rushed to the windows and shouted greetings to the artists. All the doors of the school were immediately locked and heavily bolted. The ballerina Yelena Lucom (born 1891) remembers those days at school in the following words: "Winter of 1905. I was a child then, but I remember endless talk about strikes and risings that were quite incomprehensible for me. There was a general mood of disquiet. Lessons were over in haste. Lights were hardly put on at the school and we were strictly forbidden to approach the thickly curtained windows. We wandered through the school building, peering into the faces of the grown-ups, hoping to detect and understand what was being hidden from

[1] Quoted from: M. Borisoglebsky. *Materials for the History of Russian Ballet*, vol. II, Leningrad, 1939, p. 121.

us. . . . On one such day, for the benefit of the ballerina, Olga Preobrajenskaya, there was a performance of *Les Caprices du Papillon*. When we were
taken to the theatre in the large coach, we tried to peep through the
window despite the ban of our governess. Immediately the performance
ended, our costumes were pulled off, make-up washed off our faces, and
we were pushed into the coach, that rushed at an unprecedented pace
through the dark streets. I remember to this day the whistles, the rattle of
carts loaded with something, and the shouts of the crowd. All that night,
almost until the break of drawn, we tried, with our little childish minds,
to penetrate beyond the mystery of political events that were so carefully
concealed from us by our officials."[1]

Apparently some of the pupils succeeded in solving this riddle, since
Teliakovsky made the following entry in his diary (on 15/10/1905) "I
was surprised by children—boys of the ballet department. The inspector
reported that pupils of the lower forms, having heard about various
meetings, assembled, without having obtained permission, to discuss
their needs."[2]

Meanwhile their seniors from the company, having failed to get into
the rehearsal hall, set out for the Alexandrinsky Theatre and arranged a
meeting on its stage, refusing to leave it even when the police arrived
on the spot. The lights were put out, but the meeting continued with a
solitary candle.

This revolutionary tide did not last very long. The Directorate, with
the help of its henchmen, sowed disagreement in the very midst of the
artists. Fokine and Anna Pavlova organized a petition to the Court
Ministry, but many of those who signed it began hastily to remove their
signatures. Nicolai Sergeyev (1876-1951), chief *régisseur* (company
manager) of the Mariinsky ballet, took a prominent part in these
events.

An intriguer, Sergeyev made the greatest possible use of the conditions
prevailing in the Petersburg ballet of his time. To all purposes there was
nobody to lead it. Nominally, Petipa was still regarded as chief ballet-
master and received his salary, although no longer admitted backstage
at the theatre. The Directorate attempted to engage a new foreigner.
Officials were sent all over Europe to scout for potential talent. They
were able to produce an Italian, Achille Coppini, whose main forte
consisted in arranging parading groups in Manzotti-like revues, and
August Berger, born in Moravia and educated as a linguist, but one who
had appeared in Paris as a *danseur grotesque*. Berger had to his credit a

[1] M. Borisoglebsky. *Op. cit.*, p. 113.   [2] *Idem*, p. 119.

production of *Swan Lake* (act II only) in Prague, shown in the presence of Tchaikovsky. In Petersburg neither of these choreographers was able to reveal any merit. The most insignificant member of the local company knew more about classical ballet than they did. Coppini achieved a production of *La Source* that was saved from failure only by the skill of the dancers, while Berger had to be asked to leave after the first rehearsal with the company.

Attempts were then made to find a choreographer within the company. Alexander Shiryaev (1867-1941), who had successfully revived some Petipa ballets and was very good at rehearsing and recording ballets, seemed for a while a suitable candidate. When he worked as Petipa's assistant he endeavoured to promote talented dancers from the *corps de ballet*. This was disliked by the Directorate. Teliakovsky then insisted that Shiryaev should introduce changes into Petipa's ballets, with a view to filling the post of the great choreographer. Shiryaev flatly refused to change Petipa's works, neither did he have any illusions about his own choreographic talents—he could not replace Petipa even had he wished to do so. Shiryaev was asked to resign. He worked abroad for a number of years, dancing in Berlin and London and arranging small ballets. He returned to his own theatre in 1918 (he was an outstanding character dancer), and, having retired from the stage in 1921, dedicated the rest of his life to developing the method of teaching character dancing started, in collaboration with Alfred Bekefi, before the Revolution. These efforts bore fruit in the form of a complete character *barre* and centre practice, described, with the participation of Shiryaev's pupils, Alexander Bocharov and Andrei Lopukhov, in the book *The Fundamentals of Character Dancing*, edited by Yuri Slonimsky, published in Leningrad in 1939, which remains, to this day, the first and principal textbook on character dancing.

Teliakovsky thought of transferring Gorsky to Petersburg. Such intention became fact when that choreographer was commissioned to stage *Don Quixote* at the Mariinsky. Gorsky's bold changes of accepted versions of classical ballets were met with indignation on the part of the company; he had the reputation of one who interfered with the old order and that was not welcome in the Petersburg "climate". His nomination was no longer contemplated.

The next candidate was Nicolai Legat. A good dancer and first-class teacher, he was not really gifted as a choreographer. Visions of replacing Petipa were very much to his liking. Together with his brother, Sergei, he achieved a successful production of *The Fairy Doll* to music by Bayer and with charming costumes by Bakst (1903). Although a trifle, it was at least fairly well done. But upon the tragic death of Sergei Legat it appeared that with him went the better half of the partnership. Working alone, Nicolai Legat proved to be incapable of reviving Petipa's ballets and this had to be done by the *régisseur* Sergeyev.

Sergeyev took the trouble to learn the Stepanov notation, not because he considered it his mission, as in the case of Gorsky: such a sentiment would have been entirely foreign to him. He agreed to teach the Stepanov notation without remuneration at the Theatre School in order to avoid military service. With perseverance he was soon receiving a full salary and was given two assistants, A. Chekrygin and S. Rakhmanov, who carried out the actual notation of ballets. Five years earlier the Directorate had refused Gorsky payment for doing much greater work, while the inventor of the system, Stepanov, reaped no benefit whatsoever.

Marius Petipa himself might have envied Sergeyev. With the help of back-stage intrigue he reached a situation where the Directorate paid him, in addition to a sizeable salary, five per cent from the sale of tickets for each ballet revived by him. Thus he received a similar sum for the production of *King Candaules*, at a time when Marius Petipa was alive, and nominally still on the staff of the Imperial Theatres, but never received any fee for the performances of any of his ballets.

Sergeyev was responsible for the discharge or resignation of many soloists of the Mariinsky ballet who would not tolerate his dictatorship. In 1905 he played a very ugly role at the time of the dancers' strike. Fokine openly charged him during the famous meeting in the big rehearsal hall on October 15, 1905, with being "the Directorate's spy". A contemporary caricature shows Sergeyev waving the dancers' petition at them, while Olga Preobrajenskaya is being whipped, and Teliakovsky, together with Krupensky (an official of the Directorate known for his intrigues), are looking on.

M. Borisoglebsky declared the activities of this "*régisseur*" (the quotes are Borisoglebsky's) to be "the darkest phenomenon in the history of Russian ballet during the first quarter of the twentieth century".[1]

It happened that Nicolai Sergeyev played an important role in the building up of the ballet in Britain. The classical ballets: *The Nutcracker*, *Giselle*, *Swan Lake*, *The Sleeping Beauty* and *Coppélia* abstracted by him from the files of the Mariinsky Theatre and taken abroad enabled these ballets to be included in the repertory of the Vic-Wells company.

[1] M. Borisoglebsky. *Materials for the History of Russian Ballet*, vol. II, Leningrad, 1939, p. 79.

Among the dancers who in particular revolted against the Sergeyev dictatorship was Mikhail Fokine (1880-1942). He would not close his eyes to what was going on around him—the servility, bribery, the routine that was slowly corrupting even the most gifted of artists. Fokine made no attempt to conceal his feelings and soon found himself unpopular with the officials. He was particularly opposed to A. D. Krupensky (1875-?) manager of the Petersburg Office of the Imperial Theatres, who had surrounded himself with flatterers and flunkeys, and was very much influenced by Sergeyev.

In such an atmosphere this young dancer could not be happy, despite the fact that upon graduation in 1898 he immediately started receiving leading roles. His talent was obvious. As a pupil he was noted by Lev Ivanov, who entrusted him with the role of Luke in *The Magic Flute*. While in the senior class he danced Colin in *La Fille Mal Gardée*. In the first years at the Mariinsky he danced Bernard de Ventadour in *Raymonda*, Pierre in *La Halte de Cavalerie*, Matteo in *The Naiad and the Fisherman*, Lucien d'Hervilly in *Paquita*, the Blue Bird and Prince Désiré in *The Sleeping Beauty*, Prince Koklush in *The Nutcracker*, Basil in *Don Quixote*— leading roles that would have satisfied the pride of any dancer. Fokine had an unusual range: he could perform comic and heroic parts and dance both in the classical and character style. He was not endowed with particular elevation or technical prowess, but a beautiful sense of style, his expressiveness, and, above all, a great gift of projection made Fokine into an outstanding artist.

The searching mind of the young man was ever at work. He was annoyed by the frequent lack of sense in the ballets in which he had to appear, with the conventional mime that seemed to release the dancers from any responsibility for feeling and conveying genuine emotion on stage. He was determined to find a way out of the old manner of producing ballets. At times he despaired and intended to give up ballet altogether and become a painter or professional musician. He was interested in painting and drawing while still at school.[1]

He spent many hours at the Hermitage Museum copying great masterpieces of the past and was a frequent visitor at the newly opened Alexander III Museum with its collection of Russian painters. Through his friend, Ivan Chekrygin (a dancer of the *corps de ballet* and amateur composer and

[1] A still-life of Fokine's depicting a basket of potatoes is preserved at the museum of the Leningrad school. An anecdote connected with this picture records that Fokine's classmates kept eating the fruit he wanted to paint, so he did potatoes instead.

conductor), Fokine met Andreyev, the famous organizer of the *balalaika* orchestra, and played the mandoline, *domra* and *balalaika*. Through Ivan Chekrygin, P. Mikhailov and V. Presniakov, Fokine became connected with the progressive Gogol School and entered the Philanthropic Society of the Mariinsky artists. Fokine was an active member of the "left wing" of the company. Artists met at his flat to discuss plans for further action. When Fokine distributed among them a questionnaire asking what they thought about ballet and its aims, only three of them gave answers that suited him. They were Chekrygin, Mikhailov, and Presniakov.

In 1904 Fokine was entrusted with the senior girls' class at the Theatre School.[1] This gave him an opportunity to put his ideas into practice.

At the end of 1904 he delivered to the Directorate of the Imperial Theatres a draft for a two-act ballet to Longus's *Daphnis and Chloe*, published in a Russian translation in the spring of that year. The scenario was accompanied by a memorandum explaining the principles to be observed in the production of the proposed ballet. This memorandum was not discovered in the Archives of the Imperial Theatres; unanswered and ignored, it was probably considered unworthy of preservation in the files. When Fokine recalled this in his memoirs, he reconstituted his draft from memory. Retold so many years later, backed by the experience of Fokine's entire creative life, it did sound like a complete programme of reform in ballet. Research in Leningrad, undertaken by Yuri Slonimsky, in the process of preparation of his important work, *M. Fokine. Against the Current. Memoirs, articles, letters* (Leningrad, 1962), yielded two copies of the scenario with a Preface. One came from the Fokine archives, preserved by his brother-in-law, A. P. Krupitsky, after the choreographer had left Russia; it is now available in the manuscript department of the Saltykov-Shchedrin Public Library. Another is in the archives of the composer, Andrei Kadlets, in the Leningrad Theatre Library. This important document is available in full, since it has been published in Russian in the Appendix to the above-mentioned Fokine volume:[2] (the slight differences between the text of the Preface to the scenario in the Fokine and the Kadlets archives are indicated).

This Preface, written by a young dancer and aspiring choreographer, does not contain a detailed programme. It is set down in the form of suggestions. The first of these concerns the necessity to ban applause and bows that interrupt the action to the detriment of artistic integrity.

[1] He had been teaching at the lower forms since 1901.

[2] M. Fokine. *Against the Current*. Memoirs, articles, letters. Edited by Y. Slonimsky, Iskusstvo, Leningrad, pp. 567-568.

Next comes the suggestion that in order that the production of *Daphnis and Chloe* should accord with the subject, all dances and mimed scenes should "reflect the spirit of Hellenic art".

"No ballet-master," writes Fokine, "could commit the following mistake: arrange dances for Russian peasants in the style of Louis XV or, on the contrary, create dances in the manner of the Russian *trepak* to a French theme. Then why permit the constant error in productions based on subjects from Ancient Greece: shall Greeks dance the French way?" Fokine goes on to say that it is time to "make an experiment in producing a Greek ballet in the spirit of that age". He mentions vases and sculpture as providing material with the help of which the choreographer could give an impression of the nature of Hellenic *plastique*. He says that fashionable *tours de force* are, quite naturally, incompatible with such aims.

A special paragraph deals with the *music* of the proposed ballet. Fokine says that it should also bear an imprint of Hellenic style of music and should by no means be based on banal waltzes and polkas, nor end with the ubiquitous galop. He also insists on the necessity for the music to be *uninterrupted* (with the exception of pauses required by the action of the ballet and the music itself).

In a paragraph about costumes, Fokine suggests that "the ballet would make an original and pleasing impression if, instead of the ugly *tutus* and ballet slippers with square toes, the dancers were dressed in light Greek tunics and sandals. It is impossible to invent a more beautiful and suitable costume for dancing than the one that the Greek women used to wear." In conclusion Fokine makes some detailed suggestions concerning the lighting of and settings for the proposed ballet.

Nothing came of these plans although Kadletz did write the music for *Daphnis and Chloe*, so, a little later, when the necessity arose for producing a school graduation performance Fokine proposed to revive Lev Ivanov's anacreontic ballet *Acis and Galatea*, also to existing music by Kadletz. In his memoirs[1] Fokine recalls that he had to satisfy himself with a compromise. His girl-pupils danced *sur les pointes* and the costumes were not quite conventional, but selected with some taste from the theatre wardrobe. The groups were arranged at different levels. Moreover, the boys were not his own pupils (they were from Mikhail Obukov's class) and they did not have to show how they were taught to dance on point. For them he created an original "Scène et danse des faunes" using high leaps and a type of movement that was almost acrobatic for the time. One of

[1] Fokine, *op. cit.*, p. 163.

the boys was particularly eager and possessed an extraordinary elevation. Fokine asked him for his name and was told: "Nijinsky". Fokine gave him a solo part in that dance. The boy had two more years to stay at the school, but attracted attention from that performance. The part of Acis was played by pupil Fyodor Lopukhov, the part of Galatea by Maria Gorshkova, Hymen was Nijinsky's classmate, Yelena Smirnova, the future ballerina, and Cupid was impersonated by pupil Lydia Lopukhova. There were many other names among the ensemble of the first Fokine ballet that were to win renown in the future.

Maria Gorshkova (1887-1955) recalled in her memoirs:[1] "It was a great pleasure to work with Fokine as an artist. He was very gifted, endowed with a rich fantasy, musical and rhythmic. All his movements were meticulously linked with the music. At times the movements of his arms, legs or head clearly followed one note, not only the musical phrase. It was difficult to work with other choreographers, having been educated in his method. He demanded that the pattern and style be observed. He could have torn our heads off for inaccuracy in style! He was beloved by everybody for his talent. His every word was law for us.

"When he started producing *Acis and Galatea*[2] he gave us a talk, *explaining the content of the ballet and what each of us had to represent.*" (My italics—N.R.)

This description of Fokine's work on his first ballet shows that all the salient points of his creative method were already in existence. No wonder they made such an impression on the young artists: no one was wont to explain to them what they had to portray in a ballet or what was its general significance. Neither had anyone since the time of Lev Ivanov created anything so deftly linked to the music and expressing both its structure and content. Perhaps it was not incidental that Fokine chose this Ivanov ballet to the same music by Kadletz for his first undertaking. As a boy he had witnessed Ivanov's methods of work in this production.

It is also important to note that in 1904, when visualizing the unachieved *Daphnis and Chloe*, Fokine studied sculptures and bas-reliefs of ancient Greece and was ready to use this style of *plastique* in his production *before* Isadora Duncan's initial tour in Russia. The theatre world was very much excited by Duncan's art. She could not fail to make a deep impression on young Fokine. He felt, in the words of Stanislavsky, that "in different corners of the world, due to conditions unknown to us, various

[1] Borisoglebsky, vol. II, p. 110.

[2] It was shown in a graduation performance at the Mariinsky Theatre on April 10, 1905 (Old Style).

people in various spheres sought in art the same naturally born creative principles".[1]

But there was one radical difference between Duncan and Fokine. She wanted to replace classical ballet with her kind of dancing (which, apart from not being backed by technique comparable to that of the *danse d'école*, completely ignored such an important element as the male dance) while Fokine, staunch supporter of high professionalism, never intended to break with classical ballet. Neither did he accept Duncan's imagery and costume as applicable to any kind of dance. He wanted to develop different plastic forms, idioms and costumes for ballets of different styles and periods. These ideas were formulated by Fokine later, in his famous "Five principles" postulated in the letter to *The Times* of July 6, 1914.[2]

As to the school of classical ballet, Fokine, being a highly-trained dancer, fully realized that it represents a perfect system of training worked out on the basis of anatomical knowledge by generations of teachers. He knew that it provided him with a perfect instrument, the dancer's trained body, for implementing his ideas. But he considered that the choreographer had to create his own idiom in each case. He accepted the use of *pointes*, turn-out, and steps of the *danse d'école* in the classical ballets, and new ballets requiring such idiom (as his *Les Sylphides*). But he used steps of the classical ballet with a new musicality and subtlety that produced a complete expressiveness of the dancer—from head to foot.

Fokine's most important maxim, recurring repeatedly in his writing, consisted in the necessity for the ballet to portray Man and his feelings, human beings rather than characters providing dancers with new roles. He considered that the duty of ballet was "to extol beauty and assist in the development of a healthy and harmonious attitude of mind in the spectator".

The influence of *art nouveau* and decadent trends penetrating into all branches of art, at the period when Fokine's main works were being created; the constant clash of the human and the realistic outlook with the decadent one; a long association with painters from the *World of Art* group, and the Diaghilev Ballet whose repertory was not always as harmonious as the choreographer might have wished—all this prevented Fokine from implementing his ideas more fully and realizing his dreams

[1] K. Stanislavsky. *My Life in Art.* Collected works, vol. I, Moscow 1954, chapter, "Duncan and Craig", p. 333. Also see Natalia Roslavleva, *Stanislavsky and the Ballet, Dance Perspectives*, No. 23, N.Y., 1965.

[2] Quoted in full in "Appendix A" of Cyril Beaumont's *Michel Fokine and his ballets*, London, 1955, pp. 144-147.

in their entirety. On the whole, however, his artistic outlook stood in line with the ideals of Russian art and letters in their greatest manifestations.

The next important event in Fokine's life occurred in 1907, when he collaborated with Alexandre Benois (1870-1960) on *Le Pavillon d'Armide* (to music by the then modern composer, Tcherepnin). The encounter with Benois was preceded by the independent creation of one scene from the future *Pavillon d'Armide*—"The Animated Gobelins" effected, of necessity, with the help of costumes selected from the theatre's wardrobe, for a graduation performance by Fokine's class. He was ever faced by the necessity of finding something new and interesting for the graduation. Old and tried ways were not for him. Being a musically educated man, capable of reading a score *ad libitum*, Fokine was keenly interested in the latest musical developments. He regularly attended concerts at the Conservatoire (built on the site of the former Bolshoi Theatre it was just opposite the Mariinsky) and at one of them was very much attracted by a suite from the ballet, *Le Pavillon d'Armide*, by Nicolai Tcherepnin (1873-1945), composer and conductor, and pupil of Rimsky-Korsakov. Fokine learnt from Tcherepnin that the ballet had been commissioned by the Directorate, which seemed to have forgotten all about it, and that the painter Alexandre Benois was the author of the *scenario*. When the "Gobelins" had been admired by the Directorate to such an extent that it asked Fokine to reproduce the scene for the Mariinsky repertory, the choreographer explained to Teliakovsky that it was necessary to achieve the complete Tcherepnin ballet and to invite Benois to do the settings and costumes. Though he had already had some differences with Benois in the course of the latter's work at the Imperial Theatres, Teliakovsky gave in to Fokine's insistent request. Fokine, however, advised that the three-act work be reduced to one act and three scenes, and thus a new form of presentation, to be accepted as ideal in Western ballet for a great many years, was born in Russia.

Upon returning from his summer vacation, Fokine met Benois in one of the Imperial Theatres' workshops, where the artist was already busily engaged in the painting of settings for *Le Pavillon d'Armide*. Benois was then about thirty-seven. Fokine knew him from his pictures and articles, but had not yet met the painter who was so rapidly gaining popularity as a prominent figure in artistic life as a whole.

Sergei Diaghilev (1872-1929) came to Petersburg from his ancestral home at Perm (though he was actually born in Nizhni-Novgorod Province where his father, then an officer of the Guards Cavalry, was stationed). Orphaned at birth, Sergei Diaghilev was brought to Perm at the age of ten to study at the local gymnasium and live in his grand-father's mansion. In the seventies and eighties this house on Perm's principal street served as the city's cultural centre and even won the name of "Athens of Perm". Music reigned in its spacious ballroom with a double row of windows and a balcony for the orchestra.[1]

Diaghilev's step-mother, *née* Yelena Panayeva, was a gifted amateur singer and pianist. All the members of the family were associated with music in some way, while one of them, Ivan Diaghilev, a pupil of Rubinstein, acted for a season as conductor of the Perm Opera House, founded in 1870 by the local branch of the Russian Musical Society, in which the Diaghilevs took active part. The Diaghilev music circle was replenished by the local intelligentsia and gave concerts in the grand ballroom two or three times a year. No wonder that when Sergei Diaghilev came to Petersburg in 1890 he joined the Conservatoire, while simultaneously reading law at the University at the insistence of his family. He did not make a singer, pianist, or composer, and eventually abandoned the idea of professional musical studies. Instead he became deeply influenced by the circle of Alexandre Benois, who accepted this red-cheeked provincial youth only because of his relationship to Dmitry Filosofov.

Alexandre Benois served as mentor for all the group. He brought reproductions of treasures from European galleries following each summer trip abroad, and Somov, Bakst, his cousin Lanceray, Filosofov and Diaghilev learned the history of art from those albums. Within a few years one could no longer recognize Sergei Diaghilev. He had acquired the taste and knowledge that enabled him to select unfailingly the right pictures for the exhibitions of Russian painting organized at first in Petersburg, and then (in 1906-1907) in Paris, Berlin, Monte-Carlo, and Venice.

In 1899-1901 Diaghilev served in the capacity of special missions official at the Directorate of the Imperial Theatres, editing at the same time its *Annual* and bringing this publication to an unprecedented high artistic level. He aspired to the coveted post of Director of the Imperial Theatres and no efforts were spared in this connection, though they were all of no avail. Yuri Slonimsky makes public in his detailed introductory

[1] Rare photographs from the collection of the author representing the interior of the Diaghilev house at the end of the nineteenth century are published for the first time through the courtesy of Tatiana Diaghileva-Bolshaia, daughter of Diaghilev's first cousin Dmitry and granddaughter of the conductor, Ivan Diaghilev.

article to the Russian edition of Fokine's memoirs[1] facts proving that Diaghilev's real ambitions were connected with the possibility of a career in Russia, that was cut short by dismissal from the Imperial Theatres in 1901 without the right of re-entering government service.

Slonimsky says: "In organizing the 'Russian seasons' [of painting in 1907, of symphonic concerts in 1908, of opera and ballet in 1909, and thereafter of ballet alone—N.R.] Diaghilev at first did not even dream of permanently occupying himself with this kind of *enterprise*. They served only as a goal and means for him: he hoped, as a 'triumpher', to acquire the right for governing the destinies of art in Russia. That is why Diaghilev, despite the grandiose success of the Paris seasons of Russian Ballet, resumed negotiations with Kshesinskaya [for participation in the 'seasons', in order to obtain influential support in Court circles, though he knew that she was opposed to Fokine and the 'new ballet'—N.R.]. Subsequently organizing her appearances abroad, and, over the head of Teliakovsky, Director of the Imperial Theatres, he offered the Court Ministry to organize something analogous to the programmes of the 'Russian seasons' on the Imperial stage." "With the help of Kshesinskaya" —continues Slonimsky—"Diaghilev hoped he had found a way to secure the interest and protection of members of the Imperial family. But this did not lead to anything at all. The fame of the 'Russian seasons' of ballet did not provide Diaghilev with what he had expected—with rehabilitation of his name in high life society and reinstatement in a government post. His attempts at pulling together the *World of Art* were also futile. Its members were scattered about, and their old-time programme, in the light of the new events in the life of the country, that arose after the suppression of the 1905 Revolution, failed to attract anyone. Diaghilev's memorandum to the Court Ministry, proposing the creation of a Ministry of Arts that would govern the Academy of Arts and the Imperial Theatres and, in that case, would bring him a high post, had no issue.

"Diaghilev could no longer expect a career in Russia. It was then that he decided to transform a summer touring troupe into a permanent company with Nijinsky at its head. This brought about new conditions of work for the dancers and, what was most important, resulted in a change of artistic leadership."[2]

This happened in the second period of the Russian ballet in Paris. In the first "Russian seasons" there was a sense of collective responsibility.

[1] Yuri Slonimsky. "Fokine and his time". In: M. Fokine. *Against the Current*. Memoirs of the ballet-master, articles, letters. Leningrad, 1962, pp. 5-80.

[2] Yuri Slonimsky, *op. cit.*, p. 39.

In the course of his association with Diaghilev, Fokine retained his artistic integrity. When Alexandre Benois advised Diaghilev to include ballet in the season of 1909 (Diaghilev was reticent about this and gave his agreement under some pressure on the part of Benois), Fokine had already created *Le Pavillon d'Armide*, *Nuits d'Egypte*, *Les Sylphides* (*Chopiniana*) and, for a charity performance, a version of *Le Carnaval*.

He had also created one of his greatest masterpieces—"The Swan" (later widely known as "The Dying Swan") for Anna Pavlova. In other words, at the time when he agreed to become chief choreographer for the first four seasons of Russian ballet in Paris (Benois was artistic director of the whole enterprise while Diaghilev was responsible for everything connected with its organization and management), Fokine had already carried out the greater part of his reform and was reaching maturity as a choreographer.

It was quite natural that Fokine was eager to take part in the "seasons". He was faced by conditions and vistas such as had not been envisaged in his wildest dreams. Diaghilev had transformed the Châtelet into a perfect theatre with every modern stage equipment. Fokine was surrounded by prominent painters and musicians, and a first-class company of young and eager dancers, trained either by himself, or by Gorsky in Moscow (the company was a mixed one). The choreographer no longer had to worry about stage settings, to use makeshift costumes, to create master-pieces for a limited audience at charity performances, because there was no other opportunity of putting into practice his creative ideals.

With the constellation of Russian talent in every field assembled for the Russian seasons of ballet in Paris, it was possible to create wonders. Not only Fokine but everybody present gave of their best.

The first season of 1909 contained three of Fokine's ballets already shown at the Mariinsky: *Le Pavillon d'Armide*, *Cléopâtre* (a new version of *Nuits d'Egypte*) and *Chopiniana*, now entitled *Les Sylphides*. Pavlova's poetical silhouette on Serov's famous poster of this ballet became an emblem of the "Russian seasons".

The newly-created "Polovetsian Dances" from *Prince Igor* astounded all Paris by its virile male dancing, and by the art of Bolm as the Chief and Sophia Fedorova as the Polovets Girl.

In the second season, *Le Carnaval*, *Schéhérazade*, and *The Fire-Bird*, with its poetic Russian theme and a colourful modern score by the young Stravinsky, were added to the repertory, while the French audiences were also able to see (after an interval of fifty years) their own *Giselle*, preserved in Russia and given there a new reading. Karsavina and Nijinsky danced in this ballet, creating remarkable characterizations and an incomparable partnership.

In the third season Fokine created for Nijinsky *Narcisse* (to music by Tcherepnin), *Le Spectre de la Rose*, and the outstandingly successful *Petrushka*.

In the fourth (and the last artistically fruitful) season Fokine choreographed Ravel's *Daphnis et Chloé*, Balakirev's *Thamar* (with the title-role created by Karsavina), and Reynaldo Hahn's *Le Dieu Bleu*, using poses borrowed from Indian sculpture in stylized form.

The success and the impact of the first season of Russian ballet in Paris is a generally known fact. This is what Alexandre Benois wrote in 1909 in one of his articles for the Petersburg newspaper *Rech*, sent regularly from Paris: "Every participant in the 'Russian season' . . . felt that he was bringing to the entire world all that is Russian, all that comprises his greatest pride: Russian spiritual culture, Russian art, after all of the Russian reality had been trodden upon and humiliated. . . . I felt that Russian barbarians had brought to the artistic capital of the world all that was best in art at that moment in the entire world." Benois prophesied that "with the Russian season, a new era may start in French and general European theatrical art" and his prophecy came true, though the influence was wider and included easel painting, fashions, and interior decoration.

Benois expressed conviction that "not Borodin, and not Rimsky-Korsakov, and not Chaliapin or Golovine, or Roerich, or Diaghilev were 'triumphers' in Paris but all Russian culture, all the inimitable features of Russian art, its great sense of conviction, its freshness and spontaneity, its wild force, and, at the same time, its extraordinary refinement that left far behind the sophistication of Paris".[1]

Benois went on to explain that Russian refinement consisted of the national tradition of simplicity that allowed Parisians to see Theatre such as it should be—a thing of beauty.

But with the fourth season an atmosphere of decline crept into the Russian ballet in Paris. Fokine broke with Diaghilev in 1912, not accidentally, but because with the Nijinsky-created *L'Après-midi d'un Faune* Diaghilev undertook a new artistic policy. He forsook the dancing traditions of Russian ballet that Fokine never intended to give up. After 1912 Diaghilev gradually lost his "little parliament" of advisers (it consisted of Benois, Bakst, Tcherepnin, the critic Valerian Svetlov, and General Bezobrazov, the influential balletomane and secretary of the

[1] Alexandre Benois. Newspaper *Rech* (Petersburg) of 19/6/1909, p. 2.

Russian Embassy in Paris) and drifted eventually under the influence of French art.

Of course Diaghilev succeeded in the period between 1913 and 1929 in producing some outstanding works of art in his "Ballet Russe" by attracting numerous talented collaborators. But that is a page in the history of West-European, not Russian, ballet, like the birth and re-birth of ballet in France, England, the United States of America, etc., under the influence of the Diaghilev ballet and with the help of choreographers and dancers who had worked for him.

Fokine returned to the Diaghilev "Ballet Russe" for a short time in 1914 to produce *La Légende de Joseph*, a ballet-pantomime which did not express his artistic aspirations and did not improve his relations with Diaghilev.

He tried to found a dance theatre that artistically would be strong enough to compete with the Diaghilev Ballet, and successfully to contrast its own progressive policy with the sensation-seeking ever-changing trends of "Ballet Russe". However, all the offers he received were purely commercial, promising no artistic satisfaction.

For a while Fokine joined forces with Anna Pavlova, but her small, ever-touring company was unable to interpret Fokine's former ballets at an artistic level that could have satisfied him, neither was he able to create anything satisfactory without a properly trained ensemble. However great the talent of Pavlova, his friend and closest collaborator in his early choreographic efforts, she alone was unable to breathe life into Fokine's creations, with the exception of "The Dying Swan" that gave her immortality.

Fokine possessed the gift of revealing the potential talents of dancers taking part in his ballets, and many of them became great artists through his choreography. For Tamara Karsavina he created the sparkling and mysterious title-role in *The Fire-Bird*, the fickle Ballerina in *Petrushka*, the regal and merciless Thamar, the poetic dreamer of *Le Spectre de la Rose*.

For Sophia Fedorova he created the temperamental principal role in the "Polovetsian Dances", where he also fully exploited the virile leaps and wild power of Adolph Bolm. For his wife, Vera Fokina, and Sophia Fedorova he created the "Bacchanal" in *Cléopâtre*, which was one of the greatest successes of the first "Russian season".

For Nijinsky he created the Golden Slave in *Schéhérazade*, Petrushka, and the Spirit of the Rose, exploiting that dancer's extraordinary elevation and ability to transform himself completely into another character.

In these and many other dancers Fokine invested part of his own artistic personality, inspiring them with his own great devotion to the art he chose to serve.

Upon returning to the Imperial Theatres Fokine was made staff ballet-master and given leading parts as a dancer. He created several ballets in the years preceding the Revolution of 1917. They were: *Jota Aragonessa* to music by Glinka, *Francesca da Rimini* and *Eros* by Tchaikovsky (the latter to the music of "Serenade for Strings"), Glasunov's *Stenka Rasin*, *The Sorcerer's Apprentice* by Dukas, Liszt's *Les Préludes*, a new suite of dances to music by Chopin, and dances in the opera *Ruslan and Lyudmila* called by him his "swan song"—they were premièred on November 7, 1917.

There were no revelations in these Fokine productions of his second period at the Mariinsky (altogether in thirteen years—1905-1918—he achieved over twenty small ballets for that theatre). But Fokine found satisfaction in the new type of dancer and the new way of presentation of ballets that was born as result of his efforts. The reform had taken place and its effect was felt. It would be deeply erroneous to think that Diaghilev had taken Fokine's reform away and that "Russian ballet remained outside the Fokine reform" as is sometimes suggested.

On the other hand Fokine's plans and ideals were more far-reaching than his practice. Only a few of his creations have survived the test of time and it is significant that those that live—*Les Sylphides*, "The Swan", "Polovetsian Dances" from *Prince Igor*—are done in terms of dance rather than in the dramatic mime that was often prevalent in Fokine ballets of the first "Russian seasons". Yet in its time the principles of ballet-drama, and the attention paid to content in ballet proposed by Fokine in his reform, had a great significance that continues to exert its influence on the art of choreography to this day.

Under the conditions governing the Imperial Theatres the best of plans and intentions were doomed to oblivion, the greatest of talents became sterile and lost their former enthusiasm. On the eve of the Revolution Fokine had lost most of his collaborators, and, what is more important, lost faith.

Anna Pavlova (1881-1931) was, according to papers preserved in the Leningrad archives, the daughter of a soldier from the Vyshnevolotsky District of the Petersburg Province. The circumstances of her birth are, however, not quite clear. A pass made public for the first time in Vera Krasovskaya's definitive biography of Pavlova,[1] received by the ballerina's mother, Lyubov Pavlova, for the purpose of travelling to Petersburg,

[1] V. Krasovskaya. *Anna Pavlova. Pages from the life of a Russian dancer.* Leningrad, 1964.

Mikhail Fokine and Anna Pavlova in *Javotte*, music by Saint-Saëns, choreography by Pavel Gerdt, *circa* 1906. (Collection of Natalia Roslavleva)

La Fille Mal Gardée, Bolshoi Theatre, Moscow, *circa* 1920; revived by
A. Gorsky. Anastasia Abramova as Lise, and Asaf Messerer as Colin.

makes it clear that she had a daughter, Anna, by a first marriage. Perhaps that is why Anna did not wish to bear the patronymic "Matveyevna" derived from her stepfather's name Matvey, and preferred to choose for her theatrical name the patronymic of "Pavlovna". Family legend had it that Anna's real father came from a much higher walk of life. This did not matter much in the life of the prematurely born child, delicate from birth.

The poor laundress's daughter suffered illnesses. There was not much hope that the frail girl was going to live, and the mother, busy earning the meagre means of livelihood, confided her to the care of her grandmother, who had a small house in Ligovo, close to Petersburg. There she studied at the elementary church school for peasant children. But it so happened that her mother was able to take the shy and delicate Anna to a matinée performance of *The Sleeping Beauty*, quite soon after its première in 1890. The beauty of the ballet, the magic of the music, the magnificence of the Mariinsky Theatre—all this made an indelible impression on the girl. She was determined "to dance as the Princess Aurora when grown up". She begged her mother to place her in the Theatre School where one could learn how to dance so beautifully. And the mother found protection through the ballet teacher, Eugenia Sokolova; from her Anna Pavlova received her first blessing.

In 1891 she was accepted into the Theatre School where she was placed under the care of Yekaterina Vazem; a former excellent virtuosity ballerina. Vazem was doubtful of the girl's future; she was not strong enough. But Pavel Gerdt and Christian Johansson soon noticed the pupil's great talent. They were ready to forgive a certain degree of weakness and even lack of good natural turnout because of the innate poetic qualities and the beautiful line *en arabesque* of the young dancer.

The wise Petipa also noticed the budding ballerina. When he revived for a school performance of 1898 his old curtain-raiser *The Two Stars* (created in 1871 for Vazem and Vergina) he gave the two title-roles to Anna Pavlova and Stanislava Belinskaya (1880-1916), a Cecchetti pupil in the virtuosity style, whose promise did not materialize because of insanity and premature death. The part of Adonis was given to pupil Fokine. Here, in this anacreontic ballet, Pavlova and Fokine formed for the first time an artistic partnership that lasted as long as she danced on the boards of the Imperial Theatres. And it was observed even then that this pair succeeded in dancing to the hackneyed Pugni music with an extraordinary *cantilena* quality.

A year passed and Pavlova appeared at the Mikhailovsky Theatre in her graduation performance. It was another trifle—*The False Dryads* arranged by her teacher Gerdt to selections from music by Pugni. The more sensitive among the spectators became conscious of the individual quality of this charming, but as yet rather timid, *danseuse*. Seven years later, when Anna Pavlova was already a recognized ballerina of the Mariinsky, the prominent critic Valerian Svetlov (1860–1934) wrote: "Slim, straight, and agile as a reed, with the naïve face of a Southern Spaniard, ethereal and ephemeral, she seemed as fragile as a procelain statuette. Yet at times she took poses and attitudes wherein one felt something classical, and had she been robed in those moments in a peplum of ancient Greece, she would look like a Tanagra figurine."[1]

In the same article Svetlov said: "While, in the *pas de deux* with the peasant, one could merely say that the girl was expressive and had something of her own, in the interpolated *variation* from *La Vestale* to music by Drigo, one was to sense more. It was something of the kind that enabled one, without taking the pose of a prophet, to foresee in the fragile *danseuse* a future great artist. I don't know how much pupil Pavlova won from the learned jury. So far as I was concerned, I gave her in my heart of hearts the highest mark of twelve points, and when I found myself in the cold rain of the Petersburg streets and remembered this 'false dryad', I generously added a plus to the full mark."[2]

Having been accepted into the Mariinsky ballet in the season of 1899–1900 Anna Pavlova immediately started taking private lessons from Enrico Cecchetti in order to strengthen her technique. This was typical of her—she was ever trying to improve her art, to perfect her technical abilities, to dance as much as possible. Although her position was at first relatively modest, she never danced in the *corps de ballet*. The very first season brought her solo parts, though small ones. She was noticed in the *pas de quatre* from *La Halte de Cavalerie*, in the *pas de trois* from *La Fille Mal Gardée*. Particular attention was won by Pavlova II (such was her name in the company) as one of the two wilis in *Giselle* when all the balletomanes' binoculars were focused on her alone, though old Petipa hoped for the success of his younger daughter, Lyubov, in the role of Myrtha, Queen of the Wilis. The venerable balletomane, General Bezobrazov, pronounced that Pavlova looked like Taglioni, the prototype of *Giselle*.[3] And Petipa entrusted young Pavlova with many roles in that

[1] Valerian Svetlov. "Pavlova". In: *Terpsichore*, a collection of articles, SPB, 1906, p. 297.

[2] *Idem*, pp. 297-298.

[3] Presumably this implies that Taglioni was the prototype of the *ballet blanc* and not that she was the creator of the title-role of *Giselle*.—Ed.

first season. She danced Hoar-Frost in his ballet *Les Saisons*, Aurora in *The Awakening of Flora*, the Fairy Candide—the beautiful *cantilena variation* from *The Sleeping Beauty* that first made her decide to become a dancer—and Fleur de Lys in *Esmeralda*. But in the second year she appeared as Gulnare in *Le Corsaire*—a role second only to the leading one of Medora—and as Anne in *Bluebeard*.

One of her greatest early achievements occurred when Petipa cast her in the title-role of *The Awakening of Flora* with Fokine, her classmate and permanent partner. In the third year, apart from various smaller roles, she danced her first Giselle. She was as light and as ethereal as a shadow. Her Giselle was pure and serene, she "died" loving and trusting, and this serene purity was taken through from the first into the second act. With every year afterwards Pavlova perfected her Giselle.

Recognition of her ballerina status came after Nikia in *La Bayadère* (1902), danced by Pavlova with a dramatic impact unprecedented in this great role of the classical repertory. She was in her third season at the Mariinsky. It was too early to give her ballerina rank according to the age-long heirarchy of the Imperial ballet, but the public whole-heartedly accepted her as a ballerina for the great truth of the characterization created by her, as was always the case, through purely plastic means of dance and gesture. In the "Shades" scene, the apex of the ballet's choreography, she was also superb, an "aerial Peri" as Svetlov called her.

But Pavlova was not only a lyrical and ethereal dancer. She performed many character and *demi-caractère* roles while in the Mariinsky company, suddenly surprising her audience by dancing the "Urals Dance" in *The Hump-Backed Horse* with the venerable Gerdt—then thirty-eight years her senior—and dancing it so that her partner and former teacher seemed to regain his youth. She danced many other character parts in the Mariinsky repertory, which afforded her the chance to show the different facets of her talent. She also danced the vivacious Lise in *La Fille Mal Gardée* and Ilka from *The Enchanted Forest*, though these roles were considered slight for a *prima ballerina*. She wanted to dance on every possible occasion, because dancing constituted her life. In her book Vera Krasovskaya quotes a doctor's report to the management of the Imperial Theatres that in 1904, on November 2, when suffering from influenza with a high fever, "in answer to my advice that participation in the ballet *Giselle* was harmful to her health, Pavlova II replied that she was determined to dance today, and that she released the management of the theatre from any responsibility for the dangerous effect upon her health that this action may cause".[1] There are many other proofs of Pavlova's devotion to her art, of her determination to dance on any occasion, at any time, when possible—a trait that continued throughout her entire stage career. She danced leading parts in many ballets, apart from those mentioned—*The Naiad and the Fisherman*, *Pharaoh's Daughter*, *Paquita*, etc. Pavlova was always eager to take part in charity recitals because in these she was able to participate in the new creations by Fokine, who also sought an outlet outside the Imperial Theatres. Her sudden appearance at a charity performance in Rubinstein's *The Vine* (1906), choreographed for her by Fokine, revealed another facet of her talent. This was a vivacious polka, "Champagne". After this Pavlova's collaboration with Fokine strengthened and became ever closer. Like Fokine she sought the portrayal of the human spirit in dance. That was the secret of the great impact she made. She lived her roles and *was* what she had to impersonate.

Fokine dedicated to Pavlova the best creations of his early years. For her he created "The Dying Swan", *Les Sylphides*, *Le Pavillon d'Armide* and the Mariinsky version of *Nuits d'Egypte*. In her book Vera Krasovskaya made an important discovery (derived from a study of contemporary posters) of the exact date when "The Swan" (to music from "La Vie des Animaux" by Saint-Saëns) was first performed by Pavlova. This took place on December 2, 1907, at a charity performance on the stage of the Mariinsky Theatre (though the choreographer mentioned 1905 as the date in his memoirs).

Fokine choreographed for Pavlova a dance-monologue that became an incarnation of the music, or music itself as Pavlova danced it. Lyrical in its conception, it was gradually transformed by the ballerina into a dance of tragic pathos.

The ten years of Pavlova's career in her own country were the most important ones in her life as an artist. On November 18, 1909, the ballerina had a benefit performance in the role of Nikia on the occasion of her tenth anniversary at the Mariinsky. She was received by the public with enthusiasm. However, her time at the Imperial Theatres was running short. She was not given some roles that she wanted to dance, for according to an unwritten tradition they were "the property" of definite ballerinas. She was not popular with the Directorate of the Imperial Theatres, which declined to forget the role Anna Pavlova had played in the dancers' strike of 1905. She continued being insubordinate and refused to follow the customary path. As such she was undesirable. The Directorate was not anxious to renew contracts, for after ten years' service the

[1] *Op. cit.*, p. 143.

ballerina was no longer obliged to dance exclusively for the Imperial Theatres and could appear but occasionally on its stages. She started touring abroad more and more frequently and in the end settled in London, purchasing Ivy House (in 1913) and founding a school for British girls there. Her role in the forming of English dancers, her influence on the young British ballet are well known and belong to the history of ballet in Britain. Equally important is Pavlova's influence on dancers all over the world.

But the period of Pavlova's life and work in Russia is the most important one in her own biography. It was in her own country that she danced leading parts in seventeen multi-act ballets, it was here that, despite all the limitations of the repertory on the Imperial stage, she was enabled to create complete characterizations. Anything she did afterwards consisted of reaping the benefits of that first creative period of her life.

When she danced on the Mariinsky stage one of the old balletomanes wrote: "They say that ballet is on the decline. Have you forgotten that Pavlova is dancing? And only when she is not on the stage, does ballet cease to exist."[1]

[1] See Svetlov, *op. cit.*, p. 319.

CHAPTER IX

DURING THE OCTOBER REVOLUTION OF 1917 AND AFTER

THE HISTORY OF ballet in Russia after 1917 is connected with a new phase in the Russian school as a whole, new in its very substance and quality. The great events that took place in the country radically changed not only its political order but the entire way of living and thinking. The gale of the Revolution gave a new lease of life to all branches of art, which reached an unprecedented flowering. It penetrated into the musty sanctum of the Imperial ballet that had been going through an acute state of crisis on the eve of the Revolution. While justly occupying the position of the best ballet in Europe (and, therefore, in the world), towards the end of the nineteenth and the beginning of the twentieth century, artistically it found itself in a cul-de-sac, and no single person, however talented, could have led the art of ballet, so faithfully served by Russian dancers, out of the situation. No internal reform within the ballet, no formal changes in its outward appearance, no new talents that were being constantly fed to the two companies from the schools, could have brought about the change the necessity for which was felt by every genuine artist. How many of them had departed from their own country failing to find artistic satisfaction and resenting the bureaucractic atmosphere of the Imperial ballet.

Anna Pavlova had settled in England in 1913. Since ballet in Russia was available only on the Imperial stage, she was unable to find an outlet for her great talent elsewhere in the country. Moreover, as a great dramatic ballerina she needed the surroundings of a great company steeped in the national tradition; hence her failure to find true satisfaction and application in the course of her long life abroad. Mikhail Fokine was marking time at the Mariinsky Theatre—the infrequent ballets he had created in the period preceding the Revolution no longer constituted an artistic unity and failed to attract a wide public.

Ballet continued to be looked upon as a source of entertainment for the privileged few. It could not go on living that way.

After the October Revolution the Soviet ballet started by changing the very purpose of art. It revived and developed on an unprecedented scale the best traditions of the Russian ballet, that had been combating throughout its history the principle of "spectacular entertainment for entertainment's sake."

Inheriting the great national traditions of the Russian ballet, Soviet ballet subjected them to a critical eye, selecting only those which had withstood the test of time and harmonized with the range of ideas, themes, and human content prevalent in Russian theatre as a whole.

The art of ballet transgressed the borders of pure entertainment and was raised to a more elevated plane to stay for ever in that category.

Anatoly Lunacharsky, the erudite first Soviet Commissar of Education[1] (all theatrical arts were under the auspices of this Commissariat), made a speech in March 1921 that defined the attitude of the Soviet government to the art of ballet and to the great achievements of the Russian school. Speaking of the great tradition of the past he said: "To lose this thread, to allow it to break before being used as the foundation of a new artistic culture—belonging to the people—this would be a great calamity, and, if it depends on the will of certain persons—a great crime. . . . Can ballet be abolished in Russia? No, this will never happen."[2]

Further in the same speech, extolling the "remarkable traditions of the Russian art of ballet" and the perfection of the dancers, Lunacharsky said: "We need the old art not only because it is valuable in itself, pleasant and perfect. We need it because new candles are lit from this torch and because new generations, growing around such artists, thus inherit the traditions of the school."

These words were very important, and the emphasis on the values and importance of national tradition in art and those who represented it was intentional.

It was a time when the very right of ballet to existence was questioned by those who wanted to create the new by completely destroying the

---

[1] Before the Revolution, apart from being an important political figure, Lunacharsky was a professional theatre, art, and music critic. He wrote notices on the Paris seasons of the Diaghilev ballet in 1912-1914 for Russian magazines and newspapers. His last article on the Diaghilev ballet pertained to the season of 1927 and contains an account of a conversation with Diaghilev and an evaluation of the latter's artistic outlook. Published in *Evening Moscow* of June 1927. To be found in: A. V. Lunacharsky. *In the World of Music (V Mire Musyki)*. Collected and edited by G. Bernandt and I. Sats. Moscow, 1958, pp. 343-350).

[2] From the speech by A. V. Lunacharsky at the jubilee of Yekaterina Geltser, March 6, 1921. Quoted from: Yuri Bakhrushin. "Dance in Soviet Schools," in: *The Art Education of Soviet Schoolchildren*," issue I, Moscow, 1947, p. 170.

old, particularly when it concerned ballet, so directly associated with court pleasures. Representatives of "Proletkult" (short for "proletarian culture," this organization had branches in many towns, published its own magazines and claimed a complete monopoly in the administration of art) wanted to invent "new forms" in laboratory conditions entirely divorced from life and its realities. Since they professed that their kind of art was revolutionary they often succeeded in attracting the attention of audiences. The doors of the former Mariinsky in Petrograd and of the Bolshoi in Moscow were flung open to the people—not only figuratively, but literally, since tickets were free and distributed among factories and mass organizations. A new, eager, and very responsive spectator came to the theatre. In the effort to satisfy this new kind of spectator and in the quest for a new repertory, representatives from the "Workshop of monumental theatre" in Petrograd announced that for the purpose of "revolutionizing the opera and ballet repertory the administration of the academic theatres, apart from holding competitions, has deemed it advisable to change the stories of some old operas and ballets that have great musical value, but whose subjects are alien to proletarian ideology."[1]

Experiments were made with ballets. *King Candaules* emerged with a new story having nothing to do with Théophile Gautier, from whom the original story was directly borrowed. It was now built around a popular uprising against the tyrant Candaules led by Clytia, a shepherdess. Pugni's music was newly orchestrated by Boris Asafiev, while the general plan of Petipa's choreography and the traditional *décor* by Levot, Shishkov, and three other *décorateurs* of the Imperial Theatre remained intact. It goes without saying that this version of *King Candaules* was very short-lived.

The choreography of *King Candaules* was revived and adapted to the new plot by Leonid Leontiev (1885-1942), the Mariinsky dancer and mime who had taken part in the first seasons of the Diaghilev ballet.

Leontiev was not endowed with a suitable figure for classical ballet, but possessed perfect professional knowledge of its technique (he was a pupil of Legat), outstanding mimic abilities, and a fine feeling for style and costume which enabled him to develop into a very good artist. After the Revolution he headed the ballet department of the Theatre School (1918-1920) and was manager of the ballet company (1922-1925). As ballet-master he revived and produced many ballets, revealing no mean choreographic talent. Together with Lopukhov, Monakhov, Chekrygin, and Shiryaev he was among those former Mariinsky dancers who made

[1] See: Yuri Slonimsky. *Soviet Ballet*, Iskusstvo, Leningrad, 1950, p. 47.

Final scene of Fedor Lopukhov's *Dance Symphony* (1923) to music of Beethoven's Fourth Symphony. Autographed by Fedor Lopukhov: "All the participants". Georgi Balanchivadze (George Balanchine) is kneeling on the right; Gusev over him; Lidia Ivanova is being lifted in the centre by Mikhailov; Leonid Lavrovsky (Ivanov) kneels on the right of Mikhailov; Alexandra Danilova on the left is being lifted by Ivanousky. The composition represented the cosmogonic spiral (the other title of the ballet was *Greatness of the Universe*). Note that all the participants are linked with one another.

Joseph the Beautiful, music by S. Vasilenko, choreography by Kasyan Goleizovsky. Experimental Theatre, Moscow, 1925. Scene from Act I.

every effort to maintain the normal life of the ballet after the company had lost forty per cent of its personnel, and pessimistic reports predicted the inevitable disintegration and complete annihilation of ballet in Petrograd.

Such prophecies notwithstanding, ballet continued its activity, gaining increased popularity with the audiences despite difficult conditions. Food was scarce and there were days when no bread was available upon presentation of the ration card. The theatre was unheated and ballerinas stood in its wings in *valenki* (warm felt boots), wrapped up in shawls, discarding them just before going "on stage". Otherwise nothing was sacrificed to the detriment of art; neither makeup, nor costume, nor, and that was the most important of all, the elegance of manner and the truthfulness of characterization.

The ballerina who took upon her shoulders the burden of the entire classical repertory in the first years was Yelizaveta Gerdt (born in 1891). Yelizaveta Gerdt inherited the great beauty and sculptural line of her illustrious father. She entered the former Theatre School in 1899 and was taught in the first years by Anna Johansson, daughter of the celebrated master, Christian Johansson. She graduated in 1908 from the class of Fokine. One year before graduation, in 1907, she was chosen by him to take part in the graduation performance of Nijinsky's class, dancing with him in the "Animated Gobelins"—the scene that eventually led to *Le Pavillon d'Armide*.

Having been promoted to the rank of first solist in 1913, Gerdt had just reached full maturity as a dancer by 1917, when on February 5 she danced her first ballerina part, learning in one day the role of Izabelle in the Glasunov-Petipa ballet *The Trial of Damis* (*Ruses d'Amour*) because Karsavina was suddenly prevented by illness from appearing that night. The new ballerina's lovely figure, innate grace and beauty could not have been shown to better advantage than in this Watteau-inspired Petipa ballet.

The most fruitful period in her career came after the Revolution, when most of the leading Mariinsky ballerinas had left the country. Gerdt had no less than fifteen leading roles in her repertory, from *Swan Lake* to *The Red Whirlwind*—the first attempt at the creation of a Soviet ballet (to music by V. Deshevov) made by Fyodor Lopukhov in 1924. This was a "synthetic production", wherein speech, song, and acrobatics were combined with dancing. The "ballet" was presented in the form of a heavy allegory in two "processes" (the simple word "act" was declared obsolete, standing for the conventions of the old theatre). The prologue was conceived as the victory of the red star over the cross, symbolizing tsardom. This was achieved with the help of settings and props—no dancers participated in the prologue as there was nothing for them to do.

The "First Process" contrasted the idea of socialism, symbolized by the *premier danseur*, Viktor Semenov, and reactionary ideas impersonated by Yelizaveta Gerdt, who was given languid feline poses.

The "Second Process" was done in a very naturalistic vein. It showed speculators selling their wares in the streets while the population actively opposed them.

The Prologue was done in the form of a thinly disguised apotheosis of the old ballet, and represented a "Union of the City and the Village" with peasants carrying sickles and sheaves of corn, and workers waving heavy hammers.

All this primitivism had nothing to do either with ballet or with the ideas it was trying to show in visual form. However, the *Red Whirlwind* is very typical of the type of stage performance to be seen in the early twenties. The ballet stage was not limited to the two opera houses in Petrograd and Moscow. There were numerous studios, theatres attached to organizations, mass dance demonstrations during meetings and the like. In Petrograd in particular the situation was very tumultuous as the art life of the city was seething with various groups representing modern factions.

Although the influence of the "Proletkult" was strong it did not last long. By 1922 the organization had died a natural death, expedited in particular by Lenin's famous letter wherein he condemned as "theoretically wrong and practically harmful" any attempts to invent their own special kind of culture and establish a "Proletkult autonomy". Proletarian culture, taught Lenin, has not emerged from nowhere. It should be a logical development of all the store of knowledge evolved by humanity.

Ballet was a national treasure accumulated by generations of Russian dancers, teachers and choreographers. A large group of former Mariinsky artists safeguarded this national heritage. A great event was the revival of *The Sleeping Beauty* in 1922. It was carried out by Fyodor Lopukhov (although rabidly supporting advanced and at times weird ideas, he was a serious connoisseur of the classical ballet), with the assistance of Bocharov and Leontiev. The complete Petipa choreography, including parts of it that used to be cut (the "Hunt" preceding the "Vision Scene") was carefully revived. This revival provided the company with sufficient dancing material on which to perfect itself, as modern ballets of the time had practically no dancing at all. Attention to the classical legacy was also attracted by Igor Glebov's (Boris Asafiev's) erudite "Letters on Russian

Opera and Ballet" published in the *Weekly Monitor of the Petrograd Academic Theatres*. His analysis of the music of *The Sleeping Beauty*, published in No. 5 for 1922, remains to this day an unsurpassed work, helping us to appreciate the great symphonic beauty of Tchaikovsky's creation.

In the same period Yuri Slonimsky (born in 1902) was among the first writers to lay the foundation of Soviet ballet criticism, analytical in style and scientific in its approach. At a time when annihilation of everything left from the past was in the air and the young dancers of the former Mariinsky theatre were also carried away by this wave, Slonimsky undertook a translation of Noverre's letters and wrote monographs on the history of *La Sylphide* and *Giselle*.

Yuri Slonimsky's small monograph, describing the origin of *La Sylphide* and the history of its presentations in Russia, remains a valuable source of information.[1]

La Sylphide was produced for the Vladimir Ponomaryov graduation class of 1922. The part of James was danced by Pyotr Gusev—destined to become one of the leading figures in Soviet ballet.

Among the ballerinas dancing Aurora in 1922 one may still find the name of Olga Spesivtseva. After her departure the bulk of the repertory was undertaken, in turn with Gerdt (who retired in 1928 to become a leading teacher), by Yelena Lucom (born in 1891).

An ethereal, beautifully built dancer, Lucom was one of the most interesting ballerinas of the period. She graduated in 1909 and took part in the first "Russian seasons" in Paris. From 1912 a soloist, she was promoted to ballerina rank in 1918. Her range was great—from the lyrical *Giselle* to the dramatic *Esmeralda*. Lucom was, so to speak, the last ballerina of the old Mariinsky ballet, having danced in its ranks and having been trained in its precepts. At the same time she was the first ballerina of Soviet ballet, not only because she performed for twenty-odd years in all of its repertory, but because her very art was new. Together with her partner, the excellent dancer Boris Shavrov, she was the first to use high lifts bordering on acrobatics in the numerous recitals that this couple gave in those years. She created the role of Tao-Hoa in the Leningrad version of *The Red Poppy*, danced the leading role in the controversial *Age of Gold*, and in general was the leading Leningrad ballerina until the Soviet school produced its first Soviet-trained *danseuse*, Marina Semenova.

With a whole group of people promoted from its own ranks to revive and safeguard the classical repertory, with a strong group of dancers fully

[1] Yuri Slonimsky. *Sylphida*, Academia, Leningrad, 1926.

capable of performing in it, with the resumption of a normal functioning of the school that survived repeated attempts on the part of the "Prolet-kult" to abolish all professional artistic education whatsoever, the ballet in Petrograd of the early twenties successfully passed through its critical period.

Various circumstances enhanced this state of crisis. The company lacked for a long time any definite artistic leadership. In the first years after the Revolution Fokine was still with it. He was respected and admired as a creator, some of his ballets were maintained in the repertory, and the artistic council elected at the Mariinsky, with Asafiev and Benois among its members, was in favour of mounting his *Petrushka* (rejected in previous years by the administrators of the Imperial Theatres). The company on the whole was ready to support these plans and, moreover, was ready to promote Fokine to the post of chief choreographer and ballet-master.

Fokine was inclined to head the former Mariinsky ballet but only on certain conditions: a very high fee, unconditional acceptance of his future ballets, a yearly prolonged vacation abroad and the casting of his wife, Vera Fokina, in leading roles of the classical repertory (she was a *demi-caractère* dancer). The company was agreeable to most of Fokine's demands. However, some of them caused resistance among its members, particularly the dictatorial tone of the conditions, the categorical insistence on making Vera Fokina a ballerina, and the extremely high remuneration expected. As Yuri Slonimsky says in his comprehensive introductory article to the Russian edition of the *Fokine Memoirs*, "artists, who have only recently freed themselves from the unlimited authority of the admini-strators of the Imperial Theatres, detested any attempt at dictatorship, even though it derived from a famed and honoured master".[1] Slonimsky goes on to say that Fokine always reacted hurtfully to any criticism and particularly to any belittling of his wife's professional merits. Since negotiations concerning the production of *Petrushka* and the acceptance of Fokine's conditions were being somewhat delayed, he demonstratively refused to accept the post of chief choreographer, and, having taken a short leave, went to Sweden for two months to mount *Petrushka*. From Sweden Fokine went to America.

In later years Fokine received several offers to return to Leningrad, including one from Exkusovich (Administrator of the Academic Theatres)

[1] Yuri Slonimsky. "Fokine and his time". In: M. Fokine. *Against the Current*. Memoirs of the ballet-master, articles, letters. Iskusstvo, Leningrad, 1962, p. 43.

The Red Poppy, music by R. Glière, choreography by V. Tikhomirov and L. Lashchilin, décor by M. Kurilko. Bolshoi Theatre, Moscow, 1927. Scene from Act I.

Olga Mungalova and Pyotr Gusev in *The Ice-maiden* by Fedor Lopukhov
to music by Grieg. Leningrad, 1927. (Courtesy of Fedor Lopukhov)

on behalf of Lunacharsky to mount several of his ballets in connection with the twenty-fifth anniversary of the master's artistic activity,[1] when it was proposed to arrange a gala programme to last several days. Fokine agreed, appointed a date, and never came. He was often harassed by doubts, not the least of which was the fear of losing material gain. He paid for this by being practically deprived of the possibility of creating, while still fully capable of doing so. His last ballet *Russian Soldier* significantly spoke of nostalgia experienced by a dying man for his own land. . . .

After Fokine's departure the company continued its normal activity, despite extraneous circumstances in its way. The *Weekly Monitor of Academic Theatres* for 1922 contains interesting material proving that Nicolai Legat and Nicolai Sergeyev were both aspiring to lead the Petrograd company, while the company, having vivid memories of their career-making with the Imperial Theatres and, in particular, Sergeyev's treatment of the artists, was not at all anxious to have either of them at their head.

Legat's pedagogical claims were too well known not to be appreciated, but any other claims were unfounded, as he had no particular talent for choreography and was far from welcome as a leader. Legat demonstratively went to work in Moscow. Shortly afterwards he returned to Petrograd, in the hope of having his claims satisfied. However, he was appointed to the post of supernumerary ballet-master, mime, and teacher. Legat addressed Lunacharsky with a long petition repeating his claims and presenting the position in the Petrograd ballet in the darkest possible colours.[2]

Legat was supported by the balletomane, critic, and writer, Akim Volynsky, who had organized in the twenties his own "School of Russian Ballet" employing many teachers from the Mariinsky school.[3] One of Legat's chief conditions was for Volynsky to be appointed head of the Mariinsky school. The company resented this, considering Volynsky to be no more than a dilettante in ballet and resenting his participation in the intrigues.

Particular resentment was caused by Legat and Volynsky's attempts to restore Nicolai Sergeyev to the post of director of the former Mariinsky company. Since there was hardly a person in it who had not suffered

[1] *Ibid.*, p. 44.

[2] See *Weekly Monitor of the Academic Theatres*, Petrograd, 1922, No. 7, pp. 30-32.

[3] Vaganova taught there for a while. Vera Volkova studied at this school.

in the past from Sergeyev's treatment in some form or other, such a suggestion met with a storm of indignation.[1]

All these problems were discussed, according to the custom of the time, in an open meeting of the State Academic Ballet Company of Petrograd with the participation of the Theatre School, the administration, Pressmen and representatives of the public.

I. V. Exkusovich, Administrator of the Academic Theatres, in his concluding speech, expressed the opinion that the Petrograd ballet "had not yielded anything in quality compared with prewar standards, despite the extremely difficult conditions and unexpected complications. Artists of the ballet," said Exkusovich, "are continuing to bring great sacrifices to the altar of their arts."

The resolution, passed at this meeting, said that the school had also emerged with flying colours from hardships and tribulations, and, having preserved all the best traditions of classical ballet, was energetically introducing reforms suited to the spirit of the time, being "the only treasury of choreographic art in the world".

These reforms, brought about by the new content of Soviet ballet, the new requirements posed by its choreography, were associated to a considerable extent with the name of Agrippina Vaganova (1879-1951). A graduate of 1897 (class of Pavel Gerdt), and pupil of Yekaterina Vazem and Nicolai Legat, she had absorbed much from the methods of her predecessors before working out her own. During her own career as a dancer (she was known as the "Queen of *variations*" and possessed an elevation and *batterie* that were second to none), and although she was not an actual Cecchetti pupil, she gained much from observing his classes and from watching the work of Preobrajenskaya (a pupil of Cecchetti). From all these teachers and dancers she acquired varied aspects of the classical school, re-working them, blending them into one whole and adding from her own experience and that of the young Soviet ballet.[2]

Having begun as a staunch supporter of the Mariinsky routine and opponent of Fokine, Vaganova gradually became his great admirer and follower, and the master entrusted her with the "Mazurka" in his

---

[1] It was because of this attitude of the company that Nicolai Sergeyev went to work in the Moscow Bolshoi Theatre soon after the Revolution. Having gained no popularity in the Moscow ballet he soon emigrated via Constantinople.

[2] A detailed description of the technical aspects of Vaganova's system may be found in an article by this author in: *Dance and Dancers* for January 1962, p. 17.

Chopiniana (1913). Unfortunately, Vaganova possessed neither good looks nor influential protectors, so she was given the official status of ballerina only in 1915, shortly before her retirement from the stage, according to the established practice of the Imperial Theatres, upon twenty years of service. She had performed leading roles in *La Source* (Naïla), *Swan Lake* (Odette-Odile), *The Hump-Backed Horse* (Tsar-Maiden), *The Beautiful Pearl* (one of the two pearls—a ballerina part), and numerous solos in other ballets that were even more important—the *cabriole en avant variation* in "The Shades" scene from *La Bayadère* is known to this day as the "Vaganova *variation*," at least in the Leningrad ballet.

Vaganova retired at the height of her career. She did not start teaching because she did not feel there was any particular need for her knowledge. But after the Revolution, when there was a great demand for teachers and when a new type of school was being formed, Vaganova started working with great enthusiasm and energy. In 1919-1921 she taught at Akim Volynsky's School of Russian Ballet. In 1921 she was invited to teach at the Leningrad Choreographic Technikum—the former Mariinsky School, and she soon rose to the position of its leading teacher. In 1922 she appeared for the last time in a benefit performance in *Chopiniana* and in the "Grand Pas" from *Paquita*, demonstrating her exceptional *ballon* and steel *pointes*. Her first pupils, Natalia Kamkova and Marina Semenova, took part in the performance. Vaganova trained them from their first class to the last. Later she took classes only for pupils in their last two years, and taught the *classe de perfectionnement* for the company. In those first years she was actually creating and trying out her method on her pupils.

Marina Semenova, the first *prima ballerina* of Soviet ballet (born in 1908, graduated in 1925) became an ideal embodiment of the Vaganova method.

Vaganova pupils acquired the space-conquering amplitude of movement that became a sign manual of the Soviet school. Their *tours* were more impetuous, the elevation more soaring, the back and head poised, the arms more fluid and expressive. The classical line remained as pure as ever, but it allowed greater variety. Soviet choreographers started taking advantage of Vaganova-trained pupils (they expressed not only the Vaganova system, but the *age* they lived in, with its soaring spirit). Vaganova, in turn, was also influenced by the style of Soviet choreography and this did not fail to be reflected in her work. She kept constantly studying works of Soviet choreographers and borrowing from them to keep abreast with the times.

Vaganova fostered a constellation of ballerinas and leading soloists and exerted a great influence on the style of male dancing in Soviet ballet. The Vaganova principles could not fail to find their way into teaching male dancing, inasmuch as they became the foundation of the syllabuses in all schools. To sum up the most important features of the Vaganova method, it should be stated that there was nothing in it that could be isolated from other elements in her school. Everything was subordinated to the main goal of bringing the human body into a state of complete and harmonious co-ordination of all its parts. However, the "Vaganova back" was the first thing that struck the eye in Vaganova-trained dancers. This was due to the exceptional placing of the *trunk* that, according to the professor's maxim, should be the "master of the body". She taught the pupil to "dance out of the body", so that the muscles of the trunk governed the movement of the limbs. This could be reached only after a prolonged education of muscular sensations on the part of the dancer, learning how to bring into action any part of her body and any muscles without applying unnecessary energy to its other parts. Vaganova pupils were famed for their *équilibre*. At the same time, while being firmly placed on the ground, the strength of their backs enabled them to "take off" at any given moment and soar in the air, continuing to move and to manœuvre their body *during* the flight.

In the lively experimental period of the twenties Vaganova more than taught—she *learnt* from those of her pupils who, like Olga Mungalova (1905-1942), took part in the boldest of experiments initiated by Fyodor Lopukhov (born in 1886). In the ballets of Fyodor Lopukhov the entire gamut of classical ballet was interwoven, and at times very adroitly, with numerous acrobatic tricks, particularly used by the choreographer in high lifts. Olga Mungalova, lithe, agile, endowed with a beautiful body, was ideal material for Lopukhov's experiments.

Vaganova on the whole opposed the trend that choreography was taking in those years. At any rate she was against the idea, current at the time, that new works should completely replace the classical ballet. In answer to the numerous attacks on the "old ballet" she wrote in those years: ". . . Those who assert that the old ballet has spent itself and should be forgotten are deeply wrong. . . . If art should, indeed, reflect contemporary life, it does not mean that classical examples of its past should disappear."[1]

[1] Published in the magazine *Life of Art* (Leningrad), 1925, No. 7, this article was reprinted in the volume *Agrippina Yakovlevna Vaganova* published in Leningrad in 1958 in her memory and containing all her writings, and valuable articles by her pupils. See pp. 63-64, *op. cit.*

Yet, while other representatives of the classical tradition looked upon the new ballets with distrust mingled with open hostility, Vaganova's attitude was different. When she saw that Mungalova was looking for some other means of "warming up" her entire body before performing in the taxing Lopukhov ballets, she came to her rescue. Together with Mungalova she worked out some exercises suitable for the purpose, and even started including in her own company classes (not at the School) a few acrobatic movements and even whole dance phrases from new ballets. At the same time she maintained that "so-called 'theatricalized' acrobatics or gymnastics, to be acceptable on the stage, should be based on the classical exercises. The technique of execution of the classical dance has reached unprecedented perfection. . . . Our dancers, educated according to the principles of contemporary classical training, are able to cope with *any* difficulties."[1]

In some notes written in 1929, and published posthumously in the already mentioned volume, Vaganova made the matter quite clear by saying: "Give us a Soviet theme and then we shall succeed in producing a highly artistic Soviet production even with the idiom of old classical ballet. As to eccentric-acrobatic elements they should occupy the modest one per cent that is their only worth."[2]

The fact remains, however, that many acrobatic lifts, unknown until that time in ballet, became part of the idiom of Soviet ballet and continue to remain so. In many contemporary ballets Lopukhov's discoveries appeared as powerful and convincing means of expression—if they were employed in the right place and if their use was controlled.

In the controversial *Ice Maiden* produced in 1927 to the score of *Peer Gynt* and other music by Grieg, selected and orchestrated by Asafiev, with colourful settings and costumes by Golovine, Lopukhov at times succeeded in attaining great heights of plastic expression with the help of entirely new movements. The Ice Maiden traverses the stage with sharply accentuated steps *sur les pointes*. Then suddenly this heavy stance changed into a series of "splits", followed by high, masculine jumps. All these movements, so unusual in classical ballet of the time, helped to create the merciless, "ice-cold" character of the Ice Maiden, perfectly impersonated by Olga Mungalova.

In the prologue of the ballet, when an old Norwegian told a tale about the Ice Maiden bringing death to people, Mungalova appeared on a tree to the accompaniment of Grieg's "Solveig's Song".

When the young Norwegian, Asak (Pyotr Gusev), descended into the

[1] *Op. cit.*, p. 68.　　[2] *Ibid.*, p. 67.

ravine on skis, the Ice Maiden appeared to him as a vision, now growing out of a heap of snow, and again hanging from a tree. It was in this scene that the Ice Maiden performed her weird stance, surrounded by other ice maidens and cobolds. After a realistic act with wedding dances on the occasion of Asak's marriage to a peasant girl, Solveig (another incarnation of the Ice Maiden), there followed a final scene of fantasy. Winds and Snowstorms, together with the Ice Maiden's retinue, attacked Asak. To Grieg's "Valse-Caprice" a row of ice maidens, all dressed exactly like Asak's beloved, and repeating her "ice stance" with the "splits", seemed to tease Asak. When he tried to embrace any one of them, they collapsed, melting like snow under the fire of his passion. In the finale the snowstorm became stronger, its spirits threw Asak about. The youth, trying to save himself, ran to the tree where he first saw the Ice Maiden. Holding on to a withered branch, he fell, head downwards. The Winds danced around in victory. The ballet ended with the Ice Maiden standing in a majestic pose on the tree, while Asak's dead body lay at her feet.

Ice Maiden, produced in September 1927, remained in the repertory for several years and was performed over sixty times. Its novel choreography was excellently rendered by talented young dancers headed by Mungalova and Gusev. An even more controversial production was created by Lopukhov during the summer of 1922. The daring choreographer of *Tanzsymphonia* (*Dance Symphony*), done to the complete score of Beethoven's *Fourth Symphony*, was assisted by a cast of eighteen young enthusiasts ready to give up their summer holiday after a season's hard work and come regularly and quite altruistically for rehearsals. Among the dancers there were a youth of nineteen by the name of Georgi Balanchivadze, who was to leave in a year's time eventually to join the Diaghilev company; Leonid Ivanov, who later on acquired fame as the choreographer of *Romeo and Juliet*; Professor Leonid Lavrovsky; Pyotr Gusev, celebrated Soviet dancer and ballet-master; and Nicolai Ivanovsky, future artistic director of the Leningrad school. The ballerinas of this production were Alexandra Danilova and Lidia Ivanova. The first became an international star. The latter, perhaps possessing "star" quality to an even greater extent, died tragically (drowned) the following summer having never reached the brilliant flowering predicted for her.

Tanzsymphonia was shown for the first and for the last time on March 7, 1923, to a mixture of hissing and applause, at a benefit performance for the *corps de ballet*. Lopukhov by then headed the ballet company of the former Mariinsky Theatre. This position enabled him to achieve the dance symphony that had been first conceived by the choreographer as early as 1916. It was then that he wrote the manuscript of his book *Paths of the Ballet-master* that was published only in 1925.[1]

The young dancer Fyodor Lopukhov described in great detail his choreographic *credo*. The elaborate programme of the future *Tanz-symphonia* formed part of the book. The budding choreographer conceived a grandiose symphony as the entire cycle of life in the Universe: the Birth of Light, the Growing of Life out of the destruction of all that preceded it in Death, the Joy of Existence, etc. All this was slightly naïve and at times veiled in imagery, clear, most likely, to the choreographer alone, but the symphonic principle of dance composition was unparalleled.

In a special chapter Lopukhov presented a complete *exposé* of his theory of symphonic dance: he said that the choreographer should begin by studying the orchestral parts and getting to know the score in its entirety, in order to be able to convey through dance all the subtleties of instrumentation.

In an analysis of the development of ballet music the author said that early ballets were orchestrated on the same principle as the *répétiteur* for a piano and two violins, and there was no radical difference between the piano part and the orchestra score. The situation became entirely changed after Tchaikovsky, when the choreographer risked running into disharmony with the music in almost every bar, if he failed to get acquainted with the orchestra score. Lopukhov analysed the music and the choreography of *The Sleeping Beauty* and claimed that Petipa, when working only with the *répétiteur*, produced unmusical dances such as Aurora's *variation* in the "Vision Scene". On the other hand, when Petipa did know which instrument in the orchestra was going to perform the musical theme, particularly in cases of orchestra *soli*, he produced choreography of genius that was in full accord with the music, such as in some parts of *Raymonda*. Lopukhov expressed the opinion that Petipa happened to live in a period when a study of the orchestra score was not an absolute necessity. Such a study of the orchestra score was to be begun by Fokine (the work of Lev Ivanov was not mentioned.—N.R.), although not in his earliest compositions, of which Lopukhov was both witness and direct participant.

Lopukhov also gave an account of his own views on dance and choreography. Bearing in mind that this was formulated some fifty years ago, the little-known book reads today like a manifesto of all the principles of contemporary symphonic choreography. Lopukhov maintained that

[1] Fyodor Lopukhov. *Puti letmeistera (Paths of the Ballet-master)*. Petropolis Publishing House, Berlin, 1925 (in Russian).

side by side with ballets of the classical legacy there should be "dance symphonies, with dance dominant, dance free of the close limitations of the story and accessories with which old ballets were encumbered. The art of dancing is great for the very reason that it is capable of conveying by itself, through the medium of choreography, a situation and surroundings that are in reality unseen, but felt. The art of dancing is capable of making the spectator experience such phenomena as wind or lightning far more strongly than scenic illusions of the same things."

The thirty-year-old ballet-master had a very clear idea of what his future symphony was to be like: *Dance Symphony* has no plot, and contains the development of some choreographic idea that is gradually elaborated in its several symphonic movements.

He also had worked out a theory of what the choreography of a dance symphony should be based on: "1. Choreographic themes should be worked out like musical themes on the principle of antagonism, parallel development and contrast, not on the principle of stringing together casual steps. 2. Movements and music are linked together by the discipline of rhythm. . . . Dance should flow from the music and they should both speak of the same things. Music that depicts soaring can't be bound to a choreographic theme of *crawling*, even though the dance and the music passages are identical rhythmically."[1]

There were many other interesting points, such as that "the musical curve should coincide with the dance curve", that "it is possible to convey choreographically the change in musical tonality, that the major key should correspond to *en dehors* movements, and the minor to *en dedans*," that "a ballet step properly used is capable, even when performed *sur place*, of conveying the quality of transient sonorities."

Many years had to elapse before Lopukhov was able to give visual form to that which had ripened so long ago in his mind. Perhaps he did not succeed in giving a sufficiently vivid visualization to his ideas, or, and this is a more likely explanation, the subject matter chosen by him was unsuited to Beethoven's music, and the work did not produce the desired effect. At any rate the one performance of the *Dance Symphony* had a *succès de scandale*, because some of its movements were regarded as too daring and even obscene.

True to his theory of dance idiom, the choreographer used both classical steps and a kind of *demi-caractère* free movement interspersed with elements of acrobatics. These were met with mainly in the fourth movement, subtitled "Joy of Existence" and showing "mirth of *pithecanthropi*",

[1] F. Lopukhov, *op. cit.*, pp. 101-102.

The Football Player. Music by V. Oransky. Choreography by Lev Lashchilin and Igor Moiseyev. Bolshoi Theatre, Moscow, 1930. Valentina Kudriavtseva and Igor Moiseyev.

Alexei Yermolayev as Siegfried in
Swan Lake. Bolshoi Theatre,
Moscow, *circa* 1938. (Collection of
Natalia Roslavleva)

Vakhtang Chaboukiani as Solor in
La Bayadère. Leningrad, *circa* 1935.
(Collection of Natalia Roslavleva)

etc. This caused particular perplexity. But the parts in which nothing but classical steps appeared were also not understood by the public. Here, particularly in the *grand adage* of the third movement, ordinary steps of the classical exercise were used *choreographically*. The *adagio* commenced with Danilova and Ivanova in a deep *plié*, from which they would rise performing a slow *développé à la seconde* signifying the "awakening of nature by the Spring Sun". The adagio then proceeded to increase in difficulty, arriving at steps of extreme virtuosity, that were used in an unusual way, even if they were classroom steps used at the *barre* and in centre practice. For instance the *danseuses* joined their hands and sank into a *grand plié*, one with her face to the audience, and the other with her back, thus forming a beautiful vignette. There was not a single static or purely mime moment in the whole dance symphony. These new principles could not fail to impress Balanchivadze, one of the participants already very much interested in choreography and doing some for the "Young Ballet" group. *Dance Symphony* was the first ballet to use classroom steps symphonically, and in this respect it is very important.

Subtitled "Magnificence of the Universe", Lopukhov's *Dance Symphony* ended in a finale envisaged by the choreographer as a majestic manifestation of the Universe. All eighteen participants were arranged in a pattern of great beauty. Whether the spectators realized that it was supposed to represent "the cosmogonic spiral" is another matter, but the effect was decidedly spectacular and the choreography original.

A record of this unique production has been preserved for posterity in the form of a booklet, designed in silhouette during the rehearsals by Pavel Goncharov (1886-1941), a dancer and very fine artist, who also designed the costumes. (In white and black, they were deliberately simple—white skirts and blouses with black lapels for the girls, black breeches and white shirts with black lapels for the boys. Both men and girls had black shoes purposely to attract attention to the footwork that was done in the case of the girls *sur les pointes* throughout.)

The cover of the Goncharov-designed booklet[1] shows Andrei Lopukhov, the choreographer's brother, who opened the ballet, walking in the direction of the sun and shielding his eyes from the bright light of creation.

The complex theme was not really sufficiently expressed by the dance to be fully comprehensible, while musicologists claimed that *that* particular kind of philosophy was alien to the nature of Beethoven's *Fourth*

[1] *Velichie Myrozdania. Tanzsymphonia.* Fyodora Lopukhova. S avtosiluetami Pavla Goncharova, Petrograd, 1922.

Symphony, while on the other hand its majestic monumental proportions were not matched by the chamber character of the production.

Contemporary critics did recognize that the symphonic principle of dance composition was a new thing. Fyodor Lopukhov put untold energy into the study of symphonic music. For a whole year he was coached in the art of reading an orchestra score by the conductor Emile Cooper during which the choreographer attended every rehearsal of the Philharmonic orchestra marking all the faults on the score, while Cooper would check his work after the rehearsal.

In the twenties his flair for experiments and novelty at times carried him away a little too far and some of his ballets, such as Stravinsky's *Le Rénard*, can boast the distinction of having been danced to continuous hissing on the part of the public. (A participant in this particular ballet, now a teacher in the Leningrad school, told this author that, being then a second-year pupil, she was cast as one of the hens and was obliged to "lay an egg" that remained dangling on a string.)

Lopukhov's own version of *The Firebird* had a complicated philosophy even more obscure than that of the *Dance Symphony*, and quite unsuited to the fairy-tale. The ballet was divided into seven main ideas, all signifying allegorically the struggle of evil with goodness.[1]

Its choreography was no improvement on that of Fokine.

In 1929 Lopukhov choreographed an entirely new version of *The Nutcracker* in "22 episodes", in which the settings, in the form of flat panels, were carried in by dancers of the *corps de ballet*, while the ballerina was lifted head downwards in an inverted *grand écart* ("splits"). This production seemed to be deliberately controversial like so many things that Lopukhov had staged in that period. But in 1926 he produced a charming *Commedia dell'Arte* production of Stravinsky's *Pulcinella* for which he was praised by Lunacharsky and received a diploma from Italy, and in 1927 his "choreodrama", *The Serf Ballerina*, to music by Korchmaryov, served as a vehicle for the début in the title-role of the first Soviet ballerina and one of the greatest dancers of the Soviet ballet —Marina Semenova.

However, in *The Serf Ballerina* Lopukhov went to another extreme. The scenes wherein serfs were mercilessly beaten were too realistic and the "choreodrama" on the whole lacked unity of action. Not even Semenova's youthful talent could save this ballet from its very short life. It simply did not succeed in creating a truly moving picture of the tragic plight of

[1] See *Weekly Monitor of State Academic Theatres*, Petrograd, 1922, No. 14, pp. 43-44.

serf actors. It is significant that Semenova's first important characterization occurred in a ballet that in those days was termed "old" and obsolete —i.e. in *La Bayadère*. The character of Nikia, an enslaved temple dancer, her love, her tragic suffering and death, all this was rendered by Semenova with a strength of conviction and power of impact that breathed new life into the old ballet. Through the medium of the dramatic material available in the choreography of the ballet, Semenova created a new Nikia, lending the character a heroic note.

Semenova's exceptional eloquence of *plastique* became her greatest asset, due in no small measure to Vaganova's training and her personal supervision of each role. Born in 1908, Semenova entered the former Mariinsky school in 1919 and was Vaganova's pupil from the first to the last year—she graduated in 1925 when barely seventeen. Vaganova immediately recognized this great talent and took special care of the gifted child. She wrote how at the first lesson the tiny, and at first glance unattractive, girl performed such a beautiful *développé à la seconde* that she gasped.[1] At school Semenova loved to dance and was happy when included among the children to take part in ballets on the Mariinsky stage. "It did not matter," wrote Vaganova, "what she danced in, what part she got, in the first pair or in the very last." "Anything she danced was done with enthusiasm and great regard for the purity of the dance pattern," recollected her great teacher. In the last years at school Semenova was already receiving responsible roles such as the Queen of the Dryads in *Don Quixote*. She was spoken of by the knowledgeable ballet audience: her graduation was eagerly awaited.

For Semenova's graduation performance Vaganova revived Delibes' *La Source* and coached her in the role of Naïla, Nymph of the Stream, in which she herself used to excel. However, Vaganova prepared for her pupil not those *variations* which she herself had danced, but three new ones, all composed to demonstrate Semenova's own merits—her beauty of pose, her steel *pointes*, her impetuous leaps.[2]

Semenova's début in the former Mariinsky Theatre (then called the State Academic Theatre in the season of 1925-1926) was in a ballerina role, that of Aurora in *The Sleeping Beauty*. Technically she was superb, but it was the life-asserting quality of her dancing that inspired the audience with a feeling of exhilaration.

[1] Agrippina Vaganova. "My pupils". In: *Agrippina Yakovelvna Vaganova*. Iskusstvo, Leningrad, 1958, pp. 59-60. Also in the same volume: Marina Semenova. "My teacher and friend", pp. 148-158.

[2] Marina Semenova. "My teacher and friend", *op. cit.*, p. 152.

Her greatest role was Odette-Odile performed with an incomparable regal majesty so akin to the Russian national dance with its proud bearing and poise.

Much of Semenova's experience became part of Soviet ballet and was borrowed from her by all the ballerinas that succeeded her, though her personal greatness remains unsurpassed.

In 1930 Semenova was transferred to Moscow where she became *prima ballerina* of the Bolshoi Theatre. In 1935 she danced at the Paris Opéra. She retired from the Bolshoi Theatre in 1952 and devoted herself to teaching a *classe de perfectionnement* for the ballerinas and soloists of the Bolshoi ballet, and coached them as rehearsal ballet-mistress, passing on her great stage experience to *danseuses* learning new roles.

Semenova's role of the first Soviet-trained ballerina expressing the new style and new content of Soviet ballet was duplicated in the sphere of male dancing by Alexei Yermolayev (born in 1910). Yermolayev's role in the history of Soviet ballet, equally, can hardly be exaggerated. He was the first male dancer to develop the virile, heroic manner of dancing. His position in Soviet ballet is unique because, like a few other dancers— Messerer, Chaboukiani, Gabovich, etc.—he did not start academic education as a child yet in spite of this attained extraordinary virtuosity. In 1920 Yermolayev arrived in Petrograd from the village he had been living in with his parents. It was not until 1924, at the age of fourteen, that he entered the former Mariinsky school. Within two years he graduated with honours, having passed examinations in the entire syllabus. He graduated from the class of the celebrated teacher, Vladimir Ponomaryov (1892-1951), in his time an excellent *premier danseur*. Yermolayev's début at the graduation performance in the role of Vayu, the God of Wind from the old Petipa ballet *The Talisman*, caused a sensation. He introduced a new quality, virile and powerful, into the soaring leaps that literally defied the law of gravity.

In the Leningrad ballet Yermolayev danced leading roles from the classical repertory, yet even these were transformed by him into something different. The speed of his *tours* was breath-taking, and he achieved the high and complicated lifts wherein the male dancer becomes a true and equal partner of the ballerina. Yermolayev's characters were boisterous and active. His art, while very individual, was born out of Soviet ballet. It was a challenge for the creation of new ballets with male heroic characters in them. Yermolayev's style of dancing; that of Olga Jordan (born 1907) who had graduated with him; and the art of Semenova, whose type of talent was so often compared to Yermolayev's—all were a step towards the formation of a new kind of ballet spectacle. Years were to pass, before heroic male roles were born in the ballets of the thirties. But after Alexei Yermolayev[1] the male dancer in Soviet ballet was no longer regarded as a *porteur* destined to occupy second place to that of the ballerina.

The number of dancers, both men and women, who had played their part in the building of Soviet ballet in the late twenties and early thirties was very large, and it is not possible to name them all here. Those that have been mentioned expressed to a greater extent the general efforts of the young generation of Soviet ballet. Composers, designers, theatre directors, authors—all took part in the constructive work that was now taking place in a perfect creative atmosphere.

A similar process went on in Moscow, though the ballet of the Bolshoi Theatre did not pass through the acute crises of the Mariinsky, and succeeded in maintaining its artistic unity, although it did experience some crucial moments.

Already on November 9, 1917, the Council of People's Commissars adopted a decree according to which all theatres were placed under the auspices of the Commissariat for Education, which in turn organized in 1918 a special Theatre Department. In 1919 all actors in every branch of art were commissioned to serve in units of the Red Army. A theatrical organization was formed for the purpose in Moscow. Artists from the Bolshoi, Maly, and Art Theatres were the first to perform for the benefit of soldiers. Their appearances encouraged the formation of amateur theatrical and dance groups in Red Army units.

A similar practice took place in Petrograd. Artists of the Academic theatres received highter rations (equal to that of scientists) and were usually paid in kind for appearing before Red Army forces.

Civil war conditions, lack of fuel, electricity, and transport interrupted the normal flow of life. The Bolshoi School building was taken over as a military hospital for the wounded. It was so difficult to heat the Bolshoi Theatre that the question of its closing was raised on several occasions. And each time Lenin categorically opposed any such attempts. The

[1] In 1930 Yermolayev was transferred to the Bolshoi Theatre in Moscow, where he performed more than twenty leading roles. With maturity he became an outstanding dancer-mime. His Philippe in *The Flames of Paris*, Tybalt in *Romeo and Juliet*, Yevgeny in *The Bronze Horseman*, Albrecht in *Giselle* were unforgettable. In 1959 he retired and now teaches in the company and coaches dancers in new roles. He has also done some choreography, notably *The Nightingale* at the Minsk opera (in 1939) to music by M. Kroshner.

Bolshoi Theatre was never closed. The tickets were distributed free. Workers walked many miles from the factory regions of Moscow in order to spend three hours in the theatre's magic. Lunacharsky wrote of that period: "The colossal thirst of people: Red Army men, industrial workers, even peasants, to see a performance was such that for this they were ready to part with some of their very meagre means of livelihood." The Bolshoi Theatre and its affiliated theatre (the former Zimin private opera) had to increase considerably the number of their performances.

The influence of the "Proletkult" and its pseudo-revolutionary theories was strong. There were repeated attacks on the repertory of the Bolshoi Theatre and all that it stood for.[1]

As late as 1925 Anatoly Lunacharsky was obliged to write an article "Why do We Preserve the Bolshoi Theatre?"[2] He reminded his readers of the great artistic values accumulated by opera and ballet and said that the latter in particular will find a special place in the future great mass performances (envisaged by him as a new form of revolutionary art), because "its nature is capable of inspiring the masses to an extraordinary degree and it is capable of according very fine expression to any emotion".

He expressed the opinion that the Bolshoi Theatre had to be preserved with particular care, not, however, "for the purpose of pensioning it off, but in order to continue its work, that should, at least, maintain at the present level its technical perfection, and, better still, advance it to further heights."[3]

Lunacharsky pointed out that, since there were no new works or very few of these, the repertory had to consist of old creations to a considerable extent.

The classical repertory and the precious traditions of the Moscow ballet were preserved by a group of artists devoted to the Bolshoi Theatre. Headed by Gorsky (and upon his death in 1924 by Tikhomirov), with Yekaterina Geltser as its *prima ballerina*, and a large number of talented soloists, the Moscow company did not suffer much either from the departure of some of its members (at times very talented such as Mikhail Mordkin or Sophia Fedorova) or from the considerable attacks from

[1] See Yuri Slonimsky. *Soviet Ballet*. Iskusstvo, Moscow-Leningrad, 1950, p. 43.

[2] Published in 1925 in a souvenir book issued for the 100th anniversary of the Bolshoi Theatre. Reprinted in: *V. Mire Musyki*. Articles and Speeches by A. V. Lunacharsky. Moscow, 1958, pp. 298-306.

[3] A. V. Lunacharsky. "Why do We Preserve the Bolshoi Theatre?" Souvenir book for the 100th anniversary of the Bolshoi Theatre, Moscow, 1925, p. 26.

without and from within. It was busily working, maintaining the old repertory and building up the new. It had Margarita Kandaurova, Victorina Krieger, Maria Reisen, Leonid Zhukov, Vladimir Riabtsev, Ivan and Victor Smoltsov, Lev Lashchilin, and the young ballerinas Yelena Ilyushchenko, Anastasia Abramova, Valentina Kudriavtseva, Lyubov Bank, and Nina Podgoretskaya. The Bolshoi School resumed normal activity in 1920 and by 1925 had graduated fifty-three dancers. In the early twenties there were numerous other ballet schools and studios in Moscow existing side by side with the Bolshoi Theatre School. Young talents starting studies in those private and semi-private studios would come to continue them in the Bolshoi Theatre School with its extensive and more solidly based tuition. This is how dancers like Asaf Messerer (graduated in 1924) found their way to the Bolshoi School in their late teens, and, owing to their talents, and the guidance of Gorsky and Tikhomirov, grew into outstanding dancers.

Youth is usually ready to support anything strikingly new. So it happened that the young dancers started a campaign against the very masters who had taught them, and the tradition they represented. There was a struggle of various trends in the ballet company, a struggle that in a way did it good, since it resulted in a general livening up of the artistic atmosphere. The idea that ballet had to be new and different was in the air, but there were no tried examples and no ready recipes. Most of the early attempts were primitive and so far removed from dancing that they were unable to compete with the high professionalism of the ballet.

On November 6, 1918, for the first anniversary of the Revolution, Gorsky created a one-act ballet, *Stenka Rasin*,[1] to his own scenario. Gorsky wanted to create scenes of popular protest against tyranny. The theme of this early ballet has not been preserved and little is known of its nature, but the leading mime of the Bolshoi ballet, Alexei Bulgakov (1872-1954), a participant in this production, testified that its mass scenes were particularly impressive.

Apart from arranging a children's ballet, *Ever Fresh Flowers* (1922), to music by Tchaikovsky, with interpolations by Asafiev (Gorsky was the first to seek the assistance of this gifted ballet composer), the choreographer concentrated his efforts on the preservation of the classical repertory. In reviving classical ballets he applied, as before, the principle of creating new versions while preserving the best from the past. The

[1] Based on the legendary hero, popularized by the famous song of the same title, and using Glasunov's suite, *Stenka Rasin*.

choreography of *The Nutcracker*, achieved in 1919 with Korovine's settings and costumes, was entirely new.

The first act was done very realistically in the Gorsky manner. The characteristic household of a nineteenth-century German *bürger* was shown in great detail. The rest of the ballet was envisioned poetically as a child's dream. It opened with Masha (such was the new name of the heroine) tracing designs on a frosted window with her finger. The window disappeared to give way to the dance of the snowflakes. There was no tarlatan for tutus in 1919, so Korovine was obliged to dress the snowflakes in an imitation of Russian fur coats, with muffs in their hands. Gorsky gave the music of the Sugar Plum Fairy *variation* to Masha (pupil Valentina Kudriavtseva), while Vasily Yefimov, a very talented dancer both in the classical and *demi-caractère* style, was the Prince-Nutcracker.

While Gorsky's *Nutcracker* did not survive, the tradition of giving the *grand adage* of the Sugar-Plum Fairy and Prince Koklush to Masha and the Nutcracker who, having been freed of the spell put upon him, becomes a handsome prince, has been used in all other Soviet productions of the ballet, notably the most frequently produced version by Vasily Vainonen (1934).

In 1920 Gorsky achieved a new version of *Swan Lake*, his fourth. It was done in collaboration with Vladimir Nemirovich-Danchenko in an effort to introduce the Stanislavsky method into ballet. The production was unusual. Lev Ivanov's compositions were not used at all. Only the frequent use of the *arabesque* and the general style of the *ports de bras* were reminiscent of Lev Ivanov's swan images. The dance patterns were entirely different and all the *corps de ballet* and soloists did not wear tutus but danced in loose tunics in the Duncan style, very much loved by Gorsky. The roles of Odette and Odile were performed by two different ballerinas: Yelena Ilyushchenko and Maria Reisen. They symbolized the struggle of White and Black, with a retinue of black swans supporting Odile (she also appeared in the second act) and white ones for Odette.

This Gorsky production did not survive. But the Jester, introduced here for the first time to create a role for the brilliant Vasily Yefimov, may now be found in all Soviet productions of *Swan Lake*.

In 1922 Gorsky created his final version of *Swan Lake*. This was done with greater respect for past traditions. The Lev Ivanov swan scenes were only slightly changed in pattern. The dual role of Odette-Odile was now done by one ballerina. In the first act Gorsky used to great advantage the experience gained from working with the great theatre director Nemirovich-Danchenko. It enabled him to create lively *mises*

Kasyan Goleizovsky and Yekaterina Maximova taking calls after a recital of the master's *Choreographic Compositions* at the Tchaikovsky Hall, Moscow.

Marina Semenova as Aurora in the gala performance of *Sleeping Beauty* in Leningrad on May 22, 1947, in honour of the 125th anniversary of Petipa's birth, when the name part was danced in each act by a different ballerina—Marina Semenova in the first, Galina Ulanova in the second, and Natalia Dudinskaya in the third. Each had her own partner, while the roles of the King and Queen were also taken by different leading actors in each act. Yekaterina Geltser, then 69, was one of the queens. (Collection of Natalia Roslavleva)

en scène of great impact, wherein every character had its "acting task". He now had a *premier danseur* of the first order—Asaf Messerer.

Born in 1903, Messerer started his first ballet classes when almost sixteen upon seeing his first ballet (*La Fille Mal Gardée*) in 1918. Having resolved immediately that he wished to be a dancer, Messerer studied for a year in a private studio established by Mikhail Mordkin. Within a few months he was accepted into the ballet company of the Theatre of Working Youth—one of the numerous theatrical organizations that were springing up like mushrooms in those early years. He was the only male dancer in that company and, not being engaged very often, he was able to continue his studies at the Studio. He was noticed by Gorsky who taught him privately. When the Bolshoi School was re-opened in 1920 Messerer was accepted directly into its senior class. In 1922, shortly upon graduation, Messerer was given the role of Prince Siegfried in *Swan Lake*. Although Gorsky and the group of dancers supporting him had been doing much to avoid routine in classical ballets, there was plenty of it left. Asaf Messerer boldly replaced incomprehensible conventional mime gestures with expressive acting. His changes of traditional mime caused a turmoil at the theatre. Ballet-masters responsible for rehearsals even thought that he had forgotten the correct gestures in the nervous state caused by the début. But the next performance proved that Messerer's actions were deliberate. He found that conventional gestures may always be replaced by expressive ones through acting. He was encouraged in this by actors of the Art Theatre, who frequently visited the ballet. The young generation greeted his innovations with enthusiasm, other dancers started following his example and many archaic customs disappeared from the ballet. Messerer next set himself the goal of enriching the "vocabulary" of male dancing. He was the first to perform multiple *tours en l'air* and other new *enchaînements* of known steps. Other dancers followed him, thus enriching the technique of male dancing.

Messerer's range was wide. Apart from classical dancing, which remained his main sphere of interest and inspiration, he studied character, grotesque, and folk dances. He performed *danseur noble* parts like Siegfried or Prince Désiré (*The Sleeping Beauty*), *demi-caractère* ones, such as the Fanatic in *Salammbô* and the dance of the Acrobat in *The Red Poppy* that enabled him to exploit his exceptional *ballon* and *elevation*, and grotesque character roles like the Football Player from the Moiseyev ballet of the same title. Messerer retired from the stage in 1954. But he started teaching as early as 1923 and has been conducting a *classe de perfectionnement* for artists of the Bolshoi company since 1942. A devoted disciple of the celebrated master, Vassily Tikhomirov, he acquired much from him as a teacher, developing and expanding the knowledge into his own method.

Of Messerer's numerous productions *Ballet School* is the best, and the most widely shown. Together with his sister and partner, Sulamith Messerer (born in 1908, graduated 1926), a brilliant virtuosity ballerina, Asaf Messerer was among the first Soviet dancers to tour abroad.

When Vassily Tikhomirov, master of the old school, came to head the company, the younger generation of dancers could not be fully satisfied. They did not value (Messerer excepted) the great work done by Tikhomirov and Geltser in safeguarding and preserving the treasures of the classical repertory and the school without which no professional ballet would have been possible. A long feud ensued, in the course of which a group of "dissenters", headed by Igor Moiseyev, was expelled from the Bolshoi Theatre, but re-installed in exactly a week's time.

For a while the imagination of the young generation was captured by the novel choreography of Kasyan Goleizovsky.

Born in 1892, he started ballet training in Moscow, but moved to St. Petersburg in the season of 1906-1907, spending another three years at the Theatre School and graduating into the Mariinsky company. While in Petersburg the young dancer closely studied Fokine's work, being extremely attracted by it. He was understudy to Rosai as the chief buffoon in the "Animated Gobelins". Being transferred to Moscow in 1910, Goleizovsky became closely attached to Gorsky, whose progressive artistic outlook, search for new forms of dance, and dislike of conventional classical ballet answered his own aspirations. Having known both reformers of Russian ballet, Goleizovsky equally valued them. He found them radically different—Fokine, to his mind, worked in the minute detail of an engraver, while Gorsky painted in bright rich dabs. Both masters exerted a strong influence on the young dancer, who wanted to become a choreographer and to find his own dance forms. At that period Goleizovsky met Nikita Balieff of the "Chauve Souris" and formed an artistic alliance with him not only as choreographer but as a *metteur-en-scène* of talent and imagination. He produced one-act plays, operettas, and numerous dance numbers, and had the chance to develop in the "Chauve Souris" his talent for miniatures and grotesques. He even wanted to become a theatrical director and abandon ballet altogether, but was unable to do so; his love for ballet and interest in choreography triumphed.

After the Revolution, while remaining at the Bolshoi Theatre, Goleizovsky formed a private ballet company, "The Chamber Ballet", that for a while served as a centre for new choreographic ideas and exerted considerable influence not only in Moscow, but also in Leningrad, where it gave some recitals. Only dancers with full academic education or not less than eight years of private ballet tuition to their credit were accepted in Goleizovsky's company, which in its actual work used no classroom steps of the classical ballet. If Lopukhov merely wanted to improve upon the old school and insisted upon superseding tradition, Goleisovsky, who knew classical ballet no less than Lopukhov, completely denied it. He maintained that classical steps were only good for those subjects and themes that were created in the same period as the classical ballets of the nineteenth century.

While Goleizovsky was right in saying that themes engendered by new times called for new forms, he went too far in his searches, practically doing away with classical ballet and causing serious, and in many cases quite justified, antagonism on the part of masters such as Tikhomirov, Geltser, and Vaganova who devoted themselves to preserving the heritage of the Russian school. Much of the Goleizovsky choreography of the early twenties was too acrobatic and devoid of action: the dancers were required to take intricate poses rather than to dance. The element of eroticism in his early works was very strong and that also caused displeasure, not only on the part of "purists" but to the general public as a whole. His most important work of that period was *Joseph the Beautiful* to music by Sergei Vasilenko shown at the Experimental Theatre on March 3, 1925, in one programme with another ballet *Teolinda* (satirizing classical ballet). In *Joseph* Goleizovsky, together with the designer Boris Erdman, painted the dancers' bodies to follow a definite colour scheme. Then the dancers were told to form sculptural groups on a constructed setting in the form of steps. Thus beautiful poses, passing from one to another, created the impression of living sculpture rather than dance. Critics said that *Joseph the Beautiful* belonged to the genre of *tableau vivant*.

In order to maintain his position as leader of the young generation in ballet, Goleizovsky had to create something more in harmony with the times. His ballet *Whirlwind*, produced at the Bolshoi Theatre in 1927 to music by B. Beer, was conceived as an allegorical contrast of capitalists performing an orgy expressed in terms of the foxtrot, and proletarians dancing in unison with hammers and sickles. He declared that his ballet signified the struggle of the classes without resorting to the subject matter or definite place of action. At the first presentation spectators started demonstratively leaving their seats, and the ballet was never shown again.

Having failed to formulate a positive artistic programme, Goleizovsky lost his following at the Bolshoi Theatre, and left it.[1]

The classical school won again. Much more could be said to the heart and mind of spectators when Geltser enacted Esmeralda or Krieger[2] invested Kitri of the old *Don Quixote* with the life-like features of a true daughter of the people. All this was based on the classical dance, but it served as means of characterization. This was an old custom of the Moscow ballet, born in the course of a long association first with the Maly, and then the Art Theatre. It now came to full flower, because the emphasis was on dramatic truth.

When Tikhomirov came to head the Bolshoi ballet in 1924 he started by reviving ballets of the classical heritage. It was important to revive *The Sleeping Beauty*, which had dropped out of the repertory. This was done with regard for everything that was best in Petipa's choreography. Tikhomirov realized that it was imperative to create a contemporary ballet. However, the task was too responsible to be tackled without proper preparation. A kind of bridge was needed in order to pass from classical ballets to contemporary themes. An ideal intermediary stage of this kind was found in *Esmeralda*. Tikhomirov had known this ballet in Petersburg, when Perrot's choreography had not been spoilt by later additions. He revived the remarkable *pas d'action* created by Perrot in the "Jealousy Waltz" for Esmeralda, Gringoire, and Phoebus, but asked the composer Reingold Gliere to write new music. He treated the whole ballet as a popular drama and strengthened its anticlerical theme. The cast was such that the rendering of each role reached ultimate perfection. Yekaterina Geltser created her Esmeralda in the heroic vein. Tikhomirov was Phoebus de Chateaupers, Ryabtsev—Quasimodo, Bulgakov—Claude Frollo, Valentina Kudriavtseva danced Fleur de Lys, betrothed to Phoebus and causing Esmeralda's jealousy, while Victor Smoltsov impersonated Gringoire—the role originally created by Perrot himself.

This production had no secondary roles and every dancer acted individually in harmony with the whole. *Esmeralda* had a great success and stayed in the repertory for many years. The only scene changed was the "happy end" that introduced a false note: when the tortured Esmeralda was dragged to the scaffold and the people, rallied by Gringoire, rushed to save her, and Phoebus suddenly appeared with a pardon, Claude Frollo then attempted to kill Phoebus, but Quasimodo, appearing in

[1] In later years Goleizovsky changed his views and did much valuable work that will be considered in another chapter.

[2] Her biography will be given in the next chapter.

time, turned the knife and Claude stabbed himself. His body was carried away and the ballet ended with a crowd scene that returned it to realism. *Esmeralda* served as a prologue to the introduction of the Soviet theme. This was a wise and necessary step.

The importance of *The Red Poppy* was very great. It initiated the heroic theme in Soviet ballet that became inseparably associated with its style and content. It put an end to formalistic trends in ballet for the simple reason that its success was greater than anything that could be produced by opponents of the classical school.

The Red Poppy was born within the Bolshoi Theatre ballet on the initiative of several of its members, and that also spoke of the great changes that were taking place in the company. The theme was conceived by the designer, Mikhail Kurilko, upon reading a short notice in the papers about current events in China. It was worked out in greater detail in collaboration with Yekaterina Geltser, who, as the future heroine of the ballet, was very much attracted by the creation of the dramatically authentic character of Tao-Hoa, the tea-house dancer.

Reingold Gliere composed the music after a detailed plan of the whole ballet was worked out by Tikhomirov, who suggested to him the duration and nature of each dance number. When the production was actually started, Lev Lashchilin, Tikhomirov's assistant, who, as character dancer, was better versed in folk idiom, choreographed the dances of sailors, coolies, and other characters. Alexei Dikiy (1899-1955), a well-known theatrical director, then attached to the Bolshoi as supervisor of opera productions, created the *mise en scène* of the first, most realistic and important act, and suggested the theme of the final dance of the Soviet sailors.

These joint efforts produced a spectacle that gained immediate success upon its presentation on June 14, 1927. In the first ten years of uninterrupted life in the Bolshoi repertory the ballet was shown three hundred times on its stage. It was produced on practically every ballet stage in the country,[1] while its most popular dance—the sailors' "Yablochko" (Little Apple), based on a folk song current at the time of the Civil War, the memory of which was still quite recent—exerted great influence on the formation of amateur dance groups.

In spite of this overwhelming success *The Red Poppy* was very much attacked by the self-appointed "left-wing", who accused the ballet of

[1] In Leningrad, owing to opposition on the part of formalists, *The Red Poppy* was done, with new choreography by F. Lopukhov, V. Ponomaryov, and L. Leontiev, only in 1929.

following the detestable old tradition, without seeing its obvious novelties. The whole line of Tao-Hoa's choreography, though at time done in terms of the *chinoiserie* of nineteenth-century ballet, was developed for the sole purpose of creating a heroine such as had not been met with in the ballets of the past. In Geltser's interpretation (this role provided the ballerina with the greatest possible outlet for her dramatic abilities) the image of the Chinese dancer dying in order to save the Soviet captain (Vassily Tikhomirov) acquired the nature of a universal truth, a generalised portrayal of heroism that was capable of inspiring any audience.

The dances of the Soviet sailors were performed with an equally inspiring exhilarating joy in life, typical of Soviet ballet. And even the interpolated dances of the Acrobat with a Ribbon, and the Golden Acrobat (both were at first performed by Asaf Messerer), acquired importance because they were performed with unprecedented virtuosity and for many years became part of recital programmes.

It is important to note that the first act in particular was composed by Gliere on the symphonic principle and this accounts for its greater completeness in comparison with the other three, and, in particular, with the second one, which was done as a *divertissement* of isolated numbers. The music of the Soviet sailors' dances, ending in the famous "Yablochko" theme, served as a suite inseparable from the whole action.

The Red Poppy brought Soviet ballet to the threshold of its next stage of development—the dramatic ballets of the nineteen-thirties.

CHAPTER X

SOVIET BALLET IN THE THIRTIES

Early in the thirties, when the country was going through a period of gigantic construction and reorganization, Soviet art as a whole experienced an equal transformation. New plays, new heroes, and a whole generation of new actors appeared on the drama stage; works were written that became part of the treasury of Soviet literature. Attention was centred on seriousness of theme and purpose, on broader canvases and ideas.

Ballet could not remain immune to, or ignorant of, these events. It was part of the general life of the country. Moreover, ballet was ready for new subject-matter, and, in particular, for new heroes. *The Red Poppy* had provided dancers with such material, even though it had a rudimentary form. Its choreography proved that the spirit of optimism and heroism could be conveyed through the idiom of classical dance. Roles from the classical repertory that received deep characterizations, new Soviet ballets of the late twenties and the very beginning of the thirties gave birth to many talented young dancers. They needed new roles that would enable them to probe deeply into the inner life of the characters allotted to them. They were no longer willing to be satisfied with the superficial inventions of formalistically-inclined choreographers, displaying new tricks for the sake of tricks, to the detriment of classical dancing and of dance in general. Together with interesting and powerful artistic personalities a group of talented young choreographers appeared. Both dancers and choreographers needed ballets carrying a deep and serious idea, containing a dramatic content that could easily be translated into terms of dance and mime.

Professional dramatists then came to create ballet "books" in accordance with the laws of dramaturgy. Ballets of the new type strove to interpret the content in a fusion of music and dance. The content was based on a conflict between the main protagonists. These were shown in development, with attention not only to outward events of their life but to the thoughts and feelings that actuated them.

The Soviet school of choreography taking shape in the thirties chose themes of noble passions and feelings, of heroic deeds and romantic love. In order to convey such themes and emotions the dancers had to possess a very strong power of projection, the eloquent ability to convey to the audience with conviction the message contained in the story and the music. These qualities, always inherent in the "Russian Terpsichore", received further development in the dramatic ballets of the thirties—*Flames of Paris, Heart of the Hills, Laurencia, Romeo and Juliet* and a number of other profound and moving spectacles. It was through this experience that the ballet dancer became a dancing actor, and the choreographer no longer a plain maker of dances, but also a man thoroughly acquainted with all the aspects of theatre business, a *metteur-en-scène*.

In the desire to provide choreographers with a knowledge of theatre directing, opera houses frequently called in directors from the drama theatres to lend their experience. This is how it came about that Sergei Radlov (1892-1958), the prominent Leningrad theatre director, particularly known for his productions of Shakespeare, was asked to lead the State Theatre of Opera and Ballet.[1]

Russian ballet always worked in close collaboration with the drama theatre, in the sense that both arts were inspired by the same ideals. In the thirties this influence became much more direct and, aside from the beneficent results, produced at times a predominance of mime and of naturalistic approach that was far removed from choreography and the very nature of ballet. However, at the beginning of the "dramatic" period, this participation of men of the theatre, working side by side with young choreographers, was of great help in the creation of large-scale and deeply motivated ballets.

Nicolai Volkov (1894-1965), historian of the theatre and dramatist, started ballet criticism with a notice about the première of *The Red Poppy*,[2] wherein he significantly wrote: "the first act convinces us that such a ballet, realistic in theme and in style of movement, can be emotionally moving and easily comprehended. . . . *The Red Poppy* testifies that it is possible to create ballets that are new in style."

In conclusion of his article Nicolai Volkov said that the time had arrived for ballets to be based on clearly defined dramaturgy predetermining not only the content, but also the visual form of the future ballet. Some time elapsed before he found a suitable subject and worked it out in collaboration with Vladimir Dmitriev (1900-1938), one of those designers of ballet capable of taking active part in its actual conception.

The subject was taken from the history of the Great French Revolution.

[1] Such was the name of the present Kirov theatre up to 1935.
[2] *Izvestia*, June 22, 1927.

Salammbô, music by A. Arends, with interpolations from works by A. Glasunov, V. Nebolsin and A. Tsfasman. Book by A. Gorsky, new choreography by Igor Moiseyev. Bolshoi Theatre, 1932. Igor Moiseyev in the leading role of Mato with Vladimir Riabtsev as Spendt.

Konstantin Sergeyev as Siegfried in *Swan Lake*, Leningrad, 1935. (Collection of Natalia Roslavleva)

The first act served as a dramatic exposition of the revolutionary moods in the Southern provinces. Jeanne and Pierre, children of the peasant Gaspar, joined the battalion of Marseillais that made a halt in their village *en route* to Paris. They did this in protest against the arrest and beating of their father and the maltreatment of other peasants by the Marquis de Beauregarde, the lord of the estate. The Marseillais, Philippe and Jérôme, appeared in this act, which ended with the jubilation of the peasants who had ousted the hated Marquis and his son, and freed their victims. The ensuing acts brought in other characters: Mireille de Poitiers, a court actress; Antoine Mistral, her friend and colleague; Thérèse, a Basque girl; Louis XVI and Marie Antoinette with their suite, and numerous other colourful figures.

But the real heroes of *The Flames of Paris* were the people, the *sans-culottes*. The contents were so conceived as to lead to the march of the Marseillais on Paris, the capture of the Tuileries, the fall of the aristocracy, and the final triumph of the Revolution, celebrated, according to historical custom, by a grand allegorical festival. In an article "The Scenario of *The Flames of Paris*", Nicolai Volkov confirmed his initial ideas by saying: "While working on *The Flames of Paris* we set the aim beforehand of not limiting ourselves to the invention of a plot. We intended to trace the general composition of the ballet, to preordain the style of its expressive means. In this sense the very composition of ballet "books" was deemed by us as a special branch of dramaturgy. *The Flames of Paris* was for us the first experience in the creation of ballet dramaturgy."[1]

One might add that this practice of influencing and predetermining the general outline of future ballets became the adopted method of Soviet ballet dramaturgy, particularly evident in the creations of Yuri Slonimsky.

With *The Flames of Paris* the authors of the ballet created a synthetic work, wherein music, song, and dancing were blended into one whole. Perhaps they remembered Lunacharsky's visions of monumental "song and dance oratorios", described in his article "Why do We Preserve the Bolshoi Theatre?" Or, most likely having studied, prior to commencing actual work, an immense amount of material pertaining to the Great French Revolution, they were impressed by its own artistic manifestations. At any rate huge choruses took part in the ballet, and each act was centred around a chosen song of the Revolution: "the Marseillaise", "Ça Ira" and "La Carmagnole".

The Marseillaise was used not as a hymn but as mass-song caught up

[1] Nicolai Volkov. Scenario of the ballet *The Flames of Paris*. In: *The Flames of Paris*. Souvenir booklet, Iskusstvo, Leningrad, 1937, p. 32.

by the people at the moment of forming the detachment of the Marseillais. "Ça Ira" determined the central and most impressive scene of the ballet (end of act II)—the march on the Tuileries, when all the participants, with Jeanne, Philippe, Jérôme and Thérèse in the centre, advanced, as if carried on a powerful wave, in slow and measured stances towards the footlights. "The Carmagnole" became the main musical theme of the final act.

An active and important role in the creation of *The Flames of Paris* belonged to its composer, Boris Asafiev (1884-1949). His connection with the ballet started early—around 1910, when he worked as a rehearsal pianist for the ballet company of the Mariinsky. This enabled him to acquire such a thorough professional knowledge of ballet and its requirements that an overwhelming majority of his ballets had been written without the choreographer's draft, but in full conformity with the necessary length and style of the dances. Before the Revolution, Asafiev composed but few one-act ballets: *The White Lily*, *Mischievous Fiorenta*, *Pierrot and the Masks*. Some of them, like the last named, were "ballet-pantomimes" showing the composer's inclination for dramatic content. Asafiev's multi-act ballets were all created after the Revolution. After *Solveig*, which consisted of arrangements of Grieg's music, *The Flames of Paris* was Asafiev's first monumental work. The score was partly a "montage" of music and songs of the Great French Revolution and partly a composition in the style and character of that period. With great professional skill Asafiev transposed intonations found in the heritage of the past into contemporary music. He assimilated, replenished, and developed the abundant material that he had. While the result was far removed from an ordinary potpourri of songs, the score on the whole did not always lead to symphonic completeness—though it aspired to do so. Also, in their effort to bring the content of the ballet as close as possible to historical truth, the authors at times acted against the very nature of ballet, when they wanted the actress Mireille to sing an aria from one of Lulli's operas and intended to replace the dancer with an opera singer for the purpose. (The number was written, but omitted in the course of production.) Some of the scenes were done in terms of "dumb-show" borrowed from the dramatic theatre, as when the Jacobin orator, rousing the spirit of the masses in the scene preceding the march on the Tuileries, opened and closed his mouth, or were too naturalistic, for instance the appearance of tortured peasants from the Marquis's dungeons in act I. These were introduced by Sergei Radlov, the general director of the production, and disappeared in later versions.

The importance of the ballet was connected with its spirit. "Ça Ira" as transposed by Asafiev became a symphonic piece providing the choreographer with sufficient material for *plastique* imagery. The impression made by the march of the mass of dancers in "Ça Ira" was overpowering, and ensured the success of the ballet at the very first presentation of this scene, at the celebration of the fifteenth anniversary of the October Revolution on November 6, 1932 in Leningrad, followed by the presentation of the complete ballet the next day. On the same date (7/11/1932) the third act, with the march on the Tuileries, was shown at the Bolshoi Theatre (in the Leningrad version performed by Moscow dancers) after the Anniversary Meeting of the Moscow Soviet. On June 7, 1933, the ballet was performed at the Bolshoi in its entirety.

Having introduced the heroic genre in ballet, the need for which had been felt for a long time, *The Flames of Paris* enabled many new talents to show their worth. In Leningrad the role of the leading Marseillais was created by Vakhtang Chaboukiani (born 1910); in Moscow, by Alexei Yermolayev. Both created impressive and virile characters, endowing them in each case with individual traits typical of these outstanding dancers of the new generation. Chaboukiani's Marseillais was a simple youth just entering life. He emphasized the pathos of the role in his energetic and temperamental style of dancing. Yermolayev, while also dancing with virility and temperament, stressed the determination of his hero to fight to the end. Both characterizations have not been surpassed by a long line of successors. Jeanne was created in Leningrad by Feya Balabina (born in 1910, she was a brilliant virtuosity dancer of the Kirov ballet in 1931–1956, and is now Artistic Director of the Leningrad School) and by Sulamith Messerer (born in 1908) in Moscow. But it became identified in the Moscow ballet with the name of Olga Lepeshinskaya.

Born in 1916, Olga Lepeshinskaya showed a marked ability for dancing as a child. Accepted at the Bolshoi school in 1925, she danced on the Bolshoi stage for the first time in 1926 as Cupid in *Don Quixote*, showing a power of projection and stage presence that were later to become her main characteristics. She was a hard worker and stayed for hours after school was over to perfect some step. Long before graduation in 1933 she was mentioned as a future ballerina. Deserved success greeted her appearance in *The Nutcracker* while still in the last year of studies. She was given prominent roles immediately upon entering the Bolshoi company. Her first part in a Soviet ballet was that of Jeanne and here she was given the opportunity to apply in full measure a *joie de vivre* specially her own, an exuberant buoyancy with which she performed everything she danced, and a virtuosity technique that was far in advance of the standards of the time. The role of Jeanne afforded a chance to display technique: the choreographer created for her several *variations* and a *pas de deux* (with Philippe) in the last act, that is often used in recital programmes as a separate number.

It was with the characterization of Jeanne that Lepeshinskaya proved that she was born to create on the ballet stage the image of the heroine of her times—this came later in *Svetlana*. In the thirties this ballerina stamped every role with her own personality, including those of the classical repertory, thus, as Kitri of *Don Quixote*, she created a daughter of the people, the mischievous sweetheart of the barber Basil. The technical difficulties of the part seemed to be just the stimulus she required to prove that she had no rivals in speed, elevation, and complete mastery of the *danse d'école*, yet its steps appeared to be slightly transposed in her execution into another, major key. Her *manèges* of various complicated *tours* were breathtaking and radiated youth and exhilaration. Even her perfectly classical Aurora of *The Sleeping Beauty* had the quality of impishness and delicious *coquetterie* in the "Rose *Adagio*" of the first act. With the years Lepeshinskaya's art matured. Her Assol in *Crimson Sails* (1942), Mirandolina in the ballet of the same name after Goldoni's *La Locandera* (1949) and, particularly, Tao-Hoa in the 1949 revival of *The Red Poppy* were profound studies in character.

In 1951 Lepeshinskaya was given the highest artistic title of People's Artist of the U.S.S.R. Upon retirement from the stage she devoted herself to passing on her experience to young dancers. She spent two years (1963-1965) as ballet-mistress and adviser to the ballet of the Budapest Opera. When this company presented *The Flames of Paris* on the huge stage of the Palace of Congresses in the summer of 1965, one could see that Lepeshinskaya, who had danced in the ballet at its conception, had inspired not only the performer of the part of Jeanne, but the whole company, with the right spirit.

The Flames of Paris has enabled many dancers to test their abilities and to prove their merit. One of the most striking discoveries that were made through this ballet was the talent of Nina Anisimova (born in 1909) a character dancer of the Kirov ballet. Until *The Flames of Paris*, character dancing existed in the form of interpolated dances. While the virtuosity of Soviet character dancers was very great, they were seldom given roles containing danced action. Nina Anisimova's personality and dramatic gift were so great that she contributed much to the success of the part of Thérèse, who became one of the principal heroines of the ballet. (In

Vakhtang Chaboukiani as Frondoso in *Laurencia*, music by
Alexander Krein, choreography by Vakhtang Chaboukiani
(Leningrad, 1939). (Collection of Natalia Roslavleva)

Natalia Dudinskaya as Laurencia, creator of the title-role in the ballet of the same name, Leningrad, 1939. Music by A. Krein, choreography by Vakhtang Chaboukiani. (Collection of Natalia Roslavleva)

Moscow the role was danced with almost equal impact by Nadezhda Kapustina.)

Tall statuesque Anisimova possessed a fiery temperament and *brio* coupled with a dramatic talent enabling her later to create the principal role of Nastia in another Vainonen ballet, *The Partisans*.

Contemporaries of the first production testify that the choreographic texture of the part of Thérèse in *The Flames of Paris* was actually created by Anisimova, who had shown a talent for composition when at school. She became one of the first Soviet women-choreographers, having arranged *Gayane* to music by Khachaturian, and danced the lead in the famous "Sabre Dance" at the Kirov Theatre, and created several ballets (including a new version of *Schéhérazade*) for the Maly Opera of Leningrad with which she had long been associated, simultaneously occupying the position of leading character dancer of the Kirov ballet, from which she retired in 1957 to devote her energies to choreography.

With *The Flames of Paris* its choreographer, Vassily Vainonen, introduced an amalgamation of character and classical dancing on a scale that had not been met with until then. Character dancing, on which Vainonen was a great expert, appeared here as a means of characterization used in various forms.

Vainonen (1898-1964) was placed by his widowed mother at the Mariinsky school as a resident ward of the State in 1911. He graduated into the *corps de ballet* in 1919 and rose to the position of character soloist. In a period of experiment and "search for novelties" Vainonen played Pulcinella's double in the Stravinsky–Lopukhov ballet of the same name, and was closely connected with the "Young Ballet" group. His first ventures in choreography were produced for the recitals of the "Young Ballet". It was then that he created his "Moskovski Waltz", still performed by Soviet dancers, and famed for its breath-taking acrobatic lifts. Gradually Vainonen abandoned dancing altogether and devoted himself entirely to choreography. His first ballet, *The Age of Gold* (1930), to music by Shostakovich, was still in the nature of an experiment. Cardboard characters and concentration on effective acrobatic choreography, so popular in that period, deprived the authors (Vainonen had two collaborators) of the opportunity to create deep characters although the action was laid in the present time.

Vainonen's success came with *The Flames of Paris*, a ballet dealing with history, but providing the choreographer with an idea, action, and interesting characters, a good score and artistic guidance that resulted in the creation of a work of lasting importance.

Vainonen staged several other ballets. His version of *The Nutcracker*, with entirely new choreography, is in the repertory of the Kirov ballet and has been reproduced in many theatres, including the Budapest Opera, where he spent over a year in 1950, doing much to assist in the revival and development of Hungarian ballet.

New heroes appeared in the thirties in Soviet Ballet—heroes introduced for the sake of portraying human feelings, thoughts, and emotions with the utmost possible sincerity and artistic truth. It was impossible to dance, to teach, or to choreograph in the old and tried way. The Stanislavsky method, transformed to suit the requirements of ballet, came to help the dancing actors in the creation of truthful characters, in learning the art of *being* that character on the stage. New heroes called for new ways of acting and new ways of dancing. Powerful leaps and a sweeping breadth of movement, associated in the future with the style of Soviet choreography, were introduced by choreographers in order to give their heroes visual semblance of the loftiness of their spirit. A new type of ballerina was born, an expressive dancer, absorbing virtuosity technique for the purpose of complete freedom of stage performance. The very nature of dancing, whether male or female, became more energetic, sparkling, full of an optimistic attitude to life.

In its search for new heroes Soviet ballet needed new themes and new subjects. The themes had to be deeply penetrating, the characters noble, their emotions and experience linked to definite people and circumstances.

Where could the authors of future ballets find the best source for such subject-matter? It was only natural that they should resort to the great works of literature.

The first nationwide Congress of the Union of Soviet writers, which took place early in 1934, concentrated attention on classical literature as an important part of the national heritage. The writers' congress exerted a deeply-felt influence on all branches of art. It brought about a prolonged alliance of ballet and literature, a period yielding many paramount works of Soviet choreography.

New works appeared on the Soviet ballet stage, their subjects borrowed from Pushkin, Lermontov, Gogol, Shakespeare, Balzac, Lope de Vega, and Hugo, bringing with them a gallery of characters and depth of theme that provided both dancers and choreographers with material of great potential. Not surprisingly Pushkin served as one of the first sources of inspiration. Poems of the great Russian poet had been used in the past in Russian ballet—it is sufficient to mention Didelot's *Prisoner in the Caucasus*.

The Fountain of Bakhchisarai was used on many occasions by opera composers. It is little known that Filippo Taglioni intended to create a ballet on this subject. At any rate a brief notice in the St. Petersburg *Northern Bee* of 1838 informed its readers that "before his departure from Petersburg M. Taglioni told us that he is taking with him a French translation of Pushkin's poem *The Fountain of Bakhchisarai*. He intends to create a new ballet based on this poem especially for Petersburg." Apparently the choreographer was unable to carry out his intention, for, as we know from the earlier part of this book, Taglioni's hopes of settling in Russia were cut short.

But in 1854 Yelena Andreyanova's touring company did show in Voronezh a two-act version of *The Fountain of Bakhchisarai*, while in 1892 Nijinsky senior, father of the great dancer, produced in Kiev a grand ballet, *A Victim of Jealousy*, in two scenes with an apotheosis. This followed, in addition to Pushkin's poem, a tragedy by Alexander Shakhovskoy (1777-1846) entitled *Kerim-Guirei* and written after the poem, during the poet's life. Like Shakhovskoy, Foma (Thomas) Nijinsky replaced the profound theme, concerning the moral transformation of a wild and unruly character under the influence of love, by a clash of religions.

None of these dramatizations could aspire to an adequate scenic presentation of the idea or content of Pushkin's great poem. All of them missed its main theme.

In Soviet ballet the task was approached from another angle.

Nicolai Volkov wrote a scenario that is still considered exemplary in dramaturgy for the ballet. He constructed it as a psychological conflict of characters, as a visualization of Pushkin's poetic idea. However, since Pushkin's poem does not contain a concise subject Volkov conceived many new scenes linking the plot from the beginning with the peaceful idyll of Maria's birthday celebration in the gardens of her father's castle and her pristine love duets with Vaclav, a character non-existent in the poem. The first half of this act formed the necessary contrast to the ensuing catastrophe—the raid of the Tartars, the killing of Vaclav and Maria's father, and her encounter with Guirei, who was awe-struck by Maria's beauty. The second act took place in Guirei's palace at Bakhchisarai.[1]

Here his numerous wives, guarded by Eunuchs, waited in the seclusion of the harem for the return of Guirei. The chief wife, Zarema, confident of her beauty and Guirei's love, was also impatiently awaiting his return from the wars. While much space was given to various *divertissements*, the main theme of this act was connected with the drama of Zarema,

[1] Now restored at Bakhchisarai in the Crimea as a museum.

caused by the appearance of a new inmate of the harem—the captive Maria.

The third and principal act was concentrated on the psychological state of the three main protagonists—Maria, Guirei, and Zarema. When the latter, after a passionate dialogue with Maria, caught sight of Guirei's skull-cap (*tyubeteika*) that he had dropped in her chamber, a wave of jealousy overcame her, and she stabbed the innocent Maria. In the fourth act Guirei was discovered seated in the inner court of his palace, immersed in heavy thoughts. Warriors returned from a new raid, but he remained indifferent. Zarema was brought in by his bodyguards, and thrust out her arms begging for a farewell glance, but he was immune to her entreaties. The bodyguards flung her off the high wall down a precipice.

A wild Tartar dance—one of the best scenes of the ballet—began. Nurali, Guirei's chieftain, entreated him to return to the life of a warrior, all in vain.

Guirei wanted to remain alone. In the epilogue (as in the prologue) he was seen, bent in grief, at the Fountain of Bakhchisarai, erected by him in memory of Maria. Suddenly her white figure appeared from behind the fountain, fleeting as the wind. He was unable to touch her—she was a vision. Now she put her hand against the wound, and disappeared behind the fountain. Guirei was once more alone at the Fountain of Bakhchisarai. . . .

This poetic scenario provided ample material both for the choreographer and for the composer, Boris Asafiev. The latter used the method of composition already tried by him in *The Flames of Paris*. He deliberately resorted to musical material of Pushkin's period. Even the ballet's overture was composed in the style of ballets of the first half of the nineteenth century. Since the fountain theme permeates the entire ballet, Asafiev introduced into the score the *romance* by Alexander Gurilyov (1803-1858), "To the Fountain of the Bakhchisarai Palace", with which the ballet both began and ended (originally it was sung by a soloist in the orchestra, a practice still retained in some productions).

It is also little known that Asafiev chose for Maria's musical *leitmotiv* one of the *nocturnes* by John Field (1782-1837), the Irish composer known as "Russian" Field, because he spent a considerable part of his life in Russia.[1] In Pushkin's time Field's music was played in every drawing-room! However, this does not signify that Asafiev merely "quoted"

---

[1] Having lived in Russia from 1802, Field died in Moscow in 1834. His tombstone in the so-called German Cemetery (instituted by Peter I for the burial of foreigners) is cared for by the Soviet State as a historical monument.

Anna Pavlova as Nikia in *La Bayadère*, Petersburg, 1902. (Collection of Natalia Roslavleva)

Alla Shelest as Nikia in *La Bayadère*. Leningrad, Kirov Theatre of Opera and Ballet. (Collection of Natalia Roslavleva)

Olga Lepeshinskaya in *Walpurgis Night*, Bolshoi Theatre, Moscow.

music of the past in his score. He wrote of it: "This is no restoration of romanticism, but an attempt to *hear* the epoch through Pushkin's poem and to convey the emotions that moved the imagination of the poet. The melodious idiom of the ballet is my own."[1]

Asafiev, with his colossal experience in ballet, was endowed to an extreme degree with the gift of not only *hearing* the future spectacle but actually *seeing* it; in composing he foresaw the rhythm, structure, and the very nature of the dances, thus becoming, as in the case of *The Flames of Paris*, co-author of both the scenario and the choreography.

The Fountain of Bakhchisarai was the début in choreography of Rostislav Zakharov. Born in 1907, he entered the Leningrad Ballet School in 1920, graduating from the class of Vladimir Ponomaryov in 1925. His dancing career was short. At a very early stage he decided to become a choreographer. Having resolved upon his future profession, Zakharov was determined to study all aspects of theatre craft. In those days there was no special institution for training choreographers. (The Choreographer's Faculty of the State Theatre Institute in Moscow was founded by Professor Zakharov in 1946. He heads its chair.) In the absence of such, the aspiring choreographer entered the faculty of dramatic production at the Leningrad Institute of Scenic Art. There he studied until 1932, with Sergei Radlov as his Professor. Upon graduation Zakharov was attached to the State Academic Theatre of Opera and Ballet, at first in the capacity of assistant director of operas. In 1932 he achieved his first choreography, the "Danses Persanes" from Mussorgsky's *Khovanshchina*. By 1934 Zakharov was one of the most promising choreographers in Leningrad. At the suggestion of Sergei Radlov, his former mentor at the Institute and Artistic Director of the theatre,[2] he was entrusted with the production of *The Fountain of Bakhchisarai*, carried out under Radlov's general supervision. The young choreographer succeeded in attaining unity of action by applying his experience of theatrical direction.

Being thoroughly versed in the Stanislavsky method, Zakharov applied it in his work. This was his most important step, considered quite revolutionary at the time. "I had to find new means of expression, means capable of conveying the great depth of emotion with which Pushkin's images are invested. This was a question of creating real human characters

[1] See *The Fountain of Bakhchisarai*, compiled by L. Popova, edited by Y. Slonimsky, Leningrad, 1962, p. 8.

[2] Radlov continued working in the dramatic theatre while occupying the post of Artistic Director of the former Mariinsky. In the same period (1930–1937) Agrippina Vaganova headed the ballet company.

with their thoughts, feelings, and passions. And here Stanislavsky's doctrine came to my aid. Preliminary 'table work' enabled the artists Galina Ulanova, Olga Jordan, Tatiana Vecheslova, Vera Kaminskaya, Konstantin Sergeyev and Andrei Lopukhov[1] to give material form to the heroes of the Pushkin poem. Serious and searching work during the creation of their visual images brought about the birth of a new form of *danse d'action*: monologues and dialogues, expressing the content without the help of conventional gestures."[2]

Further in the same book Zakharov writes: "At that time it was not customary to hold preliminary discussions prior to the creation of future ballet images, work without which none of our choreographers deems it possible to prepare a ballet with any company. The choreographer did not read to the dancers an account of his idea of the production to be. He simply assembled them for rehearsals and began by showing the steps of the dance, often without bothering to explain their task to the artists."

Zakharov recalled how much consternation was caused among supporters of the routine in the former Mariinsky company when, instead of a rehearsal-call, he summoned each of the main protagonists for "table work".

"How much sarcasm this caused! 'What, are we expected to start the production by rehearsing at a table? Are they going to teach us to dance sitting?' Naturally the choreographer had not invented any new way of sedentary dancing. He simply was deeply convinced that, before beginning the practical learning of the steps, every artist should be obliged to have a clear idea of his tasks in the given production, the nature and special features of his part."[3]

Starting with Olga Jordan, the future Zarema, Zakharov invited each of the principal protagonists, analysing his or her role in great detail (with Jordan he worked out Zarema's biography *before* she was captured and brought in to Guirei's harem), dividing the role into scenes, and each scene into short sections, determining the main idea and task for each one of them.

[1] Galina Ulanova created Maria and was the ideal exponent of this role. Olga Jordan, Tatiana Vecheslova, Vera Kaminskaya were the first Leningrad Zaremas. (Ulanova liked to dance with her classmate Vecheslova.) Konstantin Sergeyev created the part of Vaclav, Andrei Lopukhov that of Nur-Ali. The first Guirei was Mikhail Dudko.

[2] Rostislav Zakharov. *The Art of the Choreographer* (*Iskusstvo Balemeistera*). Moscow, 1954, p. 116.

[3] *Op. cit.*, p. 270.

"Reading *The Fountain of Bakhchisarai*, the study of literature and lithographs relative to the period, all this material enabled the artists to imagine with great clarity of perception the life of their heroes and to comprehend their psychology in a much more profound manner."[1]

One might add that the choreographer himself spared no efforts in a similar study of material. He visted the Hermitage Museum and many other famous collections in Leningrad. Persian miniatures provided him with many interesting details for the harem act, while a silver dish with prancing equestrian figures served as a "key" to all the Tartar imagery.[2]

What comprised the enduring impact of the *Fountain*? The choreography, seemingly devoid of any technical feats and *variations* calling for virtuosity, was quite simple. Yet each movement expressed some emotional state.

By selection of a definite set of movements Zakharov created a choreographic "text" capable of giving birth to a definite character—to Maria with her ethereal semi-*arabesques* immortalized by Ulanova, to Zarema with her imperious leaps and majestic stance. It is difficult to dance *The Fountain of Bakhchisarai*, and it can be adequately performed only by great artists of the Russian school, knowing how to penetrate deeply into the psychology of the roles, and how to perform the steps, simple but exactly right for each character and situation, with the necessary expression. Without them the ballet would be lifeless.

Pushkin themes continued to inspire Rostislav Zakharov for many more years, although the unity and impact of *The Fountain of Bakhchisarai* were not to be excelled. Three other Zakharov ballets on subjects from Pushkin are: *The Prisoner in the Caucasus* (1938), *Mistress into Maid* (1946) and *The Bronze Horseman* (1949). The music of the first two was again by Asafiev,[3] while the score of *The Bronze Horseman* belonged to Reingold Gliere.

---

[1] *Op. cit.*, p. 272.   [2] *The Fountain of Bakhchisarai, op. cit.*, p. 13.

[3] Seven of Asafiev's twenty-eight ballets were based on subjects from Pushkin, while a number of them followed stories taken from Lermontov. Asafiev's connection with Soviet ballet can hardly be exaggerated. There was not a single undertaking in the ballet of the period in which Asafiev did not take part, lending his knowledge, advice and experience. On his initiative many important reforms were introduced into Soviet ballet.

Asafiev's articles on ballet music serve as models of scholarship. His work, the propagation of ballet, was conducted simultaneously with activity as member of the Academy of Sciences of the U.S.S.R. (*History and Theory of Music*).

Between 1936 and 1939 Zakharov was artistic director of the Bolshoi Ballet, and between 1946 and 1949 he headed the Bolshoi School. In 1954 Zakharov published a book, *The Art of the Choreographer*, analysing in detail his method of making a ballet, based to a considerable extent on dramatic action as a vehicle for the evocation of human thoughts and emotions. In the appendix to this book may be found detailed choreographic drafts written by Zakharov prior to the actual production of his ballets, notably *The Bronze Horseman*, *Taras Bulba* (1941), and *Cinderella* (1945).

Zakharov had an ideal Maria in the person of Galina Ulanova. He created the role with her in view: "In composing the part of Maria I constantly had Ulanova in mind: that is why her personality and all the special features of her talent lived in my creative conscience. This helped me to create Maria's dance image. When I showed it to Ulanova at the production rehearsal it appeared to be also close and dear to her."[1]

Ulanova later admitted that for her "choreography started with *The Fountain of Bakhchisarai*, where the Pushkin dramatism of the scenario determined the action and the dramatism of the music."[2]

If the *Fountain* did mark Ulanova's first period as dancer-actress, she, in turn, succeeded in filling the relatively small and laconic "text" of her role with such richness of spirit that Maria *did* become the central figure of the entire ballet, as its authors had hoped.

Ulanova *was* Maria because she understood all the *nuances* in the psychology of her character. Through this understanding she gave the subtlest of changes to the choreography. Quite unforgettable was the scene of Maria's death. Pressing the wound in her back with one hand and supporting herself against a column with another, Ulanova's Maria seemed to be listening to the last ebb of life.

Ulanova's Maria was imbued with an elegiac sorrow, close to the spirit of Pushkin preserved in Asafiev's music. It is interesting to read in Ulanova's article about the circumstances of the creation of that role[3] that she liked to read at the time Pushkin's elegy about the sad maiden, ever sitting sorrowfully over the broken jug of water, and to visit again and again the statue in the "Tsarskoye Selo" park to which Pushkin's stanzas were addressed.

In the same article Ulanova said that she "continued working at the

[1] Rostislav Zakharov. *Op. cit.*, p. 286.

[2] *The Fountain of Bakhchisarai. Op. cit.*, p. 14.

[3] See *The Fountain of Bakhchisarai. Op. cit.*, p. 14. Galina Ulanova. "Poise in Dance". Reprinted from the magazine *Teatr*, No. 6, 1949, pp. 92-93.

image of Maria for many years. It seems to me that at first it had but one colour—that of sorrow. With years my Maria seemed to come to life. The pattern of the role became more complicated, the character of the heroine acquired more facets. New smiles, new expressiveness of the arms, new linear *plastique* were found for her. I think that in the end I succeeded in finding in my Maria that state of calm, so necessary for any actor, when all the nuances of the image become quite organic. I especially felt this in the third act, when Maria, alone, became immersed in nostalgic recollections."[1]

Indeed, Ulanova's nostalgic dance of recollections in the third act of *The Fountain of Bakhchisarai* was an elegiac poem of unparalleled depth and beauty. Like everything she touched, the role acquired the importance of universal interest, and this explains the reason why the art of Ulanova has transcended the boundaries of the ballet theatre and become important to art as a whole.

At the same time, while Ulanova's creations in many ways have determined the style and method of the Soviet school, she herself was born of it and is its ideal embodiment.

Born in 1910 in Petersburg, the daughter of Mariinsky dancers Sergei Nikolayevitch Ulanov (1881-1950) and Maria Fedorovna Romanova (1886-1954), who was also her first teacher, she was placed in 1919 by her parents in the Theatre School as a boarding pupil—to a considerable extent against the child's will—she was a terrible tomboy and did not like dancing! It was probably these traits, hard to believe on the strength of her Maria and other lyrical roles, that won her her first independent role—that of a boy in the "Danse Sabotière" inserted in *La Fille Mal Gardée*.

The last four years at school were spent in Vaganova's class, where her technique was polished and she acquired the fundamentals of a school that enabled her to master technique to such an extent that its difficulties passed unnoticed. Thereafter she was able to concentrate on expressive *plastique* and the building up of character.

For her graduation performance (May 16, 1928) Ulanova danced the seventh waltz and the mazurka in *Chopiniana* and the *adagio* from *The Nutcracker* in the Lev Ivanov original version. In August of the same year she was already a member of the Kirov ballet.

In these first roles the young dancer conveyed many delicate shades of meaning and won notice for the exceptional beauty of her characterizations, even though they were still tentative. Artistic maturity came much later, after years of hard work and searching. But her first year in the

[1] *Op. cit.*, p. 15.

company already gave Ulanova the reputation of an artist with a marked personal style, one seeking for clear poetic images expressed through the medium of dance. Vaganova gave her the role of the Swan (the parts of Odette and Odile were enacted by different dancers) in her romantic version of *Swan Lake* (1933) that caused much controversial opinion—with the exception of the praise accorded to Ulanova's rendering of the lyrical part of Odette the Swan.

The important turning point in Ulanova's development as a great dancer-actress came with *The Fountain of Bakhchisarai*. The ballerina wrote herself: "I can say without exaggeration that after *The Fountain of Bakhchisarai* I had to revise all my former roles. And having enacted after Maria the role of Juliet in Shakespeare's *Romeo and Juliet*, I stopped dancing altogether in those ballets which were conventional in the extreme, such as *Raymonda* and *The Sleeping Beauty*."[1]

How Ulanova worked and how she felt about her roles may be understood from the account given by Rostislav Zakharov of his work with the then young ballerina during *Lost Illusions*, the ballet based upon Balzac's novel of the same name, created by the Leningrad ballet in 1935: "I shall never forget how, when working with Ulanova over *Lost Illusions*, I was reading to her aloud Esther's letter to Lucien (from Balzac's *Splendeurs et Misères des Courtisanes*). She listened without saying a word, and tears were dropping from her eyes. It was then, probably, that the image, later so finely created by her in the ballet, was being given form."[2]

The character in question was that of Coralie, a *danseuse* of the Paris Opéra, entirely invented by the authors of the ballet, and part-inspired by certain characters from Balzac's *Comédie Humaine*. The ballet continued to be performed until 1941, and it may be regretted that it has not survived, although without such protagonists as Ulanova—Coralie and Sergeyev—Lucien (this part was also taken by Shavrov and Chaboukiani) the mimed scenes that formed the bulk of the choreography would probably fail to make the necessary impact.

The second important stage of the development of Ulanova's talent came with *Romeo and Juliet* (1940),[3] which extended the scope of her creative abilities even further and marked another, higher stage of development of the Soviet ballet.

With Prokofiev's score Ulanova received a role created to much

[1] *The Fountain of Bakhchisarai, op. cit.*, p. 15.

[2] Rostislav Zakharov. *Op. cit.*, p. 272.

[3] Ulanova's Juliet will be considered in the part dealing with the ballet, *Romeo and Juliet*.

greater music—though she frankly admitted how difficult it was for her to understand it at the beginning of the work. As a dancer Ulanova possessed a remarkable ability of conveying and understanding just what the composer wanted to say with his music. In an article "Expressive means of ballet" (*Soviet Music*, No. 4, 1955, p. 70), she said: "The dance, engendered by music, dance that may be called the *movement of music*, makes it visible. And therefore we speak of the dance as the most important among the expressive means of ballet, because it is dance that gives body and flesh to the music and discloses its content in the imagery of *plastique*." Further, in the same article, Ulanova spoke of the necessity for the artist (of course one possessing perfect technique) to attain the *cantilena* quality in dancing, when the movements form a continuous flow from one into another. Ulanova possessed this *cantilena* quality to a very high degree.

It is known that the flowing fluent style of dancing is a hallmark of the Russian school, especially developed in Soviet ballet. Ulanova became its greatest exponent.

Bogdanov-Berezovsky said in his book *Galina Ulanova*,[1] that her dance "speaks to the mind and moves the heart". Yuri Slonimsky confirmed this in his book *The Bolshoi Theatre Ballet*[2] when he wrote that Ulanova's heroines were "faithful not only to their hearts but also to their minds". This is another paramount aspect of Ulanova's genius. The intellect played a very important part in her creations. This is seen in her work, in her writing, especially in the autobiographical *The Making of a Ballerina*[3] where she speaks of her early friendship with the family of the Leningrad dramatic actress, Time, and how greatly this very artistic and intellectual environment influenced her youth.

If for Ulanova the art of dancing was invariably accompanied by inspired thought leading to the creation of images imbued with the ultimate heights of poetry, she in turn inspired authors, composers, and choreographers. All of Prokofiev's three main ballets have been composed with Ulanova in mind (*Romeo and Juliet, Cinderella* and *The Stone Flower*). *The Fountain of Bakhchisarai* became completely identified with her.

Into the old *Giselle* she breathed new life, creating a philosophical rendering of the role in the spirit of the victory of Love over Death. In this sense all Ulanova's characters possessed a quality of heroism, a deep conviction of the rightness of what they were doing or hoping for.

[1] Iskusstvo, Moscow, 1961.
[2] Foreign Languages Publishing House, Moscow, 1956.
[3] Foreign Languages Publishing House, Moscow, 1955.

This brings us to the most important aspects of Ulanova's art. With her every appearance she *ennobled* her spectators and seemed to elevate them to higher spiritual planes, so that her every performance became a new experience. Was this not the aim of Soviet art and Soviet ballet as a whole?

The significance of Ulanova in the history of ballet is as important as that of Stanislavsky in drama and Chaliapin in opera, for in her sphere Ulanova had proved that the most complicated, deep, and psychologically subtle emotions may be conveyed through the medium of classical dance.

Agrippina Vaganova gave the fruitful period of the nineteen-thirties the name of the "new spring of our ballet". In an article entitled "The New Ballet",[1] written at the time when she headed the ballet company of the State Academic Theatre of Opera and Ballet, she said that every new ballet and every new role of the constellation of talents born in those years—Ulanova, Vecheslova, Chaboukiani, Dudinskaya, Jordan, Sergeyev—"proved ever brightly and insistently that a truly realistic popular ballet theatre was being born".

Vaganova summed up the points of issue determining the re-birth of ballet in those years in the following succession: (*a*) significance of themes, dealing with historical conflicts as in *The Flames of Paris*, (*b*) tense and dramatically well developed plots, and (*c*) realistic characters rendered in artistic form.

It was time to turn to contemporary themes. Despite the considerable experience gained, the problem was far from an easy one. One of the first attempts to resort to contemporaneity in ballet ended in complete failure.

The Bright Stream, with Fedor Lopukhov's book and choreography and a score by Shostakovich, wherein he partly used music for an earlier ballet *Bolt* (1931), was first performed on the stage of the Maly Opera Theatre of Leningrad (in June 1935) and in November of the same year was produced on the stage of the Bolshoi.

Its story sounded like a travesty. A group of artists arrives on a collective farm, *The Bright Stream*, in the Kuban grain region to take part in festivities on the occasion of the completion of harvest. It turns out that Zina, wife of the agronomist, used to study at a ballet school and knows the ballerina of the group. Zina's husband becomes infatuated with the ballerina. The collective farmers decide to punish the fickle spouse. Zina, dressed as the ballerina, comes to a rendezvous with her husband. In the

---

[1] *Izvestia*, June 22, 1935. Reprinted in: *Agrippina Yakovlevna Vaganova*. Iskusstvo, Leningrad, 1958, pp. 80-81.

Raisa Struchkova in the title role of *Cinderella*. Music by Sergei Prokofiev, choreography by Rostislav Zakharov, Bolshoi Theatre, Moscow.

Natalia Dudinskaya as Raymonda. Leningrad. (Collection of Natalia Roslavleva)

morning all the misunderstandings are settled, the penitent agronomist begs for his wife's pardon, and all ends in general jubilation.

As to classical dance, Lopukhov used it in this "kolkhoz" ballet in a purely formal way. It was far removed from Vaganova's idea of classical dance as "a form of expressing human emotions in movement, the poetry of human movement, as in music and song".

"It is imperative, however," said Vaganova (in the article "New Ballet", quoted above) "to understand classical dance as a kind of movement that should originate from and be expressive of human emotion and social behaviour. It is also necessary to work it into the very substance of the action, depicting with its help the development of artistic images."[1]

In a special article on the subject of *The Bright Stream*, entitled "No Ballet Falsitudes",[2] Vaganova gave a highly professional analysis of its errors. She said that while the new type of ballet-play had already educated dozens of young dancers in the art of acting, the first error of *The Bright Stream* consisted in a scenario quite hopeless even for the old ballet. The main problem, from Vaganova's point of view, was embodied in the second error, the failure to use classical dancing in a suitable form.

"Classical dancing is changing its forms and means of expression before our eyes, depending on the subject, its dramatic purpose, the period shown, etc. Is there not a colossal difference between classical dancing in *The Sleeping Beauty* and the dialogue between Maria and Zarema in *The Fountain of Bakhchisarai*? In order to create a good contemporary Soviet ballet one needs another approach to classical dance. But the second error of the authors of *The Bright Stream* consists precisely in the fact that their kind of classical dance is indifferent to action, periods, subject, or anything else. Any of these *divertissements* may be shown in *The Bright Stream* or another ballet. An attempt to create a Soviet ballet with *such* classical dance is to discredit both the theme and classical dancing as a whole."

As a third error Vaganova cited the choreographer's failure to create national dances appropriate to the people shown, which was unpardonable in the light of the great success achieved by *The Flames of Paris*, due in no small way to the excellent and knowledgeable choreographer of its character dances.

Lastly Vaganova said: "All of our enumerated works [she mentioned

[1] *Op. cit.*, p. 81.
[2] Agrippina Vaganova. "No Ballet Falsitudes!" *Krasnaya Gazeta*, Leningrad, March 9, 1936. Reprinted in: *Agrippina Yakovlevna Vaganova*. Iskusstvo, Leningrad, 1958, pp. 89-90.

The Flames of Paris, her new versions of *Swan Lake,* and *Esmeralda,* and *Lost Illusions*—N.R.] are based on the principle of parallel development of the scenic and musical dramaturgy. The plot is expressed in action through music and dance. Musical themes, *leitmotivs* and melodies are intangibly linked to the main ideas of the spectacle. And here again *The Bright Stream* did not undertake the correct path of musical dramaturgy that is connected with the action. No, it is a score of separate numbers among which one loses sight altogether of the incoherent fragments of the plot."[1]

In the meantime the Kirov theatre was preparing a Soviet ballet, *Partisans' Days,* that was based, for the most part, on character dancing. The subject was taken from the Civil War and was connected with the struggle of partisans in the North Caucasus with White Guard Cossacks. One of the most dramatic scenes took place when Nastia, a beautiful but poor peasant, was married against her will to a rich Cossack. Drunken men mocked at Fedor, her poor sweetheart. This strengthened Nastia's decision to break with the way of life and people hated by her. Tearing off the wedding veil she threw the ring at the bridegroom. When partisans headed by Kerim, a Caucasian, broke into the village and freed Fedor and Grigory (head of the guerilla detachment), Nastia joined them and went to war. Later in the ballet Fedor was shot by the White Guards, while Nastia and her partisan friends went through many tribulations before attaining victory and uniting with the Red Army units. The ballet (shown on May 16, 1937, at the Kirov theatre with choreography by Vainonen and a score by Asafiev) was an important event. It introduced new heroes into Soviet Ballet, and the heroic spirit of the early days of the Revolution could not fail to move the audiences deeply. The production was staged in character-dance idiom—Russian and Caucasian (Vainonen visited the North Caucasus to study its dances and reproduced in scenic form the Simd, Lekuri, and a Lezghinka). This was the first ballet danced off-*pointe,* in character shoes, with the principal role performed by a character-dancer (Nina Anisimova in the first cast, Vera Kaminskaya in the second). Vakhtang Chaboukiani and Sergei Koren were excellent as the partisan leaders.

The plot afforded the dancers ample chance to create strong characterizations. The choreography of Nastia's tragic wedding dance was unanimously approved, and on the whole Vainonen succeeded most with the first act. With every next scene the story became more and more disjointed and the action lost continuity. Also, in the attempt to create dramatically impressive scenes, the authors of the ballet too often copied

[1] *Op. cit.,* p. 90.

literally the methods of the dramatic theatre, rather than attempted to recreate in terms of dance the poetic substance of the themes.

In spite of these weaknesses *Partisans' Days* was an important experiment in using folk dancing as means of characterization, an experiment that was continued and developed in many further works of Soviet choreographers.

In the meantime in Moscow the contemporary theme appeared in the form of a ballet that was partly fairy-tale. Three dancers of the Bolshoi theatre—then quite young men—Alexander Radunsky (to become one of the company's greatest mimes), Lev Pospekhin, and Nicolai Popko had their debut as choreographers when they were entrusted with the production, for the graduation performance of the Bolshoi School in 1937, of *The Baby Stork*, the music of which had been composed by the Kharkov composer Dmitry Klebanov. In the outward guise of a fairy-tale the story told of things easily comprehended by the Soviet child of the late thirties. The first and last acts were laid in the yard of a house, with a school-building nearby. If gloriously stupid Hens, a Cat (she was created by pupil Maya Plisetskaya), a Dog, a Baby Stork and various jungle animals danced in the ballet, it was also populated by Soviet children and a little Negro boy. The plot was connected with the saving of the orphaned Baby Stork by Soviet children, and a similar rescue of an orphaned Negro boy in the jungle, with his subsequent arrival in the Soviet Union where the stork, now grown-up, brought him upon return from hibernation in Africa. Some scenes, such as the one when the children taught the Baby Stork to fly, were very moving and well done. Much of the ballet, and in particular the third act, was done in the form of a *divertissement*, that, quite naturally, could not replace proper characterization and obscured the general idea. However *The Baby Stork* not only served as a stage in the mastering of the realistic method, but remained in the repertory of the Bolshoi Theatre for a number of years, being twice revived.

The Baby Stork was shown on the second affiliated stage of the Bolshoi Theatre, known in Russian as the Filial.[1]

Two years later a new realistic ballet was presented on the same stage. The three young choreographers had gained experience with *The Baby Stork* and were now ready to take a story set directly in their own time with the theme of new construction and the appearance of a new type of people.

Svetlana (the music was by Dmitry Klebanov) told of a girl, living with

[1] The building now houses the Moscow Operetta.

her father, a forester, in the depths of the Far Eastern *taiga*. She met a group of *Komsomols* (members of the Young Communist League) going to build a new town (this was a period when Komsomolsk-on-the-Amur was under construction—N.R.). Love arose between Svetlana and Ilko, one of the boys. In the second part of the ballet Svetlana performed a heroic deed: in order to signal to frontier-guards that a *saboteur* was in the *taiga*, she set her house on fire. Svetlana's fight with the *saboteur* was conceived in terms of acrobatic dance, while the ensuing pantomimic scene, in which she crawled, wounded, to fire her house, was very effective. The impact produced by *Svetlana* was due in no small measure to the excellent portrayal of the title role by Olga Lepeshinskaya. One may only express regret that more contemporary ballets were not created for this brilliant ballerina with outstanding feeling for her own times.

Yuri Kondratov (born in 1921), still in the graduation class, danced the part of Ilko, also with a great feeling of contemporaneity that never left this fine actor-dancer during his twenty years on the stage of the Bolshoi Theatre, where he danced many contemporary and classical roles.

Svetlana was far from perfect. Its music did not provide enough material for characterization. Its story was at times too fragmentary (some of it was borrowed from a popular contemporary film). In their zeal to be closer to real life, the young choreographers, inexperienced in the broad poetical generalizations more appropriate for ballet imagery, overburdened the ballet with mime and were not bold enough with the dance idiom used. Thus they made Svetlana appear in the first scene in top boots because she had just returned from the hunt. In this case the ballerina's performance was reduced to mime. In the next scene she was allowed to perform a few dance steps in character shoes. And only in the lyrical *adagio* did she dance *sur les pointes*. Naturalistic details, abundant in the ballet, reduced its artistic merit. But it provided the participants with a chance to create strong characters (the roles of the enemies: Stepan the alleged "carpenter", and the *saboteur*, were brilliantly done by Victor Tsaplin and Alexei Zhukov), and contained a few, but well-done dances.

Spectators liked *Svetlana* and the ballet stayed in the repertory for a number of years and was also staged (with other choreography) in Kharkov, Lvov, Gorki, and Vilnius.

With all its merits, *Svetlana* belonged to the type of dramatic ballet wherein all the key episodes had to be, out of necessity, enacted in mime. The number of such ballets produced in the thirties multiplied. Good dancers, capable of expressing a gamut of deep feeling in motion, were limited to roles done in terms of pantomime. Some of these refused to be satisfied with this situation. Vakhtang Chaboukiani, a brilliant dancer, needed more than such roles as Kerim in *Partisans' Days* could offer him. In the absence of such ballets he took to creating some of his own.

He was endowed with that unique gift, to be envied by any choreographer: he thought in terms of dance.

Vakhtang Chaboukiani was born in Tiflis (Tbilisi) in 1910 of a poor family. At the age of nine he had to start making baskets and toys. His entire life took a new turn when he was sent to deliver a box of Christmastree toys to the Maria Perrini ballet studio, the only one at the time in the whole of Tiflis. After having seen "the ballet" danced by children around the Christmas tree, the boy danced when and where he could. In the end, Perrini taught him, free of charge, as much as she knew of the fundamentals of the Italian school. The next turn came with the tour in Tiflis of Yelena Lucom and Boris Shavrov. The boy realized that "real" dancing was to be found in Leningrad. He arrived there in the autumn of 1926, only to discover that he had long ago passed the age when pupils are accepted for the Choreographic Technicum, as it was then called.

Luckily the school had evening courses formed in 1923 with the purpose of giving a chance to study to talented youth (especially boys) who had passed the "age" (10 to 11) required for entry into the main (daytime) department. Chaboukiani auditioned and was accepted in spite of the extreme slightness of his knowledge. Within two years the youth was transferred to the main department, and in another three he had covered the entire syllabus (ballet and general education). His exceptional physique, striking personality, dynamic style of dancing and determination to achieve his goal brought Chaboukiani, after he had graduated (in 1929) into the State Academic Ballet, to the very summit of his career. He became the company's *premier danseur* and the greatest classical dancer in the country.

Chaboukiani, like Yermolayev before him, played an outstanding role in the style of male dancing developing in those days in Soviet Ballet.

He introduced many new movements and changed known ones by transforming them through his own vigorous and impressive manner of execution. His soaring leaps and impetuous pirouettes became legendary.

He danced his first *Swan Lake* in the first season on the former Mariinsky stage, and later, in 1933, created the Count in Vaganova's version of the same ballet. In the second season he danced Basil in *Don Quixote*, a role very much suited to his temperament.

Other classical roles followed—Albrecht in *Giselle*, the Blue Bird, the *grand pas* in *Raymonda*. However, in spite of the perfection of his classical school—in those days, his outstanding roles were all in ballets by Soviet choreographers, each connected with important landmarks in Soviet ballet as a whole. The Sportsman in *The Age of Gold*, Vaclav in *The Fountain of Bakhchisarai*, the Marseillais in *The Flames of Paris*, and Kerim in *Partisans' Days*, the *premier danseur* of the Paris Opéra in *Lost Illusions* —all these provided him with experience in characterization. Yet he was not satisfied with the predominance of mime and *divertissements* in many of these ballets. He wanted to express the content of his roles directly through dance, dance in which the mime would be integrated with the general physical expressiveness.

Chaboukiani had already tried his hand at choreography in some concert numbers—the first was done while still at school. Moreover, the style of his dancing and the urge to change the old order of things was such that he virtually changed the choreography of his parts in classical ballets—it is sufficient to mention the Slave in the famous *pas de deux* from *Le Corsaire* (choreographed by Chaboukiani in the season of 1931-1932), Basil in *Don Quixote*, and Actaeon in the *divertissement* from the Vaganova version of *Esmeralda* (1935).

In 1938 Chaboukiani showed his first big ballet, *The Heart of the Hills*, to music by the Georgian composer, Andrei Balanchivadze. While the story was taken from the remote history of Georgia, the ballet was contemporary through its breadth of ideas, execution, and spirit. The image of a whole nation rising against its oppressors—such was the central theme of *The Heart of the Hills*. Its plot was based on a tragic conflict. Gardji, a young hunter, is in love with Manije, the feudal Prince's daughter. A true son of his people, he stood at the head of the peasant uprising. During the battle on the grounds of her father's estate, Manije shielded Gardji with her own body and died. The castle was set on fire, the peasants carried up to the mountains their wounded leader, Gardji, and the body of Manije.

Of greatest importance in the ballet were all the scenes connected with the Georgian people. Chaboukiani used folk-dance steps deftly inter- woven with classical ones, in order to convey action and create character- izations. In this respect his "Horumi" (a traditional Caucasian war dance of ancient origin) is still considered exemplary, and there is not a version of this dance in the present repertory of folk-dance groups that would not be based on Chaboukiani's finds in *The Heart of the Hills*. To the incessant throbbing rhythm of the "Horumi" one of the warriors, although wounded, continued his dance, supported by his comrades, holding one another by the shoulders in unity. The "Horumi" was again repeated in the finale of the ballet as a triumphant dance, performed against the background of the burning castle. In *The Heart of the Hills* Chaboukiani began a fruitful collaboration with Simon Virsaladze (born in 1909), the leading designer of Soviet ballet, an artist who never failed to leave his own imprint on the general style of the ballet for which he had created the settings and costumes. No less important for the success of the ballet was its music. Dmitry Shostakovich said that its merits placed *The Heart of the Hills* in the first rank among the compositions for ballet in the thirties. "Some parts of the score make a truly stunning impression: this especially pertains to the 'Horumi' of the fourth scene and the finale of the entire ballet. . . . In general there is nothing small-scale in this music, I would say that everything is noble and profound, while the pathos of the ballet emerges from its high poetic qualities."[1]

In creating choreography for the role of Gardji, Chaboukiani composed virile dances far removed from stereotype *variations* in classical ballets, though all the steps were based on the *danse d'école*. His dances, coloured with Georgian national tradition and filled with a kind of *bravura*, were compared with the flight of an eagle.

For Manije he created contrasting choreography in the soft and feminine style of the dances of Georgian women. The part of Manije was danced by Yelena Chikvaidze. She was a worthy partner of Gardji-Chaboukiani. Her gentle Manije grew into a heroine.

Galina Ulanova wrote that among Soviet ballets, serving as an intermediary stage to the mastering of contemporary themes, *The Heart of the Hills* was a production that "represented this stage both in its content and form of implementation".[2]

The subject of Chaboukiani's next ballet, *Laurencia*, to music by Alexandre Krein (1883-1951), was taken from Lope de Vega's famous drama, *Fuente Ovejuna*. The play was four hundred years old. But one could hardly find another theatre, with the exception of the Russian one, where it would have been adopted to such an extent as one of its own, and where its revolutionary spirit was as thoroughly understood and conveyed. When *Fuente Ovejuna* was first produced at the Maly Theatre in the seventies with the greatest tragedienne, Maria Yermolova (1853-1928), in the role of Laurencia, heroine of the uprising of Spanish peasants from the "Sheep Stream" village against its feudal lords, this seemingly

---

[1] Dmitry Shostakovich. "A Prominent Work". Newspaper *Soviet Art* 1938, June 30, p. 3.

[2] Galina Ulanova. "Debatable problems of the ballet theatre". In the magazine, *Art and Life*, Leningrad, 1939, No. 4, p. 23.

remote image became in her interpretation a symbol of Revolution for the progressive students of the Moscow University. It was a Russian *Fuente Ovejuna* and a Russian Laurencia. After that a traditional approach to the drama in a heroic key was established in the Russian theatre. Naturally several attempts were made to create a ballet on this theme—it was literally born for choreographic evocation. The Gliere ballet, *The Comedians*, produced at the Bolshoi theatre in 1931 with character-dance choreography by Alexander Chekrygin, only partly followed the plot of *Fuente Ovejuna* and entirely missed its content.

In Chaboukiani's *Laurencia*, beyond any doubt, partly from the search for the heroic theme and heroic characters, one found a reflection of the sympathy experienced by the Soviet people for the heroic struggle that had taken place in Republican Spain.

With all its shortcomings (traditionalism in the composition of the score, insufficiently developed dramaturgy of the scenario) *Laurencia* may be considered another important stage in the development of Soviet ballet. The entire population of Fuente Ovejuna became its principal hero. With this idea in its background, the character of Laurencia was its central figure. The choreography of the part was planned to convey the idea of Laurencia's heroism. However, the success of the role would not have been complete but for an ideal exponent in the person of Natalia Dudinskaya.

Born in 1912, a pupil of Vaganova (class of 1931), Natalia Dudinskaya soon proved herself to be a brilliant ballerina in the *bravura* virtuosity style. In 1932 she danced her first Odette-Odile and Aurora (*Swan Lake* and *The Sleeping Beauty*), in 1934 Kitri of *Don Quixote*, in 1935—Giselle. Perfect technique enabled the ballerina to perform a great variety of roles in classical ballets—Nikia in *La Bayadère* was preferred by her because it afforded a chance to penetrate more deeply into the psychology of the character. The nature of her talent called for roles coloured with a heroic note. Such a role came with Laurencia, bringing her full artistic maturity. Through brilliant classical dancing (Chaboukiani's choreography for the part calls for the utmost virtuosity) Dudinskaya created a passionate, realistic character.

In Chaboukiani's characterization and impersonation, Frondozo was an evocation of the fervent and unrelenting spirit of the people of Fuente Ovejuna. Frondozo's dances abounded, sometimes to an extreme, explained by the virtuosity and exhilaration of their author, in the most difficult *enchaînements* of classical steps. In this second ballet Chaboukiani resorted to a much greater extent not only to the steps, but to the

Galina Ulanova's Tao-Hoa in *The Red Poppy*, Bolshoi Theatre, Moscow, 1959.

Sergei Koren as Mercutio in the Lavrovsky production of *Romeo and Juliet* for the Bolshoi Theatre, Moscow. (Collection of Natalia Roslavleva)

traditional forms of classical ballet—thus in the wedding scene of Laurencia and Frondozo he choreographed a brilliant *grand pas* in the old style, but with a new meaning in the general pattern of the ballet. It served as a contrast to the forthcoming raid by the Comandore and his henchmen on the village, and was conceived to express the moods of the people.

The *corps de ballet* appeared in this ballet in the capacity of a mass hero, presented with the same care as the main protagonists. The people and their heroes: Frondozo, Laurencia, Jacinta, Pasquala, Mengo, formed an artistic unity unparalleled in previous productions and capable of producing the strongest possible impression.

The final scene of *Laurencia* was conceived by Chaboukiani in the manner of free *plastique* and expressive mime. It was here that the role of Laurencia reached its climax when she summoned the men of Fuente Ovejuna to rise against the Comandore, accusing them of cowardliness and timidity. Laurencia's famous "monologue", immortalized in the dramatic theatre by Yermolova, was transposed here into another, choreographic key.

The form of free movement, used by Chaboukiai in the finale of the ballet, contrasted with the more conventional idiom of the *danse d'école* and academic Spanish character dancing used in the other acts.

Since that time Soviet ballet and Chaboukiani himself have learnt more about authentic Spanish dances. The choreography of *Laurencia* belongs to its period, though the ballet still lives successfully in the repertory of the Kirov and Bolshoi theatres, affording dancers (for example Maya Plisetskaya), the possibility of creating strong dramatic characters.

Laurencia remains one of the most important milestones in the development of the heroic theme in Soviet Ballet.

The experience in dramatic ballets of the nineteen-thirties indicated that Soviet ballet had matured, that it had forces capable of tackling themes and images that earlier appeared much too profound and complicated for the ballet.

The strength of Soviet ballet in that fruitful period was due to the variety of talent. There were many choreographers and every one of them had his own inimitable quality. Among them that of Leonid Lavrovsky was one of the most mature.

People's Artist of the U.S.S.R., Professor Leonid Lavrovsky (Leonid Ivanov) was born in 1905 in the family of a Petersburg industrial worker. He was placed in the ballet division of the Theatre School in 1916 and graduated from it in 1922, class of V. I. Ponomaryov. In the repertory of the former Mariinsky Lavrovsky danced such responsible parts as Siegfried in *Swan Lake*, Jean de Brienne in *Raymonda*, Amoun in *Nuits d'Egypte*, and the male part in *Chopiniana* (*Les Sylphides*). Simultaneously with dancing in classical ballets, Lavrovsky joined the group of young dancers and choreographers known as "Molodoi Balet" (Young Ballet), founded by G. Balanchine and V. Dmitriev. Lavrovsky was ever ready to participate in any new undertaking, such as the controversial *Dance Symphony* of Fedor Lopukhov, or one of the first contemporary ballets, *The Age of Gold*, in which he danced the role of the Fascist. Soon Lavrovsky had a chance to pass his first test as a choreographer. He produced the central piece for the graduation recital of 1930 at the Leningrad ballet school in the form of dances to the music of Schumann's *Symphonic Etudes*. The young choreographer was acclaimed by the Press. He was asked to choreograph a full evening recital for the company of the former Mariinsky theatre that included the choreographic realization of Rimsky-Korsakov's *Capriccio Espagnol*. After staging Tchaikovsky's *Seasons* for the school in 1931, he choreographed his first major work: *Fadette*, to music from *Sylvia* and other compositions by Delibes, with the story taken from George Sand's *La Petite Fadette*. This was shown at the school's graduation performance on the stage of the Kirov theatre on March 21, 1934, and later revived at the Maly Opera Theatre of Leningrad (Lavrovsky was artistic director of its ballet between 1936 and 1937) on June 9, 1936.

Lavrovsky selected only good music for all his works. In order to deepen his knowledge and understanding of music he studied the rudiments of composition and learned to play the piano.

Lavrovsky worked on the scenario of *Fadette* in collaboration with the dramatic director, V. N. Solovyov, who had a considerable influence on the young choreographer. In *Fadette* he used for the first time classical dance as a means of characterization. The behaviour of each dancer on the stage was psychologically inspired, and not a single dance allowed to be devoid of meaning. This principle became the foundation of Lavrovsky's creative method.

In 1935, in the last work mounted for a graduation performance, the ballet *Katerina*, to music selected from Rubinstein and Adam, Lavrovsky created an example of major choreography.[1]

This was a ballet about the Serf Theatre, one of the brightest and most terrifying pages in the Russian art of the past, with hundreds of nameless tragedies, buried talents and premature deaths. One such story, partly

[1] In 1936 *Katerina* was included in the repertory of the Kirov Theatre.

following Leskov's *Wig-maker*, was enacted in Lavrovsky's ballet. With a great feeling for historical style, Lavrovsky re-created in this first major work a "ballet within a ballet", in other words a performance of the Serf Ballet on the stage. This inserted ballet of the serfs, finely stylized in the manner of Didelot's anacreontic ballets and Fedor Tolstoy's famed sketches for them, was, however, pursuing aims that left far behind simple stylization of a past period. The action of the serf ballet from *Katerina* corresponded to the main tragic conflict: Boreas robbed the Shepherd (Vladimir, the hero of the ballet) of his beloved Nymph (Katerina, the serf ballerina), thus predicting what was to happen to them later in real life.

In the happy finale of the serf ballet (the Nymph was returned to the Shepherd), the serenely beautiful poses that had to be performed by the serf ballerina were filled with great tragic pathos.

But the greatest dramatic impact was achieved by the choreographer of *Katerina* in its third act. Perhaps there were not many dances there. But one of them, the Russian dance of the serfs, acquired the significance of a dramatic symbol. The drunken lord of the estate, threatening the serfs with a whip, made them dance. The crowd performed the steps as if obeying his order. But in the way the movements were performed, in the broken pattern of the *khorovod's* round, in the anguish of every one of the dancers, one felt the mounting wave of the serfs' indignation. The dance was abruptly broken with a tragic note—the Governor arrived on the scene demanding his newly-purchased slave. The body of Katerina, who had committed suicide, was laid at his feet. In this ballet Lavrovsky revealed another aspect of his choreographic talent, the ability to create mime imbued with action and the content of the music, mime that was plastically done in a manner bringing it to the level of *danse d'action*. This quality became one of Lavrovsky's main methods and assets in his next major work, *Romeo and Juliet*.

It was preceded by years of study and perfectioning. While producing ballets at the Maly Opera (*The Prisoner in the Caucasus*, etc.) the choreographer literally lived at the Hermitage Museum. Much work was done in the Saltykov-Shchedrin Public Library; it was there that Lavrovsky found the idea for the famous "Cushion Dance". Based on the study of authentic material it became, in the ballet, a symbol of the dark forces of the Middle Ages.

When Lavrovsky started the production of *Romeo and Juliet*, he was already heading the ballet company of the Kirov Theatre.

In preparing an outline of the future choreography, Lavrovsky had to introduce considerable changes in the scenario offered by its authors, Sergei Radlov and Adrian Piotrovsky, a Leningrad writer and theatre scholar. *Romeo and Juliet* was conceived by Radlov as early as 1934 (in that period he had achieved a production of the tragedy in the dramatic theatre). He proposed to commission Rostislav Zakharov, his disciple from the Theatre Institute, with the production. In his book, *The Art of the Choreographer*, Zakharov confirms that he was invited by the Bolshoi Theatre in 1935 to produce Prokofiev's *Romeo and Juliet*. "Together with Prokofiev," writes Zakharov, "we discussed the composition plan of the ballet, its dances and scenes, including the duration of each separate number. But I did not achieve this production, because the Directorate of the Bolshoi Theatre turned down Prokofiev's music. . . ."[1]

Galina Dobrovolskaya, staff worker of the Leningrad Institute of the History of Music, Theatre and the Cinema, informs us in her valuable study of the circumstances accompanying the composition of *Romeo and Juliet*[2] that Radlov wrote a draft of the future "book" of the ballet in 1934, and that in the same year Prokofiev had his preliminary talks in Leningrad with Radlov and Zakharov.

In 1935 Radlov published a detailed article, in which he expressed confidence that it was quite possible to create a ballet based on *Romeo and Juliet* without departing from the profound theme of Shakespeare's tragedy: "From Shakespeare there will be a feeling of the love of Juliet and Romeo, representing youth defending its right for personal happiness against the oppression of the dying, but as yet still strong, feudal society. From Shakespeare there will be the growth and development of a personality in the course of the entire spectacle (Juliet the child into Juliet the heroine). From Shakespeare comes the sharp contrast of the tragic and the comic, and consecutive realism as the main method of vision."[3]

The original scenario by Radlov and Piotrovsky (apparently with advice from Zakharov), on the basis of which Prokofiev had composed his original score, consisted of *four* acts and nine scenes. While the action on the whole followed that of the tragedy, there were some changes, among them a very serious one. The ballet was given a happy end! Romeo was

[1] R. Zakharov. *The Art of the Choreographer*, Iskusstvo, Moscow, 1954, p. 177.

[2] G. Dobrovolskaya. "From the history of the creation of Prokofiev's 'Romeo and Juliet' ". In *Music of Soviet Ballet*, a collection of articles. State Music Publishing House, Leningrad, 1962, p. 239.

[3] *Soviet Art* (newspaper) of June 23, 1935. S. Radlov. "The Ballet 'Romeo and Juliet' ".

just about to stab himself, when Friar Laurence entered to stop him. At this very moment Juliet started breathing. Friar Laurence hid Romeo and Juliet behind a rosebush, summoned all the relatives by beating a gong (!) and showed them the unharmed couple. The ballet was to end with a lively general dance.

In the third act of this version of the scenario, Paris brought Juliet on the morning of their expected betrothal "live presents" in the form of Syrian girls and Moors (!) performing a *divertissement* that interrupted the action. In general this scenario lacked the tragic tension of the final version.

Late in 1935 and at the beginning of 1936, Prokofiev played the completed parts of the ballet first at the Bolshoi Theatre, and, in January 1936, at the editorial office of the newspaper *Soviet Art*, for the benefit of critics and musicians. The music of the ballet was unanimously praised, but its happy end caused, for the most part, nothing but emphatic opposition.

It is probable that the changes introduced into Shakespeare's tragedy were instrumental in the decision of the Bolshoi Theatre not to include *Romeo and Juliet* in its repertory, despite the numerous announcements to the effect that a contract had been signed with Prokofiev.

In the spring of 1936 Prokofiev was approached by the Leningrad School (through Yuri Slonimsky, then in charge of its "Method Department") which wished to produce *Romeo and Juliet* for its 200th anniversary in 1938. Prokofiev was very sceptical about the idea. The failure of the negotiations with the Bolshoi Theatre the disillusioned him about the possibility of staging *Romeo and Juliet* as a ballet altogether. Moreover, he had never heard of the choreographer Lavrovsky, unknown at the time outside Leningrad, where he had created only two graduation performances: *Fadette* (1934) and *Katerina* (1935). However, Prokofiev agreed to meet the choreographer. Almost simultaneously Prokofiev received a similar offer from the State Theatre of Brno (Czechoslovakia).

Since the talks with the Leningrad School were not resumed, it so happened that the actual first performance of *Romeo and Juliet*, with choreography by Vania Psota (1908-1952), took place at Brno on December 30, 1936. The end, however, followed Shakespeare's tragedy and by that time Prokofiev had, apparently, written the new finale. On the other hand the *divertissement* of "live presents" was still demonstrated by Paris immediately after his intended bride had drunk the sleeping potion. In this first version the choreographer's attention was centred on the love story. There was no question whatsoever of portraying the bitter conflict of two worlds. In 1937 Prokofiev created a second version of the scenario and piano score, with many new details providing the heroes with more definite traits of character. Juliet is described in the betrothal scene as "pure, all in white as a symbol of innocence". After the clash with her father and the visit to Friar Laurence's cell, Juliet is said to grow "into a tragic figure". In the new version much more attention was given to the portrayal of the grim and menacing world of the Capulets and Montagues. Now the scenario told not only of Juliet's and Romeo's love and death, but revealed that the reasons leading to their tragic end were embodied in the senseless hostility of two feudal families.

In the middle of 1938 the Kirov Theatre of Opera and Ballet opened energetic negotiations with Prokofiev, in the hope of presenting the ballet during the next season. Leonid Lavrovsky went to Moscow for talks with the composer. At first they did not bring about any satisfactory result. The composer and the choreographer had their own ideas of Shakespeare's tragedy. As a result of many debates the scenario was considerably changed. Radlov remained as only one of its authors. The problem of the music was much more serious. It had already been composed to the *old* scenario. Many times did the composer and the choreographer meet, differ and agree until *Romeo and Juliet* was born as we have known it now for twenty-five years.

Prokofiev at first would answer obstinately: "I have written as much music as is necessary and I am not going to do anything else. The piece is finished. It is ready. You may produce it or not as you will."[1]

In search of a dance for the first scene, Lavrovsky went to a music shop, purchased sheet music of Prokofiev's *Second Pianoforte Sonata* and choreographed to the *scherzo* movement a "Morning Dance" of tavern servants. Everybody awaited Prokofiev's arrival at the rehearsal with bated breath. A storm did follow. Prokofiev departed in complete indignation. But a few days later he brought the well-known music of the "Aubade" which matched the *scherzo* both in rhythm and in all other *nuances*. The ice was broken at last, and Prokofiev was willing to co-operate.

All the music that had been already written by Prokofiev deeply moved the choreographer. He described the music as "titanic". However, not all of it would fit his own choreographic plan. In a letter to Prokofiev (of August 31, 1939) Lavrovsky asked for a *variation* for Romeo (at the end of the balcony scene) because "Romeo is already taken up by his great and genuine love. He should, and can, be manly

[1] G. Dobrovolskaya, *op. cit.* Quoted from Ulanova's article, preserved at the Central Archives of Literature and Art Fund 1929, book 1, No. 108.

and energetic. Juliet's *variation* is not 'comfortable' for dancing in its first part. It would be preferable also to feel an indication of elevation in the music."[1]

Apart from those mentioned Prokofiev composed several new pieces for the final score of the ballet, including Juliet's *variation* in the grand ballroom scene, the famous procession with Tybalt's body, the dance performed to the mandoline orchestra on the square of Verona, Juliet's scene with Paris, Romeo's scene in the vault, and a proscenium inter-mission for carnival pairs. Several scenes, non-existent in the original score, were either created or expanded by Lavrovsky by repetition, or by a different order of pieces that had already been written. This is how he devised the music for the "Cushion Dance".

This history of the *creation* of *Romeo and Juliet* has been given here intentionally in detail because it is little known. The production, shown for the first time on January 11, 1940, at the Kirov Theatre, and on December 28, 1946, at the Bolshoi, has become universally known as one of the greatest achievements in Soviet ballet.

Romeo and Juliet proved that Soviet ballet was in possession of qualities without which it would have been quite impossible to resolve such grandiose themes. Lavrovsky succeeded in conveying the colossal impact of Shakespeare's ideas through choreography. The love of the "star-crossed couple" was shown as a symbol of the Renaissance, of a new way of life, against the background of the family feud, personifying the dark Middle Ages.

It is not surprising that the ballet of *Romeo and Juliet* attracted the attention of Shakespeare scholars. After the Moscow première of *Romeo and Juliet* (in the course of its preparation Lavrovsky asked the eminent Shakespeare scholar, Professor Mikhail Morozov, to lecture to the company on Shakespeare and his time), the Theatre Society convened a special conference of its Shakespeare department. The conference resolved that the ballet, *Romeo and Juliet*, had succeeded in translating Shakespeare's thoughts and imagery into the language of dance.

Romeo and Juliet was a new form of musico-choreographic drama, and that it has withstood the test of time (despite several new versions Lavrovsky's is universally accepted as the definitive one) serves as proof that its plan was wisely chosen.

The settings by Pyotr Williams (1902-1947) appear somewhat heavy nowadays. But on the other hand their impressive monumental breadth

---

[1] *Idem*, p. 254.

and accord with the period presented are in complete harmony with the symphonic breadth of Prokofiev's music and the colossal theme from which it stems.

Lavrovsky's choreography, born after the pangs described above, is exceedingly musical, and at times is organically linked with the score. Perhaps there is more mime than dance in the texture of the ballet, though there are now plenty of danced items, but is it possible to trace the border-line between mime and dance in this choreography, to say where dance ends and mime begins in the betrothal scene, to give but one example? The pantomime in Lavrovsky's ballet is completely integrated with the music and mirrors its rhythms and content. Everything is subordinate to the music. Every super (though in this ballet there are no supers—every member of the crowd has to be an actor) knows the exact bar when he has to start his entrance. The procession carrying Lady Capulet lamenting over Tybalt's body has to stop on the bridge at an exact moment in the score, and even the curtains are timed to music.

Of course an important role in the happy birth of *Romeo and Juliet* as a ballet was played by its first protagonists: Galina Ulanova—Juliet, Konstantin Sergeyev—Romeo, Andrei Lopukhov—Mercutio, Robert Gerbek—Tybalt, Yevgenia Bieber—the Nurse, and Boris Shavrov—Paris.

In the Moscow production the ballet found other Romeos—Mikhail Gabovich and Yuri Zhdanov, a greater Tybalt in the person of Alexei Yermolayev, and an incomparable pair of Capulets in Yelena Ilyush-chenko and Alexander Radunsky, but it was lucky to have for a number of years the same Juliet.

One can say of Ulanova's Juliet that she danced Shakespeare and, as in the case of Maria, simply was Juliet. The great dancer-actress admitted that she had difficulty at first with Prokofiev's music. She had to sing her own "internal melody" in order to breathe credible emotions into her dance. After the role had been performed by her many dozens of times, she wrote that: "Even such a great composer as Sergei Prokofiev has some pages in his ballet that have to be 'warmed' by our own inner feeling."[1]

She lived the role and completely identified herself with the character. She wrote about this: "Knowing that I am not Shakespeare's heroine, but simply Galina Ulanova, I strive to feel myself to be Juliet Capulet, in Verona, four hundred years ago. . . . I am assisted in this by all the

[1] Galina Ulanova. "Expressive means of ballet". In: *Soviet Music*, No. 4, 1955, p. 7.

Andrei Lopukhov, creator of the role of Mercutio in Leonid Lavrovsky's original production of *Romeo and Juliet*, Leningrad, 1940. (Collection of Natalia Roslavleva)

Ivan Kurilov as Sir John Falstaff, from *The Merry Wives of Windsor*, ballet with music by V. Oransky and choreography by V. Burmeister and I. Kurilov. Stanislavsky and Nemirovich-Danchenko Lyric Theatre, 1942. (Collection of Natalia Roslavleva)

expressive means of ballet—all the composite parts of the choreographic spectacle."[1]

After having created Juliet, Ulanova changed her mind about Prokofiev's music and in a tribute to the composer wrote: "If I were to be asked now what kind of music is needed for *Romeo and Juliet*, I would answer: the same as Prokofiev's! I cannot envisage it otherwise and I do not wish to have it any other way. . . ."[2]

Juliet became identified with Ulanova to a much greater extent than was Romeo with the name of the creator of that role, Konstantin Sergeyev. Justice should be done to this remarkable portrayal. It is a great pity that circumstances (after the war Ulanova did not return to the Kirov company) prevented the continuation of this perfect partnership. As Romeo and Juliet, Ulanova and Sergeyev created a duet of unmatched beauty and the fragrance of youthful love.

Konstantin Sergeyev (born in 1910), now People's Artist of the U.S.S.R. and Artistic Director of the Kirov ballet, had an unusual career for a member of an academic company such as the former Mariinsky. He started his first ballet lessons when over fourteen. Having joined the evening courses of the Leningrad Ballet School he studied under the great master, Victor Semenov. Upon graduation he had no chance to dance in the academic company; it refused dancers who had not passed through the full course of tuition from childhood. After two years as *premier danseur* in a touring ballet company headed by Joseph Kshesinski, Sergeyev, having passed his examinations in September 1929, entered the graduation class of the Leningrad School. In the autumn of 1930 he was already a fully-fledged member of the academic ballet.

In the first season he danced Siegfried in *Swan Lake*. Sergeyev's contribution to the development of Soviet ballet can hardly be exaggerated, he participated in all its important creations, and was in turn creator of roles such as Vaclav in *The Fountain of Bakhchisarai* and Lucien in *Lost Illusions*. In the forties and fifties Sergeyev turned to choreography of his own, creating such original ballets as *Cinderella* and *The Path of Thunder*, and new versions of Tchaikovsky and Glasunov ballets for the Kirov theatre.

When Sergeyev came to work at the role of Romeo, he was already a formed dancer-actor with considerable experience in dramatic ballets. Yet, as in the case of Ulanova, his participation in *Romeo and Juliet* served

[1] *Idem*, p. 76.

[2] Galina Ulanova. "Author of favourite ballets". In: *S. S. Prokofiev. Materials, documents, memoirs*. Moscow, 1956, p. 267.

as a landmark in his entire career, the starting point of a new, more deeply felt, and profoundly motivated, manner of enacting a part.

Prokofiev's *Romeo and Juliet*, as created by Lavrovsky and the wonderful cast that supported him and understood his artistic intentions, stands out in the history of Soviet Ballet as the highest peak reached by dramatic ballets of the thirties.

CHAPTER XI

BALLET IN THE SOVIET REPUBLICS

In studying the history of Soviet ballet one should not lose sight of companies other than those dancing on the illustrious stages of the Bolshoi and the Kirov Theatres. The general picture of Soviet Ballet is colossal. There are currently thirty-four ballet companies in the U.S.S.R. dancing in thirty-two cities, inasmuch as Moscow and Leningrad have two opera houses each: the Kirov Theatre of Opera and Ballet and the Maly Opera (both have the subtitles of "Academic") in Leningrad, the Bolshoi Academic Theatre of the U.S.S.R. and the Lyrical Theatre named after Stanislavsky and Nemirovich-Danchenko in Moscow.

Both of the smaller opera houses have ballet companies that in the course of their history produced many new ballets on an experimental plane. This especially concerns the early period of the Maly Opera Ballet (the theatre[1] popularly known as the "Malegot").

It was formed in the season of 1930-1931 as a "laboratory of ballet" with the intention of creating something different from the repertory of the former Mariinsky ballet. Fedor Lopukhov was asked to head the new company. In the desire not to duplicate by any means the Mariinsky repertory, and in the realization that the young company (many of its members at the time had not enjoyed a full ballet education) could not cope with the difficulties presented by great masterpieces of the nineteenth-century ballet, Lopukhov decided to found a theatre of "ballet comedy". The idea received support: comedies were very rare in ballet, which was quite capable of choreography evoking moods of mirth and exhilaration as was shown by the comic ballets of the past. Lopukhov began by reviving (in 1933) Drigo's *Harlequinade* (*Les Millions d'Arlequin*). When first produced at the Hermitage Theatre in 1900, with choreography by Petipa, it had a simple little plot from the *Commedia dell' Arte* with the entire second act taken up by a *divertissement*. Musically it consisted of a

[1] The Maly Opera is housed in the building of the former Mikhailovsky French Theatre, originally exclusive to Court circles. On March 8, 1918, a new Lyric Theatre was opened in this building on the initiative of Lunacharsky. In the beginning comic operas were shown here, and a very small ballet group was kept for *divertissements*. This group provided the nucleus of the future independent ballet company.

suite of dances, melodious and rhythmical, one of Drigo's best composi-tions. It so happened that at the beginning of the twenties Riccardo Drigo (1846-1930) was still living in Petrograd (afterwards he returned to his home town of Padua). Lopukhov had been nursing the idea of a new version of *Les Millions d'Arlequin* for some ten years. He was able to discuss it with Drigo in person, who told him that because of the necessity to trim the score to the duration of brief performances shown at the Hermitage Court Theatre, some of its best parts were deleted. Lopukhov found the complete score and restored its original content. He then transferred the action from the conventional and indefinite surroundings of the earlier version into Paris of the mid-nineteenth century. A group of young people donned costumes of Harlequin, Pierrette, and Columbine, and, in a series of mystifications, obtained the consent of a *bourgeois* father (enacted in mime by an actor from the Comic Opera company of the theatre) to his daughter's marriage to a poor student. Though at times Lopukhov resorted to rather crude buffoonery, the ballet did prove both merry and amusing. It created a gay atmosphere in the auditorium and had quite a success with the public, forming an immediate rapport between the spectators and the young company.

The production included, among other things, "vocal and choreo-graphic ensembles" in the 2nd and 4th scenes, sung by members of the opera company. It had, however, several *ballabili* performed by all of the ballet group, an *adagio* for the two enamoured couples and a *pas de deux* for Columbine and Harlequin. Lopukhov choreographed these with the intention of providing experience in the classical school for the very immature and uneven company. *Harlequinade* was more than a new production. It played the role of a classroom and welded the company, assembled from different sources, into a unified whole. After the success of the new version of the *Harlequinade* several of the dancers from the State Academic Ballet, tired of the routine still reigning in those days on the stage of the renowned Mariinsky, expressed a desire to dance in the ballet. Three of them, Pyotr Gusev (born in 1905), Alexander Orlov (born in 1889), and Nicolai Zubovsky (born in 1911), soon joined the company altogether, abandoning the academic precincts.

Lopukhov's next undertaking was a new version of *Coppélia* (1934). He again devised an entirely new plot. The new *Coppélia* was about a travelling circus. Its old master's chief attraction was a speaking doll. When the covered wagon makes a halt in one of the small towns in the Transcarpathians, a soldier and his sweetheart quarrel because he had fallen in love with the doll, taking her for a beautiful girl.

The Perm Theatre of Opera and Ballet (after reconstruction).

Le Corsaire at the Stanislavsky and Nemirovich-Danchenko Lyric Theatre, Moscow. Scene from Act II, with Eleonora Vlasova as Gulnare.

The Leningrad Symphony (to music of Shostakovich's Seventh Symphony). Choreography by Igor Bielsky. Kirov Theatre, Leningrad.

The action, with the help of Mikhail Bobyshov, a designer who had collaborated with Fokine in some earlier productions, was filled with the colour of real life, and the dances were based on the national dances of the Transcarpathians.

The attitude to classical dancing was very typical of the period. The Swanilda of the first act was more of a character dancer, dressed in a long peasant skirt and top boots. After quarrelling with her sweetheart and remaining alone she had to perform the melodious *variation*, composed by Delibes for *Coppélia*. The ballerina was made to pull up her skirt in front of the audience and take off her boots, which concealed her ballet shoes. This transformation was done in an effort to "justify" the introduction of classical dancing. We shall see later that such cases were not isolated.

Lopukhov rearranged Delibes' music to a considerable extent, particularly in the last two acts, where the new action did not at all suit the musical content. There were also plenty of rather vulgar tricks in the circus scenes that abounded in buffoonery. Yet the new *Coppélia* on the whole exerted an atmosphere of mirth and exhilaration. Galina Isayeva (born in 1915)—brilliant in *soubrette* and *travestie* roles, the dramatic dancer-actress, Valentina Rosenberg (born in 1916), Nina Anisimova (born in 1909), Sergei Koren (born in 1907), Galina Kirillova (born in 1916), Nina Mirimanova (born in 1917), all began their fruitful careers in those years, either remaining in the company or leaving it, as in the case of Koren, Anisimova, and Kirillova, for the academic stage.

The next stage in the life of the Maly Opera ballet was connected with the appointment of Leonid Lavrovsky to the post of its artistic leader (between 1935 and 1938). The company grew in his dramatic ballets and learned to create characters in ballets on serious themes borrowed from great works of literature. After a successful debut with the choreography of *Fadette*, built on the principle of *pas d'action*, and an original three-act version of *La Fille Mal Gardée*, Lavrovsky created here one of his major works—*The Prisoner in the Caucasus*. It was a "romantic drama", conceived for the most part in dance rather than pantomime. All contemporary criticisms agreed that the spirit of Pushkin's poem was successfully conveyed by the choreography. This version of the Pushkin ballet was considered to be more successful than a later one, produced by Zakharov at the Bolshoi Theatre in 1938.

In 1940 the Maly Opera produced another successful Pushkin ballet after the fairy-tale in verse *The Tale of the Priest and his Workman Balda*. The choreography served as the début of Vladimir Varkovitsky (born in 1916). A character soloist from the Kirov company, he became interested in choreography and studied at the "Balletmasters' Courses" organized at the Leningrad School, under the guidance of Fedor Lopukhov. The composer Mikhail Chulaki (born in 1908; now Director of the Bolshoi Theatre) wrote his first ballet score with imagination and in a contemporary style. The book by Yuri Slonimsky ensured the high artistic qualities of the production and in many ways predetermined its style. The choreography was full of amusing details. Samovars and kettles were made to dance. Black devils (the principal characters of the story) performed hilarious dances. Particularly effective were the dances of the Little Black Devil performed by the talented dancer Galina Isayeva *en travestie*. Balda, fooling both the devils and the priest who hired him, reminded one of Ivanushka-the-Fool, the traditional character of Russian fairy-tale, who was in reality much wiser than those who tried to outwit him.

Vladimir Varkovitsky was very much praised both for the *genre* scenes and for the lyrical Russian dances created in the classical idiom for this ballet. After the great success of *The Tale of the Priest and his Workman Balda* during the theatre's first tour in Moscow, Varkovitsky was invited to head its ballet and remained in this post until 1943, returning in further years for separate productions.

The next fruitful period of the company is connected with the name of Boris Fenster (born 1916). He graduated from the Leningrad Ballet School in 1936 directly into the Maly Opera ballet. Here, aside from dancing solo parts, he became assistant ballet-master in Lavrovsky's productions, *La Fille Mal Gardée* and *The Prisoner in the Caucasus*. This was the first choreographer to start his career directly at the Maly Opera and acquire its traditions of realistic acting from the very beginning. Between 1945 and 1953 Fenster was chief choreographer of the Maly Opera Ballet.

In this period he achieved his best productions—*The False Bridegroom* (after Goldoni's *Il Servitore di duo padrone*) and *Youth*—both to music by Mikhail Chulaki, whose collaboration with the theatre was always very fruitful. The first continued the company's tradition in creating ballet comedy. The role of Beatrice was created by Galina Kirillova, an excellent ballerina. Her transformation from the gentle maiden into a gallant officer (Beatrice did this in order to be a "False Bridegroom") was effectively done by the choreographer and perfectly carried out by the dancer. But the entire ballet centred around the personality of Nicolai Zubkovsky in the role of Trufaldino, the Servant of Two Masters. Zubkovsky was a dancer with a style of his own. Possessing perfect technique, though rather small in stature, he excelled in roles requiring characterization. *Youth* became a landmark in the history of the theatre and of Soviet ballet as a whole. This was the first truly successful work about the Civil War, one that conveyed its romantic and heroic spirit. Conceived by Yuri Slonimsky, author of the scenario, after the well-known novel by Nicolai Ostrovsky, *How the Steel was Tempered*, it followed the plot only in some general aspects. The scenario was in no way a literal translation of the book into ballet, but an evocation of its spiritual content. Slonimsky succeeded in creating growing and developing characters in the persons of the three principal heroes—Dima, Petia, and Dasha (danced by F. Shishkin, V. Tulubiev and G. Isayeva). A considerable part of the ballet was enacted in pantomime, but it had plenty of action. One act, in contrast, was carried out in classical idiom. It was a picnic arranged by boys and girls in the woods. Many of the choreographic "finds" in this ballet, effectively performed by Fenster, were, however, directly suggested by Slonimsky's scenario.

The ballet owed no small part of its success to the cast with Svetlana Sheina (born in 1918), one of its principal ballerinas, as the schoolgirl who joins the revolutionary youth of her town.

The palm in this ballet went, however, to Galina Isayeva's original and outstanding impersonation of Dasha—a tomboy growing into a dramatic figure.

Another important period in the life of the Maly Opera Ballet came when Pyotr Gusev headed it between 1960 and 1962.

A first-class teacher and great connoisseur of the classical school, especially famed for his classes in *pas de deux*, Gusev, in his capacity of the company's ballet-master, improved its professional standards to a great extent. (Of course by that time its personnel consisted for the most part of dancers with a complete ballet education.) As choreographer, Gusev produced two important works at the Maly Opera, a new version of *Le Corsaire* (in 1955), with a book by Yuri Slonimsky that brought the story closer to Byron, and *Seven Beauties* (1953), introducing the remarkable symphonic score by Kara Karayev, the Azerbaijan composer, who has since become one of the leading composers in the Soviet Union. Based on classical dance that was, when necessary, deftly transformed with the help of steps and general style of movement borrowed from dances of the Orient, the *Seven Beauties* was also a powerful dramatic ballet with most of the action expressed in dance rather than mime. The story, borrowed from the great Azerbaijan poet, Nizami, was connected with the Shah Bahram, and the punishment received by him from his own people, who banished him from his land. Shah Bahram betrayed both Menzer, the hunter who had saved his life after the treacherous Vizier had tried to assasinate him and take his throne, and Menzer's sister, the gentle Aisha, whom he killed in the finale in the hope of escaping. The theme of the vision of the Seven Beauties, directly borrowed from one of Nizami's poems, was of secondary importance in the choreography, but afforded the opportunity of creating a varied *divertissement*. The lyrical and tragic theme of Aisha and her relations with Bahram was the most prominent one in the entire ballet, though its mass scenes, choreographed by Gusev with great mastery (particularly the effective court procession on the occasion of Bahram's return and the contrasting dances of workers in the market square), also produced a great effect. *The Seven Beauties* is still in the repertory of the Maly Opera.

In the fifties the Maly Opera ballet revived a number of ballets from the classical repertoire with the idea of providing its dancers with material for improvement. Thus the "Grand Pas" from the third act of *Paquita* was revived in 1957 by Konstantin Boyarsky. Fedor Lopukhov, too, carried out an interesting experiment by reviving, in 1958, the authentic version of *Swan Lake* as created in 1895 by Lev Ivanov and Petipa. This experiment did not fully succeed. The attempt to revive scenes done in conventional mime proved that it gave the production an outdated look, so that the idea was soon abandoned. However, the Petipa choreography of the first act, the authentic Lev Ivanov patterns in the "White Swan" scenes, where Benno was introduced as in 1895—all were there. In this form and with the authentic replicas of the original settings, *Swan Lake* remained in the repertory of the Maly Opera until 1965, when Igor Belsky did a version of his own.

The inclusion of important classical ballets in its repertory enabled the Maly Opera to educate a constellation of good classical dancers: Galina Pirozhnaya (born in 1929), Galina Pokryshkina (born in 1937), Lyudmila Safronova (born in 1929), Tatiana Borovikova (born in 1924), Maria Mazun (born in 1924), Vera Stankevich (born in 1922), Georgi Litvinenko (born in 1922), Adol Khamzin (born in 1934), Veniamin Zimin (born in 1932), and Elbrus Gioyev (born in 1932). Outstanding among the male dancers was Valery Panov (born in 1938). Possessing a very wide range—from classical to *demi-caractère* style—he was particularly noticed after creating the title-role in the company's revival of *Petrushka* (in 1961). Konstantin Boyarsky (born in 1915), the company's ballet-master during that period, is a professional choreographer, inasmuch as he graduated

Swan Lake at the Stanislavsky and Nemirovich–Danchenko Lyric Theatre, Moscow. Choreography by Vladimir Bourmeister. Scene from Act IV, with Sophia Vinogradova as Odette.

Margarita Okatova, soloist of the Novosibirsk Opera and Ballet Theatre, in the ballet *Swan Lake*.

Larissa Sahyanova, People's Artist of the U.S.S.R., ballerina of the Ulan-Ude Theatre of Opera and Ballet of the Buryat Autonomous Republic, in a dance from the ballet *In the Name of Love*.

both from the *régisseur* faculty of the Leningrad Theatre Institute (like Rostislav Zakharov) and the three-year choreographer's courses instituted in the thirties by the Leningrad Ballet School (like Leonid Lavrovsky).

Boyarsky has an exceptional flair for revivals, though, as will be seen further on, he has also choreographed in the modern idiom. Since no record of *Petrushka* was available in Leningrad (where it was produced for the first time only in 1920 with a version of the *décor* made personally by Alexandre Benois), he restored the choreography by resorting to the memory of many participants, still living, not only of the 1920 production, but of the first performance of *Petrushka* in Paris in 1911 (notably Alexandre Orlov, the first Blackamoor).

In Panov, Boyarsky found a remarkable actor. Panov's impersonation was that of a puppet endowed with the capacity for real suffering, and he enacted the role with a great power of projection. His make-up was also outstanding—the young dancer, who likes to paint in his few spare hours, devised it himself.

Panov possessed an outstanding virtuosity technique and a virile quality of dancing reminiscent of such dancers as Yermolayev and Chaboukiani. Graduating from the class of Abdurahman Kumysnikov, a prominent Leningrad teacher, in 1957 Panov attended during his years in the Maly Opera the *classe de perfectionnement* of Semen Kaplan, former *premier danseur* of the Kirov Theatre. Under his guidance Panov considerably increased his virtuosity.

After spending several years with the company and creating a number of important roles, particularly that of Orpheus in the Boyarsky choreography of Stravinsky's ballet (1962), and the Soviet Pilot in the ballet *Flowers* to music selected from Shostakovich and choreography by Varkovitsky, Panov was invited to join the Kirov ballet in 1963, becoming one of its *premiers danseurs*.

Among Boyarsky's works *The Fire-Bird* is noteworthy. He staged it after seeing the authentic Fokine choreography during the Royal Ballet's first tour in Leningrad in 1961. The ballet was revived with new (but unsatisfactory) *décor* and costumes by Tatiana Bruni. However, when in 1964 Boyarsky's revival was included in the repertory of the Bolshoi Theatre, the authentic Golovine–Korovine settings and costumes, and the one Bakst costume, were reproduced after painstaking research.

Boyarsky's most successful original work was done at the end of 1962. It is a ballet to music from Shostakovich on the subject of Mayakovsky's *The Young Lady and the Hooligan*. The latter role was danced by Panov.

The subject is concerned with the transformation of a hooligan under the influence of love. The scene is laid in the early twenties, and the choreographer, whose youth coincided with that period, succeeded in conveying its features with remarkable artistic perception. In many ways the ballet continued the realistic line of the *Youth* created thirteen years earlier. But this new ballet was done in dance idiom and served as an object lesson of the company's progress.

Today it is headed by Igor Belsky,[1] one of Soviet ballet's most talented choreographers. He created in 1963 for the Maly Opera original choreography for *The Hump-Backed Horse* to a new score by Rodion Shchedrin (born in 1927) done in the spirit of the *Skomorokhi* games of old Russian. The ballet has many original touches and is very popular.

The Maly Opera Ballet of Leningrad is well known beyond that city. It appeared *in toto* in Australia and New Zealand in 1961, while groups of its artists have appeared in Finland and Scandinavian countries.

The company had a grand tour in Moscow on the stage of the Kremlin Palace of Congresses soon after its opening in 1962.

The second ballet company of Moscow, now part of the Stanislavsky and Nemirovich-Danchenko Musical Theatre, grew out of the "Art Ballet" founded by Viktorina Krieger.

Born in 1896, daughter of a well-known dramatic actor Vladimir Krieger and playwright Nadezhda Bogdanovskaya, Krieger was placed in the Bolshoi school in 1903, graduating from it into the Bolshoi Ballet in 1910. She was one of the "Gorsky ballerinas"—in other words, a dancer for whom technique (she was a virtuosity soloist) existed as a means of creating strong character. She excelled in roles requiring temperament, such as Lise in *La Fille Mal Gardée* and Swanilda in *Coppélia*. When she danced classical roles such as that of Kitri she was one of the first to give the part a contemporary note by portraying Kitri as a daughter of the people. In 1921 Krieger was in Anna Pavlova's company. In 1923-25 she toured the United States of America with Mikhail Mordkin.

In 1925 she returned to rejoin the Bolshoi Ballet. She was not satisfied with the repertory it could offer and sought broader vistas. At that time she was asked to take part in the performances of a ballet group organized by dancers of the Bolshoi Theatre, Vladimir Golubin and Nicolai Gerber, in order to bring ballet closer to people who had never or seldom seen any. Hence they toured the Moscow Region and other parts of the country. At first the limited repertory was performed to a piano, and the performances in Moscow took place in a small auditorium

[1] Belsky's biography will be given in the next chapter.

in the building of GUM, the trading arcade on the Red Square, right in the midst of various shops.

In 1927 the small group created its own version of *Schéhérazade* entitled *In the Chains of the Harem*. Beginning with 1928 the company expanded its personnel to about twenty-eight persons, and acquired an orchestra of ten musicians. The repertory now included smaller versions of ballets from the Bolshoi repertory—*The Hump-Backed Horse, Le Corsaire, The Red Poppy*. It was then that Krieger's attention was attracted to this group, and she became its artistic leader. The company was expanded by inviting some other dancers from the Bolshoi. It was anxious to create its own ballets. Its members adopted the Stanislavsky method of living the roles and creating "true-to-life" portrayals, taking these precepts much too literally at first.

In the absence of anything original, the company decided to create a new version of *La Fille Mal Gardée*. The choreography was by Nicolai Kholfin (born in 1903), one of the company's creators, and Pavel Markov (born in 1897), a theatrical director from the Art Theatre, Stanislavsky's disciple. They used the Hertel score but planned an entirely new theme by the choreographers. In this version it was given the name of *The Rivals*, and was connected with the rivalry of two girls, a rich and a poor one, for the love of Colas. It is interesting to note that at that time (the ballet was produced on May 7, 1933) the choreographer Kholfin and the Director Markov, who guided him to a considerable extent, thought that classical dancing might be introduced only when its use was "justified". Apparently considering its artistocratic origin stilted and the manner and style unnatural, the choreographers resorted to classical dance mostly in depicting negative characters. Also a dancer was permitted to perform the *jeté* if he had to reach an apple in a tree!

Of course the method was very naïve. But at the time the youthful creators of the ballet earnestly believed in its rightness. Moreover, their youth and enthusiasm enabled them to create a merry atmosphere that was infectious. *The Rivals* had success and played an important role in the growth of the company.

The production also revealed a great talent in the person of Maria Sorokina (1911-1948) who became, until her untimely death in 1948, the company's ballerina, endowed with expressive *plastique*. She danced many leading parts.

The same treatment of classical dance as needing "justification" was used in another of the company's first works: *The Carmagnole*, to music by the Ukrainian composer V. Femilidi, with choreography by the young dancers, Nicolai Bolotov (1904-?[1]) and Pavel Virsky,[2] who had just graduated from the ballet department of the Lunacharsky Theatre School, the second important ballet school of Moscow in the twenties and early thirties.

The young choreographers sincerely believed that they were following the precepts of Stanislavsky (by then, in 1932, the company bore the name of "Art Theatre of Ballet"), when they used the classical idiom only for characters of the French countries in a comic vein. This is the way the *pas de deux* of Marie-Antoinette and her favourite was treated. The choreography used a lot of character dancing, but it was interspersed with many naturalistic details and the artists were encouraged to laugh and whistle on the stage with the idea of creating "real" characters. Of course *The Carmagnole* did introduce new heroes into ballet. But the artistic method used failed to create convincing and emotionally moving images. How far removed was *The Carmagnole* from *The Flames of Paris* —created in the same year!

But the young company learned its lesson with time. It was the first to ask Rostislav Zakharov to stage his *Fountain of Bakhchisarai* and achieved a production of this ballet in April 1936 before the Bolshoi Theatre had staged it with the same choreography by Zakharov (in December of the same year). In this production the company found material that answered its aspiration in full measure and was an object lesson in the application of the Stanislavsky method in ballet. The company's production had many fine touches, absent even in the Bolshoi revival. In 1937 the company, still under the name of "Art Theatre of Ballet", produced a version of Pushkin's *Gypsies* to a score by Sergei Vasilenko, with choreography by Nicolai Kholfin. The company's reputation as a group of "dancing actors" was considerably strengthened after these two Pushkin ballets.

Vladimir Nemirovich-Danchenko, who needed dancers for ballet scenes in the operas (usually of the chamber or comic *genre*), invited the Art Theatre of Ballet to be incorporated with his "singer-actors" at the Musical Theatre founded by him. The company now had a permanent home and over the years developed into the second ballet company of the capital.

This second period of the company's life is identified with the name of

[1] He is known to have died.

[2] Born in 1905, Pavel Virsky, People's Artist of the U.S.S.R., has been occupying the post of Artistic Director and Chief Choreographer of the Ukrainian Ensemble of Folk Dancing since 1955, having created many vivid dances for this world-famous group.

Final scene from the ballet *Le Sacre du Printemps* at the Bolshoi Theatre, Moscow. Choreography by Natalia Kasatkina and Vladimir Vasilyov. Yuri Vladimirov as the Shepherd, Anatoly Simachev as the Wise Old Man.

Gorda. Music by D. Toradze, choreography by Vakhtang Chaboukiani. Paliashuili Theatre of Opera and Ballet, Tbilisi, Georgia. Scene from Act III.

Vladimir Bourmeister. Born in 1904, Bourmeister studied at the ballet faculty of the Lunacharsky Theatre School between 1925 and 1929. This was a ballet school that afforded young people, who for some reason (usually connected with their age) could not study at the Bolshoi School, the chance to receive a ballet education. A relatively small percentage reached the top and graduated. Those that did were usually gifted and determined artists with ideas of their own. As a dancer Bourmeister performed mostly character roles and also did national dances, which were more suited to his temperament; moreover, he started studying too late to make a good *premier danseur*. In *The Rivals* he danced the part of Nicaise; in *The Gypsies*, that of Aleko. His début as choreographer took place in 1931, when he produced for the "Art Theatre of Ballet" a new version of *Le Corsaire*, enacting the part of Birbanto the villain.

His most important works followed later, when the company became an integral part of the Stanislavsky and Nemirovich-Danchenko Music Theatre. In 1942 he staged (in collaboration with the brilliant impersonator of Sir John Falstaff, Ivan Kurilov, born in 1910) *The Merry Wives of Windsor* in ballet form, with a score by V. Oransky; in 1943, *Lola*, a ballet to music by Vasilenko, with a story reminiscent of *Fuente Ovejuna*. This ballet contained many scenes of great dramatic impact. The title role was danced by Maria Sorokina. Among Bourmeister's other works are a new version of *Schéhérazade* (1944), a contemporary ballet *The Happy Coast* (1956) with a score by Spadaveccia, and *Jeanne d'Arc* (1957) to music by Peiko.

He made an outstanding contribution to ballet with a new production of *Swan Lake*, achieved in 1953. Having closely studied the Tchaikovsky manuscript of the ballet, preserved at the Tchaikovsky Museum in Klin, the choreographer achieved a production following the original sequence of musical numbers as composed by Tchaikovsky. He created completely new choreography for the first and fourth acts, and considerably revised that of the third act, presenting all its *divertissements* as part of Rothbart's sorcery. Only the second act, considered justly to be among the gems of Russian classical ballet, was preserved with the Lev Ivanov choreography, restored by Pyotr Gusev, then the company's ballet-master.

In many ways Bourmeister's version of *Swan Lake* has become a definitive production to be copied either partly or fully by many companies. Even the current version of the third act as presented by the Kirov Theatre Ballet shows some influence of the Bourmeister *Swan Lake*. In 1960 he was invited by the Paris Opéra to stage his version of *Swan Lake*, which is now in the company's repertory.

Among Bourmeister's latest productions is *The Snowmaiden*, arranged to a selection of Tchaikovsky's music, first for London's Festival Ballet in 1961, and, in an expanded version, for the Stanislavsky and Nemirovich-Danchenko Theatre Ballet in 1963.

While Bourmeister's productions constitute the greater part of the company's repertory, it has invited other choreographers on numerous occasions. Alexei Chichinadze (born in 1917), a graduate of the Choreographers' Faculty of the State Theatre Institute, has grown and matured in this company.

In 1963 the theatre invited Fedor Lopukhov to create one of this choreographer's most mature works, a ballet to the music of Mussorgsky's *Pictures from an Exhibition*, which achieved exceptional impact with the peasant dance from the picture entitled "Bydlo".

Fedor Lopukhov's choreographic version of Mussorgsky's work is staged to the complete and unabridged score arranged by Ravel from the pianoforte composition.[1]

While carried out only in 1963, Lopukhov's work, like many of his other undertakings, was actually conceived some thirty-five years earlier, and partly attempted in 1927, when the master choreographed the "Gnome" episode. In a letter to this author Lopukhov stated: "I have revised some of the details, but not the fundamentals, conceived thirty-five years ago", adding that it took him that long to "give birth" to a choreographic visualization of Mussorgsky's music, because it was his most difficult ballet from the viewpoint of tackling the musical imagery.

Certainly, Lopukhov achieved success. The master proved that he had reached that period of maturity when classical dance appears in another form in every new work, and is used as means of characterization. From this point of view "Bydlo" was unanimously rated as a choreographic *chef d'œuvre*. In this piece Lopukhov resorted, it is true, to Russian dance steps, brilliantly used to form very powerful images. In many ways Mussorgsky created a whole world of imagery from the pictures of his friend Hartmann, whose posthumous exhibition moved the composer to write his famous piece. Lopukhov tried to probe at the very core of the music and guess what the composer wanted to say. As one of the musicologists put it ". . . the choreographer succeeded in looking at the music

[1] The first attempt at such a choreographic rendering was made by Bronislava Nijinska in 1944 for "Ballet International", revived in 1947 for the "Grand Ballet de Monte Carlo". However, Nijinska's version, being in nine scenes, apparently did not use the whole of Mussorgsky's music.

in a new way, in revealing through choreography something that we had not seen or heard before in this work".[1]

Lopukhov interpreted the "Bydlo" episode as a gradual awakening of the peasant "bydlo" (the word means "cattle") and the composer's sympathy with the tragic plight of the peasants in his day. In Lopukhov's "Bydlo" scene (the picture in the background is formed by barren fields and a peasant "izba" (hut of logwood)) four peasants, dressed in rags, with "lapti" on their feet, and huge crosses dangling from their necks, are first prostrated on their knees. As the music commences the men step out of the picture's frame *on their knees*, and, at first hardly unbending their stiff backs, do a dance charged with concealed emotion and a growing sense of revolt. They seem to want to rise from their knees to full height, but are unable to achieve this. As the remarkable Mussorgsky music swells to its climax, the four figures, after making several attempts, at last rise—but only for a while. The music and the tide of emotion subside and at the end of the dance the four peasants return to the frame on their knees, to the same prone poses, that now spell something else, as we know that they conceal a wealth of hidden passion. . . .

This dance was said by the late Mikhail Gabovich to be worth many a long ballet and to be compared with another miniature *chef d'œuvre*, Fokine's "Swan".[2]

Lopukhov placed the action of No. 8 from Mussorgsky's work, entitled "Catacombs", in the catacombs of ancient Greece, glistening in dull gold, with Hades, the god of the lower world, and his three Erinyes, the cruel and avenging spirits who, according to Greek mythology, pursued evildoers and inflicted madness and misfortune upon them. This was a formal kind of composition, rich in typically Lopukhian semi-acrobatic idiom. But in No. 2—"The old castle"—he resorted to pure classical dance steps in a truly romantic *pas de deux* portraying a poet's vision of some beautiful maiden who might have lived in the castle of the picture. In the same manner each of the musical episodes was given choreography suited to its content.

Fedor Lopukhov celebrated his sixtieth anniversary in art in the spring of 1965. It was indeed sixty years since the day when he danced Acis in Fokine's *Acis and Galatea* in the graduation performance of April 10, 1905. But he is still full of ideas and plans. One of them is to create pictures

[1] A Zolotov. "The New Year". In: *Nedelia* (supplement to *Izvestia*), No. 37, 1963, p. 11.

[2] Mikhail Gabovich. "Ballet large and small". *Izvestia*, October 11, 1963.

from a Soviet Exhibition to music specially composed by Dmitri Shostakovich.

Lopukhov has been called a "choreographers' choreographer" because so many of his ideas have been borrowed and incorporated in other people's works and served as a starting point for new trends in choreography. Thus, it was he who, in a version of *Swan Lake*, produced at the Kirov theatre on June 22, 1945, first used music from Tchaikovsky's original score and introduced a *variation* for Rothbart in act III.

It is also important to note that the complete and unabridged Tchaikovsky score was used for the first time in ballet at the end of 1955, not in Moscow, but at the Saratov Theatre of Opera and Ballet bearing the name of Nicolai Chernyshevsky (the great Russian writer and critic of the nineteenth century who was born in that town). This serves as proof of the vastness of the ballet scene in the U.S.S.R. and the seriousness of work done in ballet companies to whom the word "provincial" can hardly be applied.

The Saratov version of *Swan Lake* was created by Lyubov Serebrovskaya, (born in 1915), one of the first graduates of GITIS (State Theatre Institute) choreographers' Faculty. While Bourmeister in his version of 1953 rearranged the sequence of numbers and deleted part of the music (particularly that of the *pas de six*) in order to carry out his own choreographic concept, in Serebrovskaya's production the orchestra played the full Tchaikovsky score just as it had been composed. There was no Lev Ivanov second act and many familiar things were missing, while the music known as the *pas de deux* for Odile and Siegfried in act III of the Petipa–Ivanov version appeared—then for the first time—in act I.

Serebrovskaya wrote her own version of the scenario, showing in the first act the circumstances which led to Odette's enchantment. The choreography was not very successful; it failed to create the romantic atmosphere so important in this ballet. But the general level of presentation was sufficiently high.

Saratov's large ballet company (partly trained in its own studio) is at present headed by Semyon Drechin (born in 1914), one of the leading choreographers in Soviet ballet outside Moscow and Leningrad. Drechin's formative period started in 1932 in the Minsk Theatre of Opera and Ballet. It is there that he danced the principal role of Simon in *The Nightingale* in 1940, a ballet with music by M. Kroshner and choreography by Alexei Yermolayev shown in Moscow on June 9, 1940, at the Byelorussian Art Festival at the Bolshoi Theatre. This ballet had a book by Slonimsky, which, as is usual in the work of this outstanding

Le Sacre du Printemps at the Bolshoi Theatre, Moscow. Yuri Vladimirov as the Shepherd. Choreography by Natalia Kasatkina and Vladimir Vasilyov.

Natalia Bessmertnova and Maris Liepa in *The Legend of Love*, music by Arif Melikov, choreography by Yuri Grigorovich. Bolshoi Theatre, Moscow.

Vladimir Koshelev, Nina Sorokina and Yuri Vladimirov (from left to right) in *The Geologists*, ballet to music by Nicolai Karetnikov with choreography by Natalia Kasatkina and Vladimir Vasilyov. Bolshoi Theatre, Moscow.

dramatist of the ballet, provided the choreographer with many valuable suggestions. The part of Zosya, the serf girl, was danced in *The Nightingale* by Zinaida Vassilyeva (born in 1913). A ballerina (class of 1933), she began her career at the Maly Opera Theatre Ballet of Leningrad and became the leading dancer of the Minsk Opera in 1937, having been awarded the title of People's Artist of Byelorussia. Vassilyeva was an outstanding lyrical ballerina. Upon retirement she headed the Minsk School of Choreography and now teaches at the Novosibirsk School, having taken an active part in its foundation in 1950.[1]

Among the ballet companies of the country, that of the Novosibirsk Theatre of Opera and Ballet by right occupies a leading position. Numbering one hundred and twenty dancers, it is housed in the largest opera house in the country. The construction of the Novosibirsk Opera House was started before the war and completed in wartime. Opened on May 12, 1945, this theatre's auditorium is two and a half times larger than that of the Bolshoi theatre. The theatre opened a ballet studio of its own immediately after the war. It invited amateurs of any age with some experience in dancing, or at least with interest in the profession. This is how Gennady Lediakh, now one of the principal dancers of the Bolshoi ballet, started his first ballet lessons at the age of eighteen. Of course his case is a very rare exception, but in a couple of years he danced leading roles in the Novosibirsk Opera House and later, after having improved his technique at the Bolshoi School, was accepted into the Bolshoi company. In this manner the Novosibirsk Opera trained its first ballet personnel, also receiving replenishment in the persons of two Moscow-trained ballerinas: Tatiana Zimina (born in 1928) and Lydia Krupenina (born in 1928).

Now Novosibirsk has its own Ballet School, housed in a separate building. Dancers graduating from other schools consider it a privilege to dance on the huge stage of the Novosibirsk Opera and to take part in its varied and interesting repertory. This is how its *premier danseur* Nikita Dolgushin (born in 1938) and young ballerina Natalia Alexandrova (born in 1932) came to join this company, though they might have stayed at the Kirov Theatre.

In the summer of 1963 the Novosibirsk ballet had its third tour in Moscow and demonstrated a very high professional standard. Its repertory

[1] There are nineteen ballet schools (counting the Moscow and Leningrad ones) in the Soviet Union with a full nine-year course of tuition. This course is now being revised to cover eight instead of nine years (retaining the same amount of knowledge) so that dancers can start their careers earlier.

consisted of a new version of *Swan Lake* by the GITIS graduate (then still a student), Oleg Vinogradov; an excellent rendering of *The Legend of Love* in the original version by Yuri Grigorovich; *The Young Lady and the Hooligan* by Konstantin Boyarsky; and a revival of *Le Corsaire* arranged by the company's Artistic Director and Chief Choreographer, Pyotr Gusev. It was Gusev who brought the high professionalism to the Novosibirsk Ballet that within two years placed it among the best ballet theatres of the country. It was not surprising that in 1964 the opera house as a whole (and, therefore, its ballet company) was accorded the title of "Academic", like the Bolshoi, the Kirov, and Maly Opera Theatres. It is now called the Novosibirsk State Academic Theatre of Opera and Ballet, and there is every reason to expect that its ballet company will stage many more important ballets and produce some outstanding dancers.

The next in importance is surely the ballet of the Perm Opera. While the Novosibirsk house was recently built, the one in Perm was constructed at the end of the nineteenth century, when the Perm branch of the Russian Musical Society founded an Opera House in the city. Two companies—the opera and the ballet—could not work normally without proper rehearsal space, and the many excellent productions of the Perm Opera (it earned the name of a "laboratory" because many ballets and, in particular, operas by Soviet composers were first performed there) were stifled by the small stage. This situation continued until 1958, when the building was enlarged and completely renovated. Its company of fifty-eight, headed by GITIS graduate, Murat Gaziev, has produced some interesting ballets, among them a version of Ravel's *Bolero*, and, in 1964, *Checkmate* to music by Bliss, with an entirely new story (though still based on chess) and new choreography by Gaziev.

All the leading dancers of the Perm ballet have been trained by its State School of Choreography. Headed by Ksenia Yesaulova (born in 1911), former dancer of the Maly Opera ballet in Leningrad, it has the reputation of being second only to Leningrad and Moscow. This is not surprising, since it was founded in wartime by Leningrad dancers when the Kirov ballet was evacuated to Perm.

The company's *premier danseur*, Lev Asauliak (born in 1937), and his wife, the lyrical ballerina Rimma Shliamova (born in 1935), have received prizes at the Varna Ballet Festival in the summer of 1965. The company also possesses a brilliant *demi-caractère* dancer in the person of Gennady Malkhasiants (born in 1939).

There is a very good company of some fifty dancers in Sverdlovsk. Its chief choreographer, Grigory Yazvinsky (born in 1905), graduate of the

Bolshoi School in the early twenties, retired a couple of years ago, and while several younger choreographers have tried their hand, the Sverdlovsk ballet still remains without a proper artistic leader. Yazvinsky was steeped in the old tradition and some of his methods, in particular the frequent prevalence of pantomime in his productions, have become outdated. One should give credit, however, to Yazvinsky for having been the first to devise a dramatic story (told in conventional mime in the Petipa–Ivanov original) about Odette's magical transformation. In 1940, in a production of the *Swan Lake* for the Opera in the town of Gorki, Yazvinsky dimmed the light on the stage at the beginning of Odette's story, and then, behind a gauze drop, a princess was seen on the bank of a lake, gathering flowers. A magician in the disguise of an owl then appeared from his lair and enveloped the girl in his powerful wings. At the same time a white swan with a crown on its head appeared on the lake. . . . This scene, interpolated in the second act of *Swan Lake*, is, in every other respect, exactly like the prologue introduced by Bourmeister in 1953 in his own version of the ballet.

The Russian Federation has an opera house with a ballet company in many of its cities. There are also four opera houses in the Ukraine; the one in Kiev is of long standing, and has a large company of a hundred and twenty dancers headed by Vakhtang Vronsky (born in 1905), and trained, for the most part, by the Kiev Ballet School, founded and headed by Galina Berezova (born in 1909), one of Vaganova's closest disciples and herself a splendid teacher. The ballet of the Kiev Opera had a tremendous success during its Paris tour in 1964, followed by appearances in Moscow on the stage of the huge Palace of Congresses. Outstanding among the Kiev ballerinas are the young Irina Lukashova, Yevgenia Potapova, Anna Gavrilenko, and Valentina Kalinovskaya. Its present *premier danseur*, Veanir Kruglov, studied in Perm and has been for a number of years principal dancer of the Sverdlovsk company.

A talented young dancer of the athletic type (he excels in semi-acrobatic *pas de deux*) is V. Parsegov, who, together with Lukashova, was awarded the Prize of the City during the company's visit to Paris in 1964.

There is a ballet company in the capital of each of the national republics in the Soviet Union. Some are large and have a fairly long history and many achievements, as in the case of the ballet of the Paliashuili Opera House in Tbilisi, headed since the early forties by Vakhtang Chaboukiani, who is also head of the Tbilisi Choreographic School. Particularly brilliant among the Georgian dancers are Chaboukiani's pupils: Vera Tsignadze, the company's ballerina, and Zurab Kikaleishwili, its *premier danseur*, second only to Chaboukiani, who continues to dance in parts created for himself, such as the title roles in *Othello*, to music by Alexei Machavariani, first produced by the Georgian Ballet with choreography by Chaboukiani in 1957, and in *The Daemon* by Sulkhan Tsintsadze, also first shown in Tbisili in 1961 with choreography by Chaboukiani.

The Tbilisi company numbers nearly one hundred dancers and, thanks to Chaboukiani's artistic leadership (he literally moulded it anew in the forties), has a marked style of its own. Other companies, such as the more modest one in Dushanbe, Tajikistan, are still searching for adequate expression of the style and traditions of their national art in ballet form.

The youngest Opera and Ballet Theatre in the U.S.S.R. is that of Kishinev, Moldavian S.S.R., founded in the end of 1959.

But the number of opera houses does not quite exhaust the ballet stage of the country. There are some theatres, known as Musical Dramas, that have ballets, operas, and drama in their repertory. Outstanding among this kind of theatre is the role of the "Vanemuine" in Tartu, Estonia. It exists alongside the "Estonia" opera house in Tallinn, and plays a very important part in creating chamber works. Its choreographer, Ida Urbel (born in 1900) is very gifted.

In Lithuania there are two music theatres: The Opera and Ballet in Vilnius, headed by Vitaustas Grigitskas (born in 1925), GITIS graduate of 1952 with several ballets to his credit, and the Music Theatre in Kaunas, located in the old opera building.

It should also be mentioned that there is a vast chain of operetta (musical comedy) theatres all over the Soviet Union and that every one of these employs at least a small ballet group for its *divertissements*. In such circumstances the demand for dancers always exceeds the supply. Quite a few professional dancers started their first ballet lessons in amateur dance groups attached to factory clubs, to Palaces of Culture, and Young Pioneers' Clubs to be found all over the country. Many of these groups have reached such high standards that they were given the name of "People's Ballet Theatres"—such as the "People's Theatre of Ballet" of the Likhachev Automobile Plant in Moscow, or the similar group work-ing at the Gorki Palace of Culture in Leningrad. These amateur ballet groups are usually headed by present or retired dancers from the academic ballet companies. Renowned choreographers are also ready to help them. Amateur ballet and folk dance groups receive guidance and assistance from the Central House of People's Art in Moscow which publishes a number of books and sends its staff workers to other cities, when asked for assistance. Amateur art is maintained by the factories and offices.

All ballet companies are maintained by the State and are subject to, and financed by, the Ministry of Culture of the given constituent republic. The receipts from performances are applied to the needs of the opera and ballet companies of the given opera house, and are an important part of its budget.

The work of the entire system of opera and ballet presentation in the Soviet Union is supervised by the U.S.S.R. Ministry of Culture.

After twenty years of service Soviet ballet dancers are entitled to a pension regardless of their age. They may, of course, remain in the company as mimes (or continue dancing for a few more years if their professional standard still warrants it) or devote themselves to teaching if they are so gifted.

Since the formation of the Choreographers' Faculty at GITIS many dancers, with interest in choreography, start learning there some years before retirement, so as to prepare themselves for the position they aspire to occupy upon abandoning a dancing career. This explains the growth of the number of choreographers with diplomas and a high standard of professional knowledge and general education.

These manifold aspects of the life of ballet in the Soviet Union account for its high level, based on seriousness of purpose, high artistic aims, and good nationwide organization.

CHAPTER XII

THE SOVIET BALLET TODAY

We now come to the present day in Soviet Ballet. It has its own problems and its own achievements. Soviet choreography has moved into a new period, a period of active searching for new, more contemporary, more completely expressive means of conveying the content in ballet. This need no longer be tied to an elaborate plot, but must convey a momentous, significant idea. In a number of the works that sprang from the historically necessary period of "dramatic ballet", development of the plot superseded depth of thought and feeling expressed symphonically in music and dance. This applies even to the best of the most recent offerings in the "dramatic" *genre*: *The Happy Coast* (Bourmeister–Spadaveccia) and *Youth* (Fenster–Chulaki). Choreographers are now looking for a different kind of imagery and symbolism, since new times call for new songs. In order to convey themes of contemporaneity—a paramount task—they will have to revise the vocabulary of choreographic idiom at their disposal and find a way of expressing plastically the complexity of contemporary ideas. But all work will be steeped in previous experience: *The Red Poppy*, *The Flames of Paris*, *The Fountain of Bakhchisarai* and *Romeo and Juliet*, works which have enabled Soviet ballet dancers to become "dramatic dancers", capable of portraying Man in all the beauty of his spiritual world.

In the new ballets by Soviet choreographers there is a marked tendency to express action in terms of dance, to integrate mime with dancing. This does not diminish, but, on the contrary, increases the responsibility of the dancer for projecting the human content of his role, which can only be achieved through "acting craft" as developed by the entire previous experience of Soviet Ballet. Various *genres*—comic, tragic, dramatic—may arise; the more variety in choreography, the better. Choreographers with different styles and methods of approach will continue to come to the forefront, but the path of their progress is common to all.

Professor Leonid Lavrovsky, the greatest exponent of "dramatic ballet", has the following to say: "I think that one of the main merits of Soviet Ballet is the belief that the creation of human images is of the greatest importance. This enriches our art immeasurably. At one time we used to depict princes and princesses, butterflies and elves—what you will, but Man as such was never shown in ballet. This is very difficult to achieve. But when Shakespeare, Pushkin, Lope de Vega, Balzac, etc., came to our ballet they obliged us to find methods to portray *humans* with the means provided by our art. . . . Pantomime, dance, and music are closely interwoven in ballet and create that idiom, which makes ballet an art. And if, previously, the virtuoso dancer occupied a leading position in a ballet performance, the principal and decisive place is now taken by the dramatic dancer."[1]

In the same article Professor Lavrovsky expressed some of his ideas about the aim of choreography: "Music is not only the soul, but the content of the dance. Therefore the question put to me at times by my foreign friends: 'Can there be dance without content or does Soviet Ballet not recognize such a possibility?' sounds strange to my ears. What does it mean, dance without content? Can a man dance without any reason, make the slightest move, without an inner compulsion? I can't imagine such a dance. This does not mean that every dance should express action, but it should by all means express man's inner state. I cannot conceive that it is possible to come out on the stage and not express anything, neither joy nor sorrow, but simply perform some technical feats, demonstrating the dancer's virtuosity. It would be necessary to find music that expresses nothing."[2]

Lavrovsky's own post-war choreography differs very much from his style in "dramatic ballets", in the sense that it is expressed solely in terms of dance, but his general principle of creating movement engendered by the music has not changed—it has merely deepened. In the search for choreographic inspiration he has resorted to great works of music. His evocation of Sergei Rachmaninov's famous *Rhapsody on a theme of Paganini* was premièred under the title of *Paganini* at the Bolshoi Theatre on April 7, 1960. Since this was the first choreographic attempt[3] at *Paganini* after Fokine's version in 1939, that alone made it an event in the history of contemporary ballet.

Unfamiliar with the Fokine production, Lavrovsky was deeply moved by a recording of Rachmaninov's *Rhapsody* and, as he listened to the music, he found he was actually visualizing it. At that time the Rachmaninov–Fokine correspondence on the content of *Paganini* as a ballet was published

[1] Leonid Lavrovsky. "The borders of the genre are being expanded". In: *Evening Leningrad*, September 17, 1963.

[2] Leonid Lavrovsky. *Op. cit.*

[3] On May 5, 1963 Ida Urbel created another version in the *Vanemuine* Theatre, Tartu (Estonia).

in two volumes by the Music Publishing House in Moscow. Lavrovsky was not inspired by the Fokine "book" version and decided to create his own libretto. He did not agree that Paganini should be portrayed merely as a tortured soul who sells himself to the "evil spirit" for perfection in art. He wanted to show Paganini as a creator "fired with inspiration, courageously fighting for his art; a Paganini eternally in love with music, and with life that engenders it".[1] Such a solution (said the choreographer) was presented by the *Rhapsody* itself—"valiant, expressive, full of admiration of Paganini's love of life".

In accordance with this idea Lavrovsky divided his "book" into seven episodes: 1. First improvisations. 2. Enemies. 3. An encounter. 4. Solitude and despair. 5. Love and consolation. 6. Joy of creation. Death. 7. Finale. Art triumphs over death.

Lavrovsky's scenario did not attempt to depict any actual episodes in the violinist's life as would probably have been the case in the thirties. Rather it aspired to convey an impression of the emotional conflicts that troubled the famous artist, his moments of great inspiration, the bigotry and persecution to which he was subjected by the Catholic Church, and the final victory of creative art over all the obstacles.

The *Dies Irae* themes occupying a considerable portion of Rachmaninov's *Rhapsody* were not ascribed to "evil spirits" but to the Catholic Church, symbolized by sinister black figures in hooded cloaks, and carrying black chandeliers, and by the distant figure of a bishop in scarlet robes. The *adagio* part was allotted to Paganini's visions of the Muse (created by Marina Kondratieva, a lovely lyrical ballerina of the young generation, born in 1934) who at times took the form of Paganini's Beloved.

The ballet was shown against the translucent grey-blue draperies forming Vadim Ryndin's laconic *décor*. There were no stage props and much of the effect was produced by lighting. The ballet started in complete silence and a fleeting passage of clouds created an atmosphere of tension. After this the *Rhapsody* began and Paganini suddenly appeared on the stage. Rachmaninov said in one of his letters to Fokine that he would have preferred not to see Paganini with a realistic violin—it had to be something in the realm of fantasy. Very much impressed by this idea, Lavrovsky arranged movements for Paganini suggestive of a violin in his hands, while the dance to the main Paganini theme was full of staccato-like *brisés* in harmony with the *scherzo* quality of the *variation*.

With time, the qualities of an almost daemonic urge for creation,

[1] Leonid Lavrovsky. Preface to the synopsis of *Paganini*. Souvenir programme of the Bolshoi Theatre, 1960.

Dancers of the Bolshoi Ballet in class. *From left to right:* Lyudmila Bogo-molova, Tatiana Popko, Yekaterina Maximova, Yelena Riabinkina, Ella Brichkina.

Legend of Love at the Bolshoi Theatre, Moscow. Music by Arif Melikov, choreography by Yuri Grigorovich. Natalia Bessmertnova's Shirien (on the right).

Galina Ulanova prepares Yekaterina Maximova for her début in the title role of *Giselle*. Ulanova has been coaching Maximova in all her classical roles.

Yelena Riabinkina as the Tsar Maiden in the ballet *The Hump-Backed Horse*.

imperative in the character of Paganini since it is present in the music, was fully realized by the character dancer, Yaroslav Sekh (born in 1930), entrusted with the responsible role. Sekh danced the difficult role beautifully. Paganini is a taxing role because, as in all of Lavrovsky's work, it is hard to distinguish where dancing ceases and mime begins. Moreover the impersonator of the title-role has to be on the stage practically throughout the entire duration of the *Rhapsody*, dancing it, so to speak, in "one breath" and merging completely with the music.

The *corps de ballet* in *Paganini* is small and takes an active part in the emotional development of the undercurrent of action. Lavrovsky started with his early works, especially *Katerina* and *Romeo and Juliet*, by turning the *corps de ballet* into one of the active *dramatis personae*. In *Paganini* he carried this principle further, by working the dances of the *corps de ballet* into the choreography, until they became an inseparable part.

Paganini is still in the repertory of the Bolshoi ballet. The name part is now also danced by Vladimir Vasiliev (born 1940), the outstandingly brilliant Bolshoi *premier danseur*. He stresses Paganini's indomitable inspiration and in turn produces an extremely powerful impact. The Muse is also danced by Yekaterina Maximova (1939), his wife and partner, pupil of Yelizaveta Gerdt, a charming lyrical ballerina with a very strong technique, enabling her to expand the customary range of roles—Giselle, Cinderella, and Aurora, and to dance, also with Vladimir Vasiliev, the vivacious and exhilarating Kitri, with the utmost virtuosity.

Leonid Lavrovsky was next attracted to Bela Bartok's *The Miraculous Mandarin*, containing music of really superb beauty and great impact. As is known, Bartok's last ballet was composed in 1918 to the plot from a pantomime by the Hungarian playwright, Menyhert Lengyel. The story of a prostitute and the three thugs who entice victims to their den with her help was conceived with such candour that the first production in Cologne in 1926 did not survive the opening night, while in the country of its creation *The Miraculous Mandarin*, with choreography by Gyula Harangozó, was not performed until 1945.

Lavrovsky's version caused much controversy among musicologists, for he wrote an entirely new scenario. The choreographer was convinced that the Bartok score contains much lyricism. Musicologists, on the other hand, opposed any attempt to change the content of programme music, for Bartok's score is accompanied by footnotes explaining the stage situation in a way quite different from Lavrovsky's interpretation. Despite the ensuing controversy, Lavrovsky's version, emotionally, did seem to coincide well with the music, and produced an extremely moving and surprisingly chaste impression. First shown at the Bolshoi Theatre on May 21, 1961, Lavrovsky's *Night City* told of a girl and three thugs, one a Redhead, their leader. Against the din of the big city he orders the girl to start looking for a victim. An Old Dandy appears in the square, the girl lures him, he is killed, robbed, and thrown into the gutter. In the introductory part of the ballet the Bartok–Lengyel scenario virtually coincided in content with the new version, but thereafter the story and the music programme were at complete variance. (The fact remained, however, that Lavrovsky's choreography was extremely powerful and blended well with the music, thus presenting quite a problem for those who maintain that changes in composers' programmes are prohibited.)

The remaining part of Lavrovsky's *Night City* was concerned with the love between the girl from the gang and a young man—a repair-hand in blue jeans on night-duty—much like the manikin she had just been admiring in a shop window. When the Redhead and the other two thugs return, the Youth is ready to defend the girl against them. The girl fears he will be killed. Together they try to escape, only to be pursued by the thugs and caught in a dark corner. A desperate struggle follows, during which the Redhead flings a knife at the boy, mortally wounding him. The girl tries to carry him on her shoulders. (This impression was artfully conveyed in the choreography through a quick and uneven glide of the ballerina in a series of *pas de bourrée*, with the boy's limp body being supported upwards by the girl's shoulders and back. This is just one of the striking examples of how Lavrovsky's choreography, modern in idiom, was thoroughly grounded in classical ballet.) The boy's strength fails and he dies. The girl mourns her short-lived love. The Redhead and his gang run in and throw the body into the gutter. By the time the policeman arrives everything seems to be in order. The Redhead and his friends are dancing around the girl. He once again orders her to go into the street. The girl again passes the same shop windows, the same motionless dummies. Her dream has been shattered, she is no longer the same.

The score of *The Miraculous Mandarin* was "read" by conductor Yevgeny Svetlanov with an emphasis on the lyrical emotions as interpreted by Lavrovsky; therefore the music and the choreography coincided to some degree through this similarity in approach. Another reason for the ballet's success with the audiences was beyond doubt the extraordinary power of projection of Leningrad-trained Nina Timofeyeva (born 1935), in the part of the Girl. Timofeyeva, until then thought to be a strictly classical dancer in the academic style, showed unexpected dramatic depths and mimetic power. In the sixties, especially after the second Bolshoi

Ballet tour in North America in 1962, she blossomed forth as one of the finest ballerinas of the company, adding a flowing *cantilena* quality and a new radiance to her exceptional technique.

The Youth was interpreted by Maris Liepa (born 1936). Latvian born, he studied at the Bolshoi school until 1955 and, after dancing at the Riga Opera House, was invited to the Nemirovich-Danchenko Lyric Theatre, and in 1960 to the Bolshoi. Well-built, with an engaging stage presence and fine technique, he soon developed into one of the leading dancers and partners. A good actor, his repertory includes such contrasting roles as Romeo and Basil, the Youth and Siegfried.

The Redhead was created by Anatoly Simachev (born 1933), outstanding among the younger generation of Bolshoi character dancers.

After *Night City* Lavrovsky continued to explore symphonic music in Ravel's *Bolero* and *La Valse* (first presented in 1964), with an emphasis on danced action. This interest in dance as the principal medium for expressing content in ballet is evident in the work of choreographers of all generations. In Leningrad, Konstantin Sergeyev created a completely modern ballet with *The Path of Thunder* to a very colourful score by Kara Karayev (to Slonimsky's scenario after the novel of the same title by the South African author, Peter Abrahams). This is a story about a coloured youth, Lenny, and Sarie, a white girl, daughter of the master of the estate, on whose grounds Lenny spent his childhood before going to a big city and acquiring his bachelor's degree. Lenny returns to his village to become the teacher, and, ultimately, to take "the path of thunder" against racial discrimination. Naturally, Slonimsky could not (as a good ballet playwright, he had no intention of doing so) follow all the episodes of the novel. Some of the characters were somewhat changed, others not included. But the main idea of the tragedy of these two young people murdered cruelly, because "their only fault was to love each other", was conveyed both movingly and impressively.

Kara Karayev wrote the score after some three years' study of African music. He dedicated his work to the memory of Prokofiev, and the influence of that composer's style is felt in the music. Karayev created the ballet in the form of symphonic dance suites, centred upon a key episode in the tragedy. The story of Lenny's and Sarie's love is shown in four major duets, all with a theme growing out of the action. In the first two they try to overcome the feeling of love that spells tragedy, the third *pas de deux* shows their love at its height, and the fourth and last leads to the culminating tragic clash of the couple with the white crowd led by Sarie's own father.

The choreography by Konstantin Sergeyev (he also created the role of Lenny) showed evidence of a close study of African dance lore, never expressed directly, but either fused with classical dance, or woven into danced action. In the latter case the dance of the recruited Africans, led by the tribal chief (summarily shot on the spot), was particularly striking. On the whole, Sergeyev's choreography was arranged in terms of dance. Only the negative characters were given merely pedestrian mime roles of a cliché type in the grotesque style. This considerably reduced both the impact of the ballet and the chance to create three-dimensional characters for the impersonators of those roles. On the other hand the character of Sarie grew in the course of the ballet, and was interpreted in terms of classical dance, just sufficiently coloured with a change of line to convey a contemporary impression. The first Sarie, Natalia Dudinskaya, until then known as a fine classical ballerina, has not been bettered. She created a flesh-and-blood Western girl and her gradual awakening to love, and resolution leading to tragedy, were deeply moving.

The Path of Thunder was first performed in Leningrad on December 31, 1957, and, with the same choreography, danced in Moscow in 1959 by Lepeshinskaya and Kondratov. The ballet was included (with choreography by other ballet-masters) in the repertory of several Soviet Opera houses.

Konstantin Sergeyev, master of the "dramatic ballet" generation, has very much changed his style in the new version of *Cinderella* (first prepared by him in 1946), performed on June 11, 1964. This is practically a new ballet so far as the choreography is concerned. Everything is carried out in classical dance, but without blind obedience to tradition. Each of the protagonists was to portray character in the medium of dance. The title-role of this re-born *Cinderella* was performed by Irina Kolpakova (born in 1933), a radiantly charming ballerina, the last one to graduate from Vaganova's class in 1951 shortly before the Professor's death, and by Alla Sizova (born 1939), a youthful ballerina of the Kirov theatre for whom Cinderella was one of her first important roles in a ballet by a Soviet choreographer. (She danced her first Aurora in London during the Kirov Ballet performance of 1961.)

The part of the Prince, virile and manly, was danced in the revival by Vladilen Semenov (born 1932), Irina Kolpakova's husband, a perfect *danseur noble* in the academic manner, and Yuri Solovyov (born 1940), a remarkable dancer of the younger generation, who has often been compared to Nijinsky both for the quality of his *elevation* and *ballon*, and for the resemblance in physique (like Nijinsky, Solovyov has thick,

Galina Ulanova in "The Dying Swan". (Photo Houston Rogers)

Maya Plisetskaya and Vladimir Levashov in *The Hump-Backed Horse*, music by Rodion Shchedrin, choreography by Alexander Radunsky, Bolshoi Theatre, Moscow.

Galina Ulanova in *Giselle*. (Photo Houston Rogers)

strong thighs, that are not ideal from the point of view of line, but allow him to achieve feats of elevation). With this airborne quality of Solovyev in view, enabling him to hover in the air as in a state of weightlessness, Sergeyev arranged the dances for the role of the Space Pilot in his one-act ballet, *The Distant Planet*, in 1963. This is a fantasy interpreting Man (the Astronaut), Earth, and Planet, by generalized symbols. The choreography is varied and contains passages requiring extreme virtuosity. But the music (by Boris Maisel), with its rather monotonous sonorities produced by electric instruments in the orchestra, does not differentiate between the earthly and celestial characters, and deprives the ballet of serious validity.

While not, strictly speaking, a *danseur noble*, Solovyov also danced the principal roles in the classical repertory, and took part in the filmed version of *The Sleeping Beauty*. In 1963 he was awarded the Nijinsky Prize by the Paris "Université de la Danse".

Attention has been concentrated on Yuri Solovyev because of his remarkable elevation. There are other brilliant dancers in the company as well. Among them, Sergei Vikulov (born 1937) is quite outstanding not only for his good line, but for his nobility of manner, excellent technique, and elevation accompanied by exceptional lightness of landing, and his above average acting ability. These qualities have enabled Vikulov, in a few years, to come to the fore of the Kirov ballet.

Leonid Yacobson, resident choreographer of the Kirov ballet, has achieved several productions in a variety of styles differing considerably from his youthful experiments in choreography, such as *Till Eulenspiegel* (1933) to the Richard Strauss score, and, in particular, participation in the choreography of *The Age of Gold* (1930): there he worked out the choreography for the second act (which takes place in a sports stadium), comprising a very difficult semi-acrobatic dance for Galina Ulanova as the Young Communist Girl of the West and four cavaliers, he himself being one of the partners. It is important to note that, while being thoroughly versed in classical ballet (he graduated from the Kirov School in 1926, having first started, like Sergeyev, Chaboukiani, Koren, etc., in the evening courses in 1923), Yacobson from the start was inclined to use a free form of movement in his choreography. He was particularly interested in *plastique*; this led him to the creation of several dances for the Isadora Duncan studio in Moscow, maintained by several of her pupils up to 1949.

In 1941, in Kazan, Yacobson prepared his first major work, a three-act ballet *Shuraleh* to music by a gifted Tartar composer, Farid Yarullin, to be shown in Moscow for the Festival of Tartar Art. War prevented the presentation of this work, and the composer was killed in action in 1942. In 1950 Yacobson re-created *Shuraleh* at the Kirov theatre, and in 1955 this ballet, with the same choreography, was added to the repertory of the Bolshoi theatre.

"Shuraleh" is the name of a sylvan devil from Tartar lore, who enslaved Suimbike, a girl-bird. Ali-Batyr, a hunter, espies Suimbike in the woods and falls in love with her. Shuraleh has stolen Suimbike's wings; therefore she is again a mortal. She consents to marry Ali-Batyr. During the wedding feast Shuraleh purposely leaves the wings on the threshold of Suimbike's new home. She cannot resist the temptation and returns to her former ethereal element. But Shuraleh again enslaves her in his forest lair. When Ali-Batyr arrives on the scene, Shuraleh starts a forest fire. Having experienced human love, Suimbike offers her wings to Ali-Batyr; aided by them, he can fly out of the encircling flames. The youth in turn throws the wings into the conflagration: they are going to die together. This breaks the spell, the fire ceases, and the couple find themselves in a blossoming garden instead.

The music for *Shuraleh*, while totally symphonic (Yarullin was a Conservatoire graduate), is coloured with Tartar melodies and rhythms lending it a special charm. Yacobson deftly worked Tartar national steps into his choreography, even in the dances of Suimbike and other bird-maidens, performed *sur les pointes*. On the other hand, in the scene portraying Shuraleh and his forest retinue, he used a *plastique*-like idiom, grouping the various characters in expressive poses. Shuraleh himself, using this kind of idiom, was partly a gnarled and knotty tree, and partly a human being.

The part was created by Igor Bielsky in Leningrad and by Vladimir Levashov in Moscow. The parts of Suimbike and Ali-Batyr had a long line of interpreters, but were created in Leningrad by Dudinskaya and Sergeyev, and in Moscow by Plisetskaya and Kondratov.

In *Shuraleh* Yacobson used a variety of dance forms, including grotesque and national dances, but the bulk of the choreography remained classical. In his next work, *Spartacus*, with a truly great symphonic score by Aram Khachaturian (born 1903), temperamental, as only Khachaturian's music can be, rhythmically impulsive, rich in harmony and orchestration, Yacobson resorted to an entirely different principle. The story of *Spartacus* concerns a historically true uprising of slaves in Ancient Rome, led by Spartacus. Nicolai Volkov, author of the scenario, studied the works of Plutarch and Appian for the material, though he re-worked it in his writing, inventing some of the characters anew and presenting others in the light of his own creative imagination. Thus, aside from the historical characters of Spartacus, his wife (she was given the name of Phrygia), and Crassus, commander of the Roman troops, Volkov introduced, for necessary contrast, Crassus's mistress, Aegina, and Garmodius, the young Thracian, a weakling at first devoted to Spartacus and the cause he represented, later betraying him for Aegina who, after deliberately enticing Garmodius, turns him over to Crassus.

In order to give visual form to this colossal canvas of characters and events, Yacobson followed the precept of Fokine, who considered that in each case a new idiom corresponding to the subject should be created by the choreographer, whose duty it is to find the most expressive form possible for representing the given period and character of the nation portrayed.

Yacobson's decision to refrain from the use of *pointes* altogether in his version of *Spartacus* met with considerable resistance on the part of the company. It was even felt that the professional standards of the dancers were being threatened. In reality, when Yacobson created his choreography after a painstaking study of Greek and Roman vases, bas-reliefs and other sculptural and pictorial material, it was discovered that the production of *Spartacus* required professionalism of the highest possible order, and could only be performed by a company properly brought up according to the school of classical ballet. It requires a fully trained and fully expressive body in order to interpret Yacobson's idea of presenting "Animated bas-reliefs" on the proscenium apron between the acts, or making Phrygia and Aegina dance on high three-quarter point.

Yacobson himself explained his decision in the following manner: "When I began working on *Spartacus*, I was well aware that if one were to represent the life of Ancient Rome in the language of classical ballet, that is, if the Roman women and the girl-slaves were placed *sur les pointes* and the Romans made to perform *pirouettes* and *jetés*, it would look false and unnatural. The ballet would amount to nothing more than a conventional show expanded by picturesque *divertissement*. I decisively rejected any attempt to resort to steps of academic classical dancing and turned to plastic choreography. . . . Khachaturian's music—passionate, colourful, image-forming, but lacking continuity of dramatic action—suggested that it would be more propitious to present the ballet as separate frescoes, containing episodes from the life of Spartacus, rather than an uninterrupted story of the hero. . . ."[1]

[1] Leonid Yacobson. "Ballet and Contemporaneity". *Ogonyok* (magazine), No. 32, August 1962, p. 16.

In full accord with his concept, Yacobson created an impressive series of scenes: Crassus's triumphant return to Rome in a chariot drawn by prisoners, one of them Spartacus; the Slave Market that afforded the introduction of some colourful dances, especially the one of the Egyptian slave-girl, and set the scene where Spartacus was purchased by the owner of the school for gladiators, and Phrygia was sold to Aegina. Then followed other grandiose canvases: the Circus (the combats of gladiators), the slaves' uprising, Crassus's Feast, Spartacus's camp and the tragic requiem in the finale, with Phrygia mourning over the body of Spartacus.

The ballet does not contain many dances for Phrygia or Spartacus, but their lyrical *adagio*, done in the same style of *plastique*, was invested with Spartacus's chivalrous and crystal-pure attitude to Phrygia. In the first Leningrad production the title-role was created by Askold Makarov (born 1925), who seemed made for the role. Every pose of his Spartacus could serve as a model for a sculptor (having in turn been re-created by Yacobson from ancient statues). Tall and athletically built, Makarov had been particularly prominent in roles of a heroic nature, and his own share in the creation of new Soviet ballets can hardly be exaggerated. While at his best in contemporary ballets that enable him to shine in roles on an heroic plane, Makarov has danced principal roles in all the classical ballets, from *Swan Lake* to *La Bayadère*. He often dances Spartacus opposite his wife, the beautiful ballerina, Ninel Petrova (born 1924), as Phrygia. The role was created, however, by Inna Zubkovskaya (born 1928).

Aegina, as created in Leningrad by Alla Shelest (born 1919), is unequalled to this day. Shelest was a dancer with an acute sense of style in whatever she did, and an almost uncanny ability for transforming herself into the character she was impersonating. Aegina was one of the last roles created by Shelest before she retired to devote herself to coaching dancers of the Kirov ballet.

Yacobson's version of *Spartacus* did not exhaust its scenic history. On March 11, 1958, Igor Moiseyev presented his own version of the ballet at the Bolshoi Theatre in Moscow. It should be mentioned here that Nicolai Volkov had negotiated with Igor Moiseyev about the choreographic presentation of the theme of *Spartacus* as early as 1933 (the scenario was completed in 1934), and the choreographer had been nursing the idea of the ballet for many years.

Moiseyev's version was in some parts superior to that of Yacobson. This particularly concerns the gladiators' dramatic fights in the Circus; here the choreographer had the advantage of his rich experience in folk

Above: Galina Ulanova
directs a rehearsal.

Left: Galina Ulanova and
Yekaterina Maximova.

The Bolshoi Theatre, Moscow.

dancing obtained in the course of working with the famous Folk Dance Ensemble he has headed for over twenty-five years. The dance of the Gaditanae (the dancing girls of Cadiz, mentioned by Plutarch) with the tragic sonorities, precursing the advent of disaster, beautifully elaborated by Khachaturian as one of the main themes in the score, was, in a way, more original in concept than Yacobson's. And most of the dances, particularly those of Phrygia and Aegina, were done *sur les pointes*. Yet the ballet did not survive in the repertory of the Bolshoi Theatre. Apparently classical technique was unable to offset the lack of action; Yacobson's series of frescoes and high reliefs offered, strangely enough, greater continuity.

In 1962 Yacobson was asked to stage his *Spartacus* at the Bolshoi Theatre. But this presentation also did not last long. In the effort to reduce the length of the production and increase its dramatic action, Yacobson shortened it to three acts and deleted altogether the character of Garmodius, while the character of Aegina lost its importance in the intrigue and became secondary to that of Phrygia. The *raison d'être* of this abbreviated version of *Spartacus* was connected with that role. It was impersonated by the Bolshoi *prima ballerina assoluta*, Maya Plisetskaya. Born in 1925, this great classical *danseuse* reflects contemporaneity in everything she dances. Ever since her graduation into the Bolshoi ballet in 1943 (and even earlier than that, since she was given responsible parts while still in her last year at school) she has sought new roles and new idioms, to satisfy her preference for powerful, heroic characterizations. That is why she readily agreed to dance Phrygia, and, moreover, found the high three-quarter point style of her choreography interesting to explore and as complex to perform as classical dancing. Plisetskaya's remarkably expressive, "singing" body, as it has often been called, seemed to have been made for the beautiful poses copied from Greek and Roman sculpture. Instead of the customary vocabulary of classical ballets such as *Swan Lake* or *The Sleeping Beauty* the ballerina performed, in soft Greek sandals, movements worked out by Yacobson strictly without the turn-out that is obligatory in the *danse d'école*. Some people remembered Isadora Duncan. But there was a marked difference. This "duncanism" was based on a technique and general education of the body undreamt-of by the originator of "Greek" dancing. Also Maya Plisetskaya, a great actress of the ballet, applying her remarkable power of projection, evoked tears by her impersonation of Phrygia, giving the role the meaning of a universal truth. At each performance Plisetskaya's rendering of the final scene of Phrygia's mourning over the body of Spartacus met with tremendous ovations. She literally created the figure of a Muse of Tragedy, and her face, its set features looking like an ancient mask, was really unforgettable. The ballerina graced the production but a few times. She felt that her domain was that of a virtuoso demonstrating her great technical powers, then at their height. The lyrical *adagio* for Phrygia and Spartacus in the last act of the ballet and the short dance of tenderness in the first act were too far apart, and the public naturally would have liked to see more of the famous ballerina. However, in the spring of 1964, when Plisetskaya was nominated for the Lenin Prize in Art, she included the *udagio* from Spartacus in her special recital at the Bolshoi Theatre, and, presented side by side with the other classical roles performed *sur les pointes*, this choreography introduced valuable variety into the ballerina's repertory and served as an object lesson of her own versatility. It is interesting to note that in the Igor Moiseyev version Plisetskaya danced an opposite character, that of the cunning and vicious Aegina. After her success as Phrygia some people in ballet suggested that, had the sequence of scenes in *Spartacus* permitted it, Plisetskaya should have really performed *both* roles. Certainly her range as a dancer-actress would have made it quite possible. It is known that her greatest role—that of Odette-Odile—is notable not only for the remarkable fluidity and *plastique* of her beautiful arms as Odette, and the brilliance of her dancing as Odile, but for the deep insight into the dual nature of the character. Plisetskaya's musicality is also extraordinary. She has such a fine feeling for phrasing that she succeeds in interpreting the subtlest changes in the orchestration of the score. Her body is like an obedient musical instrument on which she plays in harmony with the orchestra. No wonder that she was very much attracted by Khachaturian's magnificent music. Though she no longer dances it, Khachaturian's *Spartacus* was for her a rewarding experience. Plisetskaya can hardly be imagined without her permanent partner, (so far as classical ballets are concerned), Nicolai Fadeyechev, the *premier danseur* of the Bolshoi Ballet. Born in 1923, he graduated in 1952, becoming a member of the Bolshoi company. Within two years he danced his first Siegfried. He possesses a pronounced feeling for the romantic style, and his Albrecht (previously often danced with Ulanova) is a fine and noble characterization. He danced in London in 1956 with the Bolshoi Ballet, and again in 1958 with Nadia Nerina in a television performance of *Giselle*, and partnered this ballerina, at her request, when she danced *Swan Lake* at the Bolshoi Theatre in 1961.

Strong, with an elegant manner, and good school, he is a very reliable partner. No wonder ballerinas like dancing with him. But Fadeyechev is much more than a *porteur*. When the time comes for his own *variation* in *Swan Lake*, he demonstrates perfect technique, an excellent *ballon*, soft landings and a general perfection of school, that won him his first performance as Siegfried when he danced with Plisetskaya in Milan in 1964. It was then, shortly after she had been nominated for the Lenin Prize, that Plisetskaya wrote of her partner: "Fadeyechev's every movement is academic and perfect in form. He has such a soft and high elevation, such a remarkable sense of the right pose. All his behaviour on the stage is thought out to the smallest detail. . . . Moreover, he has that rare and valuable quality for an artist: the ability to see oneself as if from a certain distance. Nothing is exaggerated and nothing is sacrificed to spectacular effect."[1]

As to *Spartacus* it has entered the tenth year of uninterrupted life in the repertory of the Kirov Theatre in the original unabridged version by Leonid Yacobson. This choreographer is a man of constant artistic unrest. He has done choreography in different styles since *Spartacus*: *The Bug* (1962) after the satirical posters drawn by the poet, Vladimir Mayakovsky, bringing to life pictures from the early twenties; and a series of *Choreographic Miniatures* (1958), in which he resorted to ideas from sculpture by Rodin or suggested by the music itself. He used many pieces by Ravel, Debussy, Stravinsky, Rachmaninov, and some works by Soviet composers. The full evening programme of *Miniatures* was filmed by Soviet television and sent on an exchange basis to TV studios abroad. In 1961 this film received first prize at Monte Carlo. On the basis of this Monte Carlo demonstration, the Paris "Université de la Danse" (founded by Serge Lifar) awarded Yacobson the first prize for choreography on the occasion of the three hundredth anniversary of the founding of the *Académie Royale de Danse*.

The most difficult, most responsible, and therefore most worthy task of a choreographer is to create both in contemporary idiom and on a contemporary theme. Igor Bielsky wanted to tackle this difficult problem from the start of his choreographic career. Moreover, at the first attempt, he succeeded where renowned masters had failed repeatedly.

Born in 1925, the son of well-known vaudeville dancers, Bielsky graduated from the Leningrad school, having had an opportunity to study character dancing under Andrei Lopukhov, one of the greatest exponents of that *genre* in Soviet Ballet. In 1942, he was accepted by the Kirov company while still at school; at that time the theatre was evacuated to Perm

[1] Maya Plisetskaya. "Nicolai Fadeyechev". In: *Soviet Artist*, (gazette of the Bolshoi Theatre), April 10, 1964.

and badly in need of male dancers. His formal debut in Leningrad took place in 1943 in the part of the chief (the "Polovetsian Dances" from *Prince Igor*). This determined his future career as a character dancer and he soon occupied the position of leading soloist. He did not restrict himself to national and character dances and always sought roles with strong characterization. Thus he created the roles of Shuraleh and Mako, the Negro in *The Path of Thunder*, one of the strongest and most important performances in that ballet. While still in the midst of an active dancing career he completed his first major work, *Coast of Hope* (1959), to a scenario by Yuri Slonimsky and a score by the Leningrad composer, Andrei Petrov, well known for his music in Soviet films. The two-act ballet brought him recognition as one of the most promising Soviet choreographers.

The style and poetic rendering of the ballet was very much prompted and inspired, as is usually the case, by Slonimsky's scenario. Slonimsky wanted, in his own words, to create "a fairy-tale about truth", a romantic poem extolling a true heart and a pure soul, a poem about a man who could not be bought or forced to his knees. Deliberately rejecting the narrative and descriptive method to which he himself had resorted on many previous occasions, Slonimsky wanted the heroes of the ballet to "live in a rich world of dance, eloquently talking to one another, loving, hating, and fighting for their own convictions—all in the language of *dance*".[1] He wanted this ballet to employ a wealth of purely poetic methods.

Both the scenario and the music of the ballet were created in close collaboration with the choreographer. This produced a certain unity. Moreover, the authors decided that they were going to do away with programme notes; the ballet had to be clear without elaborate explanations. One must say that they succeeded—the spectator was handed a slim house programme with the *dramatis personae* and the cast, and a brief enumeration of the main episodes, and that was all, yet the content of the ballet was quite apparent. It was divided into two distinct parts— the Soviet Coast and Another Coast (with a Far Eastern flavour).

In the first act, against a blue cyclorama and using no props, girls and boys dance a scene that leaves no doubt that it depicts the life of Soviet young folk in a fishing village.

Gone were the heavily-built props; the entire stage space was free for

[1] Yuri Slonimsky. "Speech before the première". In: *Za Sovietskoye Iskusstvo*, Gazette of the Kirov theatre, No. 9 (37) of June 6, 1959, p. 1. (The ballet was presented on June 11, 1959.)

dancing. Only two large sails fluttered in the breeze. The settings and costumes were created by Valery Dorrer—a designer whose work has shown profound understanding of the requirements of contemporary ballet. Many Soviet choreographers before Bielsky had arranged dances which used various work movements, including dragging in the nets. But they were simply dances, usually amounting to nothing more than a *divertissement*. Here, when the boys bent over imaginary oars, or dragged fishing nets and linked their hands together in the unity of common labour, all these motions, simple as they were, amounted to a poetic symbol and became an integral part of the entire "plastic" imagery. Later in the ballet came a veritable choreographic find.

The next scene was that of a storm. In semi-darkness girls ran pathetically hither and thither, in an atmosphere of anxiety and tension, enhanced by the flying sea-gulls. They were given a very important place in the choreography and a special theme in the music, as a symbol of freedom, motherland, and strength of spirit. The sea-gulls were impersonated by dancers of the *corps de ballet* performing darting leaps suggestive of the birds' flight. At times their role was dramatic, as when they brought hope to the imprisoned hero in a moment of trial.

In the beginning of the ballet the arrival of the fishermen—returning from the sea four by four, seemingly having climbed up a steep bank—was preceded by sea-gulls, soaring among the women. In this scene they serve as harbingers of sorrow.

After a dance suite with three notable *variations*: "Supplication", "Despair", and "Hope" (the last performed by the heroine, the Beloved), the fishermen, announced by the sea-gulls, who seem to join the tragic choir of girls, arrive in fours, as earlier. However, their entire bodies express the feeling of terrible despair and anguish. In the last line there are only three men. The place which should have been filled by the fourth forms a yawning gap. The arm of the lost man hangs limply, having failed to find the friend's shoulder. The impression of empty space is intensified, because two of the fishermen stand with bowed heads at the back of the gap, as if flanking the void formed by the loss of one of them. The heroine then throws herself right into the gap. In anguish she runs to the sea in search of the one she loves. By very simple means, with no unnecessary detail, the choreographer succeeded in creating a moving and impressive symbol.

The scene just mentioned is not really dancing, neither is it mime—it is a choreographic symbol. Otherwise classical dance serves as the foundation of all Bielsky choreography. But he has succeeded in fusing classical steps, with a mere suggestion of work and sports movements, in such a way that something new has been created from well-known elements. There is even a long *adagio* in the form of a love duet for the principals. But it is done in the form of a journey on an imaginary boat, suggested by a large sail gliding out of the wings. The young couple dive into the sea, then they stand on the prow of the "boat", and again swim to finish the dance on shore. All this is expressed by huge, broad leaps, rapid turns, high acrobatic lifts. The virtuosity required from the dancers is deftly concealed in the composition.

Entirely different kinds of *plastique* were used by Bielsky for the second act representing "the other coast". Not only did he resort to movement borrowed from a close study of Japanese and Chinese theatre and design, but the very pattern of the dance is different. Instead of the unity and continuity of energetic and vigorous movement, we see broken lines of other fishing-folk, timorous and down-trodden. In an original dance they tell a simple tale of catching a shark. When they suddenly notice that the waves have cast a man ashore they fear to show sympathy, though in the end they do. But when a patrol of black-clad soldiers arrives, they steal away one by one. The last of them, the pathetic "girl who has lost her beloved" (wonderfully impersonated by the creator of the role, Tatiana Legat, born in 1934, granddaughter of Nicolai Legat by a first marriage), is the only one to remain by the Soviet fisherman until he is led away by the patrol. In prison the Youth is tormented by his captors in a highly stylized dance and enticed by a sinuous creature in black, too much of a symbol to be convincing, in a fantastic orgy based mostly on Rock'n'roll. Having shaken off the Enticer, surrounded by a bevy of red-headed beauties, the young Fisherman again finds himself in prison. Visions of his motherland sustain him, visions in the form of sea-gulls, and his Beloved. This gives him strength. He raises his arms as if attempting to shatter the walls and soar away like an eagle, and the prison walls disappear, while the hero—it was not shown in detail just how this was achieved—is back on native soil. Greeted by the sea-gulls, he walks onward, though his feet sink in the wet sand and he is exhausted, until he comes to the front of the stage to face the audience—his people, to whom he has returned.

This simple finale, created by the choreographer in place of a long scene showing the hero welcomed by the whole village, is perfectly understood by the public, who applaud the dancer *first* as the hero of the ballet, and *then* as the impersonator of the role. The part was created by Askold Makarov. For him, the Fisherman was in line with the other heroic characters he had been working on in the course of his artistic career: Ma Lie-chen (*Red Flower*), Ali-Batyr (*Shuraleh*) and Spartacus. Makarov's Fisherman was strong and virile, with an engaging presence. His acting in the second act was charged with drama. Alexander Gribov (born 1934) alternated with Makarov when the ballet was first presented. He created a younger, more spontaneous, but also heroic character. The Beloved was danced by Alla Osipenko (born 1932) and Irina Kolpakova (born 1933). Alternating in the role, both ballerinas, contemporary in their individual styles, lent their own features to the heroine, whose character was not very clear from the rather sketchy material provided by the scenario. Osipenko's Beloved was stronger, with a marked will of her own, graceful and perfect in line. Kolpakova coloured the character with her own special radiance and warmth, and therefore was able to arouse greater compassion in the spectators' hearts. The dancing of both ballerinas was superb, their brilliant technique concealed to permit the characterization to come to the fore.

Bielsky continued his research for contemporary theme and idiom in another work, *Leningrad Symphony* (1961), using the first movement of Shostakovich's famous *Seventh Symphony*. It is a plotless work with more generalization than *Coast of Hope*. It had to be so in keeping with the form of the symphony. But the content, also determined by Shostakovich's powerful music written in Leningrad at the height of war, is quite definite; it is about the girls and boys of Leningrad who learn to defend their land through grim and severe trials. The role of the Youth was danced by Yuri Solovyov, that of the Girl by Alla Sizova. It is, however, Galeria Fedicheva (born 1935), a young ballerina of the Kirov ballet who came to the fore in the last few years, who brings a sense of contemporaneity to the role and performs it with great vitality and impact.

Yuri Grigorovich, another Leningrad choreographer of the younger generation, did not start with a contemporary theme. But everything he has done so far leads to new methods in approaching such tasks.

Born in 1927, Grigorovich was at the ballet school when war started and was evacuated with the other pupils, to Perm. There he wanted to get away in a canoe to the front, but the attempt was cut short. He graduated upon return to Leningrad in 1946 and joined the Kirov company, where he became one of the leading *demi-caractère* soloists, like his uncle, the brilliant George Rosai of the first "Ballet Russe" Paris season, 1909. At a very early stage Grigorovich showed a flair for choreography. In 1956 he did the choreography for the school graduation performance of Glinka's *Valse-Fantasia*. For the Leningrad Maxim Gorky

Palace of Culture, he prepared his own version of *The Baby Stork* and *Tom Thumb*, a forgotten ballet by Varlamov, a nineteenth-century composer.

While remaining as a dancer of the Kirov ballet, Grigorovich, together with a group of young enthusiasts, started work in 1957 on a new version of Prokofiev's *Stone Flower*, returning the original score to its pristine state as compared with the earlier Lavrovsky version of 1954. The entire production was conceived by the choreographer as a succession of dance suites. All characterizations were achieved through dance integrated with mime. Thus the character of Severyan (the bailiff), enacted in pedestrian pantomime in the 1954 Bolshoi theatre version, acquired new significance in Grigorovich's choreography, particularly as performed by the creator of the role, Anatoly Gridin, an excellent character dancer (born 1929). The role grew out of the action and was interpreted in dance, or, at the least, in dance-mime co-ordinated with the music. However, the most important character of the ballet was the Mistress of the Copper Mountain. Benevolent to the people and merciless with their oppressors (she turns Severyan into stone and causes him to sink into the earth in an impressive scene), she appears to Danila the stone-cutter, symbolizing the search for Beauty in his determination to find the Stone Flower and carve its likeness, now in the guise of a lizard and now in that of a Russian beauty. The novelty of the part consisted in the difficult acrobatic movements used by Grigorovich for the Mistress of the Copper Mountain when, as a lizard, she entwined herself around Danila (Alexander Gribov) bewitching him, and, in turn, falling victim to his youthful charms. The Mistress was impersonated by Alla Osipenko and remains her greatest creation to date. (In 1959, when the ballet was staged at the Bolshoi Theatre, the Mistress of the Copper Mountain was performed by Maya Plisetskaya with great virtuosity and powerful impact.) Katerina, Danila's gentle bride, was created by Irina Kolpakova, again presenting, together with Osipenko, two different types of character.

Of great importance was Grigorovich's use of the *corps de ballet*. It was given active choreography on a symphonic plane. For instance, in the market-place scene, the *corps de ballet* of gypsies served as a background for Severyan and reflected the tormented state of his soul, while the crowd of peasants at the fair seemed to comment in unison on the events, such as the sudden appearance of the Mistress in defence of Katerina.

The only discord was the *divertissement* of semi-precious stones that were given unseemly angular movements (when Danila arrived in the heart of the Copper Mountain). However, the choreographer's intention, perhaps not fully realized, was to portray the angularity of the stones' crystals through the use of this type of movement, borrowed directly from gymnastics and modern dance.

On the whole *The Stone Flower* was an immediate success. It not only remains in the repertory of both theatres, but has been staged by several other theatres.

In Moscow the roles of Danila and Katerina were performed by Vladimir Vasiliev and Yekaterina Maximova, both just out of school in 1959, while Severyan was impersonated with a power of projection exceeding even that of Gridin's, by the remarkable Bolshoi character dancer and mime Vladimir Levashov (born 1923).

Grigorovich's second ballet, *Legend of Love*, was a much more mature work. The music for it was specially written by Arif Melikov, pupil of Kara Karayev, another gifted Azerbaijan composer. As in *The Stone Flower*, Grigorovich worked out the decorative style of the future ballet together with Simon Virsaladze, the great designer, long before the choreography was actually started. This produced absolute unity of all composite parts, resulting in an unprecedentedly complete work of great artistic value and psychological impact. When first shown at the Kirov theatre on March 23, 1962,[1] *Legend of Love* immediately became a major event in Soviet choreography. Grigorovich, as choreographer, is a seeker after modern means of expression. But he is a firm advocate of profound dramatic content. The story of *Legend of Love* is borrowed from a play by the Turkish author, Nazym Hikmet. It seemed, indeed, a "natural" for ballet: the haughty and powerful Queen Mehmene-Banu is ready to sacrifice her crown in order to save her sister, Shirien, dying of some terrible plague. A Stranger in the disguise of a Dervish is brought to the palace. He demands a terrible price for the life of Shirien. The Queen must relinquish her beauty. After the Queen has consented to this, the real conflict starts: both women fall in love with the stone-cutter Ferhad, while he loves only Shirien. . . . A clash of temperaments and character follows. The two lovers flee from the palace. The Queen sends her retinue in pursuit. The fugitives are caught. Mehmene announces that for punishment Ferhad must hew a passage through the mountain which obscures the flow of water to her scorched kingdom. Ferhad is ready to sacrifice himself for the benefit of his suffering people. He goes up into the mountains to achieve this deed, renouncing Shirien and his love.

This fairy-tale interested Grigorovich because of the deep psychological

[1] In Leningrad, *The Stone Flower* was first performed on 27/4/1957, and in Moscow on 7/3/1959.

origins of its action. As a matter of fact, disguised as a legend, he had a very strong dramatic conflict to work on.

Grigorovich continued and developed further the method of composition started in *The Stone Flower*. Each character was given his own idiom. Particularly beautiful and appropriate were the gazelle-like movements and hand gestures invented for Shirien, based on genuine Oriental dances. Much time was devoted to the study of Persian miniatures with beneficial results. Moreover, each of the three main performers was given a *corps de ballet* that seemed to echo the thoughts and enhance the intensity of the particular dancer's feelings. This particularly applies to the red *corps de ballet* of Queen Mehmene-Banu, accompanying her tormented impassioned agony when, alone in her bedchamber, she dreams of Ferhad.

But the most important achievement in Grigorovich's choreography is contained in the three trios—one for every act. In the first, Mehmene-Banu and Shirien meet Ferhad for the first time. The lights dim, the music now sounds as though from a great distance, and the three people remain alone with their thoughts, each dancing in his own beam of light while we, the spectators, are allowed to share in what is going on deep in their hearts. In the second act a similar trio occurs just after the pursuit of the fugitives: the frenzied movement that had been sweeping all off the stage is suddenly hushed, the lights dim, and the three protagonists stand in conflict in the glare of solitary beams, while far-away music accompanies their secret thoughts.

The third trio occurs in the final act, when the two sisters see Ferhad for the last time, and part with their love forever.

There are many other touches of genius in Grigorovich's choreography—the symphonically performed march of the Queen's equestrian retinue in the first act, the pursuit in the second, the dances of Gold and the Court dancers and jesters. The character of Ferhad is not as three-dimensional as that of Mehmene-Banu, and the story about water that has to be given to the people and Water itself (danced by the *corps de ballet*) is not as well done as the rest of the choreography. But one is ready to forgive its weaknesses in view of other great merits. Beyond doubt *The Legend of Love* became the starting-point among many Soviet choreographers, particularly of the younger generation, for new approaches to their task.

Virsaladze's *décor*, conceived as a colossal book that slowly opens to reveal the changing of scenery (reduced to a minimum), greatly assists the impact of the ballet.

The creators of the main roles at the Kirov theatre were Inna Zubkovskaya as Mehmene-Banu, Irina Kolpakova as Shirien, and Alexander

Gribov as Ferhad. Grigorovich's choreography is so conceived that it is, for the most part, foolproof and conveys what it has to say.

In Moscow, where the ballet was first shown with this choreography on April 15, 1965, it found a remarkable Mehmene-Banu in Maya Plisetskaya, who succeeded in infusing greater dramatic power into the angular acrobatic idiom devised by Grigorovich[1] for the part of the queen. The gazelle-like jumps and the crystal lightness of Shirien's dances were performed to perfection by Natalia Bessmertnova (born 1941), the youngest and most promising ballerina of the Bolshoi ballet. So young that she barely has a biography, Bessmertnova, in her four seasons at the Bolshoi ballet (she graduated in 1961), had performed several leading roles: Giselle, Leili in the new ballet *Leili and Mejnun*, the Seventh Waltz in *Les Sylphides*, etc.; but none compare with her role of Shirien, where her talent seemed to have opened up like a flower. Ferhad was first danced in Moscow by Liepa, an elegant dancer and good actor. However, in the third cast, Mikhail Lavrovsky (born 1941), Bessmertnova's classmate and partner, appeared to be an ideal Ferhad, more earthy and temperamental. As a dancer Lavrovsky belongs in the same category as Vasiliev; he expresses everything in dance and is made for strong and virile roles.

On the other hand, Vasiliev showed the great versatility of his extraordinary talent when he appeared, on December 17, 1964, as Mejnun in the full-length Goleizovsky ballet, *Leili and Mejnun*, with music by Balasanyan, also based on an Oriental legend, concerning star-crossed lovers whose story is reminiscent of Romeo and Juliet. Goleizovsky's choreography is conceived in soft, almost feline movement, very Oriental in nature (the master-choreographer is a great connoisseur of dances of the Orient). Vladimir Vasiliev abandoned, for this one role, his virile style, and danced, with every part of his body, as to the manner born, creating a sinuous style of *cantilena* movement. Mejnun proved that Vasiliev has a greater range than was imagined. The role became for him a new stage in the constant progress of this truly unusual artist.

The Moscow ballet has also produced young choreographers of its own. Alexander Lapauri (born 1926), the outstanding impersonator of Guirei in *The Fountain of Bakhchisarai*, and other important roles, unsurpassed as a partner in semi-acrobatic *pas de deux* usually performed with his wife and former classmate, Raisa Struchkova (1925), started studying at the Choreographers' Faculty of the State Institute of Theatrical Art (GITIS) while still at the height of his dancing career. His first ballet,

[1] Grigorovich now heads the Bolshoi ballet.

Tale of the Woods, to music by Zhukovsky in collaboration with his fellow-student, Bolshoi dancer Olga Tarasova (born 1927), was dropped from the Bolshoi repertory after several presentations in 1961. But it was a different story with the second ballet by the same two choreographers, entitled *Lieutenant Kije*, set to Prokofiev's music for a film of the same title[1] based on Yuri Tynianov's novel satirizing the period of Paul I.

Lapauri and Tarasova used the same story and succeeded in giving it interesting choreographic form. The ballet was first performed at the Bolshoi Theatre in a triple bill on February 10, 1963. It was not easy to make it clear through choreography that the entire situation arose because one of the scribes in Paul the First's predominantly military reign made a blot with his goose-quill and thus created one more, non-existent, Lieutenant Kije. This was done by introducing the character of the Quill, created by Lyudmila Bogomolova (born 1932), a brilliant dancer capable of coping with the technical feats required by the part. The Quill symbolizes the bureaucracy of Paul's reign and appears throughout the ballet right up to the end, when the mad emperor issues one edict after another and they multiply, filling the entire stage.

The principal part of the Lady-in-Waiting, marrying the fictitious Kije in order to achieve her own career at the court, was danced by Raisa Struchkova. A strong ballerina possessing a perfect school acquired from her teacher, Yelizaveta Gerdt, she is also a first-class actress, possessing a great sense of humour. The role in *Lieutenant Kije* fits her like a glove, and it is a pity that more has not been done with her kind of talent in view. In an impish and provocative manner Struchkova's Lady-in-Waiting passes from one infatuation to another, always pretending in reality to be devoted to her phantom husband, Lieutenant (later General) Kije, and ending in a flirtation with Paul himself, for which purpose Kije is conveniently killed off. One of the hilarious moments of the ballet is Struchkova's mock expression of grief when she follows the empty funeral bier in deep mourning, and then suddenly starts a saucy little dance with several of her numerous admirers. The idiom used by the choreographers contained many forgotten steps of the *danse d'école* that were most beneficial for the Bolshoi *corps de ballet*.

Lapauri keeps to the following choreographic *credo*: he cannot envisage even a short dance number without a definite idea and content. He considers that the purpose of ballet, like any other art, is the presentation of

[1] Fokine used the same music for his *Russian Soldier* in 1942 with an entirely different subject.

great ideas, emotions, and feelings. All this, the young choreographer maintains, should be done "through the human being"—in other words through real people as characters. "I consider," says he, "that if the choreographer has come out on to the stage with a work of his own, it means that he has something to say."

This desire to state their artistic convictions is evident in the work of all Soviet choreographers. It is emphatically declared in ballets created by two young artists who have grown directly from the midst of the the Bolshoi Ballet.

Natalia Kasatkina (born 1934), one of the company's most talented character soloists, and Vladimir Vasilyov (born 1931), character dancer, are husband and wife in private life. Their first joint work, *Vanina Vanini*, after Stendhal's story of the same title, was done in 1962 to music specially written by a conservatoire graduate, Nicolai Karetnikov. It was created in the dancers' spare time, outside the Bolshoi regular plan of new productions. The cast enthusiastically supported the young choreographers. The title role was created by Yelena Riabinkina (born 1941), another talent in the roster of young Bolshoi ballerinas. The role of her lover, Pietro the *carbonaro*, was created by Vladimir Tikhonov (born 1935), a dark virile dancer from Moldavia, with a very expressive body and good technique obtained in Leningrad, where he received his initial training. The choreography was done in terms of dance integrated with mime. Galina Ulanova wrote of it: "Our spectators received the ballet well because they like what is new and fresh. And even if at first the choreographers have not quite succeeded (that is natural and logical), *Vanina Vanini* as a ballet possesses an important main quality: it is danceable, it conveys a definite idea, the images of its chief heroes are presented in action, simple and clear."[1]

In their next work, *The Heroic Poem* (1964), again to music by Nicolai Karetnikov, the choreographers were ready to approach a contemporary theme. It was a ballet about people their own age, three geologists, perhaps students, prospecting for some mineral in the *taiga*. At the moment of triumph, when after great hardships they find what they have been looking for, they are trapped by a forest fire. The leader of the party, a boy of greater willpower, loses his life helping the Girl to fight the flames. The other boy is badly burnt. He is unable to walk. The Girl remains alone with him in the scorched *taiga*. She has terrible visions of the tragedy that has taken place. A city girl who has never had to face any serious

[1] Galina Ulanova. "Début of the young". In: *Soviet Artist*, Gazette of the Bolshoi Theatre, 15/6/1962.

tests of character, she resolves to save her comrade. Improvising a stretcher she drags him through the *taiga*. (There is no stretcher, since there are no "props" of any kind and the impression is produced choreographically.) When she is about to collapse from exhaustion she meets a Yakut boy and girl, who lead the young people to safety.

The choreography is done entirely in terms of dance, at times very imaginatively. The idiom is modern, always conveying some idea. Thus, when the wounded boy performs the so-called "wrestler's bridge", he does it because he suffers from his burns. The numerous acrobatic lifts in the first part of the ballet are introduced to convey the impression of the difficult track covered by the explorers before reaching their goal. Each of the three main performers possesses traits of character that change with the development of the plot. The part of the Girl was created by Nina Sorokina (born 1942). A classmate of Bessmertnova, she is noted for her virtuosity as a soloist in such different roles as Jeanne (*The Flames of Paris*) and the Diamond Fairy (*The Sleeping Beauty*) and she flowered in the roles created in ballets by Kasatkina and Vasilyov. The leader of the small group was danced by Yuri Vladimirov (born 1942), a former classmate of Bessmertnova and Sorokina. Vladimir Koshelev (born 1935) graduated five years earlier and is a promising *demi-caractère* dancer. He, too, matured artistically in his creation of the second boy, weaker in physique and in character than the leader, but acquiring moral strength by the end of the ballet.

The Heroic Poem is invariably a great success with the public, particularly with the young generation, because it depicts their own time and the story of the three geologists strikes a familiar note in their hearts.

In the spring of 1965 Kasatkina and Vasilyov produced their major work to date in the form of a new version of *Le Sacre du Printemps* (premièred on June 28, 1965). The fact that the choreography for Stravinsky's score was arranged by many illustrious predecessors did not stop the young couple from making their own attempt. As on the two previous occasions they wrote their own scenario, placing the action in the second millennium B.C. when tribes were just being formed. The Rite of Spring takes place before an idol. The Possessed (danced by Kasatkina) is to choose, in a frenzied dance, the victim for the sacrifice, ordered by the Wise Old Men—the high priests of the tribe. Earlier, during the spring revels of the youth, a young Shepherd is attracted to a Girl. He does not know of such feelings as love—nothing but youthful lust inspires his behaviour. But when the Possessed throws the sacrificial veil on the Girl and she, moving as if also possessed, is irretrievably attracted to the sacerdotal fire, he tries to wrest her from the hands of the Possessed and the principal Old Man. For a while he succeeds, but the Girl, as if hypnotized by the Possessed, again moves, in tiny hops *sur les pointes*, towards the idol, to be slain by the Wise Old Man and thrown into the fire. It is then that the Shepherd experiences the feeling of an irreparable loss. He is ready to fight the Wise Old Man. He challenges the Idol itself and awaits in awe, together with the crowd, the terrible punishment. But nothing happens. Only the remaining girls stretch their arms towards the Shepherd beseeching his help.

The Shepherd was created by Yuri Vladimirov, who had already collaborated so fruitfully with the young choreographers in *The Heroic Poem*. The Wise Old Man was very well danced by Anatoly Simachev. But none of the characterizations so far match the power of Kasatkina's work in a role created for herself.

This version of the *Sacre* was hailed by the critics as the most successful in years. The only blemish is in the costumes (by Andrei Goncharov who has collaborated with the authors on the two previous ballets), which are not in keeping with the nature of Stravinsky's music, and do not create the necessary atmosphere. But these might be improved in time, as this version of Stravinsky's great ballet will no doubt survive its severe test. One may observe that in all the works of the young choreographers there is a search for a new dance idiom. The existing vocabulary does, indeed, require some measure of innovation if it is to express contemporary life. But in order properly to reflect it one should start with a thorough study of life itself, which is fully capable of providing choreographers with the material they need. In the best works this is achieved: for instance, the dances of the geologists in *The Heroic Poem*, and those of the fishermen in *Coast of Hope*, both depict movements of labour and every-day life in a highly-stylized art form. At times, however, the choreography of the young is a little too "busy", they try to pack everything they have learned into a few dance passages. This will pass, no doubt, and constitutes a temporary transitional period to new quality. Also, people coming into contact with Soviet Ballet for the first time expect to find something unprecedently *avant-garde*, for the reason that the Soviet Union is a progressive, advanced country. But the progressive in Soviet Ballet should be sought for in another direction. It is contained in the progressive approach to this branch of art as among other arts, and serves the same purpose of elevating the spectator to a higher plane with every visit to the theatre. The traditions of the great Russian school, with its emphasis on content (even when there is no plot), is carefully preserved in Soviet

Ballet, which is now engaged in furthering the greatest discoveries of the past, connected with symphonic choreography stemming from symphonic music. Soviet choreography has been endeavouring lately to blend dance and mime in such a manner that mime is subjected to the same rules as the dance, in other words it is subordinated to the music. Great dancers, in particular Ulanova, were always capable of conveying the slightest nuances of emotion through their entire body, and, from this point of view, Soviet ballet holds that there are no dances without content. Man, with his entire gamut of feelings, should live in any dance, first and foremost. However, Soviet ballet considers that the ballet is preferably associated with ennobling feelings and emotions. This is what Mikhail Chulaki has to say on this subject: "It is necessary to caution authors against infatuation with terrifying, repulsive, tragic, and grotesque themes in ballet. The measure of such colours is quite different in ballet as compared with that in literature, poetry, cinema, or opera. The principal force in ballet belongs to another sphere. This force is embodied in light, joyful, lyrical and lyrical-dramatic colours. It is incomparable in this domain. Great classical masters of the dance were always cautioning against the use of the ugly and the gloomy, explaining that it is an easy but unnecessary direction for ballet to take. Remember, the two most loved, most popular of all ballets are the two lyrical-dramatic ballets: *Swan Lake* and *Giselle*. This is neither a whim, nor evidence of an old-fashioned taste, but the will of the people, the will of the art itself."[1]

Soviet ballet no longer serves as entertainment for a limited audience in two theatres. It has become a multi-national art, flourishing in each of the fifteen republics of the Soviet Union. In turn, national dance lore has very much influenced the art of ballet, enriching it with idiom and content. Therefore, classical dance in Soviet ballet is not a rigid form, though by itself, especially as represented by the Russian school, it is a great treasury to be used by choreographers as the most important foundation of their work. But the technique of classical dancing is constantly being expanded and perfected with the help of borrowings from folk dance and new discoveries by Soviet choreographers. The technique itself is no longer the prerogative of a few outstanding soloists. It has been mastered by large groups of dancers, trained all over the country by experienced teachers according to a unified syllabus. The Soviet system of ballet education is in itself a new, more perfect stage of the Russian

[1] Mikhail Chulaki. "Thoughts on Soviet Ballet". In: *Soviet Music* (magazine), No. 4 for 1964, p. 60.

School, that should be considered as an independent phenomenon: the Soviet School of classical ballet.

Soviet ballet is now faced with the most difficult task, that of creating more and better ballets about our own time. It is for this purpose that it is so actively engaged in the search for the new. Works such as the *Coast of Hope* and *The Heroic Poem* indicate that great things may be expected from young Soviet choreographers.

RUSSIAN BIBLIOGRAPHY

Annual of the Imperial Theatres. 1890–1917.

Arapov, Pimen. *Chronicles of the Russian Theatre.* SPB, 1861.

Bakhrushin, Y. *A. A. Gorsky.* Moscow, 1946.

Bakhrushin, Y. "Tchaikovsky's Ballets and their Scenic History". In: *Tchaikovsky and the Theatre.* Articles and materials. Moscow, 1940.

Blasis, Carlo. *Dances in General, Ballet Celebrities and National Dances.* Moscow, 1864.

Bogdanov-Berezovsky, V. *Galina Ulanova.* Moscow, 1961.

Bogdanov-Berezovsky, V. *Konstantin Sergeyev.* Leningrad, 1951.

Borisoglebsky, M. (Editor). *Materials for the History of Russian Ballet.* The Past of the Ballet Department of the Petersburg Theatre School, 1939, now the Leningrad Choreographic School. Vol. I, L. 1938. Vol. II, L. 1939.

Chayanova, O. *Maddox's Theatre in Moscow.* Moscow, 1927.

Chudnovsky, M. *Victorina Krieger.* Moscow, 1964.

Druskin, M. *Essays from the History of Dance Music.* Leningrad, 1936.

Eliash, N. *Russian Terpsichore.* Moscow, 1965.

Evreinov, N. *Serf Actors.* Leningrad, 1925.

Famintsyn, A. *Skomorokhi in Russia.* SPB, 1889.

Fokine, Mikhail. *Against the Current.* Memoirs of the ballet-master, articles, letters. With an introductory article by Y. Slonimsky: "Fokine and his Time". Leningrad-Moscow, 1962.

Gluszkovski, A. *Memoirs of a Ballet-master.* Moscow, 1940.

Golubov, V. (Potapov). *Galina Ulanova.* Leningrad, 1948.

Gosenpud, A. *Music and Ballet in Russia of the Eighteenth Century.* Leningrad, 1959.

Gurevitch, L. *History of Russian Theatrical Life.* Moscow–Leningrad, 1939.

Khudekov, S. *A History of Dancing.* Volume IV. Petrograd, 1918.

Krasovskaya, V. *Anna Pavlova,* Leningrad–Moscow, 1964.

Krasovskaya, V. *Russian Ballet Theatre. First half of the XIXth century.* Moscow–Leningrad, 1958.

Krasovskaya, V. *Russian Ballet Theatre. Second half of the XIXth century.* Moscow–Leningrad, 1963.

Krasovskaya, V. *Vakhtang Chaboukiani.* Second edition. Leningrad–Moscow, 1960.

Kremshevskaya, G. *Natalia Dudinskaya.* Leningrad, 1964.

Krieger, V. *My Notes.* Memoirs. Moscow–Leningrad, 1930.

Kuskov, Ivan. *The Dancing-Master.* SPB, 1794.

Lisitsian, S. *Dance Notation* (Kinetography). Moscow, 1940.

Lunacharsky, A. *In the World of Music*. Moscow, 1958.

Lunacharsky, A. *Selected Articles on the Theatre*, 2 Vols. Moscow, 1958.

Lvov-Anokhin. *Alla Shelest*. Moscow, 1964.

Martynova, O. *Yekaterina Geltser*. Moscow, 1965.

Mikhnevich, V. *Essay on the History of Music in Russia*, SPB, 1879.

Moscow Bolshoi Theatre. 1825-1925. Anniversary edition. Moscow, 1925.

Musical Leningrad. Reference book. Musical Publishing House, Leningrad, 1958.

Music of Soviet Ballet. Articles. Moscow, 1962.

Petipa, M. *Memoirs*. SPB, 1906.

Plescheyev, A. *In the Shadow of the Wings*. Paris, 1936. (In Russian.)

Plescheyev, A. *Our Ballet*. SPB, 1896.

Plescheyev, A. In: Sergei Lifar. *From the Old to the New*. Paris, 1938. (In Russian.)

Plescheyev, A. *What I Remember*. . . . SPB, 1914.

Prokofiev, S. *Materials, Documents, Memoirs*. Moscow, 1956.

Rovinsky, D. *Russian Popular Prints*. Saint Petersburg, 1881.

Skalkovsky, K. *Ballet, its History and Place among the Fine Arts*. SPB, 1882.

Skalkovsky, K. *In the World of the Theatre*. SPB, 1899.

Slonimsky, Y. *At the Cradle of the Russian Terpsichore*. Introductory article to *Ivan Valberkh: From the Archives of the Ballet-master*. Moscow, 1948.

Slonimsky, Y. "Birth of the Moscow Ballet and Adam Gluszkovski". In: A. Gluszkovski. *Memoirs of a Ballet-master*. Moscow, 1940.

Slonimsky, Y. *Didelot*. Leningrad, 1958.

Slonimsky, Y. (Editor). *The Fountain of Bakhchisarai*. Collection of articles compiled by L. Popova. Leningrad, 1962.

Slonimsky, Y. *Giselle*. Leningrad, 1926.

Slonimsky, Y. *Masters of the Ballet in the Nineteenth Century*. Leningrad, 1937.

Slonimsky, Y. *Soviet Ballet*. Moscow–Leningrad, 1950.

Slonimsky, Y. *Swan Lake*. Leningrad, 1962.

Slonimsky, Y. *Sylphide, La*. Leningrad, 1927.

Slonimsky, Y. *Tchaikovsky and the Ballet Theatre of his Time*. Moscow, 1956.

Staelin, Jacob. *Music and Ballet in Russia of the Eighteenth Century*. Triton Publishing House, Leningrad, 1928.

Stepanov, V. I. *Table of Symbols for Notation of Movements of the Human Body*, after the system of V. I. Stepanov, Artist of the Imperial Theatres of St. Petersburg. Prepared by A. Gorsky. Saint Petersburg, 1899.

Svetlov, V. *Contemporary Ballet*. SPB, 1911.

Svetlov, V. O. O. *Preobrajenskaya*. SPB, 1902.
Svetlov, V. *Terpsichore*. SPB, 1906.

Teliakovsky, V. *The Imperial Theatres in 1905*. Leningrad, 1926.
Teliakovsky, V. *Reminiscences*. 1898-1917. Leningrad, 1924.

Vaganova, Agrippina Yakovlevna. *Articles, Memoirs, Materials*. Moscow, 1958.
Valtz, K. *Sixty-Five Years in the Theatre*. In collaboration with Y. Bakhrushin.
Vazem, E. *Memoirs of a Ballerina*. Leningrad, 1937.
Vecheslova, T. *I am a Ballerina*. Leningrad, 1964.
Volynsky, A. *The Book of Exultation*. Leningrad, 1925.
Vsevolodsky, V. *A History of Theatrical Education in Russia*. Vol. I., SPB, 1911.

Weekly of the State Academic Petrograd Theatres. 1922-1923.

Yakovlev, N. *Ballet-master Marius Petipa*. Petrograd, 1924.

Zakharov, V. *The Art of the Choreographer*. Moscow, 1954.
Zhytomirsky, D. *Tchaikovsky's Ballets*. Moscow, 1957.

Note: The above titles have been translated into English for the
purpose of this Bibliography.

INDEX

Note: Titles of ballets and *divertissements* are listed alphabetically under 'Ballets and Divertissements'; names of theatres are listed alphabetically under 'Theatres'